The Wordsworthian Enlightenment

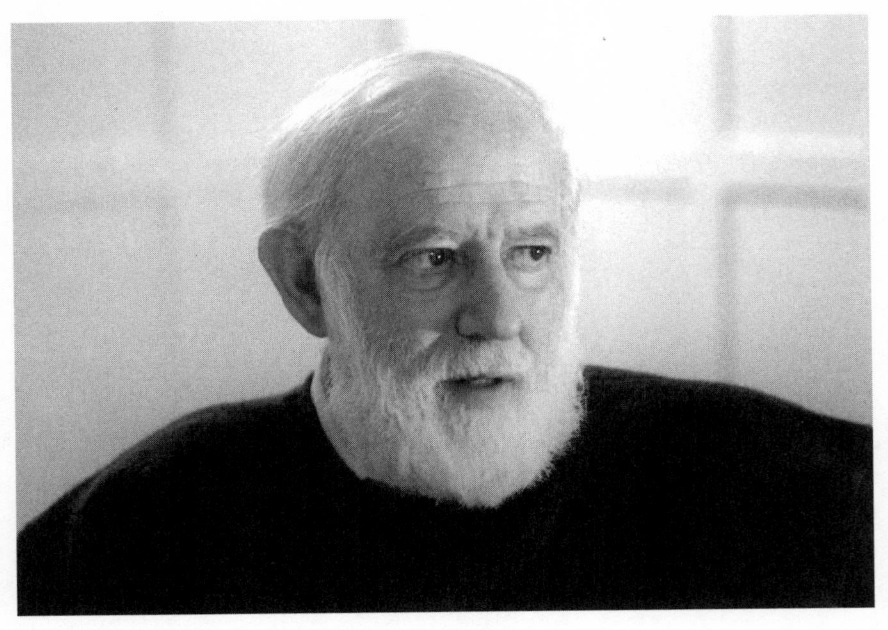

Essays in honor of Geoffrey Hartman

The Wordsworthian Enlightenment

Romantic Poetry and the Ecology of Reading

Edited by Helen Regueiro Elam and Frances Ferguson

The Johns Hopkins University Press
Baltimore

Printed in the United States of America on acid-free paper
9 8 7 6 5 4 3 2 1

The Johns Hopkins University Press
2715 North Charles Street
Baltimore, Maryland 21218-4363
www.press.jhu.edu

Library of Congress Cataloging-in-Publication Data
The Wordsworthian enlightenment : romantic poetry and the ecology of reading / edited by Helen Regueiro Elam and Frances Ferguson.
p. cm.
Festschrift in honor of Geoffrey H. Hartman.
Includes bibliographical references and index.
ISBN 0-8018-8187-0 (hardcover : alk. paper)
1. Wordsworth, William, 1770–1850—Criticism and interpretation. 2. Wordsworth, William, 1770–1850—Knowledge and learning. 3. Literature and history—England. 4. Books and reading—England. 5. Enlightenment—England. 6. Romanticism—England. I. Elam, Helen Regueiro, 1943– II. Ferguson, Frances, 1947– III. Hartman, Geoffrey H.
PR5888.W67 2005
821′.7—dc22 2004027034

A catalog record for this book is available from the British Library.

Frontispiece: Photograph of Geoffrey Hartman by Cathy Caruth

Contents

Acknowledgments

The following chapters first appeared in slightly altered form in *Studies in Romanticism* 35.4 and constituted the winter 1996 issue, a festschrift in honor of Geoffrey Hartman. Copyright owned by the Trustees of Boston University (Deborah Swedberg, Managing Editor of *Studies in Romanticism*).

"Introduction" by Helen Regueiro Elam; "Romantic Memory" by Frances Ferguson (chap. 3); "Green to the Very Door? The Natural Wordsworth" by Paul H. Fry (chap. 4); "The New Historicism and the Work of Mourning" by Alan Liu (chap. 7); "Making Time for History: Wordsworth, the New Historicism, and the Apocalyptic Fallacy" by Kevis Goodman (chap. 8); "Gentle Hearts and Hands: Reading Wordsworth after Geoffrey Hartman" by J. Douglas Kneale (chap. 12); " 'Reading After': The Anxiety of the Writing Subject" by Lucy Newlyn (chap. 13); and "An Interview with Geoffrey Hartman" by Cathy Caruth (chap. 16).

Ortwin de Graef's "Encrypted Sympathy: Wordsworth's Infant Ideology" (chap. 2) is reprinted with permission from *Partial Answers* of Hebrew University.

An earlier version of Peter J. Manning's "The Other Scene of Travel: Wordsworth's 'Musings Near Aquapendente' " (chap. 10) appeared under a different title in *Angles on the English-Speaking World*, n.s., 3 (2003), Lene Østermark-Johansen, editor.

J. Hillis Miller's "Rachel When from the Lord" (chap. 15) is reprinted in slightly altered form from *Speech Acts in Literature* © 2001 by the Board of Trustees of the Leland Stanford Jr. University.

We would like to thank Michael Lonegro for his sustained, unfailing support for this project; Juliana McCarthy for her guidance; Barbara Lamb for her insights and attention to detail; and Andre Barnett for her concern for the whole as well as its parts.

The Wordsworthian Enlightenment

INTRODUCTION

Helen Regueiro Elam and Frances Ferguson

Some years ago the *New York Times* published an article on the young men—or, rather, boys—to whom the Rothschild family had given safe haven in their country home near Aylesbury. Accompanying the story was an old photograph that looked like many a school photograph, only this one seemed as if it had been produced not for a single class but for a one-room schoolhouse, as there were boys of various ages, heights, shapes, and sizes.

The face of a very young Geoffrey Hartman looked out at the camera for the photograph. When the *Times* story appeared,[1] Hartman seemed surprised that people who had come to know him when he was a grown man were able to recognize him from that early photograph. He claimed that what they must be noticing was his ears. It was a characteristically self-deprecating gesture, a way of putting modestly Hartman's most extraordinary trait: his commitment not so much to being seen as to conceiving of himself as a set of capacities for receiving the world—what he has called his "delight in phenomena as such." To hear Geoffrey Hartman tell it, as he did in the Charles Homer Haskins Lecture "A Life of Learning," presented to the American Council of Learned Societies in 2000,[2] his entire career has been less a steady march of professional advancement and renown than the attempt to "devour new words," natural sights, and even the life of an imagined community as a way of filling "some emptiness."

"Living in a small English village from the age of nine till sixteen," Hartman grew up far from galleries and museums, surrounded by "cheap, Penguin editions" of novelists like Tolstoy and Virginia Woolf—and by a deep sense of the significance of places. Art was for him an intensification of the sensory experience of places, and he developed a commitment to photography that was all the more ardent for the way in which his "five-dollar Brownie," with the "simplest of mechanisms (no timer, no lens, just a pinhole)," did less to supplement his own sight than to challenge it: "The eyes had to think, fast." Like the Wordsworth whom he understands so well, he began very early to see that things like the home amusements of children are all the better at registering sensation when its external instruments—for Wordsworth an incomplete deck of cards, for Hartman a modest and undemanding camera—placed demands on his own sensory apparatus.

It was perhaps inevitable that someone who so appreciated being conscious of his own experience would come to be an extraordinary commentator on that experience and on its analogue, the structure of critical reflection itself. Yet the most remarkable turn in his thought was to see that the structure of critical reflection did not merely rest on personal experience but also involved, at least in the "friendship style" of amiable correspondence that Hartman took to heights that were both easy and strenuous, "an embryonically democratic ethos, at least in the domain of letters, an ideal equality of writers and readers." Hartman cites John Crowe Ransom as having "got it right when he said the literature has logical structure and irrelevant texture," and he goes on to say that a "devilish detail is part of art's economy, of a sign-system that produces large effects through micro-material means." In that observation, he says a great deal about his own characteristic practices of literary interpretation; he generously gives to his audience a sense of the importance of the modesty and rudeness of the "micro-material means" through which literature enlarges our sensory and reflective world by insisting that its effects should travel through the linguistic equivalent of a five-dollar Brownie camera.

The very range, and precision, with which Hartman moves from aesthetics to questions of culture, and in particular between poetic memory and historical disaster, is itself a powerful testimony for our times, addressing as it does the central importance of poetry, of literature, of "primal sympathy," of "reading," in a time of dearth.

The last century produced some especially rich intersections between Romantic poets and their critics, owing in large measure to the pressure theoretical discourses brought to bear on more traditional (formalist, humanistic) ways of reading and in part to the imperious demand of Romantic poetry for the kind of reading that would account for a range of issues it brings to the fore: the condition of the fragment, the relation between writing and mortality, memory as recuperation and as the realization of loss, the unsayable (knowable yet unknowable) recognitions that precipitate (and are precipitated by) this kind of poetry, and the fragmented and powerful narratives of human beings who have traversed (yet never quite traveled through) traumatic events. The categories of nature and history, the relations of event to the telling, the complex and layered imbrication of poetic and human trauma because of the way one remembers and narrates — all these have affected the course of criticism of Romantic poetry in the last half century, or rather than affected, one might say that poetry and theory have influenced one another ("thickened" one another) in the space between reading and writing.

At these intersections, no poet has been richer and more suggestive than Wordsworth, and in Wordsworth criticism Geoffrey Hartman has been one of the richest and most suggestive critics. If some of these essays weigh themselves toward his intervention in the field of criticism and theory and toward his readings of Romantic poetry, this is because his has been a powerful and sustained voice in the field of theory from the 1960s to the present and because his voice has dramatically transformed Wordsworth studies. In a long and distinguished career, which began with questions of nature and self-consciousness and is at present focused on Holocaust traumas, Wordsworth has been for Hartman the sustained obligato that bridges concerns as diverse, yet as unavoidably and relentlessly interlinked, as nature, history, and mortality.

One factor that changed the field of literary studies over the last fifty years was the opening of "literature" and "criticism" to other disciplines, themselves in turn submitted to the questioning of the literary. Hartman has been one among many forces in this enterprise. One would have to be sparse here, but the reconsideration of "writing" in relation to fields like history, psychoanalysis, anthropology, would, in its impetus, demand that such fields recognize the "literary" element imbricated in their sense of the discipline. Fields have historically repressed such knowledges (Nietzsche says that a discipline can be defined by what it forbids its practitioners to do), but critics like Hartman have brought these intersections and ambivalences to the foreground. Such reading practices have been critiqued by arguments about historicity and culture, but the relations

Hartman traces between historicity and culture on the one hand, and literary reading on the other (in his most recent work on trauma), make any swift answer to these issues problematic. What keeps the negotiation of these distances a critical problem is that in these negotiations (or contaminations) the stable categories by which each concept can be said to stay in place are instead shifting uneasily, endlessly, until the very oppositions that account for their stability seem to come undone.

Of these, none is more ultimate than that between "life" and "death," and it is telling that several of these essays point to the intimacy, in Wordsworth, between the animate and the inanimate. The distinction between the living and the dead is already dismantled by Nietzsche in *The Gay Science*: "Let us beware of saying that life is opposed to death. The living is merely a type of what is dead, and a very rare type." Nietzsche suggests here a critical process in which everything becomes something else, in which things turn into their opposites, in which nothing is its solid self, so the oppositions that allow us to classify and thus to keep chaos at bay enter into contaminatory, chiasmic, vertiginous relation with one another. In the same paragraph (which ends with the sentence quoted above), he aphoristically suggests that there are no accidents in nature because there are no purposes. That the living and the dead are types of one another is an iteration in another register of this claim that "once you know that there are no purposes [in nature], you also know that there is no accident."[3]

No accident, no purpose, no causality. Hartman's intellectual life would appear to have been dedicated to the traumatic power of accidence, of that very absence of causality that transforms the unremarkable into the remarkable, the commonplace into a moment of surprise. He speaks, in Wordsworth's own tongue, of the "unimaginable touch of time" which places upon us not only the burden of accidence, of historical or individual happening, but also the burden of response. Wordsworth's poetry "responds," in extraordinary excess, to almost negligible, accidental "passages" of nature, and that response translates itself, in Hartman's work, into the listener's own "telling"—a telling that courts silence, that enters into the perilous uncharted territory of the unsayable.

In "Reading: The Wordsworthian Enlightenment," Hartman refers to the Boy of Winander as a "moving accident," an episode "close to plotless," an event that remains unutterable as event, or as Maurice Blanchot puts it, "ungraspable as fact and fascinating as remembrance."[4] For, finally, how does one speak the ultimate accidence of death itself—a death that has not happened yet has already taken place? To read what is not there, to hear the absence of echo, to think of the failure of the owl's response as a major event, is to think of the boy's—the poet's—traumatic encounter as a recognition of death. Hartman refers to the Boy of Winander as a "posthumous figure," as if the autobiographical act were always, irreducibly, a gesture of farewell.

"Farewell" is the last word in Hartman's text, lingering both as text and as quotation with the force of the boy's absent echo. Yet "farewell" is also where the story begins, a "yet once more" that makes the poet's mind, in Hartman's words, the mind of a survivor. Indeed, despite the distance between Hartman's two major concerns—poetry (Wordsworth in particular) and Holocaust studies, the one aesthetic, the other historical or theological—the two are linked by what it means to survive (*sur-vivre*). Under Hartman's touch survival becomes a great deal more complex and layered than a response to literal death—even that of the death camps. Survival responds, in poetry and in testimony, to an encounter the trauma of which remains inarticulate and often disarticulated, so the task of the listener, like that of the boy, the poet, the critic, is of a kind of "overhearing," a term Hartman uses in his early work. One never witnesses the event, or the landscape, or the poem with any directness—or if one does, that is a way of missing what is not spoken.

There is a by-now-famous example of Hartman's overhearing in his reading of "A slumber did my spirit seal." What he hears is not exactly what Wordsworth writes:

> No motion has she now, no force;
> She neither hears nor sees;
> Rolled round in earth's diurnal course,
> With rocks, and stones, and trees.

Hartman overhears the suggestiveness of "tears" embedded in "trees." Aside from the fact that the poem is pure Wordsworth, Hartman's mingling of rocks and tears points to an active link between the most hardened element in nature and the least audible sign of human grief. The tears echo the preceding stanza's "fears" and "years," and it takes Hartman's ears to follow the inaudible but true ending to the poem. And the response is more than grief—for grief is an appropriate, measured response to the measure of accident that befalls one. Hartman deals with what is in excess of grief on the part of the survivors—a traumatic event to which neither the survivor nor the listener has an adequate response.

This fissure between an event and its telling, between speaker and listener, accounts for the profound sense of isolation in Romantic poetry. It is as if grief, and the mortality that enfolds and generates it, created a language so encrypted that the poet even as survivor cannot seem to hear his own voice or the echo of his voice. Yet Wordsworth insists on a "primal sympathy" which binds us in our humanity. Ortwin de Graef addresses this complex issue of sympathy tugged in opposite directions in his reading, in "Encrypted Sympathy," of "Salisbury Plain" and the Intimations Ode, poems in which the privileged infant nonetheless has to grapple with the "untimely tooth of time." Sympathy ought to function as a "community-generating principle," yet as de Graef argues, "sympathetic strength in the face of suffering can only be purchased . . . at the cost of denying the radical difference of death itself." Death, the ubiquitous gravesite, the lapidary inscription, the unimaginable touch of time: they are the names for a nameless thing, an otherness so pervasive and disruptive that the very insight into it is constitutive of trauma. De Graef reads the two poems across each other to bring to the fore the irreparable untimeliness of every timely utterance, the "thought" that lies too deep for "tears" and that is itself a "wound."

Wounds and scars are markers in Hartman territory. Far from being signatures of past pain, these are the tropes by which Hartman undoes a philosophical tradition whose main argument is transcendence and whose high point is Hegel. *Scars of the Spirit* takes issue with Hegel's notion of a consciousness that can be present to itself, that can rise above temporality and come to "see." From his first text, *The Unmediated Vision*, to his most recent, *Scars*, Hartman underscores the failure of the Hegelian enterprise. That failure is at the heart of poetry, of its mournful awareness of mortality as the space in which, from which, we "cannot see to see." We are here in that strange, nameless space that Dickinson marks with a well-placed comma between subject and verb. Her slant of light slashes invisibly like a knife, and

> We can find no scar,
> But internal difference,
> Where the Meanings, are —

This is no mere punctuation, but a deliberate indication of the way the poem fails to speak itself, name its meaning, make subject and verb responsive to each other. The heaviest comma in the English language, it marks the black hole into which consciousness falls, perishing from before itself for just the scrutiny that is the poem. It is as if the poem, contra Hegel, managed to trace its passage through itself and find in its place, in its own place, nothing, no space, except the comma dangling down.

Though Hartman does not address this poem, Dickinson epitomizes this refusal of transcendence which devolves into the most concrete yet elusive of signs — the comma wrongly, rightly placed. We witness here a consciousness ensconced within its own nothingness and unable to speak it, which is Dickinson's version of Wordsworth's long half hour of mute contemplation by the grave. There is in both poets an encounter with the inhuman "other" which takes the form of an encounter with nature, and which Hartman reads as an encounter with temporality.

Paul Fry engages this issue of nature as the alien presence that has the power to afflict us. Nature, he suggests, is the domain of the inhuman, and to think of nature as the inhuman, deadly element to which our own life is opposed yet to which our own mortality is linked is to articulate an unspoken bond between the human and the inhuman and, by a circuitous route, to come to see the human as the unnatural element of nature, nature's "other," as much as "Nature" is the human's "other."

This otherness is a persistent concern in Wordsworth criticism. How to tell one's own story, how to relate to a figure on the landscape, how to relate at all to this ubiquitous alterity, is a propelling impulse in Romantic poetry. What one might define as "trauma" in its most evident sense already exists as an implicit dimension in Romanticism. The more extreme examples are not Wordsworth's, yet they serve to place Wordsworth within a context in which he appears malleable and assimilable and yet is also the most resistant and ambivalent of nineteenth-century poets.

Two poems — Keats's "This Living Hand" and Coleridge's "Rime of the Ancient Mariner" — articulate some of the vexed relations of nature, memory, mortality, and trauma — the very paths that Hartman has himself thought through and traversed from his earliest work to his latest.

> This living hand, now warm and capable
> Of earnest grasping would, if it were cold
> And in the icy silence of the tomb
> So haunt thy days and chill thy dreaming nights
> That thou would wish thine own heart dry of blood
> So in my veins red life might flow again
> And thou be conscience calmed. See, here it is.
> I hold it towards you.

This is a poem that compels an answer — from Fanny Brawne, but more importantly, from the reader. A hand that is living but that is already dead, that becomes dead by the conditional "if" of the second line, proleptically imagining its own accomplished nothingness; a hand that demands payment from the living, the payment of life itself for the sake of allaying guilt; and, the final gesture of holding out this hand, as if in greeting or welcome but in fact being imperiously held forward as demand, as the imperial command to join the dead in their mortality, to understand the mortal nature of living and of writing, indeed, almost extracting such a promise from us in the very process of our reading. Even as the poem articulates an exchange—give me your life for mine, your reading for my writing—it knows full well that such exchange cannot be. Yet there is an ambivalent interaction here between reader and writer, between writer and survivor, between those who remember and those who are lost. The subtext of this poem is not exchange but an uneasy sense that we are somehow, already, in the place where breathing stops, that the act of survival entails the synonymity of memory and guilt.

One of the classic "guilt poems" of this period, Coleridge's "Rime of the Ancient Mariner," attempts, through its gloss, to allay this guilt, to regulate chaos by establishing a series of cause-and-effect relations without which we could not lead an ethical life. But the poem persistently undoes the gloss, almost as if it prefigured Nietzsche's "Let us beware of saying that there are laws in nature. There are only necessities" (*Gay Science*, par. 109). It thus tells the other story, showing cause-and-effect relations to be merely the imposition of a narrative sequence, a kind of "retroactive meaningfulness" (Freud calls it *Nachträglichkeit*). What are the causes for one's actions, and why do they precipitate the kind of guilt that never leaves the Mariner? Whether to incur guilt or exculpate ourselves, retroactive narratives are the story within the Mariner's story, and they respond to his inability to get hold of his tale, to tell his story straight. Hence his compulsion to repeat his tale, attempting to catch up with it, to grasp it, to contain it, to understand it. Despite his telling efforts it always evades him, excluding him from his own story as Blanchot and Kafka (among others) say they are excluded from their own writing, becoming exiles to themselves. Keats's demand that one give up one's life for the dead (tropologically), or that reading be in a responsive (and absolute) relation to writing, is a version of the Mariner's compulsion to repeat or to compel the compulsion to repeat.

The Mariner's tale is exemplary for a number of reasons. First, it highlights the context of narrative. Narrative, against the gloss, tells the story of random acts for which a relation between cause and sequence can only be threaded "after." The Mariner's shipmates first state that the killing was a "hellish thing" because the albatross "made the breeze to blow," and in the next stanza "They all averred, [he] had killed the bird / That brought the fog and mist." The poem in this way opens the space for a different (un)ethical tale of violent acts and violent tellings and retellings. In a sense, whatever the Mariner does or does not do has less to do with his act than with his reading of it. The reading is everything; it is a narrative that ensconces his life in a frame but that repeatedly evades that frame ("wrenches" it) and precipitates its reiteration. The Mariner's tale is fueled by guilt, in part perhaps for the violence against nature, but more heavily weighted toward the sequence of events following the random killing, which results in the death of his shipmates. The compulsion to repeat seems as connected to the guilt of survivorship as the invocation of that guilt in the Keats poem. The dead become very much present to the living, and the awareness of their presence, that is to say, of the imbrication of the living and the dead, seems to confer upon the speaker what he calls "strange powers of speech." Transported by the agony of memory, yet unable to be precise as to the nature of that agony, the poem derives its power from its inability to tell.

> Since then, at an uncertain hour,
> That agony returns:
> And till my ghastly tale is told,
> This heart within me burns.

The uncertainty of the hour suggests that the randomness that afflicts actions and their consequences in the poem also marks the return of traumatic memories that the telling cannot get past, cannot get right. The telling never results in the kind of forgiveness, of transcendence, that the Mariner yearns for. He is caught in a space of nothingness in which there is nothing to forgive and nobody to grant forgiveness, and yet, against this nothingness, what remains is guilt and the iteration of it.

Ferguson comments in her essay "Romantic Memory" that "Romanticism, in the process of charging consciousness with the revaluation of actions that can be recalled only in the sense of being remembered and not at all in the sense of being revoked or undone, creates a mental apparatus for manufacturing guilt much more rapidly than it can forgive it." Nietzsche's conflation of the impossibility of forgetting and the necessity of doing so in order to live, and Dickinson's "Remorse — is Memory — awake — " are versions of Ferguson's insight about memory's activation or reactivation of traumatic guilt. This may be why theories of the "wound" have been so persistent in relation to Romantic poetry. Harold Bloom refers to the philological connection between blessing and wound (*bles-*

sure), and one of Geoffrey Hartman's essays is entitled "Reading the Wound." A wound makes possible a certain kind of understanding—or rather, a certain kind of understanding is itself a wounding. The essays in this volume that deal with the wound recognize the intense link between guilt and mortality. Hartman narrates and Ferguson comments on a paradigmatic story of a woman forced to relinquish her child, which she has bundled up and which she later refers to no longer as a "baby" but as a "bundle" after having been forced to give it up to the guard at the deportation site. Ferguson suggests that the slippage (she calls it "connection") between "baby" and "bundle" enables this survivor to "single herself out in her own mind as someone forced into an act that she cannot accept as one she would willingly remember herself committing." The trauma that is made visible, or overheard, in this woman's account is linked to an act that is "retrieveless" and to which guilt accrues precisely because there is death.

Ferguson's essay takes on the exploration of guilt in relation to memory and bridges the distance between Romantic poetry and current studies of trauma, history, and identity. Ferguson suggests that what we remember is less a function of remembering the act or the event and more a function of remembering the consequences of our actions. These are consequences that may have been unmeant, and certainly unforeseen, yet we suffer the effects as if they had been meant in full foresight; we are responsible despite our blindness, as Oedipus is. The ancient Greeks had a very different way of thinking about responsibility and guilt than we do, because for them pollution inhered in the act, regardless of motive. In Ferguson's reading, we might say that responsibility inheres in the consequences. Her astute comment that one remembers the act not for itself but for what it precipitates opens up a space for rethinking history and poetry as well as the legal system and the way it thinks about acts of witnessing. Memory, in her reading of Hartman, constructs retrospective action, and that retrospection has the capacity to haunt and to wound. The living hand that is already dead as we read Keats's poem is also very much alive, since its demand has the capacity to wound *even when no act has been committed that would account for the guilt that it elicits.*

It may be that the wound, according to Freud, is always already there, what Lukacher calls a "preexistent earliness that precedes conscience and the superego." If this is the case, he argues, then "primal guilt lies on the threshold between organic life and inorganic existence, and between life and death; it is at once life's protection against death and the work of death always already at work in life itself."[5] Harold Bloom's essay on Kafka in *The Western Canon* arrives at a similar insight: "Hamlet suffers guilt only for the murder he has not yet performed. Shrewder in this regard than Goethe, Kafka seems to have understood that guilt, in Shakespeare, is not to be doubted and precedes all actual crimes."[6] Bloom goes on to say that for Kafka we are guilty "precisely because our deepest self is indestructible." That is a rather Dantesque notion, but it is also the Derridean argument in *The Gift of Death:* "This guilt is originary, like original sin. Before any fault is determined, I am guilty inasmuch as I am responsible."[7] This is not the place to expand on this notion of an "always already" or "from the very first" wired-in mental apparatus, but these arguments open up an interesting path that links concepts as apparently distanced from one another as nature, mortality, accidence, history, and trauma. Lukacher's arguments on this contaminatory relation between the living and the dead, between protection and infection, calls forth the Nietzsche of *The Gay Science* and the telling connection Nietzsche makes between there being no accidents in nature because there are no purposes with the fact that one cannot oppose living and dying. Death is an "accident" in the human world of reason and laws, but nothing more than a minor event in the world of nature, where there is nobody who commands and nobody who obeys. Mortality has no "meaning" in nature, and perhaps that absence of meaning is part of its traumatic power in the human world. It is because Wordsworth so subtly interlinks mortality and nature that his poems provide an opening for a study of crisis in its most intense yet also in its most untellable forms. Hartman suggests this relation between intensity and untellability when he connects trauma and sublimity in his interview with Cathy Caruth.

The reason to focus on Hartman's work in this volume is that his work on Wordsworth and his work on Holocaust studies have bridged the apparent divide between poetry and history, between textuality and culture. The critic who thinks of Wordsworth as the poet who turns the commonplace into the remarkable is also the critic who works with dramatic tellings of catastrophic events. Hartman mentions, in the interview with Caruth, that "the reflective moment is not just a moment of pastoral safety and rest but *one in which you can be equal to your experience.*" To be equal to your experience, you would have to catch it, speak it, know that you have traversed the interval between saying and being, something that neither the Mariner nor the Boy of Winander can do. The gap between saying and being is another register of guilt being inbred, of the poet's inability to state, directly and unmediatedly, what the scene meant. Meaning is the subtext—what the poem cannot know it knows and from the simultaneity of which it derives its power. At times, that subtext erupts into the poem's surface with considerable force. Hartman quotes an abrupt Coleridgean line from the "Rime" in this regard: "At one stride comes the dark." He posits a difference between the suddenness of the dark in Coleridge and the slower, Wordsworthian "gentle shock of mild surprise," yet the gentleness of the conversational style in Wordsworth overlays traumatic episodes that break through (interrupt) the apparent gentleness and seamlessness of the narrative. If trauma and sublimity are linked by intensity, gentleness is the clothing for a very deep distress that the poet contends with and that "humanises his soul" only to the extent that it lays it open to the experience of the inhuman in the guise of mortality. Robert Griffin aptly captures this feeling of one's own elusiveness when he suggests, in "Wordsworth's Horse," that the horse "is a figure for the human borderer between this world and the next and for poetry as the appropriate middle space." In Griffin's reading, the horse passage epitomizes a "dynamics of bordering" synonymous with self-consciousness itself, with a movement not distinguishable from arrest, the living and the dead entangled and "hanging" in this space.

This "space between" is crucial in Hartman, because he appears to travel a great distance between two unlikely subjects: Romantic poetry and Holocaust testimonies. The philosophical link exists because sublimity (Kant) is in some sense always traumatic, but Hartman activates the subtlest nuances between the two and connects the question of "reading" to the register of ethics. We seem to be here at some distance from the Wordsworthian concern with "nature," but nature is the name for the most intense and difficult-to-read moral teachings. Hartman's earliest work, *The Unmediated Vision*, posits the problem of the poet's relation to nature in terms of cognition: the production, by nature entering into the mind, of "thoughts of more deep seclusion." Although in that work Hartman moves from cognition to the principle of generosity, to the transcendence of seclusion, there is already in it a concern with the poet's "internal difference" from himself, with the rift of self-consciousness which Nature appears alternately to deepen and to heal. It is in this sense that Nature is a moral teacher, wounding the child with lessons that can hardly be apprehended even in later years, and thus memory of childhood and the moral wisdom one might draw become thickly interlinked in Wordsworth's poetry. Gerald Bruns, in a discussion of *The Unmediated Vision* in "Poetic Knowledge," points out that already in his earliest work Hartman is trying to "get the subject out from under the furniture of consciousness as representation, including such representations as the 'self.' " Pierced by otherness, the "self" in Hartman's early readings of Wordsworth is already a problematic entity requiring the "subduing of the eye" for understanding to take place. Bruns points out that the act of sight becomes, in *The Unmediated Vision*, "a moral responsibility" to which Hartman responds as he returns, pointedly, to the connection between poetic knowledge and moral wisdom. Testimony in Hartman's hands follows upon the very high sort of hearing that the Boy of Winander is attuned to, in particular, the acute hearing of silence and the trauma that swirls around and at its center. The poet/survivor, the "posthumous" speaker, elides the unspeakable, willing to say but not saying, speaking inaudibly. In her introduction to *Writing and Madness*, Shoshana Felman asks: "Might not literature indeed be defined as that which speaks, precisely, out of what reduces it to silence? That which speaks by virtue of its own muffling?"[8] If silence and speech are not opposite but overlaid, then historical, personal, poetic traumas bespeak the rhetorical impossibility of naming the shock or fully understanding it, of reaching past the "deep seclusion" to which Hartman refers.

In recent years a variety of historicisms have returned issues of representation to the simpler version of the eye and what it sees and knows for real. Hartman's readings of both poetry and history have sustained the problematic density of thought itself, and his subtlety has provoked a wide range of critical responses, responses that, even when contestatory, attest to the critical power he commands. Essays by Paul Fry, Alan Liu, and Kevis Goodman take up the question of history in Hartman's writing. Fry comments, in a suggestive phrase, that "the subversion of meaning itself becomes a technique for making nature appear." That would mean that "meaning," as Felman puts it, is the opposite of "truth," and that "the real" can only presence itself in the absence of human (or humanly constructed) meaning" (*Writing and Madness*, 120). This is an issue that arises between Fry and Liu. Liu says that "nature is the name under which we use the nonhuman to validate the human," whereas Fry's reading is that "nature is our own nonhuman existence, forgotten once named"—or, as Dickinson says, "forgotten, as fulfilled."[9] Fry's telling phrase is that Wordsworth realizes, in the Boy of Winander, that "inanimate things came before animate ones" and that such an understanding puts into question "the priority of language to the being of death disclosed in the sensory object." Death, the most abysmal absence, is rendered present, in Fry's reading, through the vehicle of nature. Nothing, in this "return to ecology" reading of nature, allows for return—only for the doubt of that return, for the doubt that temporality inscribes in us. Contra Bate, Fry undoes the "certainty of the following spring's return" by arguing "the imposition of pastness by extinction." To be "on the verge of life," as he argues, is to be traversing (almost) that borderline between life and death, between a "body" and Liu's concept of the body that "becomes no longer quite a body," fluttering, as Wallace Stevens says, its empty sleeves.

This emptiness responds to Liu's sense of a connection between history and Wordsworth which links New Historicism with "loss." Liu critiques New Historicists and post–New Historicists who think of poetry as the loss of historical truth and comments that they labor under a "secret Romantic ideology," since this mourning for the loss of history is itself elegiac. Liu's argument that "history is the absence that is the very possibility of the 'here and now' " is a complex one that links loss with gain and "regret" with "jubilation": "for only if we conserve the possibility of real loss can we also hold the world open to the notion of real, and miraculous, gain."

Liu critiques "presence" and "absence" as ways of thinking about loss and about history because they promote the illusion of the possibility of absolute losses and gains. To the extent that history is for him the absence of the here and now, the ending of his essay ("for us—here and now—it is loss that is the 'unpresentable' ") reopens the question of representation around which much of the controversy between historicisms and poststructuralisms have danced. Goodman takes up this question in her essay: "How events become history necessarily entails questions about work performed by acts of representation." By representation she means not a simple relationship between inside/outside or between text and event but a concern "about the operation and the limits of the aesthetic dimension in the transmission of historical event." Goodman's insistence on the role of the aesthetic in relation to history and trauma is a way of marking off and responding to what she calls the historicist suspicion of psychoanalytic and (by extension) trauma studies. She teases out a connection between Liu's sense that "denial is the strongest engagement with history" and contemporary studies on trauma. Current controversies around the terms "history" and "aesthetics" mask for Goodman a yearning for an unmediated vision of history that would translate itself into advocacy. Her contestation of Liu is that history surfaces "not only *in* but also *because* of an aesthetic medium that seals, sets some limit, to terror and makes representation possible."

Yet "terror"—the failure of representation to contain—remains a constant in Romantic poetry, at once lending itself to and resisting political discourse. An easy version of twentieth-century criticism might oppose the political and the textual, but Hartman's work complicates and undoes that opposition, and these essays return, in manifold ways, to the consequences of an unstable "boundary" between them. Hartman's overhearing of "trees" and "tears" in "A slumber did my spirit seal" is an example of the terror (linguistic, autobiographical) that can be unleashed by this "play," a play whose seriousness Hartman underscores by the word "wound." Not in Wordsworth alone but across the Western tradition Hartman hears something "other" than the word, a "spectral dimension" made explicit in Lear's "Look with thine ears." Patricia Parker's study of the "metamorphoses of eye and ear" in *The Winter's Tale* points to this movement between what may appear to be play, "mere" pun, and what devolves, of its own force, into a chaos that stretches all the way to the politics of the proper name. Parker points out that Shakespeare was writing at a time when sound and the aural were still far more important than later print culture would lead us to suspect. When Shakespeare was edited in the eighteenth century according to the principles of neoclassicism, most editions were biased against wordplay, and they produced the influential textual tradition we have inherited. Parker's insistence on "seeing with the ear again" stems from a sense that the modern pun "anachronistically suggests the contrived joining of what was not yet clearly separate." To hear what in Shakespeare was not yet separate is to hear a relentless and unstoppable multiplication that begins, and ends, in Lear's "nothing." From "bear" to the breeding of this "nothing" underlying orthographical regulation is a "negative generation" that, like a black hole, engulfs what it has bred. Hartman's own reading of what begins, perhaps, with the adjacency of trees and tears, ends up threatening the very edifice of the autobiographical self.

Representation and, at the other end, terror. It is not surprising that Hartman, who tells us that "every understanding is built on the undoing of a previous understanding," should generate the liminal questions raised by these essays. The arguments about nature, history, aesthetics, transcendence, trauma are ultimately arguments about the labor of "reading." One assumes that the act of listening requires a "sympathetic imagination" and that the ethical dimension of reading is built upon this premise. Yet de Graef suggests the very opposite: that the failure of such sympathetic imagination, which is in some register the complication of the question of representation, is productive, even constitutive, of the "material effectiveness" of literature. "The fact," he says, "that this ethicopolitical resistance to a rhetoric of sympathy is generated by the text itself indicates that there may be more than one way to be caught in the ethical turn: not only by understanding the literary text as a vehicle for the sympathetic imagination, but rather by reading its failure to cover difference with the cloak of sympathy." What is interesting about this mode of reading against the grain is that de Graef links the sympathetic imagination to certain transparencies such as representation *and* transcendence. Thus, the "failure" of sympathy becomes the most profound ethical act, because it is an acknowledgment not only of the mortality of the human community but of the abysmal isolation with which we must confront our mortality.

Peter Manning's erudite essay "Musings Near Aquapendente" gives us another window on the writer's (in this case Wordsworth's) relation to mortality. Neither solitude, nor the proleptic living of a death that has not happened yet, but a calculated move to regulate his own posterity. In his reading the "hanging" motion of the waterfall (*pendente*) leads to a quite different account of the poet's response to recognitions of mortality. Here Manning departs from, and recontextualizes, what Griffin calls the Wordsworth "signature" around the verb "hang." The musing of the poem, Manning suggests, is less an elegy for Scott or proleptically for himself than it is an expression of the joy of sur-vival. Wordsworth's persistent returns to the scene of autobiography, his meditations on eventual absence, are a different sort of signature inasmuch as they signal the poet's "multilayered resituating of himself in literary history." Manning's exquisitely researched argument tracks the "friendship" between Wordsworth and Walter Scott and the complex ways in which Scott's decline finds its way into—indeed, accounts for—Wordsworth's anticipatory elegies, among them "Tintern Abbey," "Yarrow Revisited," "A trouble, not of clouds," "Extempore Effusion upon the Death of James Hogg," and "Essay on Epitaphs." The force of Manning's argument is that Wordsworth's elegies in advance of a death are not expressions of friendship but a construction of the poet's own place in literary history. Far from these recognitions of mortality emphasizing the poet's solitude and laying him open to the unimaginable touch of time, Wordsworth's musings are for Manning "no longer a form of solitude" but an active, ongoing "public self-construction," a "performance that he scripted and directed."

Yet this self-scripting is not antithetical to the consciousness of mortality which may in part underlie it. Andrzej Warminski's reading of Hegel articulates this connection:

> Consciousness can die because it can know its own death; it can represent its own death to itself—indeed, such self-representation is the "truth" of consciousness (i.e., self-consciousness). In other words, a condition of consciousness is its having to represent its own death to itself, but such representation is not possible without a subterfuge. . . . We have to die while watching ourselves die. We require a spectacle, theater, sacrifice, a comedy in which we can represent our own death to ourselves and survive it.[10]

The consciousness *of* death which appears to be constitutive of consciousness itself marks both poetry and criticism in the last two centuries. And that marking—Donald Marshall calls it a "blow"—makes Wordsworth's intimations of immortality both suspect and indispensable. Like a cello's lingering note, the Immortality Ode ends with that braiding of the two. Perhaps it is in his self-scripting, in his attempting to create for himself a place in a historical spectrum he can only imagine, that the poet simultaneously eschews immortality and attends (in acts of almost "pure" attention) to the "material" and the "concrete"—to objects, events, "things" that ground him in a history he also wishes to transcend.

Marshall, in "Writing Criticism," engages the question of historical understanding by insisting that a poem's movement away from the specificity of historical circumstance "does not mean that the poem flies away from concrete life, leaving it behind, but that it calls upon concrete life, deflecting it with a blow that is historical in the sense that its ramifications are unpredictable and endless." What de Graef terms a failure of the sympathetic imagination and Marshall "a blow" suggests not only the dismantling of transcendence but an accompanying insistence on concreteness or materiality, as well. Marshall's metaphor of a "blow" is percipient, for it addresses simultaneously the poetic and the historical, the Boy of Winander's shock ("gentle" though it may be) and the force of testimony. It points to the heart of Hartman territory, to the unexpected force of reading itself. Kafka writes to Oskar Pollak that "what we need are books that hit us like a most painful misfortune, like the death of someone we loved more than we love ourselves. . . . A book must be the axe for the frozen sea within us."[11] This violence, so different from the resignation in so many of Kafka's characters, describes the disruptive force of thought itself—a thought that in Wordsworth, in Hartman, in testimonies, is at once distinct from the literality of death and inseparable from the otherness that haunts it. Not an axe but a gentle shock, yet one as compelling as the other.

It is precisely in relation to a violence that is often described and even at times enacted that J. Douglas Kneale's focus on "gentleness" in relation to reading (both Wordsworth's and Hartman's) takes on a particular and welcome charm. The halted traveler in his essay is not violently wrenched (as he is in Coleridge's "Rime") or violently suspended but gestures toward a human capacity to relate to nature under the terms of this generosity or "gentleness." Wordsworth is ambivalent on this topic, because while gentleness is an aim, it becomes almost (in "Nutting," for instance) a retrospective wish to undo the history of an act, of an event of destruction. The wish aims to undo the act, yet reminds us in the very gesture that it stems from an act opposite the wish. Kneale is right that Hartman's reading in relation to Wordsworth has always been "gentle," yet there is also to Hartman's readings a piercing and searing quality that could almost be compared to the violence of the trauma his understanding unleashes.

Part of the Sturm und Drang is the complex double-step Hartman engages in when he "reads." J. Hillis Miller, in his extraordinary tribute, comments on Hartman's "notice" of "just those passages that most challenge or put in question his own commitments." At the same time, he quotes what for him is one of Hartman's most telling descriptions of Romanticism: "the emergence of the gentle out of the haunted mind."

The closeness, through these essays, of gentleness and wounding (another register of the intimacy of representation and terror) is in itself an insight into Wordsworth. It is almost because something has wounded him (either in the sense of trauma or in the sense of being "moved") that gentleness surfaces so often in him—as reality, as illusion, or as wish—perhaps because almost invariably the first instance of relation in Wordsworth is not communion but wrenching. Even when there is generosity and gentleness ("there is a blessing in this gentle breeze"), this blessing is soon followed by a correspondent breeze that is tumultuous and "vexes its own creation." To ask why this should be so is to return to the question of mortality. Lucy Newlyn, in her response to Kneale, highlights the wrenching effects of this "aftering," the other word for which is "mortality." "No amount of continuity between voices can do away with death or the belatedness it incurs." Newlyn links reading and writing to this recognition of mortality. She suggests that for Hartman the act of reading is an act of listening to prior words that might otherwise be drowned. She responds to Kneale's reading of "Nutting" with a reading that foregrounds, as in Kneale, Hartman's sense of the importance of gentleness, or as Hartman also puts it, "generosity," since the end of "Nutting," for Newlyn, is "somewhere between admonishment and a blessing." But implicit in Newlyn's reading is a cautionary note: to listen is to bless, but blessing is also a wounding, perhaps, through the piercing insight of a reading, but also through the acknowledgment of a shared mortality. Newlyn refers to "a will-to-power that reflects on our own survival as readers" which would, as in the Keats text, point to an uneasy and tense relationship between reader and text, no matter the level of generosity or sympathy.

As distant as "ecology" might appear to be from "reading," Newlyn's notion of ecology (a concept that Fry takes up in relation to Bate) no longer refers to nature but belongs to the textual field, to the appropriateness or misappropriation (the gentleness or violence) of reading and writing. The gentleness (or generosity) of reading responds to the "magic in the web," to the poet's simultaneous revelation and occlusion of his subject, to his simultaneous muteness and speech. When it is translated onto this register, ecology opens into the political as well as the institutional and aesthetic activities of reading and writing. For Newlyn, the paradigm for this intersection is the "echo." In this untellable "echology," the echo marks off and yet connects these intricate and circuitous relations — between poet and nature, between nature and history, between the living and the dead, between the critic and the poet.

These echoes traverse even — and especially — the biblical text, and do so, in Leslie Brisman's and Hillis Miller's essays, in political and ethical registers whose "call" for justice is precisely dependent on understanding the complexities of reading. Brisman points out that what is at stake in Hartman's reading of midrash is reading as risk, as "daring to go wrong." To read is to be capable of hearing something other: "Do not read *kirivyah* — like a child — but *kilivyah* — a little dog." At first glance no more than a pun, the slippage of a consonant, in Brisman's argument this hearing-otherwise disallows any simple "historical" understanding or any identification of scripture with either "purely tautological" or "unquestionably local" pronouncements. At the very point at which the weight of history is felt most keenly, midrash engages in a playfulness that is serious to the precise extent that it dislocates. That dislocation is the call to justice. Moving between the New Testament and the Old, Brisman focuses unerringly on the performativity of the prophetic mode ("But I say unto you . . .") and on the links thus forged between the political and the prophetic in the movement across testaments — between Moses and Jesus. The call to justice is heard — is overheard — in the slippage or echo that turns "daring to go wrong" into "daring to do right."

A call to action from the dislocation of reading. Miller's "Rachel When from the Lord" is a complex and layered performance of a reading in which Proust and the biblical text unfold upon and within one another. St. Loup's infatuation with Rachel can be designated as a "reading into," a seeing what is not there; Marcel's seeing what is there ("Rachel when from the Lord"), however, is no less performative and no less constitutive of a memory ("a memory without memory"). Miller's analysis underscores the incompatibility between performativity and knowledge, and at the same time and for that very reason he reads "act" as a "call," laden with echoes and reverberations and given weight by them. Like Griffin's borderer, inhabiting a space between this world and the next, Miller's example of Rachel and her precursor, Magdalene, as "threshold figure" gives the call substance, makes of it an unsettling of accounts, an imperious demand, and an ethical responsibility.

This reading of the call as demand and as gift, as a necessity, offers a glimpse into the complex movement in Hartman between poetry and testimony. In an interview with Ian Balfour and Rebecca Comay, Hartman speaks of Moses's call to "give ear" and to bear witness.[12] Witnessing, he says, "begins by being a physical fact involving eye and ear, but a moral dimension—the issue of responsibility for attestation, for continuing to make known what was (is) seen and heard—immediately appears." The urgency seems to be less death-related, as Hartman says later, and more a matter of acknowledgment, of discharging in part the indebtedness that comes from having "seen" and "heard." But whether Moses or Wordsworth, in Hartman's keen ear testimony is not different in kind from the mute speech of the poet or the gentle shock that leaves the Boy of Winander suspended. Because, in the final finding of the ear, both poet and critic must speak around a lack that haunts what is "seen" and "heard": a self that is marked by evanescence and a future and past that can be acknowledged only in a movement in which prophecy is not distinguishable from testimony or celebration from mourning.

All these essays, in their own ways, respond to the act of telling, and many of them turn to the act of listening, to the muteness, to the speech, of the Boy of Winander episode. This is a far more traumatic and untellable scene, perhaps, than "Nutting," because there is no "gentleness" to assuage the violence of the temporality that intrudes. The act of reading in this case is an act of listening to the silence of the owls and all that it portends. The suspense, the halting, the listening for something that does not come, the gentle shock of mild surprise, the reversal, as Paul de Man says, of heaven and earth in that "uncertain heaven," and then the reflection of the grown man upon the boy who is already—always—dead—point to the paradoxical conjunction of muteness and speech, to the voice of the poet and the deadness of what he wishes to voice. "The Boy of Winander" is a far cry from Wordsworth's wish that the child be father of the man. This poem holds forth and at the same time disrupts the promise of such continuity. Hardly any other poet can appear so gentle and yet unleash such violence upon an unsuspecting reader. The echo of the boy's voice is in itself traumatic because at that point he cannot tell which is which—what belongs to him and what belongs to nature. The inability to sever one thing from another, to constitute an either/or situation, opens the path to the contaminatory energies that Nietzsche addresses and to the as well contaminatory energies between reading and writing, between, we might also say, Wordsworth and Hartman. And they collect in the Boy of Winander episode.

What in Keats's "This Living Hand" and Coleridge's "Rime" surfaces as the guilt whose telling cannot allay the trauma of it, in the Boy of Winander episode comes through as the unspoken recognition of mortality that renders the poet mute and that nonetheless makes him speak without speaking it. Ferguson's remark in her essay that actions (in this case it would be events, scenes, episodes) become memorable less because we remember them than because of their effects is dead center here. In the Boy of Winander episode, nothing much seems to happen, yet what happens is of such intense, searing importance that nothing can be the same after the unspeakable recognition. The poet returns to the scene, recalls it, in order to understand the muteness that enfolds him, the untellable hidden in the folds of the telling. As Caruth puts it in *Trauma*, the historical power of the trauma "is not just that the experience is repeated after its forgetting, but that it is only in and through its inherent forgetting that it is first experienced at all."[13] The poem in this case becomes both the process of uncovering trauma and the locus where that trauma occurs, contained by the aesthetic, as Goodman suggests, yet also unleashed through it. The untellable is the boy's and the poet's mortality, and, as Fry so succinctly puts it, the natural channel of communication between the human and the natural breaks under the weight of another barely tellable recognition: that of "a silent being in nature which, somatically signaled, is also a being toward his own imminent death." The sensory object enfolds "the being of death," an insight that de Man, in his essay "Time and History in Wordsworth," articulates as Wordsworth's "anticipating a future event as if it existed in the past."[14]

In first-person mode, in the autobiographical *Prelude*, the Boy of Winander episode moves into the third person as the poet recognizes his own death, not yet accomplished. This seems to be both the secret and the trauma connected with Romantic poetry, yet also stretching back, as Ferguson indicates, to the ancient Greeks. Trauma is linked to secrecy precisely because there is something unsayable that can be "voiced" in the mode of the inaudible in poetry. Oedipus begins and ends with a secret. Although many critics have read the Oedipus cycle as the movement from ignorance to knowledge, the two plays do not provide such certainty. Oedipus is very good at solving riddles, that is to say, problems for which there is an adequate solution. But when it comes to his own secret, we are told that his feet wander far from the navel of the earth. The navel is a knot, a crux, a connecting point or intersection that might be the locus of revelation, and one expects the cycle to bring forth that revelation. Yet the cycle moves in the opposite direction, from the errancy away from the navel, to recognition and understanding of a certain sort of truth, to the final "space unseen," where Oedipus disappears without really dying, without ever surfacing again in classical underworlds. That space unseen repeats the condition of the secret, of a trauma that cannot be relieved because it cannot be read. In object-relations psychoanalysis, as Rudolph Eckstein and Elaine Caruth have so eloquently pointed out, once the last layer has been peeled off, "the hideous, frightening furies escape, one by one, until, finally, there emerges the last secret: that soft but persistent voice of hope."[15] In this reading, past the last occlusion is hope. In Wordsworth, however, certainly in the Boy of Winander episode, the ultimate secret is not hope but a vision of mortality, of his own mortality, traumatic enough to render it present and yet, as de Man says, in the mode of prefiguration. The past and the present are as interwoven and as inextricable as the boy's hands calling to the owls.

This complex fold in temporality marks off the question of what "reading after" means. Newlyn addresses the "Boy of Winander" as "a poem whose central activity dramatizes 'reading after' in ambivalent ways," the Hartmanian reading of which "has held at bay its anxiety and resurrected its dead," a very suggestive insight, because it links the act of interpretation with the activation of mortality and its effects. Memory and prefiguration are interwoven for the poet in relation to the boy, but they are also interwoven in relation to Hartman's reading of Wordsworth, and to our reading of Hartman.

This interlinking of speaking and listening, of hanging listening, of listening for the echo, of responding in kind, goes to the heart of the genre of the interview, which, as Caruth guides it, foregrounds the relation between the speakable and the unspeakable, between what is seen and how what is seen is remembered, between the figurations of the past and the figurations of the future. At the heart of these intersections is "trauma" in a variety of registers, from the reversal of expectation to the collapsing of recollection and event.

In the interview, Hartman suggests that the unshielded eye or the unshielded senses increase the potential for trauma. Certainly Wordsworth speaks of a time in which the bodily eye was the most "despotic" sense, and the ocular problem with which Ferguson opens her essay also recurs in the closing interview. We presume, of course, the importance of the ocular when we think of witnessing, but the ocular in Wordsworth is also linked to muteness (the visible scene that enters into the boy's heart is in some relation to the poet's muteness, a muteness he nonetheless articulates), to the inability to articulate what one has seen and what its meaning was. This is what Caruth refers to as both development and an impasse to development. The ocular has to be filtered through, made audible, less despotic, and this passage from visibility to audibility in Wordsworth marks Hartman's passage from his *Unmediated Vision* to his most recent studies on Holocaust trauma. Caruth asks Hartman how "pause" and "shock" are linked in the Boy of Winander episode, and his response is that there is in it a "lengthened pause" that makes the boy reflective of mortality. Hartman is consistent in *The Fate of Reading* and *Criticism in the Wilderness* in seeing that nature is a force in relation to the boy's muteness and the poet's speech. In his interview with Caruth, he is more explicit: nature is apprehended, at first, through the ocular, but the ocular occasions trauma, a halting of development, as Caruth calls it, so Wordsworth has to get past the ocular into the audible (i.e., Derrida's "otobiography" and "how to avoid speaking"),[16] into the mute speech that the poem occasions and acknowledges.

This silent acknowledgment responds, as in the "Rime," though far more gently, to the relationship between living and dying and to the random occurrence of their intersection. Hartman mentions, in the interview, that natural development depends on accident and that accident is always defined as something you cannot prepare for. His insight here connects with Liu's and Fry's, for if nature is the domain of the inhuman then Nietzsche is right to call it the space where there are no accidents because there are no purposes. Though the definition of "accident" is different in Hartman and in Nietzsche—indeed, opposite—what Hartman calls accident and Nietzsche the absence of it nonetheless closes in on the psychic wound upon which development, for Hartman, comes to rest but the necessity of which *The Prelude* occludes ("from all internal injury exempt"). De Graef and Manning in opposition over the question of sympathy, Manning and de Man in opposition over the accidence of death: the opposition is rather an overlaying in which the opposites are bound inextricably by the echoes that constitute them.

Necessity and occlusion signal the adjacency, or overlaying, of muteness and speech. When Hartman asks, How is this muteness poetic? the answer is right there: poetry is the gesture, the endlessly repeated desire, to speak silence, to traverse the interval between life and death. Muteness intimates the untellable and unknowable secret, but it also intimates the secret's relationship with what Hartman calls "ecstasy." It would seem strange to link ecstasy and trauma, sublimity and trauma, except by virtue of their intensity. Fry terms the boy's reaction to the failure of response (of the owls) "an ecstatic correlative to death," and

Hartman refers to the boy's (and the poet's) silent recognition of mortality as "the shadow cast by ecstasy." Ecstasy in this reading is neither pleasure nor transcendence but the recognition of a depth that the poetic self dreads but is nonetheless forced to acknowledge.

This overlaying of apparent opposites turns visibility into the "uncertainty" that traverses the poem like a wound. Visibility is causative of trauma not because of its too-potent presence but because its "presence," as it turns to audibility, is proleptic of the viewer's (and listener's) absence, of the shock of listening when one "hangs listening." The traumatic episode in the Boy of Winander is not the moment in which the poet is mute, "looking at the grave in which he [himself] lies," but just prior to it, when the echo stops, when the boy's echoing voice stops pealing, when the rebound of nature has ceased its response and propelled him into the domain of the inhuman. The moment in which the echo does not return, does not return his voice to him, does not return the certainty of his self to him, is the moment in which the remembering and prefiguring of mortality become simultaneous. The crisis here is so undervoiced that it can be said not to be a crisis, but the gentle shock of mild surprise is a result of the absence of one's echo coming back, that is to say, of one's absence to oneself, so that muteness (or as Claire Nouvet calls it, "mute voice")[17] is a listening for what does not come, a listening to one's absence to oneself, so that the visible scene enters with the power of death. The loss of echo prefigures the silence at the heart of the poem, and the muteness of the poet is merely a replication of it. The visible scene enters with the power of inaudibility, as boy, poet, and reader hang listening.

The underlying dramatic element of a well-conducted interview is its own interplay between visibility and audibility (one is present to one another, yet rendered present primarily in the mode of speech). The interview replays, in a distant yet telling way, the interactions between listening and speaking that the Boy of Winander episode stirs. Voicing and listening cover a wide range of activities, including those between patient and psychoanalyst, between trauma victim and interviewer, between critic and poem. The boy's shock is preeminently the shock of recognition, of something already known yet not acknowledged. At its best, the interview does just that: it teases the unspeakable into speech, intervening in the muteness that halts the poet's speech yet also propels it, so that the muteness and the speech interact in provocative ways. Hartman thinks of the interview as a "social act," as a story that, "even if it describes a universe of death, is communicated by a living person." But there is a fissure in the Wordsworthian autobiographical act. As with the "Rime," one lives one's speech, and one's memories, as another, or, as Blanchot puts it, "we have only lived it as though having always already lived it, lived it as other and as though lived by another" (Blanchot, 232). This inability to take hold of one's own experience lies behind the Mariner's obsessive repetition of his ghastly tale and his desperation to find the appropriate listener. The listener for the Mariner is never the right one, even if at the moment he seems "certain": "I pass like night from land to land / I have strange powers of speech. / The moment that his face I see / I know the man that must hear me / To him my tale I teach." His interlocutor is never the last one (in the sense that there are no last words), and in that sense no listener can help the Mariner become present to himself.

Wordsworth is far more reticent and cautious about who listens. In the Boy of Winander episode, in *The Prelude* as a whole, Wordsworth's interlocutor is his own past self, lost yet tauntingly just beyond reach, beyond telling, and thus inviting the telling with compelling force. The entire poem is a gesture, a plea for an act of listening that will restore him to himself, that will allow him to establish a sustained and unbroken conversation with himself, listening to himself through the "other" that is no longer "other." This is the impossible self-presence that poetry promises and the promise of which it betrays, and out of whose breaking emerges "voice." Hartman suggests that "it is voice as well as memory that is recovered from moments of silence and impotence." Voice is thus marked by a fissure, a hiatus that peels off the poem's occlusions. If trauma, as Hartman says, disappears into the stammer we call poetry, then it behooves the listener to listen between the lines, to hear that stammer, that hiatus, as Wordsworth does in the moment when he comments on his muteness, and earlier, in the moment in which the boy hangs "listening." Wordsworth here functions as his own witness, listening to himself, to his already dead self, to his proleptically dead self, witnessing the prefiguration of his own mortality, "listening" to it, in the retrospective and privative form of the poem, yet not so privative that it is not overheard, recalled, refracted in Caruth's interview with Hartman and in the responses each text in this collection enacts. In the final finding of the ear, the Boy of Winander speaks around a traumatic absence, and Hartman's entry into that liminal space — his work — is itself the "call" to which this volume, in its own minor key, responds.

Part I / Nature and Memory in the Post Era

CHAPTER ONE

Reading

The Wordsworthian Enlightenment

Geoffrey H. Hartman

> . . . the poem of one who all the time
> is still in the act of perceiving,
> still turned toward appearances,
> questioning and addressing appearances;
> it turns into conversation;
> it is often a desperate conversation.
>
> — PAUL CELAN

In October 1796 Coleridge published in the *Monthly Magazine* a poem written the previous year, which is now known as "Reflections on having left a Place of Retirement" but which was originally titled "Reflections on entering into active life. A Poem that affects not to be Poetry." In 1797 he prefixed a motto from Horace: *Sermoni propriora* (i.e., more suitable for a sermon, or the kind of poetry Horace called a *sermo*). This blank-verse meditation gives the impression of being an extract from a more continuous self-scrutiny that has no definite length and indeed no good formal precedent.[1] It describes and eulogizes the "Blessèd Place" (line 17) Coleridge felt constrained to leave, as, like Wordsworth in Book 8 of the poem on the growth of his mind, he attempts to go from "Love of Nature" to "Love of Man," from pastoral to philanthropy. Coleridge's poem is too complex — or confused — to be given a short summary, yet it has the virtue of associating to the theme of "coming out" or leaving a place of retirement a problem of style. The question, What is the proper style of a poem like this? keeps company with an explicit moral reflection on what is socially proper in the career of Coleridge as husband, professional, and fellow citizen, who should be engaged, as he called it, in "honorable toil." It is a poem, in short, about a vocation that in conscience cannot be purely contemplative.

Whatever psychological interest the verses have, their linkage of proper style (poetics) and proper style of life (ethics) is puzzling. The association indeed evokes an older, canonical career idea, whereby poets advance from a lower to a higher action, from the apprentice and playful genre of pastoral to the high-serious, heroic epic. But did Coleridge have to bring in the issue of the *genera dicendi*, the theory of levels of style? That there should be some career uncertainty in a twenty-three or -four year old is hardly unusual; yet what has that to do with poetic style—unless the career uncertainty includes poetry itself, and Coleridge did not know whether he was cut out to be a poet or what kind of poetry he should pursue?

"More appropriate to a sermon" alludes to a Horatian genre that was not a sermon in the modern sense but thoughts on society distinguished by their moderation from the more savage satire of Juvenal. It is possible, then, that Coleridge foresaw—and resisted—having to enter a life that was not only more active but also more bloody-minded; one that, even if it pursued the "bloodless fight" waged by writers, could not be devoted, as this poem still is, to benevolence and philanthropy. It is also possible that the tag is a schoolboy joke, mildly self-satirical, since the author, contemplating a career as a Unitarian Minister, knew his propensity for preachment, apparent in this as in other productions. Both life (contemporary social and political duties) and temperament (that of a garrulous sermonizer) seemed to be against Coleridge turning into a poet.

Coleridge's lines coincide with the period in which he first met Wordsworth; and in the political and intellectual debates of 1795–97 (some of which are taken up in *Prelude* 11), the theme of the *poetical* character must have played a part. The theme focuses less on how to find the right genre or style than on what it meant to be a Poet at that revolutionary moment. Coleridge's phrase "honorable toil" (63), though a cliché, is an antonym to Virgil's *ignobile otium* ("dishonorable" or "unglorious" leisure) at the end of the *Georgics*, where the Roman author compares his bucolic activity (*carmina lusi pastorum*) with Caesar's martial exploits.

The most telling sign, however, of Coleridge's doubt about the poetic vocation is his subtitle: "A Poem that affects not to be Poetry." This may simply be a modesty topos directed to magazine readers who might not appreciate loose thoughts strung together in a relaxed sort of blank verse. "I am just thinking aloud, I am not really writing poetry." Indeed, Horace's *sermones* were famous for being at once chatty and elegant, the perfection of the middle style.[2] A first determination of the subtitle, then, is that it evokes a principle of decorum that limits the poet's ambition. He is not prospecting a high style, or the low style of indignant social critique, but something sociable, something "conversational"—and that strain, of course, Coleridge would develop in the so-called Conversation Poems, named after his famous "The Nightingale: A Conversation[al] Poem," first published in the 1798 *Lyrical Ballads.*

Recent commentary has focused on the conversational in Coleridge and Wordsworth and has even seen it as dialogic in Bakhtin's sense.[3] I sympathize with any analysis that breaks down the monologic; but here I am trying to understand how a certain stylistic change came about and so prefer to retain the term "conversational," which suggests that whenever we deal with style we also deal with social decorum and with a historically specific situation. The style is the man or the woman, but the style is also a compromise between integrity—the sense or illusion of an inviolable personal character—and the pressures of public life. Even the most antitheatrical poet, by "coming out" in poetry, subjects himself to the eyes of others and so plays a role in a drama not completely of his choosing. Coleridge, I surmise—and this is a second determination of the subtitle—has a difficulty in "coming out," not so much from a place of retirement, but, paradoxically, *into* the retirement of an absolute commitment like Wordsworth's.

It is Wordsworth who will define poetic election and all the vainglory and scruples, the ups and downs, the "Was it for this?" that make up, relentlessly, the daily life of the poet and expose him to the danger of a solipsistic fixation—that "Sole True Something" (acronym of STC in Coleridge's Greek lettering) that is at once desired and feared. It is desired, because it may spring the poet out of Limbo, and feared because it might define him as nothing but one thing, jeopardizing the middle ground of sociality. "A Poem that affects not to be Poetry" sends a loaded message. It implies: "I will not seek greatness in poetry, for to do so would mean, in effect, never coming out of retirement, leaving life itself behind." And it also implies: "If I write poetry, it will be in the middle style, in a conversational mode that keeps me close to friends and away from a terrible self-isolation."[4]

Wordsworth—to whom I now turn—was yearning at this very time for the retreat Coleridge apparently rejected: the famous preamble that opens *The Prelude* looks forward to a "work of glory" (another antonym of *ignobile otium*) to be composed in a "chosen Vale," a country "hermitage" (Rousseau's name for his own retreat), as he journeys from the vast city—either London or the Bristol where he and Coleridge first met—to Racedown, Alfoxden, and, ultimately, Grasmere. He moved, then, in a direction opposite from that of his friend: *toward* a place of retirement.[5] In his most characteristic poetry, moreover, such as "There was a Boy" (drafted before but published in the 1800 *Lyrical Ballads* and later incorporated into *Prelude* 5),[6] a powerful suggestion is conveyed that the worldly concept of "entering into active life" has no relevance for the poetical character; it sets up a false antithesis reflected in the pastoral/heroic distinction and its illusion of progress. The episode, which I want to look at closely, contains not only a critique of Enlightenment pedagogy and its new scholasticism, its mechanically progressive program based supposedly on nature rather than on authoritative tradition; the episode also revises the locus of *action* as radically as Milton's critique of martial heroism or "tilting Furniture."

Wordsworth is explicit in Book 3 of *The Prelude* about this revision of "heroic argument":

> Of genius, power,
> Creation and Divinity itself,
> I have been speaking, for my theme has been
> What passed within me
>
> O Heavens! how awful is the might of Souls
> And what they do within themselves, while yet
> The yoke of earth is new to them, the world
> Nothing but a wild field where they were sown.
> This is, in truth, heroic argument.
>
> (3.173–84)[7]

Being so caught up, however, we must not forget that the very strength of this moment—the heroic age of childhood—could obstruct as well as found later growth. In "There was a Boy," Nature, as a tutorial agency, so encompasses and binds the developing imagination that she in effect takes the child to herself. The Boy never leaves his birthplace; the "beauteous spot" where he was born is also his grave. However buffered and benevolent, what is described is a trauma in which the skin of the psyche is pierced, as the sounds and sights of the natural world enter so far into the heart that a kind of ecstasy, or little death, ensues. Nature intends—in Wordsworth's understanding—to naturalize a wild imagination so that it can later be socialized; yet it is the height of irony that in our first great poem on developmental psychology impasse overshadows the promise of psychic growth. On one side of the divided episode is the "action" of Nature that marks the child and perhaps singles it out; on the other side is the "contemplation" of the mature poet looking at the child's grave, at a mode of being recoverable only in memory. "Together" in "A full [1850: long] half-hour together I have stood" could be read as qualifying "I have stood," so that what lengthens or fills the pause is a (visionary) rejoining of the divided I: of present and past modes of being. The poet re-members himself.

Let me insist on the peculiarity of Wordsworth's picture of poetic development. There is a sense in which the Boy of Winander episode shows that mute, inglorious Miltons do exist. (We remember also Wordsworth's characterization of his brother John as a "*silent* poet.") Indeed, this elegy in a country churchyard may suggest that all human beings are potentially poets. What prevents their poetic gift from developing? One of the puzzles in Wordsworth's depiction is that muteness and maturity are not dissociated: the mute look of the poet lengthens into a "full half-hour" and climaxes the "lengthened pause" in the Boy's experience.

I am not sure we can go from this to the pausal sensitivity of poetic style, which meters experience in a distinctive rather than a mechanical way. What I *am* sure about is that the muteness of the inglorious child, which persists in the poet aspiring to fame, is based on intimations of immortality as well as on a mortifying sense of loss. If the poetic gift, the talent, is buried, if a repression of the poetic sensibility, "great birthright of our Being," occurs, it is because of a weight of glory rather than simply because the celestial light fades owing to daily realities. The youngster's early experiences were so charged and powerful—despite Nature's gentler aspect—that the mind becomes mute. These moments of fearful beauty cannot pass through, they block themselves: the aphasic child never gets beyond the relative muteness of mimicry and enters nature's, as if that were Abraham's, bosom.

The mind of a poet, then, is a survivor's mind. Its philosophic quality, its way of looking through death, differs from a ratiocinative and dissecting mimesis. *The Prelude* as the genealogy of a reflective that is also an imaginative self-consciousness undoes the opposition between poetic language and thought which is present at so many levels in our disciplinary and social ontologies. The muted child returns in the mature poet, not as a sublimated, dialecticized or lapsed mode of being but as an ecstatic and active memory, a discontinuous and disruptive source of joy, at once solicited and defended against.[8]

Wordsworth, I have suggested, complicates the notion of maturity in a counter-Enlightenment way. For him the issue of growth, both personal and collective, leads to the question: Is poetry an essential part of the active life? Can it be carried over into maturity and that new epoch the Enlightenment claimed to be? The maturation of the poet and the progress of poetry vis-à-vis the march of time become culturally sensitive matters. When I read "There was a Boy," a Goethe ballad breaks in like static from a radio signal: "In seinen Armen das Kind war tot." The dead child (in the Erl-King ballad) also points to a power of imagination which the age denies but which is strong enough to kill—and perhaps the age denies it for that reason. At a time when the dogma of progress demanded a turning from poetry to philosophy, and even a rejection of poetry as childish, Wordsworth intervened with a concept of visionary action whose locus is childhood and whose maturity is poetry.

That maturity remains precarious, however. The Boy dies, "retired by Nature," like a child of whom we say that heaven loved it so much that it was taken back. The sublime itself, scorching a sensitive soul or one unable to adjust to common day, is one way the imagination decays. The other way is the soul's successful adjustment to common day, a repression of imaginative desire as the transition to social life is negotiated. That second fatality (social domestication) could result in a "Poem that affects not to be Poetry," one that damps the sublime and the visionary, the crucial Romantic strain. Wordsworth's own revolt against poetic diction, his experiment with "the language of conversation in the middle and lower classes of society" ("Advertisement" to the *Lyrical Ballads* of 1798), often brings his diction perilously close to prose and could have played into the wrong hands.

It may have been this daring compromise by a socially defensive man that allowed the emergence of a new and idiosyncratic verse, conversational in idiom yet not at all urbane. In a society where *negotium* prevailed and *otium* was suspect he had to recreate the vocation and character of Poet. *A poet must pass from the passivity of receiver to an action for which his intense life in Nature has destined him, but whose social form is missing.* Wordsworth gave birth to modern poetry, not by his realism alone or by his class-conscious experiment with language, but principally by a struggle with inactive, otiose, trivialized representations of the sublime. An all too normative sublimity not only occults, with its vapid, unnatural terminology,[9] manual or georgic labor; it also elides a very special kind of "action"—that of heart and mind in "the act of finding / What will suffice" (Wallace Stevens).

This test of sufficiency is strictly imaginative, yet not at all unempirical. The poet records, or involves in the record, the pulse of the imagination, as it responds to (sometimes fails to respond to) both inner and outer experience. The stress of this criterion of imaginative sufficiency is rarely communicated as language-stress and so does not result once more in a highly rhetorical, labored, compensatory diction. A new notation appears, a "language of the sense" closer to prose in its excursive motion and casual force, but also in its thoughtful recovery of ordinary experience. "Without him," the *New Monthly Magazine* wrote about Wordsworth in 1835, "a grey cloak seen in the distance on a lonely moor would have no meaning."[10] Just because poetry has made it through, we now feel it was never in danger, yet it may be more than a need for dramatizing literary history that makes me think of poetry as mortal and that Wordsworth, rather than Blake, Keats, and Shelley — though this needs arguing — assured the continuance of great poetry by a strange and still not entirely understood revolution of style with implications for the way we read.

I turn to these implications via the bold Wordsworthian move to take on the ballad: not just to participate in its revival but to make it display an entirely different kind of plot or image of action. Wordsworth's design is especially striking in "There was a Boy," a ballad that pretends not to be a ballad.[11] Creating a new poetry rather than a new genre, Wordsworth invented a different mode of disclosure, or "representation" as we now say. It shifts the worldly locus of news, of where the action is. Dismissed from other lyrical ballads, the "moving accident" (the phrase, from *Othello*, is found in the earliest *Prelude* and also in "Hart-Leap Well") returns here in a radically contingent, ordinary guise.

"There was a Boy," like many of these new "lyrical" ballads, epitomizes a life by way of a single incident or accidental encounter. That chance happening, however, leaves a decisive mark: it provokes something close to an epiphany or periodizing recognition. In the youngster this marking effect remains unconscious; not so in the retrospective poet. He knows that the boy's experience of emotive dissonance, near trivial from an adult point of view, has disclosed Nature's invisible hand. The potential for trivializing such experiences is based, in fact, on their unconsciousness during childhood. They are as common, say, as death — and death is the second surprise here, where all the signs pointed to life and development. The unexplained death of the boy is also an accident, a "sad occasion deare" with echoes of *Lycidas*.[12]

There is no logical connection between the two accidents depicted in "There was a Boy." They are incommensurable: How can a momentary failure of response (during the contest with the owls) belong to the same plot as death? Only if a visionary thought intrudes; only if Wordsworth's concern with the ebbing of imaginative sympathy (the disconnection of nature from the imaginative life) becomes prophetic and projects a plot of this kind. But this perception cannot be ascribed to the boy, only to reader or poet: it is a negative insight that associates failure of response with death.

That insight overflows the strict economy of interpretation, for now the reader is drawn in as co-developer of the poet's design. I have said that the boy's death could be understood as Nature taking him back: his growth is arrested, blocked by early, ecstatic encounters.[13] This interpretation, which I began with, does not require a special *Wordsworthian* type of reading. But the negative insight that associates a failure of conversation with death[14]—eliding all intermediate possibilities and all the euphemistic, even utopian talk about a marriage (or good fit) between mind and nature—this insight does call for a special kind of reader willing to cooperate with a technique of reticent, perhaps involuntary, disclosure.

The reader can easily miss the negative insight. Like Francis Jeffrey, for instance, he may not be moved—though the formation of a sensibility, and responsiveness in particular, are the focus of the episode. Jeffrey, totally unwilling to cooperate, could not understand the point of "There was a Boy." He has no clue. "And for the sake of this one accomplishment [the game with the owls] . . . the author has frequently stood mute and gazed on [the Boy's] grave for half and hour together!"[15] In worldly terms, the episode is indeed close to plotless.

We have, then, the representation of a "moving accident" after all. The owls' nonresponse appears to be accidental, but so does the boy's death, through the manner in which it is reported. Wordsworth had mocked contemporary educational efforts to "control / All accidents" in the *Prelude* verses preceding this episode; but is he not also mocking himself? For this is one accident no one can redeem, not even a poet who claims (though many years later) that in recalling the episode he was guided by a consciousness of how internal feelings cooperated "with external accidents to plant, *for immortality*, images of sound and sight, in the celestial soil of the Imagination."[16] And if the boy, or later the poet, is "moved," the emotion passes through what Jacques Lacan has called a "missed encounter," linked to trauma and its devious action. Compare the missed or delayed recognitions that characterize the poet's crossing of the Alps.

A "missed encounter" also characterizes the scene of reading. Many reactions to Wordsworth's text are like Jeffrey's, even today; and the enigmatic picture of the poet looking at—or is it reading?—the boy's grave intensifies the sense of a missing point.

Wordsworth's graveside image depicts something more than pensiveness or "recollection in tranquillity." Sentimental pictures of the reader abounded in the eighteenth century, most typically of the female reader, dreamy and holding a letter. But here we are closer to the Intimation Ode's "philosophic mind" and "faith that looks through death," where the "through" suggests what has to be passed through: a necessary medium or perceptual shadow. Wordsworth talks about growth, joy, and primal strength, but the mood music and accompanying pictures often evoke a bleak sense of the suffering creature, explicitly Christian in later years. What makes things "cling together / In one society" we would now be tempted to identify as trauma: Wordsworth describes it as a "passion" on a cosmic scale,[17] which operates in too dark or death-related a manner for rhetorical extroversion.

In the Boy of Winander episode, reading is, precisely, *not* a medium of vision, since the direct, tutorial agency of nature is emphasized, working independently of book-related schemes of education. But there is a medium, nevertheless; the mature poet, certainly, cannot look in an unmediated, unshadowed way at childhood experience. The medium is human time, at once mortifying and bonding, in short, traumatic; but it might also be identified with nature, history, or language. Though para-theological battles are presently being fought to determine which of these mediations is the unfairest or most de-idealizing of them all, Wordsworth's emphasis lies elsewhere. He sees through a glass darkly; the medium enables knowledge while deflecting a more direct—traumatic or apocalyptic—vision that is always incipient.

The poet's "while here I stand," then, as in the second part of "There was a Boy," is not purely static or contemplative; it betrays a destabilized awareness as the poet tries to figure out exactly where he does stand. Place and time conscious, as if the very spot, the very moment, had a bearing, he describes, as a limit, the sort of ghostliness we have all experienced and discounted: Am I standing in nature, in this world, or also in another dimension? Am I the agent and locus of what I feel, or are there presences who know me better than I know myself? Even, perhaps, Is this poem my own speech?[18]

Yet Wordsworth does not cross the border into a visionary mode of representation. He expresses those feelings without relying on supernatural personae or incidents, on a system characterized by epiphanic structure.[19] His practice, at the same time, especially the attack on Poetic Diction which helped to fashion a new, more conversational style for poetry, is not exempt from the ambiguous "through." The poet rejects traditional thickeners that stand in the way, but he also replaces them with a nature-derived darkness, or with the density of *internal* time consciousness. At the end of *Prelude* 5, lines 600ff., he maximizes the paradox of linguistic mediation; by a process that remains temporal ("the turnings intricate of verse"), words become "as" a home for a reality that lies beyond that home:

> Visionary Power
> Attends the motions of the viewless winds
> Embodied in the mystery of words:
> There darkness makes abode, and all the host
> Of shadowy things work endless changes there,
> As in a mansion like their proper home.
> Even forms and substances are circumfused
> By that transparent veil with light divine;
> And, through the turnings intricate of verse,
> Present themselves as objects recognised
> In flashes, and with glory not their own.[20]

Let me now focus more directly on *reading after Wordsworth;* is the reading he solicits compatible with the conversational style that is both his and Coleridge's most striking innovation? That style suggests, on the one hand, an easier, more equal relation between poet and reader, their sensibility differing, as Wordsworth says, in degree, not in kind. On the other hand, Wordsworth's style often makes a very special demand. In general, that demand comes from the fact that it is no longer the poet who amplifies experience by rhetorical and visionary devices; now it is the reader who must amplify what is often a reticent kind of exclamatory voicing, a sort of echo-response to a powerful darkness. When this happens, the text becomes a "Bride of Quietness."

While this stylistic shift, with implications for reading, is by no means absolute, writing as a mode of conversing becomes ghostly once more. Like an ellipse, Wordsworth's poetry has a double center, and therefore, perhaps, no firm center at all; isolated and isolating sense experiences (one focus) are intensely particularized, while a self-haunting mind (the second focus) seeks to understand their "incumbent mystery." The impact of incidents is comparable to what psychoanalysts call *ideas of reference:* they impinge on observer or narrator with the indeterminate resonance of omens.[21]

What is it, for example, that engrosses the poet's attention in "The Solitary Reaper"? Without our ability to amplify the poet's own sympathies, without that "co-operating *power,*"[22] Wordsworth cannot create the taste by which he hopes to be appreciated. If, "dull of soul," we fail to respond, it bodes ill for the sympathetic imagination collectively, for its capacity to be stimulated and take nourishment from ordinary sights and sounds. It would be a sign that poetry may have to become ever more crude, sensational, didactic, even apocalyptic.

Yet there are those who feel that Wordsworth's appeal to the reader is too palpable, too pressuring: they understand the "Behold her" and "Stop here, or gently pass!" as a "coercive summoning . . . that enforces an attitude of reverence."[23] Wordsworth can certainly lapse into "palpable design" (Keats) or a didactic vein. But as Cleanth Brooks has shown, his structuring of episodes is very different from Metaphysical wit or any forceful reconciliation of opposites. In his subtler mode, an exclamation mark does not coerce response or cap a well-fashioned paradox. It hints at something unstated, as at the end of "Strange fits of passion": in effect, it asks us to exert that "co-operating *power.*" Such exclamations evoke the future reader as interior paramour—or as the "Stranger!" hailed in epitaphs.

So it is with the scandalous or enigmatic "often I have stood / Mute—looking at the grave in which he lies!" (from the *Prelude* version of the Boy of Winander episode). Wordsworth gives no clue as to what his thoughts are, no psychological specifics; he does not botanize on the grave. Yet we sense that he is looking at, as well as into, himself—that he is a *posthumous* figure. He stands toward a prior stage of life as a reader, even an epitaphic reader. By extension we gain a ghostly glimpse of ourselves: readers as intent on Wordsworth as he is on the dead boy. We may also recall Milton's "gentle muse" (*Lycidas*, 19–22), even without a formal allusion.[24] Already the poet's opening apostrophe, which turns from the boy to "Ye Cliffs / And Islands of Winander," adds a posthumous frame to the story. "The grave preceded me—" Emily Dickinson wrote.

Thus, at the very time a conversational and philanthropic style is being achieved in poetry, the idea of conversation comes under pressure again. Wordsworth's originality cannot be reduced to a reform of poetic diction, though much remains to be said about the fortunes of the colloquial in poetry from his time to ours. To present ears he introduces a new conceptual tone, rather than the colloquial itself; how sensitive and complex a tone is clear from the initial and interruptive apostrophe in "There was a Boy." The poet retains the strong rhetorical feel of "Ye knew him well," even though it breaches the conversational level of style—indeed, throws doubt on the conversational ethos. For although this formal cry can be said to have a "sufficient foundation in humanity" as a passionate mode of address, as a *turn* from one audience (or subject) toward another, here that other, Winander, is mute and insensate, and responsive only by a pastoral fiction.[25] No conversation is possible; the cry falls into the void, or . . . summons the reader to make the fiction true, to view Nature as animate and conscious.

I have mentioned in passing echoes of Milton's *Lycidas*. Wordsworth's handling of myth is as remarkable as his conversational yet precarious reclaiming of other types of figuration. It is as if Wordsworth wanted to overcome a discontinuity extending from Milton's time to his own, as if *he* were the gentle muse anticipated by Milton. The technique, whereby a classicizing machinery fades into natural perception and receives a new, inexplicit life, cannot be called refinement or attenuation: Wordsworth achieves, rather, a "cure of the ground." As in all such cures, of course, the question is whether the figure survives the cure. I think it does; lateness is not weakness here, since Milton's myth of the dead poet becoming a *genius loci* shows through.

The Boy of Winander is the genius of the shore in all but name; he halts the traveler and is intimately linked to place — so intimately, in fact, that he seems to be *of* Winander, that is, not only born there but its offspring, Nature's child. He dies, like Lucy, before emerging from a nymphal state into full and mortal consciousness. He is a *puer aeternus*, or what in the poet cannot grow up.

The link to *Lycidas* is through the *genius loci* myth but also through the introductory words of the apostrophe already partially discussed. "Ye knew him well"[26] takes the classic pastoral formula "Who knows not" (Spenser, September *Eclogue*), "Who would not sing for" (*Lycidas*), and combines it with another formula: "Well could he wayle his woes" (Spenser, June *Eclogue*), "He knew [well] / Himself to sing" (*Lycidas*). Rather than refining, once again, English pastoral elegy (already a second or third growth), Wordsworth's "Ye knew him well" mutes such literary self-consciousness by a conversational turn, even as it deepens the theme of coming-to-knowledge. It transfers knowledge from the human to the natural realm (from the mortal observer to the Cliffs) by a figure that seems to be a conventional prosopopoeia, yet looks toward the final words of the episode in *Prelude* 5 — "Knowledge not purchased by the loss of power."

To "know well," which refers in the context of pastoral to literary skill, now evokes an ideal that resolves the antinomy of knowledge and life and insinuates a question that must have had considerable pathos in an era in which philosophy put literature in doubt. What kind of knowledge is poetry? Can poetry *know well*, that is, integrate a knowledge even though that is based on trauma,[27] or a knowledge whose effect can be injurious as it marches on to enlighten and emancipate humanity? Such knowledge threatens the poetic text with obsolescence: whether conceived in philosophical or political terms, the Enlightenment's demystifying drive identifies poetry with a childlike and primitive practice or a pastoral and delusive mode of perception.[28]

We come, finally, to the question of art's relation to knowledge (and so to philosophy). This question is formulated explicitly by the German thinkers of that time.[29] Coleridge's wish to boost Wordsworth as a philosopher may be related to his appreciation of German idealism as well as to his discernment of Wordsworth's distinctive poetical character. Hegel, taking a historical and prophetic position, argues that the great period in art, the classical, is over; that the concept of the beautiful was fulfilled at that time; but that this concept is not the highest end of humanity. In the modern era, therefore, which Christianity introduced, the unity of spiritual and sensual embodied in classical art is broken; modern life is characterized by "romantic" excess, by the spiritual in subjective form, yet through that imbalance it leads to a more perfect self-realization. Hegel concludes not only that modern art no longer satisfies our highest needs, because it has been overshadowed by reflection ("Der Gedanke und die Reflexion hat die schöne Kunst überflügelt"), but that art as such has come to an end for us, except as an object of knowledge. "Art invites us to thoughtful contemplation, not in order to call itself back, but in order to understand in a scholarly mode [*wissenschaftlich*] what art is" (*Lectures on Aesthetics*, "Introduction").

As a theorist Coleridge was struggling with a parallel concern, but he does not place art in a historical progression that transcends art. He recognizes, for example, that in Milton's works it is Milton himself you see: "The egotism of such a man is a revelation of the spirit" (*Table Talk*). Subjectivity is acknowledged as a spiritual force. Emerson, similarly, in "Thoughts on Modern Literature" (*Dial*, Oct. 1840), describes in an upbeat way the "subjectiveness" of the "poetry and speculation of the age . . . marked by a certain philosophic turn, which discriminates them from the works of earlier times. . . . The eye is withdrawn from the object and fixed on the subject or mind." It is also Emerson who remarks in his *Journals* (Feb. 17, 1838), after reading the prepublished skating episode from *Prelude* 1, that it required an amazing "self-reliance" to record so simple an occasion. Whether or not we include Milton among the moderns, subjectivity in art becomes a serious issue only when it is seen as a symptom of decadence or as a sign of the end of art. Hegel, interestingly enough, separates the end of art from its decadence: art has fulfilled its mission, and it is simply the destiny of the self-realizing, progressive, and therefore also negating spirit to pass beyond art into a philosophical stage. There is a *désoeuvrement* of art, though we still recognize its contribution to the historical progress that made it obsolete.

One does not have to agree with Hegel to observe that in comparison to Milton and other great poets Wordsworth is more — I don't know how else to put it — *unemployed.* It is as if an "end" had come, at least to previous occupations of the artist, who must now discover a "revelation of the spirit" in what may seem trivial or accidental; in short, not entirely honorable. Wordsworth's self-chosen leisure, his not entering active life as his social world conceived it, and what Coleridge describes as the "station of a man in mental repose" — do they signal the end of art or a revolution of style that extends its life? How can we distinguish between the radical and the reclusive in Wordsworth, between an "unemployed negativity"[30] with revolutionary potential and the *otium* of a poet declining into countrified gentility because his art has no true, modern function?

By now you must know where I stand on this. But I do not intend to close on so feisty a note. Coleridge, with whom we began, can help us conclude with his own picture of the child on the way to becoming a poet-philosopher. He offers a vignette of his infant son at the end of "The Nightingale." Hartley is being brought up on associationist principles, as befits a child with that name. His father wants him to be familiar with the songs of the nightingale, "That with the night / He may associate joy." Coleridge increasingly did not take joy in the night, as we know from other sources. His picture of the infant is part of a farewell that extends this "conversation" with William and Dorothy. The farewell is made to linger, as if Coleridge did not wish to take his leave, either from the nightingale, "Farewell, O Warbler," or his friends, "And you my friends! farewell, a short farewell!" The thought of separation anxiety does cross one's mind; in any case, the thrice-farewelling is extended further by verbal snapshots of baby Hartley:

I deem it wise
To make him Nature's playmate. He knows well
The evening star. . . .

This "knowing well" foreshadows the poetic skill to come, but it is not without a darker emphasis. The "well" picks up on the "farewell," echoes it, draws it out; and it accrues, therefore, the meaning of "knowledge for the good," not just intimate knowledge. Such repetition begins to turn the word into a wish: may it be for the good, this knowledge, may it prevent a melancholy leave-taking or withdrawal from nature. "Well!" Coleridge continues a few lines later, in his best conversational-casual manner, "It is a father's tale." The poem is indeed as much the story of father as of son; and so the sphere of the wish or its hopeful sound expands to include him in an extended family of nightingale, friends, child, evening star, moon. His solitude is comforted.

Or is it? By the time he closes, "Once more, farewell," we sense that the wish has intensified into a charm, and that the well—"WELL!" his most famous ode, on dejection, begins, "If the Bard was weather-wise"—has deepened. All is not well. Coleridge's genial spirits, their link to the well-springs of joy and benevolence, fail.

Symptomatically at the beginning of his Great Ode,[31] and consistently in "The Nightingale" (which affects not to be an ode), imagination is diverted into conversation. Coleridge tries to hold on to each leave-taking as it becomes an ominous event, foreshadowing the loss of a world of shared sensations and threatening to plunge him into the solitude and melancholy he is exorcizing. Indeed, once out of nature, the nightingale could revert to its *penseroso* image and confirm the dependence of word on wound, of song on solipsistic pathos. The poet's farewells are shored against that ruin:

Once more, farewell,
Sweet Nightingale! once more, my friends! farewell.

APPENDIX

There was a Boy: ye knew him well, ye cliffs
And islands of Winander!—many a time
At evening, when the stars had just begun
To move along the edges of the hills,
Rising or setting, would he stand alone
Beneath the trees or by the glimmering lake,
And there, with fingers interwoven, both hands
Pressed closely palm to palm, and to his mouth
Uplifted, he, as through an instrument,
Blew mimic hootings to the silent owls,
That they might answer him; and they would shout
Across the watery vale, and shout again,

Responsive to his call, with quivering peals,
And long hallooes and screams, and echoes loud,
Redoubled and redoubled, concourse wild
Of mirth and jocund din; and when it chanced
That pauses of deep silence mocked his skill,
Then sometimes, in that silence while he hung
Listening, a gentle shock of mild surprise
Has carried far into his heart the voice
Of mountain torrents; or the visible scene
Would enter unawares into his mind,
With all its solemn imagery, its rock,
Its woods, and that uncertain heaven, received
Into the bosom of the steady lake.

This Boy was taken from his mates, and died
In childhood, ere he was full ten years old.
Fair are the woods, and beauteous is the spot,
The vale where he was born; the churchyard hangs
Upon a slope above the village school,
And there, along that bank, when I have passed
At evening, I believe that oftentimes
A full half hour together I have stood
Mute, looking at the grave in which he lies.

(1805)

CHAPTER TWO

Encrypted Sympathy

Wordsworth's Infant Ideology

Ortwin de Graef

The province of ethics and literature is arguably one of the more prominent places where the study of literature has been acting out its constitutive legitimation crisis over the past decade or so. As Steven Connor remarked in a 1996 review of, among others, David Parker's *Ethics, Theory, and the Novel*, "the word 'ethics' seems to have replaced 'textuality' as the most charged term in the vocabulary of contemporary cultural and literary theory,"[1] and in his introduction to the 1999 special topic in *PMLA* on ethics and literary study, Lawrence Buell makes much the same point, be it slightly less confidently, when he states that "ethics has gained new resonance in literary studies during the past dozen years, even if it has not—at least yet—become the paradigm-defining concept that textuality was for the 1970s and historicism for the 1980s."[2] As Buell's reservation suggests, it is still doubtful whether the ethical tremble running through literary

This essay was first published in *Partial Answers: Journal of Literature and the History of Ideas* 2.1 (Jan. 2004): 21–51. For their many valuable comments I am grateful to Leona Toker, the editor of *Partial Answers*, and to Benjamin Biebuyck, Gert Buelens, and Sigi Jöttkandt, my colleagues in the Research Programme on Literary Ethics of the Fund for Scientific Research—Flanders (Belgium).

scholarship is likely to gather to a thunder. In fact, there are indications that it is already dying down or has been swamped out by alternative thrills such as "globalization," which, we are told by the organizers of an international summer seminar in literary studies that took place in 2000, is the real "literary-critical catch-all" for the 1990s.[3] That the 1999 edition of this seminar was called *Reading Text, Constructing Theory, Thinking Ethics* confirms that ethics was on the agenda in the 1990s, though not, it would now appear, as a genuinely core-building concept.

At any rate, it is clear that contemporary literary scholarship has witnessed a marked increase in the deployment of ethical rhetoric and that this turn to ethics is received as a turn away from, typically, "text" and "history." A plausible, if brutal, account of the paradigm parade of literary studies over the past few decades could run more or less as follows: in the 1970s and early 1980s, deconstruction with its textual fixations figures as a dominant point of reference in the then-current critical discourse; during the 1980s, deconstruction's alleged textualist idealism increasingly comes under attack and is gradually ousted by approaches such as New Historicism and postcolonial studies, which profile themselves as both more properly responsive to "real" issues of history and politics and less starry-eyed about the supposed privilege of (Canonical) Upper-Case Literature, thereby relocating the study of literature within the larger project of Cultural Studies. The ethical turn of the 1990s, then, appears to herald—at least on the face of it—a dismissal not only of the sterile impersonality of textualist idealism but also of the ideology-critical overkill of resolutely politicized reading and of the paradoxical leveling abstractions of historical particularism.

Reading literature under the aegis of ethics promises a recovery of a more human and humane appreciation of literature as humanism in personal practice, an intimate exercise in increasing awareness and fostering understanding. In the words of Martha Nussbaum, who has established herself as a prime representative of the principle, if not therefore the practice, of ethical criticism, the "literary imagination" released in this reading is "an essential ingredient of an ethical stance that asks us to concern ourselves with the good of other people whose lives are distant from our own" and thereby in turn releases us "from a stifling confinement into a space of human possibility."[4] The literary imagination so conceived, Nussbaum contends, "is an essential part of both the theory and the practice of citizenship" (*Poetic Justice*, 52). As this last claim indicates, the ethical turn that is at stake here is emphatically not a matter of private imaginings alone; to the contrary, the release of sympathy effected by the literary imagination is seen as a powerful catalyst in the formation of political community. The question this raises, though, is how the literary text actually performs this saving release, or perhaps more accurately, how it saves — records, stores, preserves, encrypts — the civic virtue of sympathy itself.[5]

Europe's Latter Hour

In *The Fateful Question of Culture*, a series of lectures delivered in 1992 and reworked for publication in 1997, Geoffrey Hartman offers an extreme example of this putative participation of the literary imagination in the formation of good citizenship. Hartman's track record as a scrupulous reader of literature is such that placing him in the company of Nussbaum comes close to committing a category-mistake — but this may not be inappropriate in the context of ethics, characterized by Geoffrey Galt Harpham as "the locus of otherness [which] perhaps ought to be considered a matrix, a hub from which various discourses, concepts, terms, energies, fan out and at which they meet, crossing out of themselves to encounter the other, all the others."[6] More substantially, however, what unites both scholars is their emphatically stated belief in the civilizing power of the literary imagination.

In Hartman, the twin convictions that "the work of a great artist can have a strong and long-range impact on the way we look at ourselves as a culture" and that the "beneficial" nature of this impact as he discovers it in his test-case Wordsworth in principle characterizes all "great" literature as such, amounts to a veritable profession of faith.[7] Appealing to our critical charity in his opening movements, he first concedes that "since Wordsworth's poetry is only one example, and I do not test other explanations for the specific influence it exerted in England, I claim for my thesis no more than heuristic value," but no sooner has he made this concession than he reclaims an unassailable authority of feeling for his faith in literature as a salvific force: "But were my conjectures to be disproved or shown incapable of being proved, I would continue to feel as Mr. Henshaw does, in Willa Cather's *My Mortal Enemy:* 'How the great poets do shine on . . . ! Into all the dark corners of the world. They have no night' " (*Fateful Question*, 7).

The level of defiance and the manner in which it is voiced here are nontrivially reminiscent of Tennyson's outcry in the face of the corrosive impact of science on faith in *In Memoriam:*

If e'er when faith had fallen asleep,
  I heard a voice "believe no more"
  And heard an ever-breaking shore
That tumbled in the Godless deep;

A warmth within the breast would melt
  The freezing reason's colder part,
  And like a man in wrath the heart
Stood up and answered "I have felt."
(Sec. 124, 9–16)[8]

The resonance of this unsolicited Tennysonian echo in Hartman's profession of faith is richer than may appear at first sight, for Tennyson's uneasy appreciation of the advances of evolutionary theory and geology finds its latter-day translation in Hartman's uncomfortable recognition of the claims of deconstruction and New Historicism. To the former, to whose genesis into literary scholarship he was a privileged participant witness, Hartman now addresses a question on the verge of meeting its end in a disenchanted answer to end all questioning: "The question of our speech, the contemporary question, asks how long critical discourse must remain critical: that is, questioning; that is, in a negative mode. Can an affirmation emerge from all this splendid—cerebral, demystifying, deconstructive—'labor of the negative'?" (*Fateful Question*, 43). Yet the affirmations emerging from the New Historicism also fail to satisfy him. In a footnote added to the lectures prior to their publication in 1997, Hartman takes some pains to distinguish his own concept of "cultural causation" (16n.13) (the aforementioned "strong and long-range impact on the way we look at ourselves as a culture" issuing from "great artists" [7]) from that of the New Historicism. More specifically, he approvingly registers Louis Montrose's attempt to chart the dialectic of "social text" and "shaping fantasies" in Shakespeare's plays, but he ultimately finds Montrose's argument wanting in precision: "What is hard to distinguish here is the precise influence of the artist's work: there is often a dialectical blur as Shakespeare becomes a sort of primal historical scene, the paradigm case of a rich interplay that could go on and on, without a clear result except the work of art itself. The so-called dialectic, then, ends in a swollen moment of stasis" (16n.13).

If deconstruction, then, fails to come up with an enabling affirmation, and New Historicist interpretation does not succeed in establishing its affirmations by dint of its failure to convincingly demonstrate "the actual sociopolitical impact" of the literary work, the question is what, precisely, Wordsworth allows

Hartman to affirm as an alternative. Given the substance of his self-confessedly immodest claim about Wordsworth's "precise influence," Hartman's defiance in the face of potential disproof or reservation is not entirely surprising—for the stakes involved are quite as decisive as the existence of God was to Tennyson. It is thanks to Wordsworth that England has been spared the disastrous deployment of "a cultural and political antimodernism vulnerable to vicious dichotomies" (79) witnessed on the European continent; it is Wordsworth's poetry that "helped to create the sense of a particularly *English* culture," and "this saved English politics from the virulence of a nostalgic political ideal centering on rural virtue, which led to serious ravages on the continent" (7). Hartman's carefully imprecise phrases—"vicious dichotomies," "serious ravages"—barely conceal the breathtaking thrust of the thesis advanced: it is Wordsworth's poetry that prevented the Holocaust from crossing the Channel; it is thanks to Wordsworth that England witnessed the emergence not of National Socialism but of the National Trust.[9]

It would be all too easy to simply dismiss this thesis as the idiosyncratic expression of gratitude from a Jewish German who was forced to leave his home country at the age of nine and who found refuge in England for the duration of World War II—though there is no doubt that this experience powerfully marks Hartman's thought.[10] Neither would it be adequate to debunk Hartman's argument by merely marshaling as counterevidence the very existence of the British Union of Fascists, or by complicating and compounding the brutal pun on the National Trust by confronting it with the National Front. Hartman does, after all, carefully weigh his words, and his reluctance to drive home the thesis he intimates deserves to be respected, precisely because it involves a crucial component of the special power of cultural causation he credits to Wordsworth's literary imagination.

The Fateful Question of Culture opens by invoking an all too familiar challenge to literature and the study of literature: "Everyone, it seems, wants to make art more accountable, to prove its social or material effectiveness" (1). The interest of Hartman's response to this challenge is what he calls his "main purpose": "to restore literature's specificity as a focus for thinking about culture" (2). This specificity involves literature's peculiar power of representation, a power that, in Wordsworth at least, "does not reflect in any simple way, an existing situation [but] surrounds it, rather, with an imaginative aura" (7): literature "does not represent what is the case but brings something virtual in existence, which then has the force of imaginative fact" (13). Wordsworth's particular achievement in using this power is that he has succeeded in mediating modernization, the "catastrophic transition" (147) from an agrarian-rural to an industrial-urban society, and that in doing so he has provided England with a nonaggressive alternative to the sinister "unprogressive, overidealized, image of what is lost," which, on the Continent, led to "serious political consequences" (73). If culture can, among other things, be seen as a "harmony-restoring function" that "cures the alienation and loss of community inflicted by society's emergence from a more primal and unreflected unity" (8), its intent on "unity of purpose and unwoundedness of soul and body" (123) is also always in danger of fulfilling itself in the "perverse Nazi concept of *Kultur*" (127), in the "sinister unification" of *Mein Kampf*, and in the "absolute integration" of genocide (123). The "specificity" of Wordsworth's poetry, then, is that its "rhetoric of community" (66) envelops the trauma of transition with an imaginative aura that heals and thus preserves the wound instead of disastrously denying it in an absolute and phantasmatic reintegration.

But what, precisely, is this "imaginative aura"? What are Wordsworth's "imaginative facts" that have ushered England into modernity while preserving it from the serious consequences ravaging the Continent? What is the nature of Wordsworth's healing power, disastrously denied to Europe in its latter hour? Toward the end of his high argument, Hartman identifies this power with reference to the Blessed Babe passage of *The Prelude:*

> The slogan of the Enlightenment, which Kant affirmed in his pamphlet on the subject, was "dare to know." The romantic poets added "afford sympathy": dare to feel. Wordsworth stated his hope that mature knowledge would not have to be "purchased" by the loss of power, where by "power" he meant the "Infant sensibility / Great birthright of our being" and its evolution into "A virtue which irradiates and exalts / Objects through widest intercourse of sense." (159)

In Wordsworth's text, however, the relation between "infant sensibility" and "virtue"—phrases separated by some twenty-five lines, with the latter, moreover, preceding the former—is not quite one of straightforward "evolution." But rather than worry away at this well-worn early passage of *The Prelude*, I propose turning to another infant, one who occupied Wordsworth a few years earlier and who may cast an alternative light on the purchase of his virtuous sympathy.

Plain Speech

Ever since their publication in 1975 as the inaugural volume of the Cornell Wordsworth, the Salisbury Plain poems have been a favorite site for critical

Wordsworth scholarship. Particularly the substantial rewriting of the first text, *Salisbury Plain*, itself composed and abandoned in 1793–94, into *Adventures on Salisbury Plain*, which took place between 1795 and 1799, has proven to be an inevitable obstacle to be overcome in any conspective account of Wordsworth's literary history. Stephen Gill's editorial preface to the 1975 volume characterizes these two texts, neither of which Wordsworth published, as "poems that troubled Wordsworth in his youth" but "recaptured his imagination in old age," when he returned to this "intractable material" and finally published what he then made of it as the 1842 poem *Guilt and Sorrow*.[11] Gill gingerly steps around the question of why Wordsworth failed to develop the Salisbury Plain matter into publication in the 1790s; the "poet's struggle," he notes, "was left unresolved as Wordsworth entered the period of his greatest achievement," and since the aim of the Cornell edition was "to give the factual evidence of Wordsworth's efforts to be true to his developing vision," the editor decided to "avoid critical pronouncements" in his introduction and notes, "confident that the evidence presented here will speak plainly enough to the reader of Wordsworth's artistic integrity, energy, and power" (*SPP,* xv).

Gill's confidence in the plain speech of Salisbury Plain has not, however, been rewarded in any straightforward fashion; to be sure, there is a generally held vague consensus about the way in which the revisions sustain Wordsworth's "developing vision," but it is by no means clear what that vision actually reveals. In order to appreciate this confusion, a cursory survey of the fields is required.

Salisbury Plain is a poem emphatically framed by an explicit narratorial voice. The opening stanzas deliver a critical historical exercise in comparative suffering, in which the present is diagnosed as a time in which the poor are far more radically depressed by pain and "Penury" (*SP,* 27) than was the "hungry savage" (3) of prehistoric times, precisely to the extent that the latter never knew any better, while the present-day deprived are tormented by "memory of pleasures flown" (21) and by "reflection on the state / Of those who on the couch of Affluence rest" (24–25). The poem then homes in on one representative of the "many thousands" (34) suffering deprivation today, a solitary traveler looking for shelter on Salisbury Plain. He comes upon the ruin of a "lonely Spital" (123), which he finds already occupied by "a female wanderer" (138), who eventually begins to relate her life's story.

The female wanderer recollects her happy childhood "By Derwent's side" (226), rudely interrupted when "cruel chance and wilful wrong" (255) ruined her father. Fortunately, "There was a youth" (271) who saved them: the woman's young lover, who had been ordered by his father to a distant town "to ply remote from groves the artist's trade" (281), takes them in. They marry and have children, the father eventually dies, just as the British-American War breaks out, and the family once again descends into poverty. Too proud to beg, the husband joins the army, and the family follows in his train to America, where all but the woman perish. At this point, the tale is briefly interrupted by a scene suggesting some therapeutic effect in confiding in a friendly ear, after which the woman resumes her story up to the present. She was taken on board a British ship, lost her mind for a while, and was finally dropped off in England again, where she has been wandering for the past three years. The closing stanzas return us to the oratory of the narrator, who bursts into a full-blown performance of Enlightened revolutionary rhetoric, calling on the "Heroes of Truth" to "uptear / Th'Opressor's dungeon from its deepest base" (541–52) and to wield "the herculean mace / Of Reason" (544–45).

The most immediately striking change in the revision of the poem, most of which was completed in the following year, is the near-total erasure of the outer frame—as Gill puts it, "the poet as homilist," addressing "the statesmen of England on the corruption and oppression that are ravaging the nation," "has almost disappeared" (*SPP*, 3). The oratorical opening of the first poem is cut and in its stead we are immediately confronted with the lonely traveler, who meets an old Soldier on his way to help out his destitute daughter. The traveler offers the Soldier friendly support, secures a place for him on a passing post carriage, and resumes his journey alone. If in the first poem the character of the lonely traveler was not given much by way of personal history, in the revision he is now turned into a Sailor with a fully fledged and pathos-laden past. Returning from a long sea journey, he was seized by a press gang and spent years in battle. Back in England, he was denied wages and found himself forced to return home "Bearing to those he loved nor warmth nor food" (*ASP*, 94), but just before he reaches his house, his desperate mood drove him to rob and murder a traveler, "And when the miserable work was done, / He fled, a vagrant since, the murderer's fate to shun" (98–99). Having imparted this background knowledge, the poem returns to the present. Traveling along, the Sailor passes a gibbet with a human body hanging from it; the spectacle shocks him into an anguished "trance" (126), which, having passed, leaves him with a soul "S[u]nk into deepest calm" (129).

The text then picks up the narrative of the earlier version: the Sailor meets the female wanderer in the Spital, and she relates her life's story.[12] The principal difference between this story and that in the first Salisbury Plain poem concerns the period between the woman's return to England from America and her encounter with the Sailor. In the first poem, this period was covered by the mere elliptical indication "Three years a wanderer round my native coast" (*SP*, 388); in *Adventures on Salisbury Plain*, it is packed with further detail. The woman loses her mind, falls unconscious, and is borne away to a hospital; upon recovery, she is dismissed and finds her "first relief" among a "wild brood" (503) of "The rude earth's tenants" (506) who make a living from "midnight theft" (524). Unable to accept this way of life for long—she feels she has "abused" her "inner self" and "Foregone the home delight of constant truth" (547–48)—the woman resumes her solitary wandering and eventually encounters the Sailor.

Eschewing the inflammatory flourishes enlightening the first poem's conclusion, the second poem pulls itself together in an extended melodramatic resolution. The Sailor and the female vagrant travel on together, the former plagued by renewed anguish, the latter blessed with a sense of "new delight and solace new" (574). They arrive at a cottage where they are welcomed and fed, after which the female vagrant sets out again on her own. She encounters a horse-cart with a dying woman on it and escorts it back to the cottage, where it transpires that the dying woman is the Sailor's wife, who was turned out of her house when suspicion arose that her husband had murdered the traveler. The Sailor cries for forgiveness; on hearing his voice the woman dies, and the Sailor confesses and is duly hanged.

These, then, are the bare bones of the case for what Gill calls Wordsworth's "developing vision" (*SPP*, xv). Despite his professed intention to avoid "critical pronouncements," Gill does sum up his understanding of this developing vision in terms that are commonplace to Wordsworth criticism:

> *Adventures on Salisbury Plain* is both a continuation and a consummation of *Salisbury Plain*. It continues the social and political interests of the poem, and even extends them, but this continuing attack on the government of the country does not draw on any really new response to contemporary conditions. There were many good reasons why the attack should continue, and it is successful because the rhetoric of *Salisbury Plain* has been replaced by a fully dramatized presentation of the human calamities consequent upon war, but Wordsworth's interest was rapidly shifting from social and political phenomena to the more complex phenomena of human motives and behavior. (12)

From "rhetoric" to the "presentation of human feelings through fully realized dramatic situations" (13); from social and political phenomena to the more complex phenomena of the human: these are not only commonplaces in critical accounts of Wordsworth's growth to maturity—they are what many take to be the organizing terms of the ethical turn in literary studies today.[13] The standard chart of "Wordsworth's progress towards a more mature art"[14] prefigures the shift from "the paradigms of 1970s textuality and 1980s historicism" to "the scene of interpersonality, or interhumanity" (Buell, 16) occupying, and occupied by, a considerable section of contemporary literary scholarship. The move from *Salisbury Plain* to *Adventures on Salisbury Plain* offers an intimation of the imitation of Wordsworth that appears to be upon us. A more detailed examination of one particular passage in this move, however, will allow us to complicate this pattern and to reconnect it to Hartman's healing power.

The Invention of the Infant

On their way to the cottage at the close of the poem, the Sailor and the female vagrant are disturbed by a shrill scream, followed by a blaspheming "hoarser voice" and "female cries" (*ASP*, 609–11).

> Their course they thither bent
> And met a man who foamed with anger vehement
>
> A woman stood with quivering lips and wan,
> Near an old mat with broken bread bestrown;
> And pointing to a child her tale began.
> Trembling the infant hid his face
>
> (613–16)

The woman relates how the child had taken the place of the father, who got up to fetch a pitcher, and had failed to obey when asked to move, upon which the father began to beat the child "as if each blow had been his last" (627). The Sailor orders the father to stop and is answered with "bitter insult and revilings sad" (634), including the unwittingly appropriate prediction that he will meet his end hanging from the gallows. The Sailor does not reply but strokes the child still lying on the ground; when the boy turns his head, the Sailor notices that he is bleeding from the very spot where he had "fix'd" the "deadly wound" on the man he murdered (644–45), and the sight reduces him to tears and to interior monologue.

Within himself he said, "What hearts have we!
The blessing this the father gives his child!
Yet happy thou, poor boy! compared with me,
Suffering not doing ill, fate far more mild."

(649–52)

The father, in turn, comes to his senses, kisses the boy, and "all was reconcil'd" (655):

Then with a voice which inward trouble broke
In the full swelling throat, the Sailor them bespoke.

" 'Tis a bad world, and hard is the world's law;
Each prowls to strip his brother of his fleece;
Much need have ye that time more closely draw
The bond of nature, all unkindness cease,
And that among so few there still be peace:
Else can ye hope but with such num'rous foes
Your pains shall ever with your years increase."
While his pale lips these homely truths disclose,
A correspondent calm stole gently on his woes.

(656–66)

Several critics have singled out this beaten-child episode as a privileged moment in the poem's progress. John Rieder, in *Wordsworth's Counterrevolutionary Turn*, sees this "crucial turn towards the poem's resolution" as "a scene of lower-class corruption being conquered by sympathy and domestic virtue" (105). As such, it fits in with what Rieder diagnoses as "a partial displacement of the paradigm of political virtue operating in *Salisbury Plain* by that different set of virtues associated with the sympathetic passions rather than rational judgment" (93), a displacement that, in turn, is indicative of Wordsworth's recognition that his characters are not in a position to appreciate political virtue since they are "excluded from political participation" (105). Rieder argues that the principal effect of the Sailor's "homely truths" consists in the disclosure of "a drastic gap between the limited sphere in which the 'bond of nature' can assert itself and the 'bad world' of legal oppression and commercial rapacity":

In *Adventures on Salisbury Plain* public problems find only private solutions, as the entire poem moves progressively from the disclosure of the miseries inflicted upon

> its main characters in the bad world to a more intimate setting where the characters' virtue is competent. In the sailor's speech, as in the poem, this region of self-determination, so to speak, is first that of the family and finally, in the stanza's final line, contained within the conscientious individual. (106)

Rieder recognizes that this entails a disturbing plea for a "resignation to the unbridgeable gap between public vice and private virtues" (106), which, moreover, sits uncomfortably with the characters' unflinching devotion, as witness the public execution of the Sailor, to the organizing discourse of the public world which is the law. Yet that inconsistency, it would appear, is the price to be paid for a proper representation of the politically unrepresented. If in the first poem Wordsworth comes close to "exhibiting [his characters] as evidence in a brief against the state" (93), his attempts to rewrite this evidence in terms of what Rieder identifies as an "ethical problematic" (50) appear to risk dumping them into the last-ditch retreat of a dumb domesticity so enclosed upon itself that it cannot see citizenship as anything other than an incomprehensible curse. Practitioners of ethical criticism following Nussbaum's call for a release "from a stifling confinement into a space of human possibility" (Nussbaum, 362) are not likely to find it in this passage on Salisbury Plain.

Rieder concludes his reading of the Salisbury Plain poems with his version of Wordsworth's developing vision:

> The development of Wordsworth's thematics moves from public discords toward their private, individual roots. But this kind of radicalization passes from explicitly addressing itself to political actors to the contemplation of those who *suffer* politics from afar. In the process, Wordsworth's poetry becomes more reflective precisely because the poor lack the competence to understand their problems from the broader perspective available to the poet, and thus the polemical force of representing them derives from their mute objectivity, in which the poet of humanitarian protest finds his own sympathies reflected back to him in a socially pertinent way. (Rieder, 107)

Precisely what remains, however, of "the broader perspective available to the poet" in this process? Put bluntly, How does the poet understand the relation between the bad world of the state, which "the poor lack the competence to understand" (107), and the limited sphere of the family, where their "virtue is competent" (but competent for *what*) (106)? Does he understand it at all? And if so, how exactly do the "sympathies" informing his developing vision contribute to the practice and theory of citizenship? What *is* the "polemical force" and the social pertinence of Wordsworth's imagination?

In his recent study, *Romanticism on the Road*,[15] Toby Benis, also focusing on the child-beating episode, goes some way in addressing the contradictions Rieder here leaves suspended by turning Wordsworth's vision in an entirely different direction. Benis's perspective is partly governed by his productive misreading of the four opening stanzas of the original poem, which set up the contrast between the suffering savage and the present-day poor. In the first stanza, Wordsworth evokes the plight of the savage:

Hard is the life when naked and unhouzed
And wasted by the long day's fruitless pains,
The hungry savage, 'mid deep forests, rouzed
By storms, lies down at night on unknown plains
And lifts his head in fear . . .

(*SP*, 1–5)

The second stanza then gilds the pill:

Yet is he strong to suffer, and his mind
Encounters all his evils unsubdued;
For happier days since at the breast he pined
He never knew . . .

(10–13)

In addition, the savage's strength in suffering is increased because around him he only ever sees "men who all of his hard lot partake, / Repose in the same fear, to the same toil awake" (17–18). Those who suffer in the present, by contrast, are deprived even of this grim consolation, for they have known happier days, and they are confronted with other humans who have been spared their "sad reverse of fate" (22). The fourth stanza then drives home the point:

Hence where Refinement's genial influence calls
The soft affections from their wintry sleep
And the sweet tear of Love and Friendship falls
The willing heart in tender joy to steep,
When men in various vessels roam the deep
Of social life, and turns of chance prevail
Various and sad, how many thousands weep
Beset with foes more fierce than e'er assail
The savage without home in winter's keenest gale.

(28–36)

It is hard not to see the point of Wordsworth's comparison, but Benis convincingly succeeds in doing so. For him, the opening stanzas show "how truly radical Wordsworth's position is": by indicating how the savage "gathers strength from his isolating condition and the general lack of developed society," Benis argues, Wordsworth actually "implies that any systematic reform [of society] predicated on existing extended, organized communities is doomed" (67). Where Wordsworth sees the savage as stronger, not happier, for not having received the mixed blessing—but nonetheless a blessing—of "Refinement's genial influence," Benis sees the savage as positively blessed in his state of unmixing isolation: "The opening stanzas, repeatedly emphasizing that the fortunate savage was 'without home,' conclude that any dealings with 'the deep / Of social life' inevitably lead to misery and oppression" (67–68).

On the strength of this strange insight, central to his intent to turn early Wordsworth into an advocate of homelessness, Benis rereads the Salisbury Plain poems as teaching us that "only in individual moments of human contact, which are now best epitomized by associations among vagrants, can even a splintered sense of personal freedom and fulfillment reside." For Benis, therefore, the "most damaging overtly confronted ideologies in 'Salisbury Plain' concern the family and the home" (68). In striking contrast to Rieder, Benis sees Wordsworth discovering not a gap between the good world of the family and the bad world of the state, but rather a highly effective strategic alliance between the two spheres zealously cultivated by counterrevolutionary ideologues such as Burke, who "went on to make the patriarchal family the linchpin in his crusade against revolution: 'To be attached to the subdivision, to love the little platoon we belong to in society, is the first principle (the germ as it were) of public affections. It is the first link in the series by which we proceed towards a love to our country and to mankind' " (69–70).

Armed with this understanding of Wordsworth's vision, Benis unsurprisingly interprets the beaten-child episode as an illustration of Godwin's attacks on domestic life in the first edition of *Political Justice:* "The family, like the state that is modeled on it, creates discord and misery" (87). Where Rieder reads the Sailor's speech that concludes the episode as a defense of the family as the "more intimate setting where the characters' virtue is competent" (Rieder, 106), Benis sees it as yet another plea for the "sympathetic contact" and "unimpeded interchange" (Benis, 86) which are the blessings of homeless life alone: "The sailor invokes a generalized 'bond of nature' as the element that should keep peace in the family of humanity. He also recognizes that, in both his own life and the scene before him, the sense of this ancient bond had been riven by the new laws of nation and family. The encounter itself bears out that the only bond that has any positive power is a provisional sense of engagement" (88). Needless to say, the fact that the text explicitly qualifies this putative praise of homelessness as a disclosure of "homely truths" (*ASP*, 565), and further characterizes the female vagrant as a woman susceptible to the "homefelt force of sympathy sincere" (*ASP*, 704), goes unnoticed in Benis's account.

The interest of Benis's misreading in the present context is that it articulates what is missing in Rieder's reading, to wit, "the broader perspective available to the poet" (Rieder, 107) which could make sense of the acknowledged contradiction in Rieder's interpretation regarding the relation between family and state. Notwithstanding the questionable exegesis underpinning Benis's argument, it does help to put in clearer relief the central problem worrying Wordsworth in his turn from "social and political phenomena" to the allegedly "more complex phenomena of human motives and behaviour" (*SPP*, 12). What both Rieder and Benis recognize is Wordsworth's faltering attempt to formulate Hartman's law — "afford sympathy" — in the socio-political context in which it is meant to matter. Rieder locates this sympathy in the home but, by his own admission, fails to demonstrate how it is supposed to travel to the public field of state politics, if at all; Benis recognizes the potentially sinister ideological service to which domestic sympathy can be put and consequently locates Wordsworth's sympathy as he understands it outside both home and state, but thereby effectively confirms the real irresolution that the poem's melodramatic resolution cannot control. What neither critic queries, however, is the provenance of the infant figure triggering this ethical inquiry into the virtues of sympathy: Where *does* that child come from?

Rather than dressing it in the New Historicist detail of turn-of-the-century child-beating, there is something to be said for pursuing this infant in Wordsworth's text. As it happens, the word appears in two passages in each poem. One of these passages, shared by both texts, occurs in the woman's narrative, when she relates how, in the happy early years of her marriage, "Three lovely infants lay within my breast / And often viewing their sweet smiles I sighed / And knew not why" (*SP*, 291–93; *ASP*, 345–47). The other occurrence of the word "infant" in the first poem gives articulate voice to that sigh. Just before the woman begins her tale, the narrator fixes his gaze on her breasts:

> Like swans, twin swans, that when on the sweet brink
> Of Derwent's stream the south winds hardly blow,
> 'Mid Derwent's water-lillies swell and sink

In union, rose her sister breasts of snow,
(Fair emblem of two lover's hearts that know
No separate impulse) or like infants played,
Like infants strangers yet to pain and woe.
(*SP*, 208–14)

Discarding the swans and the lovers as appropriate tropes, the poem eagerly seizes upon the infants as figures releasing a damaging insight into the trauma of human existence:

And are ye spread ye glittering dews of youth
For this, — that Frost may gall the tender flower
In Joy's fair breast with more untimely tooth?
Unhappy man! thy sole delightful hour
Flies first; it is thy miserable dower
Only to taste of joy that thou may'st pine
A loss, which rolling suns shall ne'er restore.
New suns roll on and scatter as they shine
No second spring, but pain, till death release thee, thine.
(*SP*, 217–25)

The argument clearly recalls, inverts, and radicalizes the sketch of the hungry savage in the opening stanzas.[16] As suggested, the point of this sketch was clear, but what its modulation in the present passage primarily reveals is its absence of purpose — an absence symptomatically denied in redemptive misreadings of the savage situation such as Benis's. The four opening stanzas merely posit a contrast between the past and the present as a difference between the homogeneity of unallayed suffering and the heterogeneity of modern differentiation, this latter explicitly linked to the function of memory as a difference device. Yet the poem fails to coherently develop this posited point into a purposeful rhetoric of community for the present. The trope of the breast-infants, then, triggers the climactic culmination of this failure in the hyperbolical assumption of radical trauma. The strength of the savage is that, having always "pined," even "at the breast," and having never encountered anything "But men who all of his hard lot partake, / Repose in the same fear, to the same toil awake," he is immune to the workings of memory as a faculty producing difference. The curse of the present writ large on the faces of the infants, "strangers yet to pain and woe," is that they are destined for a difference Wordsworth can only envisage as the life-long misery of "Unhappy man" as such. What this vision effectively reveals is the etymological literalization of sympathy itself as, precisely, shared suffering. For what is the state of the savage imagined by Wordsworth if not a state of pure sympathy, in which each and everyone suffers the same? And what is our state as fallen infants if not this same condition of sad sympathy?

Read in this light, the infant trope thus bridges the gap between the past and the present from which the poem sets out by rewriting difference as more of the same, thereby at once disabling the very notion of sympathy as a core element in an affirmative rhetoric of community ready to register difference. In the context of Wordsworth's attempt to develop the ideology predicated on sympathy that Hartman, Gill, Rieder, Benis, and others have accurately identified as his chief intent, the infant passage in the first Salisbury Plain poem is a disastrous moment of excessive imaginative reduction from which the second poem is still trying to recover.

The way in which *Adventures on Salisbury Plain* sets out to control the damage done is remarkably systematic, showing Wordsworth painstakingly trying to rescue the maximum: the woman's breasts that gave rise to the passage are cut out; but the figural swans they also invited are literalized into real swans swimming on Derwent, now completing an unfinished stanza of the original poem (*ASP*, 287; cf. *SP*, 243); while the figural "infants" develop into a real child—catachrestically called "infant" (*ASP*, 616, 623) yet significantly endowed with no language but a shrill scream—suffering real violence rather than the universal trauma of humankind. Most importantly, perhaps, the homiletic opening line of the first poem—"Hard is the life when naked and unhouzed" (*SP*, 1)—is modulated into the opening line of the Sailor's response to this infant suffering in his disclosure of "homely truths": " 'Tis a bad world, and hard is the world's law" (*ASP*, 658). With this last recovery, Wordsworth at once rehearses and erases the connection between savage sympathy and infant trauma which short-circuited the first poem, just about literally domesticating the infant figure by inserting it into the admittedly as yet "unhouzed" nuclear family as sympathy's last, but politically incompetent, resort. It is perhaps one of Wordsworth's most revealing, because least confidently developed, attempts to establish the oxymoron of infant virtue that haunts his political imagination throughout. Read brutally, by rewriting the figure of the infant into the second poem, Wordsworth tries beating it into the ideological service it failed to perform in the earlier text. His failure to fully perform this salvaging operation by finishing the poem to his own satisfaction signals at least a residual resistance to the trope of infant sympathy unsettled in *Salisbury Plain*.[17]

It is important to emphasize that the second poem should have attempted this rhetorical child discipline at all. True, it must seem perverse to imagine Wordsworth simply abandoning the infant as a governing trope; he is, after all, the canonical blesser of babes at the breast, infants fathering their own future virtue by the force of sympathy. Even in the Immortality Ode, with its curious curse of the infant's fall into family and society, the child remains the focus of redemptive vision: "Heaven lies about us in our infancy" (66), and what remains of this "primal sympathy" (184) is a lasting source of strength.[18] Yet as the compositional history of the Ode indicates, this lofty confidence comes at a price. As a sustained rereading of the Ode and its complicated genesis cannot be undertaken here, I will merely rehearse what I take to be the decisive turn in the text under way to its final version as "Ode: Intimations of Immortality from Recollections of Early Childhood." Unsurprisingly, that turn proves to be yet again the invention, or, rather, the recovery of the infant as a trope producing release from difference.

Recovered Infancy

The clear break in diction between stanzas four and five of the Immortality Ode is generally received as a controlled shift in the poem's overall argument. Yet, as is well known but rarely reflected upon, Wordsworth probably wrote the first four stanzas some three months prior to its continuation.[19] Looked at in their own right, these lines make strange reading, as witness this admittedly plodding prose paraphrase: "There was a time when I saw things I now can see no more; things are beautiful now, but something's missing, grieving me alone; then I heard something giving me relief, and now I'm happy again and feel at one with all. But there's a tree and a field and a flower telling me that something's missing and asking where it went." It does not take too much effort to read this account as a sober and self-concerned first-person-singular version of the sympathy crisis in the earlier visions of the savage and the infant. Importantly, however, that effort is not made by the text itself; in fact, the text as it stands in March 1802 makes no efforts to furnish any scheme in which its mild mood swings make sense. It charts a movement from isolation as a result of unspecified loss, over joyous sympathy generated by an unidentified "timely utterance," to renewed isolation articulated by singular objects, but it strikingly stops short of deriving any lesson from this movement.

The later continuation of the Immortality Ode famously *is* such a lesson: it recovers sympathy as a community-generating principle, bringing "soothing thoughts that spring / Out of human suffering" (186–87), and the vehicle for this recovery operation is, crucially, the instant infant, miraculously emerging in the first-person plural in the resolutely homiletic opening line of stanza 5: "Our birth is but a sleep and a forgetting" (58). The decisive difference between this infant and the beaten child in the second Salisbury Plain poem, however, is that its home is not in the family but quite emphatically outside human society—in the "imperial palace" (84) of God. The price to be paid for a solid foundation of sympathy is, it would appear, a resignation to religion, displacing the source of sympathy to the transcendental realm, which is its all too familiar home. Yet for Wordsworth's text, which Stanley Cavell has felicitously characterized, be it with alternative intent, as a "text of recovery,"[20] this reactionary resignation yields material gains, for it allows him finally to reintegrate the trauma-tropes of *Salisbury Plain* he was unable to salvage in the course of its revision:[21]

And are ye spread, ye glittering dews of youth
For this—that Frost may gall the tender flower
In Joy's fair breast with more untimely tooth?
Unhappy man! thy sole delightful hour
Flies first . . .

(*SP*, 217–20)

This insufferable insight in the untimely tooth of time itself is now released into the Ode's interpretation—or productive misreading—of the timely utterance its opening stanzas failed to frame:

What though the radiance which was once so bright
Be now for ever taken from my sight,
  Though nothing can bring back the hour
Of splendour in the grass, of glory in the flower;
  We will grieve not, rather find
  Strength in what remains behind,
  In the primal sympathy
  Which having been must ever be,
  In the soothing thoughts that spring
  Out of human suffering,
  In the faith that looks through death,
In years that bring the philosophic mind.

(178–89)

Here at last, the critical contrast between the savage mind's unsubdued strength in pure sympathy and the utter despair of the imaginative reduction of timely difference to unallayed suffering which paralyzed Wordsworth's imagination appears to be mastered. By relocating the infant in heaven, Wordsworth manages to positively posit human suffering as conducive to soothing thoughts. Yet this sympathetic strength in the face of suffering can only be purchased, it seems, at the cost of denying death itself. The textual trace of this transaction is the grave to which the infant is consigned, the "place of thought where we in waiting lie" (123) and where Wordsworth's sympathy quite literally rests encrypted.

This encryption of human sympathy into death-denial invites a more focused return to the contrast between savage indifference and postsavage differentiation at the outset of *Salisbury Plain.* Memory and comparison — the faculties crucially unavailable to Wordsworth's fictional and, by dint of this lack, strictly prehuman savage — institute the time and the space of difference through material inscriptions that produce "social life" as constitutively "various" (*SP,* 32–34). These inscriptions — language — take place and acquire time in matter that is dead to the processes of life: dead not for having once been alive, but "dead" because, as the medium of inscription, this matter belongs to an order altogether different from life, including the death of life. As Paul de Man, transcribing Wordsworth's *Essays upon Epitaphs,* keeps reminding us, "death is a displaced name for a linguistic predicament,"[22] and Wordsworth's savage fiction allows us to read this linguistic predicament as the retrospectively recognized traumatic collapse of the prehistoric life of nature into the history of material inscription we call culture — a practice of transmission radically alien to the genetic transmissions of life and which can survive only in the passage through dead matter. What is recorded in this passage is difference, the displaced name of which, as witness Wordsworth's narrator's breakdown in the face of the infants in *Salisbury Plain,* is indeed death: *displaced,* because rather than naming difference, the trope of death releases it into the order of natural life which difference has always already interrupted: "No second spring, but pain, till death release thee, thine" (*SP,* 225).

Effectively failing as a response to difference, this release into death merely rehearses the erasure of difference in the literal rendering of sympathy as the shared suffering of savage indifference, thereby missing precisely the "various" nature of "social life" sympathy is supposed to address. The Immortality Ode's triumphant death-denial, prepared as it is by an entirely consistent dismissal of human society as artificial shape-shifting and "endless imitation" (107), fully assumes this failure as a success and calls it "primal sympathy" (184); denying death, it simultaneously dismisses language as the material predicament of difference by encrypting it, *sub specie aeternitatis*, as a mere epiphenomenon of the lived immortality of the soul born in and borne by God, "who is our home"(65). The awaited relief of real and general human suffering which Wordsworth's earlier infant sympathy failed to imagine even in the bosom of the nuclear family is transferred to an eternally thoughtful wait for the bosom of God—a wait in which the harrowing inarticulateness in the face of overwhelming iniquity is redeemed as the wisdom of infants who know their father near, to echo once more one of Wordsworth's chief successors in the tropological exploitation of infant virtue.

> And like a man in wrath the heart
> Stood up and answered, "I have felt."
>
> No, like a child in doubt and fear:
> But that blind clamour made me wise;
> Then was I as a child that cries,
> But, crying, knows his father near;
>
> And what I am beheld again
> What is, and no man understands;
> And out of darkness came the hands
> That reach through nature, moulding men.
> (*In Memoriam*, 124, 15–24)

If such is the price to be paid for sympathy as the regulative principle of an ethical rhetoric of community which can save us from the ravages of the last century, perhaps we should resist affording it. Such resistance is not a gratuitous resistance to religion: rather, it refuses the translation of both ethical and sociopolitical issues—the difference between them being delusive but not therefore nonexistent—into professions of faith on the back of a powerful trope; more succinctly, it refuses the abandonment of suffering for the sake of a figure. That this ethicopolitical resistance to a rhetoric of sympathy is generated by the text itself indicates that there may be more than one way to be caught in the ethical turn; not only by understanding the literary text as a vehicle for the sympathetic imagination but also by reading its failure to cover difference with the cloak of sympathy, a failure rendering it unreadable on its own temporal terms, though supremely intelligible in the recovered eyesight of God. To register this failure is to allow for a different articulation of literature's "material effectiveness"—its power as a discursive practice releasing material traces of the crisis of imagination which can justifiably be called an ethical predicament inasmuch as it registers the resistance of the other — all others — to smooth and soothing sympathetic incorporation. The cry for resolution attending this crisis itself demands to be read rather than to be recovered as the answer whose ineffectiveness generated the crisis in the first place.

"No second spring, but pain, till death release thee, thine" (*SP*, 225). The additions to the manuscript of *Salisbury Plain* show Wordsworth's attempt to recover this "second spring" trope too, but it is not until he revisits the matter in *Guilt and Sorrow* nearly half a century later that he appears to succeed in reintegrating it. The narrative generated by this textual sequence is further evidence of the resistance to reading difference attending this recovery. In *Salisbury Plain*, the absence of a "second spring" names the crisis of sympathy in the face of human difference, a crisis evaded in the decisive erasure of difference, through death, in nature, where spring springs eternal. In a first revision, probably undertaken as early as 1794, Wordsworth attempts to restore the phrase by inserting it into an expanded description of the traveler's words of consolation in response to the female wanderer's narrative. It now figures, as "Joy's second spring," alongside phrases like "the general care man pays to man" and, especially significantly, "social orders all-protecting plan" as a fixed formula from the discourse of wishful thinking seeking to cover up distress by imagining a benevolent power governing society in much the same way as the ahistorical cycles of regeneration govern nature.[23] Qualifying these tropes as so many mystifications by no means amounts to a demystification of Wordsworth; the manuscript itself explicitly designates them as "Delusion fond" and as "Sounds that but served her deep breast to beguile" (*SPP*, 111). The wanderer's breasts, which prompted the crisis of sympathy in the narrator of *Salisbury Plain*, return here as a "deep breast" receptive to a form of trauma management on the part of the traveler from which the narrator continues to measure his distance.

A second stage of revision soon after, in which the dramatic development of *Salisbury Plain* into *Adventures on Salisbury Plain* begins to take shape, shows Wordsworth recovering the "second spring" trope in a new passage depicting the traveler wandering the world in fear. At this stage already burdened with the guilty conscience of a murderer, the traveler is said to be still receptive to "nature's tendency to pleasure known before" in the sense that "common cares" can "to his [heart or breast] a second spring restore," allowing his "heartstrings [to tremble] with responsive grief" in the face of "wretchedness" (*SPP*, 115). If in the first revision the "second spring" figures as a mere phrase by means of which the traveler tries to sympathetically engage with the suffering woman, in the second revision it names that engagement itself as evidence of the beneficial power of nature. The narrator's critical reservation toward sympathy as not just a necessary but, more importantly, a sufficient response to suffering gradually diminishes, and when the phrase finally reappears in *Guilt and Sorrow*, restored to its position in the consolation passage, the ideology of sympathy seems to be firmly in place:

> True sympathy the Sailor's looks expressed,
> His looks — for pondering he was mute the while.
> Of social Order's care for wretchedness,
> Of Time's sure help to calm and reconcile,
> Joy's second spring and Hope's long-treasured smile,
> 'T was not for *him* to speak — a man so tried.
> Yet to relieve her heart, in friendly style
> Proverbial words of comfort he applied,
> And not in vain, while they went pacing side by side.
>
> (*GS*, 451–59)

Gill notes that in this final version, the notion of "social Order's care" is no longer qualified as a "delusion fond"; instead, he adds, "the suggestion is that there is a benevolent order and that hope is possible, but that the sailor has put himself beyond them" (*SPP*, 257). Such would indeed be the suggestion embraced by the ideology of sympathy. Yet it is equally possible to read the passage as an ironic repetition of the first revision's demystification of "social order's all-protecting plan" as a wishful trope intent on naturalizing the social. The Sailor's own trials at the very least invite this alternative construction, in which the "proverbial words of comfort" come to figure as impotent sympathy's final recourse in the face of an injustice it is unable to address: the timeless utterances of pure ideology, whose marked repetition here *as* ideology's *disjecta membra* can hardly fail to dislodge the fond delusion that "social Order" was a living body in the first place, even as the performance of these prosthetic proverbs is emphatically credited with success.[24] The fact that *Guilt and Sorrow* immediately moves on to the child-beating scene and its "appropriate lesson" (512), that only the "bond of nature" (508) can remedy the inexorable "increase" in "pains" (511) wrought by the "Bad . . . world" (505), indicates that, on Salisbury Plain, the miraculous recovery of the infant ideology of sympathy in the Immortality Ode continues to be undone as a fond delusion by the material inscriptions riddling Wordsworth's writing.[25]

Intolerable Thought

More concretely, the errant infant in Wordsworth's text suggests that Wordsworthian sympathy itself, derived as it is from the intimate imaginary identifications whose phantasmal model is that of childhood, may not be such a good idea in the development of visions addressing the incommensurable differences riddling what we must still call the human community to the core. To trace this suspicion in the textual recovery operations constituting Wordsworth's tropology is to invite the thought of what Lisabeth During has hinted at as an ethics "on the far side of sympathy."[26] This suspicion is evidently not lost on the best apologist of Wordsworth's sympathetic imagination. Exploring what he calls the sympathy paradox—"the more successful an expanding sensibility becomes, the more evidence we find of actual insensibility" (*Fateful Question*, 144)—Hartman forcefully registers what he calls "the crucial question":

> The crucial question is now as always: how does one maintain compassion; what familial or formal pedagogy can achieve a widening of sensibility when that widening soon exhausts itself? The pro-life debate in America as well as the animal rights movement are symptoms of a deep unease: they exhibit an imagination drawn to whatever is mute or helpless and they view that extension of feeling as the test of our humanity. But feelings are finite and so, as the sympathy paradox teaches, become overinvested, dogmatic, and even schizoid. As one segment of a forgotten or neglected reality is recovered, another fails, is not responded to, or is constructed as irredeemably alien. This self-protective indifference, however, does not always anesthesize conscience: often what is rejected hurts like a phantom limb. The perceived absence of compassion can then turn into a deliberate and dangerous coldness and seek to justify itself ideologically. . . . What we see mainly around us is pathology: a stressed sympathetic imagination and doctrines or defenses resulting from that. This pathology emerges most blatantly when cultures or nations different from us are demonized or one's own country is viewed not as a beloved community, an extension of family and a way of accommodating the finiteness of our energies and feelings, but as a sacrificial abstraction. (156–57)

Yet even as he here intimates his recognition of the disturbing family resemblance between fascist demonization and familial ideology, Hartman refuses to abandon sympathy and returns to Wordsworth's infant virtue as a source of salvation ultimately unaffected by what he clearly recognizes as the "specter of a failure" (154) haunting its genesis. In *Guilt and Sorrow*, that specter appears as "True sympathy" (451): a sympathy that is essentially mute and that loses itself in a wishful resignation to injustice the moment it is performed as proverbial comfort proffered by a sensitive soul to a sensitive soul in an intimate exchange of timeless sentiment divorced from the structures of political representation.

What remains unthought in Hartman's return to Wordsworth's infant ideology here—a faithful echo of Wordsworth's inability to abandon his disturbingly marked ideologization of sympathy as surrogate justice—is the possibility of a credible alternative supplementing both the extended family and the pathological sacrificial abstraction of extreme nationalism, powered as they both are by personally imagined sympathy. In his perceptive review essay on *The Fateful Question*, Geoffrey Galt Harpham puzzled over Hartman's "almost purposeful" avoidance of the concept "society" (*Shadows of Ethics*, 218), which, as it is defined by Raymond Williams, "actually corresponds closely to Hartman's sense of Wordsworth in that it denotes a diverse polity, an ethical and civic structure held together by voluntary association based on shared interests and values" (219). Yet this avoidance, I would argue, if such it be, is less decisive than the avoidance, in this specific connection, of an alternative structure in which personal volition and substantially subjective sharing are themselves displaced, and which is consequently doomed, at least from the perspective of sympathetic society, to appear only as a vaguely threatening "apparatus of power" (13), rather than as a genuinely radical, because profoundly unnatural, implementation of the political representation of sympathy beyond lived sentiment.

What remains unthought here, to hazard an affirmation at last, is not so much "society" but a notion of the state (or State) materially representing an order of care we cannot afford to feel or even think for ourselves by instituting a resolutely timely structure of difference that offers real relief rather than charity, impersonal responsibility rather than the gratifying glow of a good conscience lying in waiting to recover from the sympathy paradox. Performing sympathy as a "productive paradox" (Rieder, 224) rather than aestheticizing it all the way to immortality, this necessarily expensive structure (only two things in life are certain) would require the recovery of, say, for now, the welfare state as an alternative response to the pathology of the present; but it would have to be a welfare state complicated beyond recognition, predicated on an ethics that challenges private conscience by exceeding its imaginative grasp, not the now-outdated compromise consigned to the suspended animation of English national heritage that goes by that name.

Perhaps Hartman is right: Wordsworth did shape a specifically English — and increasingly global — culture unable to entertain, let alone join, a genuinely political structure which it is hard to sympathize with precisely because it does not suffer intimate imaginative identifications — least of all perhaps as a family. And for once, the then-leader of the British Conservative Party may have been right, too, when he declared in 2000 that high taxes drive out good conscience.[27] But instead of leading to "a deep cynicism about the institutions that give our lives moral shape," the impersonal bad conscience constituting the superstate at least entertains the promise of a shift in the shape of our lives that would translate sympathy beyond the confines of domesticated justice. Wordsworth's memory deserves this "intolerable thought" (*GS*, 659).

CHAPTER THREE

Romantic Memory

Frances Ferguson

Locke pointed, now some three centuries ago, to the importance of memory for anchoring a sense of individual continuity over time. If, he suggested, human beings were capable of continual rearrangements of the elements of their thought and behavior, one could nevertheless see, through an examination of memory, that memory could provide testimony that one was still the same person despite the contradictions between what one said and what one did, despite the inconsistencies between what one had done earlier and what one had done later. Locke's treatment of memory meant that one didn't have to stake one's identity on the claim that a particular person must always be able to persuade others—and oneself as well—that one has remained the same person by being characteristic of oneself and, hence, recognizable. The persistence of memory relieved one of the need to continue to look the same or to produce consistent and predictable patterns of behavior. Locke was, in this, lending his support to a remarkable feature of the philosophy of everyday life—that we don't imagine

I am grateful to audiences at Tel Aviv University and the School for Criticism and Theory in the summer of 1996 for their responses to an earlier version of this essay.

that the continuity of an individual's identity rests on a series of ocular proofs, that we most often take someone who behaves differently from one day to the next to be the same person in a different mood rather than a different person altogether.[1]

Memory, from the vantage of the Lockean account, provided two very palpable services. First, in a fashion that is only superficially paradoxical, memory opened the way for considerable flexibility and innovation; it freed individuals from having to repeat the same actions continually and introduced them instead to a vision of their own possible progress and development.[2] Moreover, memory provided a theater that one could regularly open to compete with the theater of immediate experience. As historians of the novel have long recognized, an intensification of attention to memory underwrote the phenomenal rise of literature in the centuries after Locke.[3] It was, in that sense, regularly implicated in what we mean by the internalization of experience, the psychologization of everyday life that we connect with modernity, inasmuch as memory was identical with reflection, and with a reflection that did not simply reproduce an image of one's past but adapted it in the process.

Now there is probably nothing more common than to move from such an account of memory in all its self-revising aspects to the claim that our history is a version of memory. Indeed, the function of the humanities in the university and the school is, these days, regularly and routinely described as one of cultural memory. The justification for all of the humanities occurs in terms of a justification of a kind of history that models itself on individual memory, and we thus continually encounter a notion of a memory that is constituted largely outside of individuals, a social or collective memory that an individual comes to produce rather than to recall, in a kind of Jungian mutual recruitment between personal memory and phylogenetic memory.[4] The purpose of this essay is to examine, through a few key examples, the uses that romanticism develops for memory and the consequences that such uses of memory have for both history and the notion of individual identity. It will, in the process, try to indicate how memory became more individualized in the romantic period and, second, how this process includes reference to the claims of the collective.

Of course, the first difficulty with history—one that develops with the eighteenth century's intense interest in history-writing—is that the increasing popularity of this kind of writing establishes what we might call pure history as an absent ideal.[5] Modern history arises with historiography, which is to say that pure history is regularly described—by both historians of literature who are marking out the differences between historical and pseudo-historical chronicles and by Freud—in essentially archaic terms.[6] History in its pure form would record actual events that are confirmable by more than one witness. Moreover, historical witnesses are taken to be most credible—most fully historical—when they describe events in which perception requires only minimal instruction. The history of battles and wars thus represents a paradigm for such a notion of history. By contrast with social history, the history of battles and cataclysms is a very pure form of history. It relies upon the fact that one can imagine a variety of witnesses, who might come from different cultures and speak different languages but who would nevertheless be able to confirm one another's sense that a flood or an earthquake had occurred or that thousands had perished on the battlefield.[7] For if Rousseau's account of history makes it look like a problem for an event that might be susceptible to more than one description, the catastrophic event always seems to qualify as an event because the description of it as a catastrophe is imagined to drive out all others.

Such an image of pure history does not cease to have an impact because of its comparative rarity—indeed, its existing as a null set. If pure history sets a standard of historical adequacy that other versions of history continually chafe under, it is the scarcity of pure history that prompts most of the important accounts of history that we have. Social history, the "history" produced by the novel, and individual psychoanalytic history all provide images of how one might produce historical facts in the absence of such universal agreement as pure history seems to require. Social history defines itself against pure history by insisting upon analyzing different periods in order to see how the training of a particular society contributes to the ability of witnesses to observe anything like the same events. Literary history, as instanced in Ian Watt's important account of the rise of psychological realism, traces the rise of psychology as the emergence of an interest in memory as the record of how formal procedures of completeness—well-madeness—come to produce their own characteristic ways of identifying facts. Psychoanalytic history, as Freud argued in making his claim that the Wolf Man could remember having observed his parents' coitus in infancy, recalls the ancient law of testimony—that there must be two witnesses to corroborate one another—to present his case study as a legitimate representation of memory even though it revolves around the belated testimony of an adult recalling or imagining an experience from his infancy.[8]

What is striking about most of these versions of testimony is that they might appear to replace the old (or virtually unavailable) model, the one in which persons can regularly corroborate one another's perceptions, with a resolutely individualistic model in which both the perception of a pattern and its confirmation lie in the same hands. Memory, as recorded in history, seems thus to become not what all possible observers would confirm but instead a process of internal matching, in which memory or its formal simulacrum qualifies an individual to count as his own corroboration. The formal scheme of the fiction writer produces a conviction that needs no evidence from the real world; and Freud's psychoanalytic model is in the somewhat peculiar position of producing permutations for the patient's testimony that are simultaneously formal—insofar as they are merely translations of what has been said—and evidentiary—in that the original material is seen as evidence of experience.[9]

In the trajectory of arguments about evidence, the most surprising element in Freud's treatment of the Wolf Man is his claim that the only plausible evidence must be original with the patient. Indeed, the very corroboration that would once have served to confirm an individual's testimony—the testimony of a second witness—comes to seem less like confirmation than contamination. Thus, Freud takes great pains in his discussion of the Wolf Man not just to insist that he, Freud, had not influenced the patient but also to argue that no others compromised his recollection of the imagery that constitutes his account of the primal scene, something he is said to have identified as an event.[10] Memory, in this latter psychologized form, is memory less because it confirms the identity of an event (its occurring for all observers in terms that can be agreed upon) than because of its assertion of the identity of apparently dissimilar events (the intercourse between the parents that the child did not understand as he would later come to understand intercourse as an adult).[11] Moreover, psychological memory comes to register the sense of the uniqueness of this identity; although it could have been any one of a number of persons who might have recognized such an identity, it was only one—the Wolf Man—who recognized it in this particular case.

We may now take stock of the difference that the psychological or individual account of memory makes. For if it seems to supplant the archaic (or mythic) model of testimony in which numerous witnesses confirm one another in the production of the facts of the world, it is not, even so, subjective in the sense of simply producing the facts of the self, the individual's point of view that is valued precisely for being the individual's. Moreover, it goes well past the epistemological problems that the critics of the novel routinely raise—the recognition that fictions, as descriptions of things we have never experienced, may inflect our sense of what we do in fact experience. That set of epistemological problems regularly resolves itself into two worries: first, that our descriptions can come to count as creating the real but unjustified belief that we have ourselves experienced something; and second, that our descriptions come to create skepticism about the plausibility of any well-formed story (so that it looks as though experience is only credible when it seems to have the most minimal appearance of design).[12] This is as much as to say that the individual, psychologized memory comes to be charged less with a relationship to truth as such than with the capacity for recognizing oneself in the world, seeing oneself as connected to one's actions.

Thus, the most important effect of the charge that memory takes on is to make the deficiencies of memory look as though they are anything but trivial. For memory has become not merely a way of asserting a basic continuity of the observer in the face of continual lapses and confusions; it has developed into something that must be treated as a right, and to just the same extent as it has come to be treated as a duty. If romantic psychology expands the repertoire of the individual to emphasize moods, anticipations, and memory in one's life, it concomitantly imposes those enlarged powers, so that the right to have a memory becomes very nearly identical with the right to psychological life. Thus, even if countless observers were to attest to an individual's existence by affirming that they were there at the event of that person's birth, the psychological account would make it clear that this kind of information about one's life isn't what's in question at all. For memory here stands less for the ability to know that certain events happened or even that one was there to witness them than for the possibility of reflexiveness itself, for a faculty of mind that can only imperfectly be translated into public law or be received from the testimony of another.[13] Memory, that is, comes to be less important for the facts that it produces than for its ability to produce facts with personal application, for what I'll be examining as the ability to move from one description to another. Moreover, as I will be suggesting in this discussion, the looser, or more expansive, romantic sense of what memory ought to be opens on a claim that memory is important for producing what we ought to designate "moral certainty," the sense of certainty about what must have been the case and how an individual feels involved with it even if there is no possibility of producing an actual confirmation. (Moreover, inasmuch as memory comes to be an expression of the sense of knowledge from acquaintance rather than from reports, we even come to see descriptions of reports that are treated as if they were experience. Thus, Stanley Fish's account of how *Paradise Lost* leads the unsuspecting reader to be "surprised by sin"—and thus to experience *in propria persona* Adam's fall—anticipates the work that Shoshana Felman and Cathy Caruth have recently done to argue that reading reports of trauma is itself traumatizing. What is most important, from our perspective, is the urgency with which the insistence upon the dispersion of individual experience is pressed in these various cases, as if to provide evidence of the premium being placed on the personalization of memory, in which even a report is seen as producing experience.)[14]

To try to sharpen this account of the importance of memory, I shall be examining a series of examples—the first from Geoffrey Hartman's recent work on videotestimonies of the Yale Holocaust Archives, the second from Wordsworth's account of one of the famous spots of time in Book 12 of *The Prelude* and Hartman's commentary on it, and the third from James Hogg's *The Private Memoirs and Confessions of a Justified Sinner.* As my repeated reference to both the eighteenth century and the twentieth will, I hope, make clear, what I am calling "romantic memory" is by no means confined to the early nineteenth century but is a characteristic modern way of identifying the stakes of memory in relation to the individual.

The first question that presents itself concerns the relationship between the faculty of memory and the media of its representation. In a series of recent articles, Geoffrey Hartman has argued that the videotestimony has become—and ought to be recognized as—a significant new genre. In essays such as "Learning from Survivors: The Yale Testimony Project" and "The Cinema Animal: On Spielberg's *Schindler's List,*" Hartman identifies a variety of genres that aim to represent memory—histories and psychoanalytic case studies, Hollywood cinema and poetic fictions.[15] Yet while he is concerned to identify all of these various representational modes as versions of memory, he would distinguish the videotestimony from all of them. Thus, he acknowledges that the videotestimony cannot claim the kind of corroboration that historians might require of a proper history and admits that the videotestimony does not always have the density and detail of a cinematic representation of a fictional or fictionalized memory. In his view, however, these differences mark out the comparative strength of the videotestimony. The videotestimony does not fail to meet the standards of other modes of memory; rather, its example reveals their previously inconspicuous deficiencies.

Time and again, he rehearses the power of one representational mode after another, only to end in a statement of the suspicions that their successes arouse. Thus, while Hartman asserts that "it is important not to sanctify witness accounts," he also claims the videotestimony "as a representational mode with a special counter-cinematic integrity" ("Learning from Survivors," 198). Writing of *Schindler's List,* he talks about the effectiveness of the film "as a film that conveys to the public at large the horror of the extermination" ("Cinema Animal," 127), only to begin to register his unease with "the premium placed on visuality by such a film" and with the way in which seeing "things that sharply, and from a privileged position is to see them with the eyes of those who had the power of life and death" (128). In his view, the formal vantage that Spielberg's camera provides ineluctably captures its viewers in the same angle of vision as the Nazis. However sympathetic 1990s viewers might take themselves to be with victims whom they see tormented and tortured in the past that the film depicts, they cannot escape this privileged vision. Such power corrupts, for the modern spectator as well as for the historical actors in the past who shared it and acted viciously on it.

Notice that Hartman is basically arguing here against what might seem to be the fundamental premise of the Spielberg film. *Schindler's List* recounts Schindler's story in order to suggest that it was and is possible, even for someone who shares an extraordinary number of circumstances and life experiences with the murderous, to take an active role in preventing such murderous acts; but Hartman is essentially arguing that Spielberg's use of the cinematic medium itself compromises such a view. The moral dilemma he is interested in locating is this: if one's way of gaining information about a crime involves one's being put in the privileged position of witnessing it but never running the risks of victimization, doesn't that position of superiority compromise one's judgment? If we were to tease out the implications of his remarks here, it would be possible to talk about two distinct ways of suggesting the problems that are raised by Spielberg's representation of moral choice.

The first is to argue, as Hartman seems to, that the conditions of viewing lend viewers all too much of an invitation to participate in a power structure that they would repudiate were it not camouflaged as the discreet charm of visuality. Adapting the argument that critics like Laura Mulvey and Mary Ann Doane have made about the misogyny that attaches to the "male gaze" of viewers of women in film, Hartman suggests that the conditions of viewing may override the particular views that we might have and express.[16] Seeing like a Nazi may thus be, in Hartman's account, being like a Nazi, so that persons come to occupy positions that they would never independently have chosen.

The second approach acknowledges the power of the visual perspective in Spielberg's film but does not argue that this perspective aligns modern viewers with the Nazi's power. Rather, in this view, the problem with the perspective from Spielberg's camera is that it imagines that viewers need too much coaching in moral action. This is not a matter of Spielberg's protesting too much and saying murderous things in an apparently innocent way. It is, instead, a matter of suggesting that what Hartman calls seeing "with the eyes of those who had the power of life and death" is problematic because it works especially hard at directing us toward choices that ought to be easy. For the distant perspective, the all-surveying perspective, doesn't make us imagine that we would make the Nazi choice. Instead, it makes us imagine that we can enter that field of vision just as if there had been no war fought and won to affirm the rightness of the moral decision not to murder, just as if there had been no commitment to the internationalizing of justice at Nuremberg. For what the camera eye does is to give one the sense that virtually any viewer could see what the Nazis saw and make a different moral decision, the right moral decision.

The point to be made about *Schindler's List* and the position it puts its viewers in is not that there is anything wrong with visual representations—even when they are visual representations of issues of morality. It is that in a world in which it is easy to recover the technologies for the Nazi choice (in the commitment to a system that continually spurred itself onward without pausing to deliberate about the consequences of the system's success), it is comparatively difficult to imagine what it would be like to recover the choices that they made. For seeing with the eyes of those who had the power of life and death here means getting to sit in the comfort of a movie theater and congratulate oneself on having chosen life for those in one's power, on rewarding oneself with the pleasure of being able to predict of oneself that one would do better. It is, in short, to trivialize moral action by acting as if we are doing heavy lifting when we reaffirm the choice that has been made by public morality for half a century.

Now I don't mean to suggest that popular morality is always at odds with individual choice, or that one's moral strength is always in inverse proportion to one's power to use it. Nor do I mean to suggest that there isn't any interest that attaches to the moral problems that fictions enact and exemplify. (Were we to leave aside Hegel and Nietzsche, the accounts that Bernard Williams and Martha Nussbaum give of the moral significance of Greek tragedy are more than merely persuasive on that score.)[17] But what strikes me as important is something that I take to be at the core of Hartman's remarks about the perspective of the audience, which is that the effectiveness with which the film enlists us into its moral judgments represents its success and its failure simultaneously. For the film's very effectiveness in working out Schindler's exemplification of his moral problem makes it all but unimaginable that one would, in the same circumstances with the same desire to think well of oneself, do anything but what he did. What we see, in other words, is the conflict between the well-made story and moral action. For the basic impulse that Hartman registers in seeking out the false moves in the film is the sense that the film's unerringness both perfects the exemplification of this particular moral case and withdraws it from the realm of moral action for its audience by allowing us to know its lesson all too well. The film becomes a version of Thetis's immersion of Achilles. In enabling us to imagine that we could do the right thing, it deprives us of the moral credit that would attach to doing it without benefit of so much certainty. Like Achilles in Rousseau's description, we are left comparatively invulnerable but, precisely on account of that comparative invulnerability, not courageous.

Now I have advanced this account of Hartman's discussion of *Schindler's List* to get at what I take to be an enormously interesting feature of his discussion of the Yale Videotestimony archives. For Hartman, in recording his struggle to explain why survivors of the Holocaust should want to renew their grief in the exercise of memory, continually describes the importance of allowing "survivors to speak for themselves." And in doing so he refers to the necessity of reticence — or what he has called "restraint" in a variety of different contexts throughout his career — on the part of interviewers.[18] It becomes clear, moreover, that he sees such reticence as striking an important contrast with Spielberg's eager formal helpfulness. For Spielberg's helpfulness now comes to seem like a way of extending the theatrical actor's moral problem to the theatrical audience in general, so that the ability to follow the description of Schindler's courageous action highlights the split that has developed between the understanding of that particular action and the weight of its value for future action. The interviewer for the Holocaust videotestimonies, by contrast, would never anticipate, never supply any of the work of the recollection; he or she would not diminish the value of the recognitions gained through that recollection by seeing its point too quickly and extending the conversation too eagerly.

Such eagerness would, in his view, prevent the videotestimonies from serving a beneficial function, the healing function of enabling the survivors to know their experience as their own, to separate it out from the experience of others. Thus, he writes, "as I have indicated, the more technically adept we are in communicating what we call our experience, the more forgettable the latter becomes: more interchangeable and easily simulated. Yet Holocaust testimony, in particular, uses video to counter a video-inspired amnesia. A homeopathic form of representation is being developed" ("Cinema Animal," 138). What Hartman is projecting here is a kind of videotestimony, one in which the "interchangeability and replication of experiences—a replication implicit in the technological means of their transmission" is redeemed (138). "The visual medium has its hypnotism," he writes, "but it becomes clear, when one views the testimonies, that its effect is, in this instance, more semiotic than hypnotic, that the medium both *identifies* and *differentiates* persons who have been through a wasting and disidentifying experience" (138).

The problem that Hartman has been interested in is the inaccuracy of memory, its susceptibility to "error and unconscious fabulation," its way of recruiting other people's lives or mistaken names (so that Hartman can remark that Mengele would have had to have worked forty-eight hours a day in order to have been directly and personally involved with the huge number of witnesses who take themselves to have seen him and been seen by him) ("Learning from Survivors," 141). And he has three distinct claims to make about the errors of memory that would distinguish the recorded testimony from historical evidence—first, that "there are moments that recur so frequently that they seem to be archetypal"; second, that some survivors come to appropriate "the stories of those who perished, as if they were one's own story"; and third, that the process of overidentification from viewers is itself a kind of memory lapse, a "defensively ennobling comment" that tries to avoid laying blame to such an extent that it involves "expressing an anxiety that the survivor may be tainted" (199–200). Now, what seems most interesting about this series of descriptions of the way in which memory may be improved by its fictionalization (which for Hartman is here its ability to move outside of the individual to the archetypal or the substitutive), is that it encounters an immediate impasse, in the form of "overidentification," the suggestion that someone else could know an individual's memory. "Let me," he writes,

> give an example of that temporal complexity, inseparable from the rhythm of memory when expressed in words. In one of the Yale videotestimonies a woman tries to describe her state of confusion during a Nazi "action." She wraps her baby in a coat, so that it appears to be a bundle, and tries to smuggle it by a German guard who is directing the Jews to left or right. She says she holds the bundle on her left side, thinking she will rescue it that way; but that memory is already a confusion, showing the strain she was under in making choices. As she passes the guard, the baby, who is choking, makes a sound; the guard summons her back, and asks for "the bundle."

> At that point in her story she utters a "Now," and creates a distinct pause. It is as if by that "Now" she were not only steeling herself to speak about what happened next, but seeking to recapture, within the narrative, the time for thought denied her in the rushed and crucial moments of what she had lived through. She goes on to describe her traumatic separation from the baby: she wasn't all there, she claims, or she was numb, or perhaps, she implies, she is imagining she had a baby—perhaps she has always been alone. Even Jack, her husband, she says later on—slipping to another now-time as the camera pans to him (and for a moment we think she is saying that even with Jack she has remained alone)—even Jack didn't know her story, which she revealed to him only recently, though he too is a survivor. When, just before this moment, she admits she gave the officer the baby, she does not say "the baby" but "the bundle" (a natural metaphor, sad and distancing, yet still affectionate, perhaps a Yiddicism, the "Paeckel"): "He stretched out his arms I should hand him over the bundle and this was the last time I had the bundle." ("Cinema Animal," 139–40)

Hartman ends one section of his essay with the bare description of the woman's story: and begins a new one, in which he talks about how the "ability to reproduce simulacra, or to think that we *see* memories" has become "a need of the soul" in the modern era (141). Better, he suggests, to have other people's memories than to have no memories at all. Yet there is something that we might characterize as "non-responsive" about Hartman's frame narrative if we were using the terms that a lawyer might use. For the problem that emerges in the particular anecdote is not that the woman finds herself uncertain about the accuracy of her memories and about the question of whether these memories are really hers. It is, rather that her memory preserves a connection between "baby" and "bundle" that constitutes a rebus peculiarly available to one who was there to experience the conjunction and that this connection enables her to single herself out in her own mind as someone forced into an act that she cannot accept as one she would willingly remember herself committing.[19]

Hartman is well aware of the difficulties facing interviewers who solicit such stories, and he speaks eloquently in "Learning from Survivors" of the danger that interviewers may be "too protective," may not "allow the survivors their voice" (200). Yet, as becomes clear when Hartman continually returns to the image of children, the protectiveness that the interviewers must guard themselves against is virtually inevitable. For the issue that prompts Hartman to focus on Spielberg's preoccupation with children in his films and to describe Nazism's distinctive horror in terms of its willingness to murder children on the mere basis of their being classifiable as Jews, is the fact that at least western and modern societies accord children a special relationship to their own actions ("Cinema Animal," 141–42). Children cannot, in the full sense of the word, act; by the legal stipulations that establish ages of majority and ages of consent, children are thus said not to be able to do the things that they often in fact do. The significance of stipulations of legal infancy, in other words, is that they demonstrate how society suspends its judgments even of the authors of negative actions when it regards them as incapable of being conscious of the consequences of those actions.

Now the similarity between the woman in the story that Hartman recounts and a child is obvious in one respect. The protectiveness that an interviewer might want to accord her is the protectiveness that involves telling her that she was not really responsible for the death of the baby or the bundle—that she was constrained by violence to act as she never would have had she had any degree of choice in the matter. It is merely an interpersonal version of the legal standard by which any jury would acquit her of having acted wrongly. It registers the fact that no one could reasonably blame her or suggest that she had any preferable course of action open to her. And if Matthew Arnold recounts Wragg's story to suggest the horror of seeing the circumstances of deprivation finally coming to seem like the only real motive for action, the woman's videotestimony documents a different kind of moral incapacity—the woman's inability to act as she chose—for herself and for the baby-bundle.[20]

This is to say that, whether or not the videotestimony represents a new genre, it represents a peculiarly modern moral problem. Newspapers revealed themselves to Matthew Arnold to be, among other things, the literature of the awfulness of moral choice when they could describe the case of a woman who had murdered her children under the pressure of hunger and need and when they could conclude the description by saying, "Wragg is in custody." The newspaper story in that case depicted circumstances described in such a way as to make it seem plausible to the point of inevitability that the mother would be forced into an action that would put her at odds with her society and call down its negative judgment. Yet the videotestimony provides a different dilemma, one in which no amount of blame or forgiveness from others can suffice to overcome what Hartman characterizes as the woman's aloneness—her memory that it was she and no one else who was singled out by the organized fate that Nazism administered to participate in the death of her child ("Learning from Survivors," 200).

The aspect of the woman's videotestimony that is particularly remarkable here is the maximal stress it places on the tension between an individual and what seems like pure and almost random circumstance. Anyone could have been in the grip of those circumstances; anyone could have done what the woman was forced to do; but only she, by contrast, could remember that it was she who did. Bernard Williams characterizes Oedipus's situation in terms that could easily be applied here: "This is not just a regret about what happened, such as a spectator might have. It is an agent's regret, and it is in the nature of action that such regrets cannot be eliminated, that one's life could not be partitioned into some things that one does intentionally and other things that merely happen to one" (*Shame and Necessity*, 70). In considering the tragedy of Oedipus, Williams is concerned with the way in which Oedipus's situation does not revolve around the devastation of his life but with his having caused it: "*What has happened to him, in fact, is that he has brought it about.* That is the point of Oedipus's words at Colonus. The terrible thing that happened to him, through no fault of his own, was that he did those things" (70).

Oedipus is, of course, a figure for a certain problem about consciousness. For his tragedy does not simply revolve around his having unintentionally brought about the ruin of his life but also his ability to know that he has. His abilities as a riddler constitute his abilities as a moralist: being able to see an identity for "man" in the different descriptions of mobility that he hears from the Sphinx is an ability closely related to his seeing that the man he would describe himself as having slain is also the man he must describe as having given him life, that the woman he would describe himself as having slept with is also the woman he must describe as having given him life. And it is in this regard that Oedipus has become such a haunting figure for the modern conception of morality, because Oedipus emblematizes the ongoing pressure for interpretative ingenuity that the modern structures of public morals encourage but cannot enforce. For legal forms like the law of torts, with its injunction that we identify ourselves as responsible for an act that is different from any action we intended to initiate, call for something more than simple memory. They require that we see our own actions as memorable less because we remember having performed just those actions than because we are able to establish connections between our conscious actions and their effects that make them memorable under redescription.

Were we to imagine ourselves responsible for all the possible negative consequences of all our actions, memory would seem a particularly troublesome capacity, one that the Greeks mercifully bestowed only on heroes and kings, as if the mere possession of memory with its adaptive commitments would seem to call for heroic courage at the least. What is at issue, then, is not the possibility that other people will judge one differently from the way in which one judges oneself. It is, rather, that the impact of one's actions on other people come to cause one to reevaluate what one's actions were—and that the extension of the time of such remembrance increases the liability that one incurs in the process.

It is at this point that we are in a position to return to the notion of pure history and to comment on its recurrent attractions. For pure history is nothing other than the sense that an event has been established so definitively that one is unlikely to alter its basic shape. The testimony of various witnesses and the circumstantial record in these cases resolve themselves into comparatively uniform definitions of acts and events. (Whatever work historical fiction may do to alter such agreements, it is unlikely to alter the agent's sense of the value of his or her actions.)

Yet there are a host of ways in which external circumstances operate to cause one to change one's sense of the value of an act that one has already committed. The most familiar occurs in what Benjamin describes as the victor's history; history as written from the perspective of whatever position, in having triumphed, seeks to establish its own genealogy.[21] Or, the simple movement from one place to another can drastically alter the value of one's actions. Thus, Burke (in *An Enquiry into the Origin of Our Ideas of the Sublime and Beautiful*) singles out the Homeric description of a fugitive who, though conscious of his crime, crosses a territorial boundary and thus escapes all the external sanctions that would before have punished it.[22] The sense that history might have been written differently if a war had turned out differently, like the sense that a crime would be punishable in one place and go unrecognized in another, may seem to make action look like an especially fragile notion. For if a moral action comes to look like an action at all from having had an impact on another person, the circumstances that permit such an action to occur are themselves continually being acted upon in the process of being formalized and enforced, ignored and allowed to lapse.

This is as much as to say that insofar as external structures like laws and histories make actions perceptible, they contribute to the process of making actors of us all. Laws can teach us to extend the range of consequences that we see as capable of contributing to an action, can teach us to understand omissions as possibly forms of action and not merely insignificant gestures. Histories can at least encourage us to recognize the present in the mold of actions that have already been recognized as such. In providing formal or actual ways of imagining what an action would be or has been, they do not so much ask for exact duplication as provide a standpoint for comparison.

Yet it is clear that this way of talking about action constitutes a departure from both pure history and from the model of individual memory. Inasmuch as it does not restrict the notion of action to a time period confined enough to simulate the unity of time that the drama lends to action, it is not always susceptible of the kind of instantaneous multiple confirmation that pure history might seek. Inasmuch as it does not restrict action to an individual's private assessment of whether or not he has acted, it does not claim that individual intention must remain forever unrevised by outcomes or that one would never feel retrospective grief over an action that one had entered into under the happy conviction that it was a quite different action from what one later had occasion to discover it to be.

The kind of problem about action — the blending of the notion of action with description — that I am interested in here is one that finds some of its starkest and most exact illustrations in romantic writing in general and in Wordsworth's poetry in particular. Think, for instance, about Wordsworth's statement, when he is looking at Tintern Abbey again for a second time, that "the picture of the mind revives again." He is describing an immediate experience almost as if might it be a memory, as if the process of seeing were indistinguishable from the memory of having seen. And in saying of the landscape, "I remember this," rather than providing a description of a previously unobserved scene, Wordsworth is suggesting the ways in which memory is not simply a preservation of past experience but also a contribution to it. For in the poem's careful calibrations of how this viewing of Tintern Abbey is better than the earlier one in some respects, worse than the earlier one in others, the efforts to sharpen memory are not so much about creating the sense of having a history as about using memory to install comparative experience within individual consciousness.

In other words, the Wordsworth of "Tintern Abbey" is attempting to treat memory as a process that involves, simultaneously, both continuity — the connection between one experience of the same place and another — and differentiation — the bench-marking that keeps holding the two experiences up for comparison. The almost completely retrospective movement of that poem may make it seem easy to assimilate Wordsworth's depiction of memory to the pattern of simple recollection of the past, but the anticipation of how "in this moment there is life and food / For future years" (64–65) continually projects memory forward. It repeatedly describes memory in the future perfect tense.

The conundrum of memory in "Tintern Abbey" has prompted some of the most interesting critical speculations we have on Wordsworth's attitude towards memory — on his confidence or uncertainty about its efficacy. For our purposes it may be sufficient merely to note the starkness with which the problem of memory is presented. On the one hand, memory is able to establish continuity in the face of—and through the means of—an ongoing process of alteration in both the speaker (as he is aware) and the landscape (as he can infer). On the other, memory is treated as if it could be converted into static images, squirreled away for future use and occasionally deployed to patch up what come to look like gaps in an individual's experience. Yet its interest for us is in establishing a point of contrast against which we can measure accounts of memory like those that Hartman takes up in his essay "The Poetics of Prophecy."[23]

There Hartman is commenting on an attitude that he sees as linking Wordsworth with figures like the Old Testament prophets: "The ambivalent sympathy shown by the prophet for the powerful and terrible thing he envisions" (165). And he specifically ties that sympathy with the "seduction that power exerts, when seen as an act of God or Nature" (166). The major point of this portion of Hartman's discussion will be that the very ability to see—or foresee—events, even events that one dreads, involves something approaching an acceptance of—indeed, an endorsement of—those events. And he will go on to mention in particular one of the famous "spots of time" episodes in *The Prelude* (1850, 12.292–333) as an instance of this pattern. In that passage, Wordsworth describes how he had strained with expectation as he waited to be transported from school at the Christmas holidays, and how he had climbed a "crag overlooking two highways to see whether he [could] spot the horses that should be coming" (168). As he recalls the particular episode, which is in itself no more notable than what someone waiting for a bus might produce, he extends its range. Without introducing a single hostile thought or murderous intention, Wordsworth recounts that his father died within ten days of his return home, concluding (in part) that "the event / With all the sorrow that it brought, appeared / A chastisement," a divine correction of his desires (1850, 12.309–11; 314–16).

In Hartman's reading, the passage raises the question of temporality, and enables him to note the powerful lack of apparent connection between one term and another: "There is no hint of anything that would compel the mind to link the two terms, hope against time and its peculiar fulfillment" (170). Yet if it describes what Hartman calls "a sin against time," in its anticipation of futurity, the passage also prompts him to distinguish between two different stances toward time: one, the apocalyptic, which involves "an anticipatory, proleptic relation to time, intensified to the point where there is at once desire for and dread of the end being hastened," and in which "there is a potential inner turning against time, and against nature insofar as it participates in the temporal order" (167); the other, the prophetic, which represents "a perfectly ordinary mood [that] is seen to involve a sin against time" (170). As Hartman puts it, "the aftermath points to something unconscious in the first instance but manifest and punishing now" (170).

Since Hartman's concern with the passage is its usefulness in getting at the relationship between religious and secular (literary) language, I am necessarily departing from the terms of his discussion at this point. For the question that I want to address in this discussion of memory is the relationship between what Hartman has called "the seduction of power" and the kind of retrospective action that conscious memory is capable of constructing. For the passage is one in which Wordsworth links two memories that have nothing in common except that he experienced the awareness of them at roughly the same time in his life, and in both the distinct, if subdued, sense of guilt appears to emerge from nothing more than a kind of *post hoc ergo propter hoc* logic. That logic suggests that, because Wordsworth's father's death occurred later in time than Wordsworth's boyhood experience of expectant waiting, it has been brought on by it. Moreover, because that logic makes the process of perceiving objects or events look as though it were an endorsement of those objects or events, a participation in the objects of experience that amounted to some kind of implicit ratification of them, it makes the experience of living in a world in which undesirable things happen look like its own variant on the notion of original sin. Neither the purest of motives nor the greatest attention to things apparently indifferent would protect one from the experience of illimitable guilt in the face of any negative outcome or undesirable event.

I produce this gloss to suggest that romantic memory, particularly in Wordsworth's handling of it, is more than just a capacity for recording events, and that the special pressure that romanticism brings to bear on memory is the pressure of an expanded moral obligation, an obligation to reexamine one's own past actions to see if their value has been altered by subsequent events. In this, romantic memory is allied with the kind of mental techniques that Weber described so vividly in *The Protestant Ethic and the Spirit of Capitalism*.[24] Like such techniques of spiritual and material development, it involves subjecting one's own experience to a standard more demanding than that of truthfulness or even accuracy, because it makes every individual's memory stand in the same relation to experience as Rousseau's general will does to the individual. It requires a continual review of actions through the lenses of a variety of different sets of consequences.

From this vantage, it begins to appear that romanticism, in the process of charging consciousness with the revaluation of actions that can be recalled only in the sense of being remembered and not at all in the sense of being revoked or undone, creates a mental apparatus for manufacturing guilt much more rapidly than it can forgive it. From this perspective romantic memory might seem to be completely identical with liberal guilt, with its sense of regret at the possibility that one's very identity might involve the appropriation of some resources that would have been more useful to another existence. Yet if the possibility of being a conscious subject capable of identifying events and actions would seem from this perspective to be an entirely undesirable state, it becomes especially difficult to reconcile that account with Wordsworth's gloss on his memory of the expectation now tinged with a lurking sense of guilt:

> And, afterwards, the wind and sleety rain,
> And all the business of the elements,
> The single sheep, and the one blasted tree,
> And the bleak music of that old stone wall,
> The noise of wood and water, and the mist
> That on the line of each of those two roads
> Advanced in such indisputable shapes;
> All these were kindred spectacles and sounds
> To which I oft repaired, and thence would drink,
> As at a fountain. . . .
>
> (1850, 12.317–26)

That combination of anxiety and pleasure is particularly difficult to sort out. If, as Hartman's reading powerfully argues, Wordsworth's description of his experience is "prophetic" because it recruits his earlier experience as a kind of participation in the later event of his father's death, why should Wordsworth "repair" to this memory cluster as if it were a pleasurable one? Memory, in this case, provides sustenance by presenting a set of kindred elements, "spectacles and sounds" that don't cohere to produce an accusation of guilt: Wordsworth tells over the beads of memory to see that they never sort themselves into a causal chain, so that the work of memory comes to involve the sense of *still* not yet having the evidence to accuse himself of having brought about his father's death. What Wordsworth's "spot of time" enables us to track is not just romanticism's stress on memory as memory solicits a consciousness of what one has done—insofar as one judges oneself by the actions that one has performed. It also registers the increasing pressure that romanticism will come to put on the memory that can provide convincing evidence *that one hasn't acted*, that one hasn't yet seen things that would make one regret one's past for the consequences that have attended it.

The phenomenon I am describing here is what we might think of as circumstantial memory. And what I am arguing is that circumstantial memory entails something more than the cultivation of the capacity to have and harvest exceptionally vivid memories that numerous studies of memory from Wordsworth to Proust have focused on in talking about the combination of extraordinary detail and apparent randomness that attach to them. For circumstantial memory provides a kind of balm to the potentially corrosive memory that might seem to make an individual responsible for all the events that he was capable of knowing about from experience or report; it sets a limit to the extent to which the theater of memory can recruit any of us to a particular action and provides its own alternative history, which relies on the exceptional vividness of its various images precisely to the extent to which it resists assimilation to narrative's tendency to produce events. The good news of the memory of these clustered elements is that *there is no news*, that nothing has happened.

Thus, if Wordsworth's account of circumstantial memory enables him to accuse himself of having, perhaps, been at fault in the occurrence of events that he never meant to originate, it also seeks to cure such potentially illimitable self-accusation by producing a transcript of images that never cohere into a causal pattern. *The Prelude* seeks to address this question of expansive moral consciousness in almost exclusively autobiographical terms—only occasionally adverting to Coleridge or Dorothy Wordsworth or Mary Hutchinson Wordsworth to thank them for their confirmation. Yet even in those rudimentary gestures, gestures that in no way overstep the bounds of the autobiographical account of Wordsworth's attempt to cultivate and manage his own memory, we can discern the outlines of an important charge that the nineteenth century directs to the publicness of circumstance.

What we have been tracing *in nuce* is a rise in the importance of circumstantial evidence in an analysis that infers actions from circumstances as they might be observed by anyone at all, not simply by their initators.[25] Moreover, insofar as one's sense of having acted involves an expansive time frame, the consciousness of oneself as a moral agent—as a better or worse moral agent than one meant to be—continually charges the memory with the task of observing and retaining the materials that may come to be actions. Were this expansive memory to expand forever, it would produce a kind of anticipatory guilt of massive—indeed, paralyzing—proportions (so that it would fund the infinite anxiety about our relationship to the unborn that is a ready resource for social conservatism from Burke to Buchanan or, conversely, the cultivation of simple unconsciousness—the drunkenness, for instance, that George Eliot describes in *Adam Bede*). Were the individual to become responsible not only for what she was conscious of at the time she initiated each of her actions but also for all their unsuspected consequences, then the kind of memory I have been describing as romantic memory would come to include both the actual memory of immediate experience and the memory of all that one had come to know—the circumstantial record interpreted by consciousness.

Various commentators have pointed to the disadvantages that memory seems to present for the individual in the romantic account. Indeed, Foucault's critique of the political morality of nineteenth-century liberalism has revolved around just this issue—that the existence of other people continually enables one to assume a constantly escalating set of moral liabilities that constitutes an oppressive burden on the individual, so that the apparent permissiveness that enables romanticism to replace an older regime that combined physical with political force with a newer appeal to individual psychological self-government actually yields few advantages for that individual.[26] Law, in this view, provides a public record that increases the demands on individual action, in a fashion that can seem to destroy all the positive incentives for action, because it destroys one's security in one's capacity to endorse one's own actions.

The question that thus becomes particularly urgent for romantic accounts of the relationship between memory and moral evaluation is whether memory that is public and circumstantial is of any use in forwarding an individual's aims, whether it might assist individuals to see themselves as having succeeded greatly in a way that counterpoises its role in assisting them to see themselves as having erred greatly. And one fictitious account, James Hogg's *The Private Memoirs and Confessions of a Justified Sinner*,[27] is particularly useful to us in tracing romanticism's commitment to public memory as it is represented by circumstance.

The novel identifies itself immediately as the story of one Robert Wringham, a zealous Calvinist who identifies himself as "consecrated," or "elect," under the Calvinist doctrine of predestination, which contends that God, and God alone, makes the decision about one's moral worth and that it is not within the power of the individual to choose to be as he or she is. On the one hand, Robert recognizes himself as a sinner, as someone who has committed acts that have had disastrous consequences for others. Yet this consciousness never strikes him as personal, because it seems like an inevitable application of the doctrine of original sin, the view that "in Adam's fall, we sinned all." On the other hand, he seems to see himself—or at least to represent himself—as incapable of being guilty for his actions under the doctrine of religious justification, which is here taken to involve the extreme statement that one's religious standing—one's having been chosen by God to be a personal representative of his intention—might completely alter the value of his actions, might convert even crimes like murder into entirely innocent actions because they were part of the divine plan. On this account, once again, Robert's actions never strike him as personal, because they are continually referred to an intention that overrides his. Agency always looks as though it couldn't be entirely resolved into an actual person.

Indeed, though the novel is a twice-told tale, with one version of the story appearing as if it had been compiled from local reports and another as if it were related in Robert's first-person account, the most interesting aspect of the novel is its difficulty in locating individualizd agents. From the very moment that Rabina (the bride of the Royalist George Colwin and future mother to George Colwin and to Robert Wringham) returns to her father to complain of her new husband, George Colwin, characters in the novel have a way of losing their distinctness as individual actors. Rabina's father can, thus, hear her complain and proceed, improbably enough in her view, to punish *her*, taking her as a surrogate of her husband and thus as someone who stands to be punished for her husband's impertinence to his daughter. In this circuit of accusation and punishment, the plaintiff and the defendant can be the same person. In what will come to be a standard move in the detective story, with its recurrent discovery that one was someone quite different from the person one had taken oneself to be, people regularly come to be the people they complain of.[28]

Yet if the novel echoes this pattern of consolidating accusation and punishment in the same person when it depicts young Cavaliers and Roundheads fighting, only to recognize that they have been attacking their own supporters, the question of the relationship between individual and collective agency becomes even more pressing for the novel's account of Robert Wringham. For the novel's brilliant turn on the question of religious fanaticism—or, seen from the other perspective, the question of religious toleration—is that it puts Robert Wringham out of the reach of all human evaluative structures in a way that foregrounds the importance of personal memory. Wringham's apparent invulnerability to correction—his ability to escape punishment for his half-brother's murder in the Scottish courts, his ability to forgive himself for not having broken "above four out of the ten commandments" (123)—turns out to be only a temporary version of getting off Scot-free. His collusion with his mysterious friend, a creature who is capable of entering into his own thoughts and thinking what he thinks almost before he himself has done so, may mean that it no longer makes sense to accuse Robert Wringham himself of the various crimes that he—or someone very like him—commits. In the novel's perfect inversion of hard-line Calvinism, what Robert does always looks as easily ascribable to Satan—or to Adam—as to Robert.

It would be easy enough to assimilate the picture that the novel provides to some account of Calvinism as religious fatalism, a strong historicist view that would emphasize the inseparability of individuals' actions and the circumstances in which they perform them. Yet what is perhaps most interesting about Hogg's novel is that its plot turns on its protagonist's memory. In what first appears as a mild limitation of memory, Robert has found himself having a hard time with Latin, which is represented as a dead language precisely because schoolboys never learn it from experience but only by rote. His sense of the deficiency of his memory has led him to commit his first real act of perfidy, which is to frame the best Latin student as the author of his own caricatures of the Latin teacher, out of nothing other than envy at the superiority of the other student's memory. And his final punishment lies not in the judgments of others but in his despair at being unable to remember what he has done. (Accused of seducing a young peasant woman and murdering her and the child she conceived with him, for instance, he denies ever having known her.) The important point is that in a world in which everyone else comes to take him for an egregiously bad and brazen liar, Robert is merely stupid—with that stupidity involving the simple incapacity to know what he has done—indeed, to know that he has done anything at all. He dies (in one of the novel's chilling details) a suicide, having hanged himself on a straw rope that ought, under normal conditions, to be too flimsy to bear "the weight of a colleydog," as if his inability to sense and remember a world he has shared with other people has led him, finally, to be preternaturally susceptible to the sensible world he can identify (232).

Yet perhaps the most striking feature of Hogg's novel is that it makes the loss of memory serve simultaneously as the occasion of wrongful actions and the punishment for them. Robert Wringham is never punished by any civil authority acting at the behest of a court of law, and the novel ends without any smell of sulphur or any ominous obtrusion of an afterlife of torment. Yet his self-murder makes it clear what a price he has paid for exemption from the consequences of his actions; in not ever being able to recognize what he has done, he has, Hogg suggests, lost an ability that has come to amount to a very complicated right under the Enlightenment insistence upon the expansion of the person to produce rights in the past and the future—to things like life, liberty, and the pursuit of happiness, which no one actually has in their gift. When Wringham loses his memory, that is, he also loses his future, because memory comes not to record the past but to represent the power of seeing a past that one didn't experience at the time of its occurrence. To lose romantic memory is to lose the ability to act by losing the ability to see oneself in one's own past actions, to be able to recognize one's action most vividly in a redescription.

Part II / Boundaries and the Problem of Knowledge

FOUR

Green to the Very Door?

The Natural Wordsworth

Paul H. Fry

There is dazzling and varied revisionism in the Wordsworth criticism of the last thirty years, yet all the most influential rereadings have but one refrain: Wordsworth was not a nature poet. The seventies' commentaries stressing visionary apocalypse took their point of departure from the dialectic between the tyranny of the senses and the dark, unpleasant moments of "blank misgiving" in "the abyss of idealism," moments when as a child Wordsworth had to grasp a wall or a tree to be sure that such things existed.[1] The rhetorical analyses suspending anthropomorphic language rather than imagination over this abyss argue that Wordsworth is one of "the first modern writers to have put into question, in the language of poetry, the ontological priority of the sensory object."[2] And in the eighties' return to the issue of social determinants theorized in its most sweeping form by Alan Liu, history manifested as ideology takes over the role hitherto played by language or imagination and reveals, through commentary, a parallel truth: "There is no nature except as it is constituted by acts of political definition made possible by particular forms of government."[3]

Infighting aside, all the criticism identifiable with these positions — together with the feminist criticism that reflects either the psychoanalytic leaning of the first position or the social historiography of the third—has continued to envision itself in collective reaction against a grand metanarrative about Wordsworth which is purportedly so durable, so indifferent to changing reception horizons, that only Paul de Man's knowingly period-blind expression, "Wordsworth and the Victorians," has a sufficiently focused energy of condescension to wrestle it into submission. In this view, there is enough of the old Leslie Stephen remaining in every successive Wordsworth scholar and critic to warrant the repetition, ever and anon, of the Matthew Arnold mantra, "poetry is the reality, philosophy the illusion"—but always with the proviso that Arnold was, as he finally admitted, no better than "a Wordsworthian" himself. According to this whole tradition—or stubborn prejudice—nature not only exists but it responds to human desire by communicating, among other things, ethical lessons ("philosophy"), and Wordsworth is the supreme poet of this communion.

Within the last thirty years, a good many critics have continued to uphold this latter view in one form or another but in most cases have not attracted much attention because the determined simplicity of their argument and procedure, sometimes calculated, sometimes apparently innocent, has left little for more intricate thinking to attach itself to (better to dismiss "the Victorians" once more with a wave). And the more formidable critics who have come forward to champion the "humanist" nature poet, preeminently M. H. Abrams and Jonathan Wordsworth, have seemed compromised, ironically enough, by signs of complicity with the positions they attack. Revisionary critics have always been too generously aware that they stand on Abrams's shoulders, many having drawn their apocalyptic bent from his teachings, to want to quarrel with him as vigorously as he might have wished. And Jonathan Wordsworth, despite his affiliation with the Cornell–Dove Cottage network of textual scholars who consider interpretive dispute an idle exercise best left to amateurs lacking the ability to date holographs, nevertheless betrays too many symptoms: his deep engagement with the spots of time, his preference for the earliest possible *Prelude* manuscripts, and his intense dislike of the later Wordsworth make him an antinaturalist *malgré lui.*

In response to these tendencies, one point to be made in passing is that both sides of the "nature" controversy exchange positions more readily than they realize. It is worth at least sketching in the view, as I shall below, that within the traditional mainstream there have been plenty of blank misgivings about nature, while for the newer mainstreams the abyssal elements in Wordsworth are themselves, in their most uncompromising forms, the very prior sensory objects that were supposed to have been put into question. But these imputations are not meant to seem surprising or controversial; far from appearing as the glamorous result of antithetical critique, they arise merely from the almost inevitable confusion anyone is likely to feel when trying to say what nature *is.* (It is not surprising that so many distinguished minds have taken refuge in saying, in a certain sense correctly, that it is nothing.) A glance or two therefore at the historians of ideas who took an interest in Wordsworth's "nature" will resolve very little, undoubtedly, such is the hermeneutic circularity that undoes all such projects, but at least it will provide a kind of multiple definition to appeal to as need arises.

And need will indeed arise, if anything comes of the prognostication by Jonathan Bate, in *Romantic Ecology: Wordsworth and the Environmental Tradition,* that a "green" criticism of the nineties—supplanting the "red" criticism of the eighties—will make Wordsworth a nature poet once again.[4] I too think that Wordsworth is a nature poet, and realize now that I thought so even when I was most deeply influenced in manner, tone, and selectivity of perception by the visionary wing of the "Yale School."[5] But I still prefer to emphasize the *via naturaliter negativa* that I learned to recognize from that school (differing from Hartman—and from Hegel—only in doubting that this road points, or is meant to point, beyond itself), and I am inclined to criticize the notion of nature as "environment," as organic-systemic totality rather than ontological unity, which governs the polemic of Jonathan Bate. It is by way of engagement with Bate's interesting book in particular, then, that I shall try to bring some measure of discrimination to bear on the difficult plight of not being very green yet still wanting to claim that Wordsworth is a nature poet.

In the sections that follow, I attempt first to reconsider and relocate the nature topos in the diverse traditions of Wordsworth commentary; to participate in the return to nature heralded by Bate as much as possible on my own terms (with remarks in passing on *Home at Grasmere*); and to show how and where nature remains even and especially in Wordsworth texts privileged by the commentaries of the last thirty years—and in the commentaries themselves.

By Wordsworth's time, "nature" was a "technical" term (the expression is C. B. Tinker's), rather like our "physics," referring to the laws and operations of the physical world. Being "closely connected to the brutal and anti-Christian views of nature in the minds of Helvétius and Holbach," this sense of the term, which can be traced back through Locke, tended to be used by those who were hostile or condescending toward poetry.[6] Part of Wordsworth's novelty consisted then simply in reinvesting the scientificity of the term with poetic aura—"the breath and finer spirit of all knowledge," as he called such mediations of science in the 1800 Preface. He owned the 1781 edition of Holbach's *Système de la Nature* and criticized it sharply in 1809, but not without having absorbed its physics.[7] All he needed was a metaphysics, and that, we generally assume, was the "*active* universe" of the "Blessed the Infant Babe" passage (1805 *Prelude*, 2.266). As Basil Willey summarizes: "His 'creative sensibility' had taught him that he was not alone with an 'inanimate cold world,' but with an 'active universe.'"[8] H. W. Piper, the historian of ideas who has done most with this concept, perhaps overextends its pantheistic implications and its influence on the Unitarian thinking to which Coleridge especially was exposed in the 1790s, but he is able to argue authoritatively, citing Priestley, Erasmus Darwin, Hutton, and Cabanis, that "the belief that inanimate objects were in a literal sense alive came nearest to establishing itself as a scientific orthodoxy during the years of Wordsworth's most active poetic life."[9] It is to such an "external World," Wordsworth writes in 1800 (the same year as the Preface and "Blessed the Infant Babe"), that the "individual Mind" is "fitted," and vice versa, authenticating the imagination's "spousal verse" with nature.[10]

This is the basic information that has stood behind the debate about nature in Wordsworth—and did so implicitly even before it was set down in order by the historians of ideas. It would be obstinate to deny that there are many passages in Wordsworth, passages indeed reflecting something like an overall conscious design, which conform to this general outline, leaving traditional critics to disagree about questions of metaphysics: more or less pantheism, more or less mechanism (active or reactive), more or less of the insistent transcendence one finds in the Pisgah view from Snowdon or in the assertion that the spots of time make us feel that "the mind / Is lord and master." For all such critics, no matter how much they stress transcendence, Wordsworth is a nature poet.

But scientific and metaphysical ideas about nature do not exhaust the subject. There is also the ontology of nature: its mode of being, its status as beings or as a being, its relation to human being, and the being of its being. These are the issues, both in Wordsworth himself and in the history of his reception, that begin to confuse the way he has been and can be read. The results of this confusion can seem unproductive (it is in its ontological register that nature in the critic's hands gets lost in a chaos of referents); but for all who feel that the most characteristically brilliant verse of Wordsworth is always in some way an evocation of being as such, the subversion of meaning itself becomes a technique for making nature appear. It is with respect to the ontology of nature that I wish now to reconsider certain strains that can be heard, albeit faintly, in the criticism preceding that of the last thirty years.

De Man calls it a "temptation" to condescend to Victorian Wordsworth criticism but himself perpetuates the notion that the nineteenth-century reading of Wordsworth was "moral and religious" (*Rhetoric of Romanticism*, 85). Yet Pater, for example, stresses "the quiet, habitual observation of inanimate, or imperfectly animate, existence." He speaks, to be sure, of the "sense of a life in natural objects," but he notes the "sensuousness" with which this sense is perceived (playing, in anticipation of Empson, on the senses of "sense" in Wordsworth); and he places the "active universe" theme in the service of an onto-phenomenological project which I am inclined to call *a leveling of being:* "By raising nature to the level of human thought [Wordsworth] gives it power and expression: he subdues man to the level of nature, and gives him thereby a certain breadth and coolness and solemnity."[11] Wordsworth's observation is trained, in other words, on the point of intersection between human and nonhuman being in order to reveal something about the "widest commonality" of being. Hazlitt had written repeatedly (in *Lectures on the English Poets* and again in *The Spirit of the Age*) of this "leveling" in socio-political terms, and from this standpoint he noticed how many of Wordsworth's characters ("female vagrants . . . idiot boys and mad mothers"—joined, he might have added, by the very young and the very old)[12] are only marginally possessed of normative human consciousness. The ontic common denominator sought by Wordsworth is what makes his "philosophy" seem illusory to Matthew Arnold, in his turn, precisely because it is undifferentiated, a universal diffusion, in widest commonality *spread*, of "joy." To say, then, with Arnold, that Wordsworth "has no style" is also to say that, having successfully resisted the "false secondary power, by which, / In weakness, we create distinctions" (1805 *Prelude*, 2.221–22), Wordsworth also has no meaning—or, more precisely, that he underdetermines the signifier.[13] According to the lines from Arnold's 1850 "Memorial Verses" that seem most to have influenced the language and purport of Pater's assessment, Wordsworth "laid us as we lay at birth / On the cool flowery lap of earth."

This way of looking at Wordsworth did not disappear in the first half of the twentieth century. Agreeing that philosophy in Wordsworth is the illusion, F. R. Leavis remarks that the poetry of *The Prelude* looks like a "paraphrasable" argument but in fact is not.[14] Here again is the "muddle" ascribed to "Tintern Abbey" in William Empson's *Seven Types of Ambiguity*, pointing toward Empson's analysis of *The Prelude*'s "unintelligible" confusion of sensation and imagination in

The Structure of Complex Words—readings which de Man considered to be the sole flickerings of truth in antediluvian Wordsworth criticism.[15] Leavis too finds no coherent argument and imputes the "wisdom" of Wordsworth's very incoherence to "his sense of communion with the non-human universe" ("Revaluations" 250). By the time Basil Willey wrote his "Background" books, what he called the "mergence with the inanimate" in Wordsworth was commonplace.[16] It had already inspired the clear-sighted invective of Irving Babbitt against Wordsworth's "primitivism." Quoting Emile Legouis at length on the prevalence of children, crazed and idiotic persons, animals, and plants in Wordsworth (Legouis, as we have seen, was following Hazlitt), all of them beings "whose senses, not yet distorted by analysis, yield them immediate perception of the world," and citing with approval Byron's joke in *English Bards* ("the Bard himself" is the hero of *The Idiot Boy*), Babbitt expresses the fervent wish that Wordsworth had rehabilitated his "secondary power," misguidedly called "false."[17]

"It is no longer necessary to protect the Romantic poets from the charge of neoprimitivism," wrote Geoffrey Hartman in 1968.[18] Hartman aligns Wordsworth's "nature in its childhood or sensuous radiance" with Blake's Beulah, arguing that "from Francis Jeffrey to Irving Babbitt," Wordsworth's "*labor of the negative* (Hegel) was mistaken for . . . a crude nature worship" (*Beyond Formalism*, 307; *UnRW* 147). In emphasizing dark transcendence in Wordsworth, Hartman, Harold Bloom, and their disciples have always scrupulously acknowledged an antecedent tradition: Pater on "the abstract expression of desolation in the long white road" ("Wordsworth" 129) inspiring A. C. Bradley's memorable pages in the *Oxford Lectures* on "the sublime" as "visionary power" in Wordsworth, followed by G. Wilson Knight on "the hidden eternity-music in the inanimate" (the stone carried by the Arab) and D. G. James (appropriating Bradley for Christian purposes) on "visionary dreariness."[19] But even in this tradition there are moments of naturalism, signaled by Knight's mystical disclosure of the eternal in the mineral. For James, the Beulah state revealed through Wordsworth's struggle for "unity of prehension" is the *only* state that can be known without the aid of Christian revelation, and he sees Wordsworth as the prophet of his own belief that the imagination's meretricious way of achieving unity is necessarily linked to skepticism (*Scepticism and Poetry*, 115). In this he resembles John Jones, another precursor acknowledged by Hartman, who attacks the notion that Wordsworth is a unitarian poet, yet speaks of "the relational and monistic coherence" of *The Prelude*.[20]

Just so, naturalism in the criticism of the past thirty years persists as a moment to be overcome dialectically. Hartman's dismissal of the primitivist view reflects his powerfully articulated belief that Wordsworth is an Enlightenment thinker—which is to say, a strong and knotty thinker.[21] And yet, Hartman would agree, Wordsworth's intellectualized version of anti-self-consciousness, his chief gesture as Schillerian Sentimental Poet, is precisely to think the primitive, to make the primitive an object of phenomenological reflection: "The desire of the Romantics is perhaps for what Blake calls 'organized innocence,' but never for a mere return to the state of nature" (*Beyond Formalism*, 300–301). Still more problematic for the sublation of nature is the monism Hartman concedes in Wordsworth, in common with James and Jones: "There are no sharp breaks or ritual passings between one state of mind and another: vision is always continuous with sensation. Even such licensed rapture as Keats's 'Already with thee!' is avoided" (*UnRW*, 11). For Hartman here, as for all commentators at such moments, questions pile up (showing, I have said, that the issue being skirted does not concern physics or metaphysics but touches, compulsively, on the being of being): "Vision" of what? "Sensation" of what?

Vision of nature, sensation of spirit: whatever it is, it is what remains when the owls fall silent, suspending the Boy of Winander's belief that there is a natural channel of communication ("responsive to his call"), a fit between human beliefs about nature and nature itself. As the pathetic fallacy hangs in the balance, a new vision of the "visible scene" possesses him, a vision not of life, as all modern critics who have been fascinated by this narrative agree, but of a silent being in nature which, somatically signaled, is also a being toward his own imminent death. As he once hung in life, so the site of his burial hangs now, suspended in permanent estrangement above that social scene of instruction ("the Village School") where nature continues to seem significant, as typically it does in those "Books" on which Book 5 remains an ambivalent critical meditation. If this account of the Boy of Winander, introduced as it is by Wordsworth's trademark reduction of the loco-descriptive to sheer ostension ("There was"), appears merely to be a paraphrase of de Man's account in "Wordsworth and Hölderlin," a comparison can prove useful. Here is de Man: "The sudden silence of nature was an anticipatory announcement of his death, a movement of his consciousness passing beyond the deceptive constancy of a world of correspondences into a world in which our mind knows itself to be in an endlessly precarious state of suspension: above an earth, the stability of which it cannot participate in, and beneath a heaven that has rejected it" (*Rhetoric of Romanticism*, 54). What I for my part am not saying, though, is that "the mediation of poetic language" (54) puts into question the priority of the sensory object. Poetic language is in "books" and makes the owls hoot like people. The absurdity of Coleridge's having reproved Milton for anthropocentrically calling nightingales melancholy and then having called them cheerful drunkards himself cannot have been lost on Wordsworth. This is what happens when you talk about the "jocund din" of birds; you are always "already with" them by unlicensed means.

But poetic language can think the primitive, again, without being primitive. Lionel Trilling relates the children sporting upon the shore in the "Intimations Ode" to the passage in *Civilization and Its Discontents* in which Freud describes the "primary ego-feeling" as "oceanic."[22] But it is the dark interpreters of Wordsworth themselves who have altered our taste in Freud—and Wordsworth—and refer us now to *Beyond the Pleasure Principle:* "The aim of all life is death." Where it was, there shall poetic language be. What the Boy of Winander realized is that "inanimate things came before animate ones," putting into question the priority of language to the being of death disclosed in the sensory object. In response to Alan Liu's recent version of the modern critics' revolt against nature—"nature is the name under which we use the nonhuman to validate the human" (*Sense of History*, 38)—the reader who still thinks Wordsworth is a nature poet might want to say that nature is our own nonhuman existence, forgotten once named.

Jonathan Bate rightly attributes Liu's insistence on the construction of nature by "particular forms of government" to the recent "interest in questions of landownership" among romanticists inspired by the work of John Barrell (*Romantic Ecology*, 15). In response to such questions, Bate wants to say that environmental peril transcends—and has outlived—political peril: it is as true now as it was before the fall of the Iron Curtain that for every Three Mile Island there is a Chernobyl.[23] Well, yes, the issue of ownership is long overdue for a rest; and Bate's repeated quotation of Edward Thomas's "lord of that he does not possess," together with his reminder that John Clare could write of dwelling itself as possession despite never having owned any property (see 100–101), make for a welcome change of tune. Not that these very citations could not easily be demystified as exceptions proving the hegemonic rule of proprietary figurations of home: the point is, despite this available rejoinder, that feelings which are unquestionably in some sense proprietary (and not just the communist nationalism of "This land is my land" but the transitory sojourner's "This is my kind of place" are involved here) run deepest at the very moments when one is most conscious of exemptions from the burdens of ownership. That is why people feel proprietary about public parks, "historic districts," and the like. When "man" (the word is Hölderlin's) dwells poetically, he is on someone else's property, even and most especially in those poems on country seats written by guests and beneficiaries of patronage that have been laid bare in successive critiques of pastoral from Raymond Williams to Annabel Patterson. To further complications of this issue we shall return in commenting on Wordsworth's *Home at Grasmere.*

Bate's position, then, is the environmentalist position (its rallying-cry, as every first-grader knows, is the undeeded possessive "*our* planet"), and he wants to say that it is Wordsworth's position too—that for Wordsworth the only important thing about owning a cottage, in *Home at Grasmere*, is that it surrounds one with a "deep vale," a "concave" mirror image of the whole earth that can become a regional "haunt" in "the mind of man" (92, 40, 102). This position is certainly congenial to the much older author of *The Guide to the Lakes*, featured in Bate's second chapter, and congenial also to the tradition of British Wordsworth readers passing from the Ruskin of *Fors Clavigera* through William Morris to Edward Thomas and to Seamus Heaney (the name of John Berger might well be added), which Bate identifies as a genuinely left-leaning genealogy of literary Greens. (I think his patriotism justified, by the way. In most other countries environmentalism has been most typically a plank of rightist platforms and has served, not always by design, the interests of privileged classes, as is well documented in Anna Bramwell's *Ecology in the Twentieth Century: A History*, an extremely intelligent book which appears in most respects to shape Bate's understanding of the complex relation between environmentalism and politics.)[24] But Bate's position remains—to revert to my earlier distinction—a metaphysical view of nature, and fails to take into account how an ontological view might differ from it. "Wordsworth," in other words, is still at stake.

To make my point as clear as possible, let me juxtapose two descriptions of a nuclear power plant against the backdrop of a seacoast. The first is Bate's, to the tune of "Wordsworth, thou should'st be with us at this hour":

> If we ascend Coniston Old Man, the mountain beneath which Ruskin lived in the years when he was writing *Fors*, the most prominent sight on the coast is the Sellafield nuclear reprocessing plant, with its abysmal record for dumping contaminated waste. "Still glides, the Stream, and shall for ever glide," wrote Wordsworth of the Duddon in his concluding sonnet; but now it is not only water that glides inexorably into the sea off Wordsworth's coast. (61)

American readers can no doubt put hands on comparable descriptions of Seabrook on the coast of New Hampshire, juxtaposed perhaps with evocations of Thoreau on the Merrimack. The real plangency of Bate's sentiment, expressed over against the odds Wordsworth wagered upon in the Duddon sonnet (unlike the late Ruskin, Wordsworth was evidently untroubled by environmental panic), consists in his distress at knowing that *things don't stay the same.* Thoughtless human beings tamper with the metaphysics, the Aristotelian "natural form," of nature's essence. It was not "meant" to have a power plant in it. The hanging in independent suspense of this "meant" ("it" means in the same way that "it" rains) is what shows us still to believe that "nature," with Wordsworth its prophet, is in fact intrinsically meaningful, at once the subject and the object of human agency. But the amazingly *un*ecological, athropocentric hubris of thinking human threats to planetary health too powerful for the earth to pass through and beyond, just as it has passed through catastrophes in which humans have played no part (not only the massive ones that changed the course of living forms but also such threats to species as rabies, elm blight, and hemlock disease), can perhaps be humbled, and our burden lightened, by a more truly Wordsworthian kind of nature description.

In the ontological view, things *qua* things do stay the same, they just may not be the same things. Ontic sameness, not this or that visible form, stays the same. Here is a passage from a recent detective novel by P. D. James. Having detailed a panorama that includes a ruined abbey, a village, and a church as surveyed by her detective, Dalgleish, James continues:

> To the north the view was dominated by the huge bulk of the power station, the low-roofed administration block with, behind it, the reactor building and the great steel, aluminum-clad building of the turbine house. Four hundred metres out to sea were rigs and platforms of the intake structures through which the cooling sea water passed to the pump house. . . . Directly to his left the flint walls of Martyr's Cottage glistened. . . . less than half a mile to the north, set back among the Californian pines which fringed that part of the coast, was the dull cottage . . . a neatly proportional suburban villa incongruously set down on this bleak headland and facing inland as if resolutely ignoring the sea. Farther inland . . . was the Old Rectory, set like a Victorian dolls' house.[25]

History is welcome here, as is geography, each period and place jumbled together with its inharmonious characteristics, yet from flint to aluminum, it is implied, walls remain walls. Modes of dwelling, as of power (God, witchcraft, cosy imperial culture, nuclear energy) recirculate like coolant through a pump. The author revels in the mastery of detail (I have left out a lot), and while the passage is not without value judgments (the specific "nature" of objects as well as the mutuality derived from their very distinctness of being is emphasized), its overwhelming purpose is simply to place the discrete parts of the scene before the eye in their indiscriminate vividness. The nuclear power plant figures importantly in James's plot, just as it does in this panorama, but in both cases she carefully avoids aligning its role with either its messianic or its diabolical public images. Like Mont Blanc, it is a soulless image on the eye but no less for that reason a power source, timeless *as* power despite being a latecomer in the scenery. This is a "bleak headland," says James; it has the visionary dreariness of Wordsworth: a gibbet, a naked beacon, a girl with a pitcher making her way against the wind, all just unforgettably there together. That they are what they are is interesting, and suggestive, but strictly for the purpose of furnishing the ontological shock that makes them a spot of time, they could have been anything else: a road, a blasted crag, a tree, and a sheep, for example—anything, that is, in which an aestheticized symbolism of spiritual shelter and nurture, the hostelry of meaningfulness, has been effaced or carefully neutralized.

Judging from the example of Bate, an environmentalist criticism is prone to conclude that description is valuable because the things it describes *are those things*, and somehow in fact depends for this value on their continued (and, for that matter, their past) real existence. Thus Bate on reading Keats's "To Autumn" once global warming has increased the severity of winds in northern Europe: "The swallow has the greatest difficulty in coping with wind. . . . The poem will look very different if there is soon an autumn when 'gathering swallows twitter in the skies' for the last time" (2). In addition to the bad ornithology entailed here in Bate's having forgotten that swallows don't just twitter when preparing for autumn migration but also twitter every evening, when returning to their barns and chimneys, from late spring until autumn (these are not idle facts but serve to complicate Keats's already complex conclusion in important ways)—in addition to this there is also a deeper issue, touching on a matter that may be said to contradict even the bird-lore I have just supplied. *Will* the poem look very different in the sad aftermath of global warming? I think that, supposing there is then anyone around to read it, the poem will in fact look much the same, or perhaps even better. The identity of the swallows is not compromised in their real present existence, and certainly not in an exact description of their habits (though it is fostered by the impression of exactitude), but in their having been realized as a present existence; and this form of identity if anything would gain in poignancy, I am sorry to say, in ways foreseen by the poem itself, from the imposition of pastness by extinction. (Why does Bate speak of "the certainty of the following spring's return" [2]? Isn't Shelley, insofar as even he is certain, writing about the need for a violent wind during that same autumn?) Just so, on the awful day when all the trees are gone and we shall finally be entitled to say, *pace* Liu, "there is no nature" (*Sense of History*, 56), just then and not before, if we survive, we will realize, concerning what de Man called "the ontology of the poetic" in a passage cited by Bate (104), that poetry is an epitaph, not a landscape. Taking his turn with the Boy of Winander episode, Bate writes: "Let us not forget that it is . . . about a boy alone by a lake at dusk blowing mimic hootings to unseen owls. Which are there to answer him" (115). And then to stop.[26]

I should like once more to compare the position I have been taking with that of de Man on Wordsworth in order to show where I differ: "The miracle of Wordsworth's figural diction is that, by stating its own precariousness so to speak face to face, without aesthetic evasion, it recovers the totality of the phenomenal world of sky and earth and thus, in a deeper sense than any color or melody could achieve, recovers the aesthetic in the process of its refusal" (*Rhetoric of Romanticism*, 87). "Aesthetic," is a difficult, evermore important word in de Man's later work which I will not attempt to unravel. Here, though, clearly enough, it is aligned with "totality," the Kantian "purposive, not purposeful" manifold which modern criticism calls an "evasion" because it suspends historical engagement. The "refusal" de Man speaks of is Wordsworth's insistence that all phenomenality without exception is in fact purpose*ful*, while the return of the aesthetic is the all-inclusiveness of this very insistence, making the realized phenomenal world a world-picture or song of the earth after all. It seems to me that this aesthetic is after all very close to an ecology, and results in a view of Wordsworth that surprisingly resembles Bate's. It turns, I believe, on the failure to distinguish between *totality*—the comprehensive manifold or "multeity in unity" dear to Coleridge of which, in my view, there is very little in Wordsworth—and *unity*, unity to which the presence or absence of multeity is immaterial, which I take to be Wordsworth's essential subject.

Undoubtedly this is a fine point of distinction on which all too much may depend. Where, for example, does this eloquent passage in Whitehead, so impressively evocative of Wordsworth, fall between totality and unity? "Of course he recognizes, what no one doubts, that in some sense living things are different from lifeless things. But that is not his main point. It is the brooding presence in the hills which haunts him. His theme is nature *insolido*, that is to say, he dwells on that mysterious presence of surrounding things, which imposes itself on any separate element that we set up as an individual for its own sake."[27] It falls, I would say, on the side of unity, the mysterious presence obtruding itself on the poet as the being of beings. Karl Kroeber, in a 1974 article called "*Home at Grasmere*: Ecological Holiness" (*PMLA* 89) acknowledged by Bate as his forerunner in the field, offers comparable conflations of terms that I am less confident of enlisting in my cause. He sees Wordsworth's indifference to environmental prettiness (the "natural beauty" that apparently makes some ecosystems worthier than others) placed in the service of an all-embracing "ecological unity," or, again, of "wholeness," and that sounds like the return of the aesthetic in totality; but in saying that Wordsworth makes "the finest poetry out of the commonest and most everyday *beingness*, merely 'what we are,' " Kroeber, with his Native American–influenced perspective on dwelling in the presence of the inanimate, decidedly does not look forward to a "green" criticism. Indeed, perhaps it is finally a question whether the nature poetry of Wordsworth is green or *gray;* and critical insight should perhaps be commended in proportion as it serves to remind us that "rocks and stones" make up two-thirds of the Wordsworthian cosmos, the other third being Lucy — "thing" that she once seemed and now is — and the trees.[28]

An offensive, in some ways authentically Thoreauvian article in the current *Harvard Alumni Magazine* shows very clearly what happens when environmentalism becomes selective.[29] The author contrasts a beach that is difficult of access, hence frequented by ordinary, unattuned people with all their obtrusive equipment ("apparatus of happiness," Jane Austen called it in *Emma*, satirically yet not without fondness). In apparently total ignorance that his article is a humorless attack on the Great Unwashed, otherwise known as the American people, the author implies that his "kayak elite" is classless, as though the outdoorsy shabby gentility he evokes for his already-converted audience were not the very essence of patrician, quiet-money New England. Of course outsiders can join this class, just as outsiders can rise or sink to any other American class, but the snobbery and exclusiveness of each and every class (the public beach crowd with its gas barbecues and aqua-socks is capable for its part of some pretty keen satire on the narrow Yankee soul) remains always the key sign of the false secondary power whereby we multiply distinctions.

Hence, although there have certainly been plenty of occasions on which what Bate calls the "red" criticism of the eighties has been simply malapropos, a breach of scale, there is one purpose for which it is evidently still needed, and that is the demystification of green criticism. Consider this startling distinction without a difference in Bate:

> Wordsworth's concern for the preservation of the Lakes has often been put down to a selfish desire to keep away artisan day trippers from Manchester. But in his 1844 letters to the *Morning Post* concerning the projected Kendal and Windermere Railway, Wordsworth's principal objection was to large-scale organized Sunday outings. . . . It is precisely this problem of *mass* tourism that threatens the Lake District today. (de Man, 50)

Indeed, by the 1840s, Wordsworth *was* an Environmentalist "considering," as Bate says, "the evolving and increasingly disruptive influence of man on his environment" (45) and more and more concerned to select his human and non-human company during the successive editions of the *Guide to the Lakes* that Bate documents. "Is then no nook of English ground secure / From rash assault?" he inquires in the sonnet published with his 1844 letters against the Kendal and Windermere Railway, ranging the "pausing traveller" of his early poems and the small yeoman landowner with his "paternal fields" over against "the false utilitarian lure" of mechanized mass tourism—including, needless to say, the artisan day trippers. Keep "nature" hard to reach and only the right people will make themselves at home in it, leaving everyone else stranded in environmental limbo.

By contrast, in *Home at Grasmere*, which is one of the relatively few early poems that Bate can have much to say about, Wordsworth says that it takes all kinds—"I came not dreaming of unruffled life, / Untainted manners" (MS. B, 428–29)—just as he honestly admits, in the same year, that even rustic language stands in need of bowdlerization. This more forgiving view points to inclusive unity rather than any subtly exclusive totalization ("aesthetization") of the natural. "Bleak season was it" when he and his entourage arrived (218); he and Dorothy identify with a pair of swans that chose arbitrarily to live in Grasmere Vale despite lacking roots there and may have been shot—hard pastoral indeed!—by a thoughtless shepherd (see 322–56); the unself-consciousness of "sensation" and natural want among "untutored shepherds" is not "unhallowed" (see 665–72); and the spirit of leveling first noticed by Hazlitt here as elsewhere promotes ontic equality:

> I begin
> Already to inscribe upon my heart
> A liking for the small grey Horse that bears
> The paralytic Man; I know the ass
> On which the Cripple in the Quarry maimed
> Rides to and fro.
>
> (723–28)

This is not the author of the *Guide to the Lakes* but the earlier poet moved by intimations of somatism, attending to the human creatures Alan Bewell has called "marginals"[30] (in "Animal Tranquility and Decay," for instance), discovering and delineating the human by feeling tentatively around the edges of humanity in that moment of being, never far from bedrock, where death and life graze each other.

That is the moment within which he imagines himself to be embraced in the much pawed-over first verse paragraph of "Tintern Abbey," and indeed in the whole poem ("If I should be where I no more can hear / Thy voice"). This moment calls, in my view, for a criticism that is neither red nor green but gray, not dull gray but gleaming at times the way rocks, depending how you look at them, gleam at times. The "soft inland murmur," the thought of "more deep seclusion," the poet's "repose" under a dark tree from which he can view other "plots"—these are indications that the speaker is on the extreme verge of life, which is also of course to say (and here red criticism pounces) of social existence. All social forms, including the notoriously "repressed" village charcoal burners and homeless persons in the Abbey a few miles distant, are reduced, leveled, to that mode of being in which the aestheticized features of their distinctness—pastoral farms, beauteous forms—vanish. Orchards hard to distinguish from groves and copses, hedge-rows hardly hedge-rows: all specificity of cultivation and habitation is obscured by the ubiquitous monotony of green to the point of being, at most, an "uncertain notice." It is here that "the breath of this corporeal frame / And even the motion of our human blood / Almost suspended, we are laid asleep / In body" (43–46). The burthen of the mystery is *not explained*, Wordsworth never says that it was or is; he only says that it is "lightened," meaning that in the ontic moment it no longer seems to matter that the world is "unintelligible." Or so the "philosophic calm" of Wordsworth's nature poetry appears, in any case, from the standpoint of a stone-colored criticism.

CHAPTER FIVE

Poetic Knowledge

Geoffrey Hartman's Romantic Poetics

Gerald L. Bruns

Romanticism as Critique

I first read Geoffrey Hartman's *The Unmediated Vision* in the late 1950s as part of an effort to clarify what was, in those days, the question of questions in literary theory: Is there such a thing as poetic knowledge, and, if there is, what sort of account of it should be given?[1] The urgency of the question was traceable, by common agreement, to I. A. Richards, who had divided discourse into referential and emotive categories and then identified poetry as "the supreme form of *emotive* language," which meant, to speak strictly, that poetry could no longer be called meaningful or true except out of courtesy to tradition.[2] Much of what came to be called the New Criticism was a loose family of attempts to answer Richards by conceptualizing poetry as a form of cognition at the level of particularity, complexity, or immediacy of experience.[3] None of these attempts was very satisfying, possibly because of an irresistible tendency, in the absence of any sustained reflection on language, to think of poetry as a kind of seeing—for example, as a "presentational" as opposed to a "discursive" form (Susanne Langer), or as something made of imagery and symbols (Wellek and Warren), or as a "verbal icon"

(W. K. Wimsatt).[4] In Northrop Frye's *Anatomy of Criticism* (1957) there is no such thing as language; a word is whatever comes between pictures and music: it is a little bit of both but nothing in itself.[5] Even Walter Ong, otherwise critical of the way we map spatial and visual analogies onto human speech, thought of metaphor as "twinned vision."[6] Following Aristotle, Elder Olson thought that in the poetic (that is, mimetic) order of things "words are the least important element; they are governed by everything else in the poem" — for example, plot and character.[7] Evidently, if cognition could be attributed to poetry, the poem had first to be allegorized as an organ of perception or, prosthetically, by analogy with mirrors, lamps, or whatever helps us to get things in focus.[8]

Meanwhile, in the 1950s, the question of poetic knowledge began to be reformulated, or at least recontextualized, as part of an awakened interest in Romantic poetry. Following T. E. Hulme, Irving Babbitt, F. R. Leavis, Yvor Winters, and who knows how many others, the denunciation of Romanticism as "irrationalism" had become a standard classroom exercise, but after World War II students of poetry began to discover that Romantic writing was deeply philosophical and that it was oriented toward something very like what we would now call a critique of subject-centered rationality. On this interpretation Romanticism asks not only how knowledge is possible but also what its consequences are, and it dramatizes the way our consciousness of objects disengages us from the world, as if depriving us of a place we could inhabit. Knowledge is a condition of separation (or, alternatively, separateness is a condition of modern subjectivity).[9] So ideas of perspectivism and world views are born to accommodate a theory of subject as observer of the passing show. However, Romantic poetry shows that subjectivity is not exhausted by consciousness as conceptual determination or by making things present to view. At ground level our relation to the world, as Heidegger would later say, is not one of perception and representation, but neither is it one of *not* knowing, that is (among various possibilities), it is not simply a noncognitive, emotive, or purely empirical relation of sensation or brute feeling. What is it, then? Suddenly it became plausible to think of Romanticism not as a riot of feeling but as an attempt to fill in the gap between concepts and sensations or, more exactly, between transcendental and empiricist notions of subjectivity. At all events what critics began to find in Romantic poetry were, among other things, new conceptual resources for thinking about human experience. Thus, for example, in *The Poetry of Experience* (1957), Robert Langbaum identified *Einfühlung* as "the specifically romantic way of knowing" in which *one becomes what one knows.*[10] Poetry is no longer simply the art of writing verses but is, prior to writing, the experience of things (and of others) in their proximity and singularity as if they were part of ourselves or, for that matter, we of them. Subjectivity in this case extends not so much toward transcendental apperception as toward the earth, that is, in the direction of responsiveness, receptiveness, and practical reason, or in the ability to inhabit the world as well as to observe it. The irony, of course, is that Romanticism in this sense is exactly what the New Critics had been after, namely, a theory of poetic knowledge as the restoration of an *intimacy* with things that conceptual or subsumptive thinking destroys. Only now the trick is to understand poetic knowledge as a mode of being (a species of *Mitsein*) rather than as a special category of consciousness of the sort that doctrines of imagination and appeals to the immediacy of feeling, for example, were meant to exemplify.[11]

Poetry as Immediacy

Still, if consciousness is not all there is to subjectivity — if subjectivity is not to be understood on the model of perception and representation — how exactly is it to be understood?[12] One could take this as the regulating question of Geoffrey Hartman's early research. At least a question of roughly this sort helps us to get a clear sense of what Hartman was after in *The Unmediated Vision*, which is an absorbing but characteristically recondite book of close readings, filled with improvised concepts whose aim is to understand poetry as a mode of reflection, where reflexiveness is not, however, a mirroring of subjectivity but rather a critical reversal that tries to get the subject out from under the furniture of consciousness as representation, including such representations as the "self" (or, indeed, any of the representations of the subject that come down to us in modern tradition: the *cogito*, the "bundle of sensations," the transcendental unity of apperception, consciousness as spirit, intentionality, or material construction). Reflexiveness is thus not a kind of seeing turned in upon itself. On the contrary, one of its conditions is what Hartman, following Wordsworth, calls "the subduing of the eye" (185), which is the kind of spiritual exercise practiced by Wordsworth's beggars, wanderers, hermits, and other solitaries who comprise a type of the poet of experience in contrast to poets of art or writing. The hermit, Hartman says, "exemplifies contemplation, having retired to the desert or woods in order to 'subdue' his eyes and await the flood 'fast anchored.' The Hermit of 'Tintern Abbey' is an image of transcendence: he sits fixed by his fire, the symbol, probably, for the pure or imageless vision" (34).

What sort of vision is "imageless vision"? It has the form but not the content of religious ecstasy. It is a kind of intransitive mysticism in which the subject is transported, not to another world, but to the other of all worlds, other than even the inner world that introspection searches for to small effect. Transcendence is the *pure exteriority* of the subject, subjectivity turned inside out like a pocket, not in order to be filled by something else — a divine light, for example — but simply to be free of the activity or function of mediation as such. "Imageless vision" is thus a kind of gratuitous expenditure of consciousness, as if there could be a consciousness purified of intentionality or a subjectivity without any such thing as a subject conceived as a cognitive ego. In the concluding chapter of *The Unmediated Vision* Hartman calls this a subjectivity of "pure representation," as if parodying Kant's idea of aesthetic experience as conceptuality without concepts: "In pure representation, the poet represents the mind as knowing without a cause from perception, and so in and from itself; or he will represent the mind as no less real than the objects of its perceiving" (128). So a distinctive feature of poetic knowledge would be its iconoclasm; it is, whatever else it is, free of idolatry. Conceivably such freedom is poetry's main idea.

What happens to reality, or to things, in this event? The paradox is that in poetry things do not recede but are closer than any observation of them could bring about. A condition of poetry, Hartman says, is suspension of "the will toward relational knowledge" — relational knowledge being that sort in which things no longer exist in themselves but become objects or essences, phenomenological furniture of the world that consciousness constructs for itself (35). Such knowledge is the kind that Husserl understood as intentional: consciousness is nothing except consciousness *of* something. Hartman, perhaps in defiance of philosophy, wants to be free of intentionality, which is to say free of mediation, as if to be *with* the world rather than *about* it. Poetry means that we "forgo relational knowledge" (38). Poetry is, so to speak, a relation of being-with rather than one of being-for-oneself. Hartman, improvising, calls it simply "being *in relation*," to underscore the intransitive nature of the case: "The poet, insofar as he writes poetry, feels himself, and is able to express himself, as fundamentally in relation, not with any particular, in any particular way, for any particular reason (though with some thing, in some way, for some reason), but *in relation;* so that poetry is more immediate, that is, less dependent on a relational use of symbols, than ordinary discourse" (39).

The question is how to clarify the notion that "poetry is more immediate" than any other form of language, whether propositional, symbolic, or whatever. "Immediacy" is a keyword in *The Unmediated Vision*, as it was for the New Critics, but Hartman reinterprets the term away from the idea of apprehending things directly or by way of feeling toward ideas of proximity and receptiveness. The "suspension of the will toward relational knowledge" is essentially a refusal of the power that is inherent in cognition—the German word for concept, *Begriff*, derives from *greifen*, "to grasp." As Emmanuel Levinas says, "Knowledge as perception, concept, comprehension refers back to an act of grasping. The metaphor should be taken literally: even before any technical application of knowledge, it expresses the principle rather than the result of the future technological and industrial order of which every civilisation bears the seed. The immanence of the known to the act of knowing is already the embodiment of seizure."[13] In Hartman's analysis, the suspension of the will shows itself in the materialization of poetic language, as if poetry were an attempt to connect up with reality, not conceptually or semantically, but by approaching the physicality, density, and self-subsistence of things themselves.

This comes out most persuasively in Hartman's readings of Hopkins and Rilke. "Hopkins' poetry," he says, "is first an expression of sense experience and wants at first to be taken as such. *The act of sight has become a moral responsibility*" (53). But this means that perception is never merely the act of a disengaged punctual observer; experience is always physical contact with the world, where things are kinetic, as much energy as substance. When seen, things press themselves against the eye as if it were an exposed surface. As Hartman says, "The sense of pressure or stress is the sixth and radical sense in the experience of Hopkins" (55). This pressure is ethical in character; things do not just appear, they make a claim upon our senses. Disinterestedness would require that we reflect ourselves out of the conditions that make experience possible, constructing an attitude of indifference (observing unobserved: the propositional attitude of formal philosophy). One is reminded of Emmanuel Levinas's analysis of sensibility, which is not so much a mode of perception as a mode of being touched. "Qua sensible the concrete is immediacy, contact, and language. Perception is a proximity with being which intentional analysis does not account for. . . . Sight is, to be sure, an openness and a consciousness, and all sensibility, opening as a consciousness, is called vision; but even in its subordination to cognition sight remains contact and proximity. The visible caresses the eye. One sees and one hears like one touches."[14] Sensibility in this sense captures precisely the whole idea of "unmediated vision."

The crucial point is that Hopkins's way of being "in relation" with the physicality of things applies to his relation with language as well. There is in Hopkins,

Hartman says, "an unwillingness to release his mind from the physical contact with words, which are conceived not only as the means but also and very strongly as the materials of expression, and used with the undiluted stroke of some modern painters who wish to let color or *touche* speak for itself" (52). For Hopkins words are not prosthetic extensions of a sovereign subject but share the ontology of things. "We may," Hopkins wrote, "think of words as heavy bodies, as indoor and out of door objects of nature and man's art." Hopkins is not being metaphorical, because for him the relation between language and reality is not one of naming or predication; rather, the grammar of words belongs as much to physics as to semantics:

> Now every visible palpable body has a centre of gravity round which it is in balance and a centre of illumination or *highspot* or *quickspot* up to which it is shaded. The centre of gravity is like the accent of stress, the highspot like the accent of pitch, and as in some things as air and water the centre of gravity is either unnoticeable or changeable so there may be languages in a fluid state in which there is little difference of weight or stress between syllables or what there is changes and again as it is only glazed bodies that shew the highspot so there may be languages in which the pitch is unnoticeable.[15]

Hopkins's interest is in the thingliness of language—language on the hither side of predication, where "speech is to be heard for its own sake and interest even over and above its interest of meaning" (*Journals*, 289). He thus anticipates the radical poetics of Stéphane Mallarmé (and much of twentieth-century North American poetics), in which poetry is said to be made of words but is not a use of them; that is, poetry is made of language but not of any of the things we use language to produce: meanings, assertions, descriptions, expressions. Not that the poem dispenses with these things; it just no longer needs them. Poetry's language is no longer a form of mediation; it has the thickness and impermeability of things themselves.[16] So we can no longer make our way among its words as if they were extensions of ourselves, subject to our command.

It is as if the project of poetry (or of "unmediated vision") were to return language to a world inhabited by bodies rather than by minds. Whether such a thing is possible or not, Hartman shows that this was, nevertheless, Rilke's project: "How to discover the meaning of the body and of the physical world, and how to render this meaning in a language which, anthropomorphic, has lost the power of concreteness" (*UV*, 79). The question of what an "anthropomorphic" language might be is worth some serious and extended thought. Possibly the question is whether there is any other kind. In our intellectual environment (from Frege and Saussure to Chomsky, structural linguistics, speech-acts theory, and most poststructuralist appropriations of semiotics) theories of language have been basically Kantian or subject-centered, with language serving mainly as a stand-in for the idealist's concept of the spirit (structuralism, for example, is essentially Kantian idealism with language replacing reason as the origin of intelligibility). In the 1950s the same was true of reigning empiricist theories like W. V. O. Quine's, where language is conceived as a conceptual scheme, which is basically a super-subject conceived as a vast man-made fabric of sentences held together by inferential reasoning. A true statement is not so much one that squares with the world as one that fits into the scheme of things (whatever follows the law of noncontradiction with respect to the whole). What we call the world is only what can be woven into the fabric, which, as Quine says, "impinges on experience only along the edges."[17] And at the edges there are only brute sensations, or "raw feels." "Physical objects are conceptually imported into the situation as convenient intermediaries—not by definition in terms of experience, but simply as irreducible posits comparable, epistemologically, to the gods of Homer" ("Two Dogmas," 44). So objects, as things observable at all, are allegories of reason. Being a realist means being "ontologically committed" to such objects, where, in the modern world, physics is apt to be the mode of commitment with the highest rate of return.[18]

But could poetry, in the modern world, be an avenue of ontological commitment to real things? What form would this commitment take? This is basically the question that Hartman's reading of Rilke tries to answer. It is also arguably the fundamental question of Hartman's thinking, perhaps even to this day. Not many think of Hartman as a realist, but on a certain view he has never tried to be anything else.

Hartman shows that Rilke tried to break out of the constraints of mediation by conceptualizing poetry on the model of sculpture, where a sculptured object is not so much something to be seen as something to be felt as a resistance to touch, a thing of density and weight and not just of form and shape. Even the eye recognizes that the realism of sculpture is its impermeability: the statue, like the Cubist collage, is as much a limit as an object of perception. Hartman remarks that "the very text of Rilke is the 'body,' its weight and balance. . . . His conception of 'thing' tends to negate generic differences between the objects of nature, man, and art. Whether a tree, a young girl, or a column, Rilke will always understand it as an object in which a physical force has sought a certain kind of weight and balance" (*UV*, 91). Valéry thought that a defect of poetry is that its material cannot help signifying something other than itself, in contrast to music, whose forms exhibit nothing but themselves — one hesitates to ask of a sonata what it is about. Rilke would say that a defect of poetry is that it cannot achieve the physicality or, better, corporeality of paintings and sculpture. A poem cannot obtrude into the world as one thing among others the way a statue can. Yet it was this limit that Rilke sought to challenge. As Hartman says, he modeled his poetics explicitly on the work of Rodin and Cézanne as a way of inserting poetry directly into the physical world. "Rilke attempts to create a new idiom which would neglect the anthropomorphic for the physical basis of language. The commonplace sense of words is neglected for their seeming origin as signs signifying weight, direction, and invisibly oriented gesture" (95) — as if a poem were not reducible to a form of mediation but could become a thing among things, part of the world and not about it. The metaphysics of such a project would be worth trying to construct.

The Thickness of Words and Things

There are a number of writers who could help us imagine such a construction. One would be the last poet studied in *The Unmediated Vision*, Paul Valéry, who gave a distinctive interpretation to Mallarmé's thesis that a poem is made of words, not of ideas or images. Valéry's theory is that the mind or intellect naturally expresses its occupations in concepts and propositions, but the mind as such is never visible in these abstract forms. Logic is only a mediated form of rationality; it is not the thing itself. Poetry, by contrast, gives us the intellect in all of its concrete formal processes — for the intellect is not a kind of thing but rather a purely formal mechanism of construction. In poetry this operation is visible in all of its purity — or perhaps one should say, almost visible, or almost pure, since language cannot reduce its forms of predication to zero. The idea that poetry is made of words means that poetry is always, at some level, a structure of mediation. However, poetry can materialize words so radically that they approach the condition of music. Valéry's distinction on this point has become canonical:

> Ordinary spoken language is a practical tool. It is constantly solving immediate problems. *Its task is fulfilled when each sentence has been completely abolished, annulled, and replaced by the meaning.* Comprehension is its end. But on the other hand, poetic usage is dominated by *personal* conditions. . . .

> Here language is no longer a transitive act, an expedient. On the contrary, it has *its own value*, which must remain intact *in spite of the operations of the intellect on the given propositions.* Poetic language must preserve itself, through itself, and remain the same, *not to be altered by the act of intelligence that finds or gives it a meaning.*[19]

However, poetic language is not purely formal—that is, it is not merely a foregrounding of the rhetorical features of language; it is also ecstatic. In "Poetry and Abstract Thought," Valéry writes, "The moment this concrete form takes on, by an effect of its own, such importance that it asserts itself and makes itself, as it were, respected; and not only remarked and respected, but desired and therefore repeated—then something new happens: we are insensibly transformed and ready to live, breathe, and think in accordance with a rule and under laws which are no longer of the practical order—that is, nothing that may occur in this state will be resolved, finished, or abolished by a specific act. We are entering the poetic universe" (*Art of Poetry*, 65). The "poetic universe" is purely mental. Valéry describes his experience of it as the experience of creation itself, that is, the experience of his own mind in the act of composing the poem. Poetic experience is just this experience of composition; it is an experience of the purely formal operations of the mind as these become visible in language, which is to say in the poem itself. So the poem becomes the body of the mind in a way that concepts and propositions, being about the world, can never be. Poetry in this sense is an "imageless vision," not of things, but of the intellect.

It follows, however, that Valéry's would still be an essentially anthropocentric poetics, however much poetic language is constituted as something physical and impermeable. This comes out sharply when one reads Francis Ponge (as Ponge read himself) *against* Valéry. Whereas Valéry writes to experience his own mind, for Ponge, as the title of his first volume of poetry announces, writing means "taking the side of things." In *Le parti pris des choses* (1942), the poems address utterly nondescript things of everyday life: a wooden crate, a cigarette, an oyster, a doorknob, a loaf of bread, snails, a pebble.[20] Yet the purpose here is not so much to elevate these things into objects of description as to approach them casually and even intimately in the spirit of playful talk, as if to scale poetry down from the transcendence of genius to the small and the near: "Notes pour un coquillage," for example, contrasts a seashell with assorted wonders of the world—the pyramids, the temples of Angkor, and also the Louvre, which Ponge imagines surviving the end of man as a dwelling place for birds and monkeys.[21] Taking the side of things means taking sides satirically *against* man, as in Ponge's anti-industrial

"Les morceaux de viande," or in "R.C. Seine n⁰," which, Kafka-like, regards the modern office in terms of the office stairwell and its traffic of things and thing-like people, including the poet himself, who is basically a conduit for the daily mail. In fact, taking the side of things means principally occupying their ontological plane, being with them at the level of thingliness or body-to-body contact:

> LE PLAISIRS DE LA PORTE
> Les rois ne touchent pas aux portes.
>
> Ils ne connaissent pas ce bonheur: pousser devant soi avec douceur ou rudesse l'un de ces grands panneaux familiers, se retourner vers lui pour le remettre en place,—tenir dans ses bras une porte.
>
> . . . Le bonheur d'empoigner au ventre part son noeud de porcelaine l'un de ces hauts obstacles d'une pièce; ce corps à corps rapide par lequel un instant la marche retenue, l'œil s'ouvre et le corps tout entier s'accommode à son nouvel appartement.
>
> D'une main amicale il la retient encore, avant de la repousser décidément et s'enclore,—ce dont le déclic du ressort puissant mais bien huilé agréablement l'assure. (*PP*, 44)

> THE PLEASURES OF THE DOOR
> Kings never touch doors.
>
> They're not familiar with this happiness: to push, gently or roughly before you one of these great, friendly panels, to turn towards it to put it back in place—to hold a door in your arms.
>
> The happiness of seizing one of these tall barriers to a room by the porcelain knob of its belly; this quick hand-to-hand, during which your progress slows for a moment, your eye opens up and your whole body adapts to its new apartment.
>
> With a friendly hand you hold on a bit longer, before firmly pushing it back and shutting yourself in—of which you are agreeably assured by the click of the powerful, well-oiled latch.[22]

It is often repeated that Ponge's poetry is about the indescribability of things, but taking the side of things means engaging them on the hither side of description—emphatically at the level of touch, smell, and sound. One remembers Wittgenstein's remark that one can't describe the smell of coffee, but this does not expose a shortfall in our language or in our powers of description; rather it bears witness to how we are with things, which are apt to grasp us before we can grasp them, because at ground level (inhabiting "forms of life") our relation to things is not one of conceptualization and control:

> L'eau m'échappe . . . me file entre les doigts. Et encore! Ce n'est même pas si net (qu'un lézard ou une grenouille): il m'en reste aux mains des traces, des taches, relativement longues à sécher ou qu'il faut essuyer. Elle m'échappe et cependant me marque, sans que j'y puisse grand-chose. (*PP*, 62–63)

> Water escapes me, runs through my fingers. And again! It's not even very clean (unlike a lizard or a frog): it leaves traces, marks, on my hands that take a good while to dry, or have to be wiped off. It escapes me and nonetheless marks me, and I can't do very much about it. (*SP*, 59)

Likewise, it sometimes appears that Ponge's poet is on closer terms with things than with people, yet when people are encountered at the level of thingliness they become more human than those seen en masse ("Le gymnaste," "La jeune mère"). Recall Hartman's point about the way in Rilke's poetry proximity to the physical world obscures the difference between things and people. One sort of Levinasian would say that this is because proximity is an ethical relation in which things make a claim on us in the way people do. They achieve the height of alterity.[23] But another sort would say that Ponge regards things not so much face to face as flesh to flesh, in a relation of sensibility rather than alterity. For him ground-level existence is just physically *eudaimonic*, as it is for snails:

> Seul, évidemment l'escargot est bien seul. Il n'a pas beaucoup d'amis. Mais il n'en a pas besoin pour son bonheur. Il colle si bien à la nature, il en jouit si parfaitement de si près, il est l'ami du sol qu'il baise de tout son corps, et des feuilles, et du ciel vers quoi il lève si fièrement la tête, avec ses globes d'yeux si sensibles; noblesse, lenteur, sagesse, orgueil, vanité, fierté. (*PP*, 53)

> Alone, obviously the snail is quite alone. It hasn't many friends. But it's just as happy without them. It's so intimately attached to nature, enjoys her so perfectly from so close up; it's the friend of the earth it kisses with its entire body, and of leaves, and of the sky towards which it proudly lifts its head, with those so sensitive eye-stalks; nobility, deliberation, wisdom, arrogance, vanity, pride. (*SP*, 43)

Clearly, Ponge doesn't hesitate to moralize upon such things as snails, oysters, and pebbles—Ovid-like, metamorphoses to and from the human are always occurring—but Ponge's moralizations are parodies of seriousness, and in any case they are also on the side of things. Thus the snail's shell is likened to an ideal work of art, not so much because of its form (contrast Valéry's seashell) as for its restraint and acceptance of finitude: "Et voilà l'example qu'ils nous donnent. Saints, ils font œuvre de leur vie,——œuvre d'art de leur perfectionnement. Leur secrétion même se produit de telle manière qu'elle se met en forme. Rien d'extérieur à eux, à leur nécessité, à leur besoin n'est leur œuvre. Rien de disproportionné—d'autre part—à leur être physique. Rien qui ne lui soit nécessaire, obligatoire" (*PP*, 54). "And here's the example they set us. As saints, they make works of art of their lives—of their self-perfecting. Their secretion is so produced as to shape itself. Nothing exterior to themselves, to their necessity, their needs, enters the work. Nothing disproportionate, alien, to their physical being. Nothing not necessary, imperative, to it" (*SP*, 45). We think Michelangelo's David a great work of art, but a greater work would be a niche or shell proportioned to fit a human body exactly (*PP*, 76). The problem with images or mimetic works of art is that they require special environments in which to exist (frames, galleries, museums, art books). As Levinas puts it, images are "disincarnations" of things, the way a corpse is an image of the departed.[24] Ponge's idea is that the poet should insert his poems into the world the way the snail secretes its dribble. (Taking the side of things also means taking sides against the poetical, which is one reason why Ponge refuses to call his poems "poems.")

In his "Introduction au galet" (1933) Ponge says that he writes not to make things transparent to view but to thicken them (*PP*, 176). And to the thickness of things corresponds the thickness of words. However, unlike Hopkins, Ponge takes words as historical rather than natural objects: their thickness is semantic rather than somatic. The density of a word consists in the layers of contexts and usages through which it has passed and by which it is constituted. A word is its history, which dictionaries record and to which etymological dictionaries and dictionaries of puns give us even richer, more pungent access. For Mallarmé and Valéry this semantic layering was a defect; the word is soiled by its use (who wants to touch what has been in everyone's mouth?). But for Ponge this soiling is the stuff words are made of. In an interview with Serge Gavronsky, Ponge said that writing should before anything else be tuned to the history of words. We should be able to find

> in each sentence, in each paragraph, in the whole text, all the semantic levels, all the successive definitions [of a word], beginning with its roots, simultaneously respected. Naturally, that is an impossible expectation. . . . It is an impossible absolute that all words, that the texts, be written in such a way as to allow the words their

> complete semantical thickness. . . . But if one has that sensitivity to the thickness of words, to the fact that they do have a history, that they have provoked associations of different ideas in each language and in each of the periods of the evolution of language, then this provides a much thicker material, graver, much graver in the sense of weight, a material that is not superficial, which is a thing that one can mold precisely because it has the quality, the thickness, of potter's clay. It is a physical object with many dimensions.[25]

In "My Creative Method," Ponge writes: "PARTI PRIS DES CHOSES *égale* COMPTE TENU DES MOTS."[26] Yet this is less a poetic principle than a disposition to abide with words as one does with things, regarding them in their exteriority and self-possession and not as extensions of oneself or as instruments of reason. In any case, the history of words sets a limit to subjectivity, as Heidegger remarked when he observed that we no longer know how to translate many philosophical terms that come down to us from the prehistory of philosophy (as if the history of philosophy were a history of catachresis rather than a history of spirit); and as Derrida says, we are, Joyce-like, always inevitably speaking several languages at once, know it or not. Words are thinglike not simply in their inescapable physicality but principally because they are self-standing or self-withholding (*Selbständigkeit*, *Sichzurückhaltung*), resisting conceptual determination quite as powerfully as things do (*Ursprung des Kuntswerkes*). This is Ponge's insight, and it accords with his idea that a poetry of things is not so much *about* things as alongside of them.

The Time of Things

The possibility that the relation of words and things is a relation of proximity rather than mediation suggests why "immediacy" is not a word in Ponge's lexicon. His disposition toward things is finally one of reserve or discretion—*Parti pris* concludes with: "Je n'en dirai pas plus, car cette idée d'une disparition de signes me donne à réfléchir sur les défauts d'un style qui appuie trop sur les mots" (100). "I shall say no more about it, for this idea of signs disappearing makes me reflect on the faults of a style that relies too much on words."[27] As if, to get along with things, one had finally to stop speaking about them. It has never been the case that things are indescribable or that we *can't* speak of them or take them in hand by means of concepts and images; it is all too easy to picture the world. It is no trouble to depict it truthfully, whether in propositions or on film. The question is, What happens to things in this event?

This is a basic question in Maurice Blanchot's early poetics: What are the consequences of mediation? In "Littérature et le droit à la mort" (1948), for example, Blanchot takes up Hegel's model, in which speech is a dialectic of negation and signification in which things are replaced with concepts:

> I say, "This woman." Hölderlin, Mallarmé, and all poets whose theme is the essence of poetry have felt that the act of naming is disquieting and marvelous. A word may give me its meaning, but first it suppresses it. For me to be able to say, "This woman," I must somehow take her flesh-and-blood reality away from her, cause her to be absent, annihilate her. The word gives me the being, but it gives it to me deprived of being. The word is the absence of that being, its nothingness, what is left of it when it has lost being—the very fact that it does not exist. Considered in this light, speaking is a curious right. In a text dating from before the *Phenomenology*, Hegel, here the friend and kindred spirit of Hölderlin, writes: "Adam's first act, which made him master of the animals, was to give them names, that is, he annihilated them in their existence (as existing creatures)." Hegel means that from that moment on, the cat ceased to be a uniquely real cat and became an idea as well. The meaning of speech, then, requires that before any word is spoken, there must be a sort of immense hecatomb, a preliminary flood plunging all of creation into a total sea. God had created living things, but man had to annihilate them. Not until then did they take on meaning for him, and he in turn created them out of the death into which they disappeared; only instead of beings (*êtres*) and, as we say, existents (*existants*), there remained only being (*l'être*), and man was condemned not to be able to approach anything or experience anything except through the meaning he had to create.[28]

So mediation is death—in Hegel's language, the life of the spirit endures death, maintains itself in it, in order to redeem the world through consciousness: "When I speak, death speaks in me. My speech is a warning that at this very moment death is loose in the world, that it has suddenly appeared between me, as I speak, and the being I address: it is there between us as the distance that separates us, but this distance is also what prevents us from being separated, because it contains the condition for all understanding. Death alone allows me to grasp what I want to attain; it exists in words as the only way they can have meaning. Without death, everything would sink into absurdity and nothingness" (*PF*, 313; *WF*, 323–24).

The carnivorous nature of consciousness casts doubt upon the possibility of "unmediated vision," but it is also a provocation in its behalf.[29] Thus, like Ponge, and partly in response to him, Blanchot seeks to take the side of things against consciousness by figuring literature as a refusal of speech as predication, or even as a self-refusal, that is, a refusal of the classical model of literature as representation—Blanchot will later call it "Le grand refus," or the "refusal of death."[30] In "Littérature et le droit à la mort" Blanchot writes (invoking Ponge): "The language of literature is a search for the moment that precedes literature. Literature usually calls it existence; it wants the cat as it exists, the pebble *taking the side of things*, not man but the pebble, and in this pebble what man rejects by saying it" (*PF*, 316; *WF*, 327). The key to taking the side of things lies in "the materiality of language": in literature "language . . . tries to become senseless. Everything physical takes precedence: rhythm, weight, mass, shape, and then the paper on which one writes, the trail of the ink, the book. Yes, happily, language is a thing: it is a written thing, a bit of bark, a sliver of rock, a fragment of clay in which the reality of earth continues to exist" (316–17; 327–28). By thickening language, interrupting the dialectic of signification, literature lets things be, preserves their self-subsistence. Literature now is no longer a form of mediation through which a writer expresses himself: "Literature now dispenses with the writer: it is no longer this inspiration at work, this negation asserting itself, this idea inscribed in the world as though it were the absolute perspective of the world in its totality. It is not beyond the world, but neither is it the world itself: it is the presence of things before the world exists, their perseverance after the world has disappeared, the stubbornness of what remains when everything vanishes and the dumbfoundedness of what appears when nothing exists" (317; 328).

"Literature now dispenses with the writer": but Blanchot's writer, unlike Mallarmé's or Foucault's, does not die—cannot die in the nature of the case. It is precisely here that Blanchot's interest in literature engages its subject: What is it for the writer to experience this moment ("before the world exists"—"after the world has disappeared") when the language of literature interrupts the dialectic that transforms things into concepts? What is it to experience the disappearance or cessation of mediation? On Blanchot's analysis it is like experiencing the interruption of the temporal order of things, which is to say, their passage into the future (or is it into the past?—does anyone know which way time moves?). In any event the past recedes into an ineffably ancient time that never was, and the future, like the Messiah, never arrives: time before αρχε (*arche*) and after τελοσ (*telos*), "a time that can no longer redeem us, that constitutes no recourse" (*EC*, 163; *IC*, 44), the interminable interval of dying, waiting, suffering, wandering (errancy)—and writing. The spatial equivalent of such an interval would be a surface without volume, pure exteriority uncorrelated with any interior: the space of exile ("the Outside"). The disappearance of mediation means being exposed to such a space, which Blanchot doesn't hesitate to call "the space of literature" and which has nothing to do with literary form but is rather the space inhabited or, more accurately, traversed — or, more accurately still, *experienced* — by the one who writes.

So what is writing? According to the temporality of the *entretemps*, it would be speech that is foreign to the category of completion: the fragment — speech that interrupts the dialectical movement of signification.[31] It is freedom from mediation (that is, not autonomy but the freedom of things from subjection to consciousness). Let me conclude by suggesting a symmetry between this kind of speech and Hartman's "imageless vision," because what Blanchot tries to imagine, and to achieve, is speech that breaks with the category of seeing altogether. This break is announced in an essay from 1957, "Parler, c'est ne pas voir," which is a dialogue in which one voice asks another what it is searching for and which the other struggles tortuously to answer with an idea that speech is not a way of picturing the world: "Speaking is not seeing. Speaking frees thought from the optical imperative that in the Western tradition, for thousands of years, has subjugated our approach to things, and induced us to think under the guaranty of light or under the threat of its absence. I'll let you count all the words through which it is suggested that, to speak truly, one must think according to the measure of the eye" (*EI*, 38; *IC*, 27). Most of literature, to be sure, is ocularcentric: "The novelist lifts up the rooftops and gives his characters over to a penetrating gaze" (40; 29). But what Blanchot's voice seeks is speech outside the alternatives of light and darkness: "A speech such that to speak would no longer be to unveil with light. Which does not imply that we would want to go in search of the joy, or horror, of the absence of the day: just the contrary; we would want to arrive at a mode of 'manifestation,' but a manifestation that would not be one of veiling-unveiling. Here what reveals itself does not give itself up to sight, just as it does not take refuge in simple invisibility" (41; 29).

Can things manifest themselves otherwise than as phenomena? In the dialogue I have been citing a voice considers the duplicity of the image, which is not a duplication of a thing but an "initial division that then permits the thing to be figured; still further back than this doubling it is a folding [*ploiement*], a turn of the turning, the 'version' that is always in the process of inverting itself and that in itself bears the back and forth of a divergence. The speech of which we are trying to speak is a return to this first turning — a noun that must be heard as a verb, as the movement of a turning, a vertigo wherein rest the whirlwind, the leap and the fall" (*EI*, 42; *IC*, 30). This is a bit dense, but the effect is to displace the image from the order of the visible/invisible onto the order of figuration as a turn of speech away from what is straightforward and continuous toward "an interrupted line that turns about in a coming and going" (42; 30)—"the voice of the shuttle" is Hartman's term for it, borrowed from Sophocles (*Beyond Formalism*, 337), as in the pun in which multiple and heterogeneous words resonate within the same phonetic interval.

Blanchot calls this "plural speech," or "the speech of writing," or the "non-dialectical experience of speech" (*EI*, 90; *IC*, 63). In fact, he has a bagful of names for it, but basically what he is looking for is speech that is nonviolent—that is, a speech outside possibility where possibility is a category of power. In "Comment découvrir l'obscur" (1959) Blanchot writes: "When I speak I always exercise a relation of force [*puissance*]. I belong, whether or not I know it, to a network of powers of which I make use, struggling against the force that asserts itself against me. All speech is violence, a violence that is already exerted upon what the word names and that it can name only by withdrawing presence from it—a sign, as we have seen, that death speaks (the death that is power) when I speak" (60; 42). Plural speech accomplishes the impossible, where "impossibility—a relation escaping power—is the form of relation with the immediate" (54; 38). One could say that plural speech restores the "immediate presence" of things, that is, the presence of things without mediation—"presence of the non-accessible, presence excluding or exceeding any present. This amounts to saying: the immediate, infinitely exceeding any present possibility by its very presence, is the infinite presence of what remains radically absent, a presence in its presence always infinitely other, presence of the other in its alterity" (54; 38). Vertiginous language, as Blanchot admits. It were better to say that such speech restores *us* to an intimacy with things by removing us from the modality of the present, that is, from site of the spirit, or consciousness, or the disengaged punctual ego: "The immediate is a presence to which one cannot be present, but from which one cannot separate; or, again, it is what escapes by the very fact that there is no escaping it: the *ungraspable that one cannot let go of*" (65; 45).

Perhaps this would be what poetry means: knowing how to enter into the *present* of things whose presence is no longer present to view—knowing, if such a thing is possible, how to live outside of consciousness. Hartman calls it learning how "to accept and live the lack of mediation" (*UV*, 173). The stress should be on living. If there is such a thing as "unmediated vision," or poetic knowledge, it would have to be a knowledge of *how*, not *what*, things are, which means a knowledge of how to abide with them. On this line of thinking, poetic knowledge is, classically, a species of practical or, if you like, moral wisdom.

CHAPTER SIX

Wordsworth's Horse

Robert J. Griffin

> For all the objects of our manifold experience, for every unity, there is an action of the mind which cuts off roots, melts away context—or indeed we should never have objects or ideas or anything to talk about.
>
> —WIMSATT AND BEARDSLEY, "The Intentional Fallacy"

The text I consider here is a brief sixteen lines, a self-contained incident intended by Wordsworth as one of several illustrations of the principle that Nature works in ways similar to the Imagination. Originally related to the epiphany on Snowdon, these lines, composed in early 1804 as part of the expansion of *The Prelude*, were left in manuscript and came to light only in the De Selincourt edition:

One evening, walking in the public way,
A peasant of the valley where I dwelt
Being my chance companion, he stopped short
And pointed to an object full in view
At a small distance. 'Twas a horse, that stood
Alone upon a little breast of ground
With a clear silver moonlight sky behind.
With one leg from the ground the creature stood,
Insensible and still; breath, motion gone,
Mane, ears, and tail, as lifeless as the trunk
That had no stir of breath. We paused awhile

In pleasure of the sight, and left him there,
With all his functions silently sealed up,
Like an amphibious work of Nature's hand,
A borderer dwelling betwixt life and death,
A living statue or a statued life.[1]

It's a wonderful passage, and as Jonathan Wordsworth noted, characteristically Wordsworthian.[2] Coleridge might have said of it what he said of another, more famous passage: "Had I met these lines running wild in the deserts of Arabia, I should have instantly screamed out 'Wordsworth!' "[3] I propose to review briefly two approaches to reading the Horse passage and suggest a third. The first two approaches—broadly, humanist and antihumanist—are those of Geoffrey Hartman and Mary Jacobus. Hartman gives us Wordsworth "from the inside," as Paul de Man remarked; the poet's point of view is reconstructed and the poems are read in the spirit with which they were written.[4] While many consider this kind of hermeneutic essential to the critic's task, few have done it as well as Hartman. Jacobus's penetrating feminist-deconstructive reading, however, participates in a line of inquiry that precisely disputes the poet's point of view, frequently by investigating in the poems what lies outside the range of represented consciousness as well as inquiring into strategic absences. In the discussion that follows, I propose to return to Hartman and make use of his discussion of the role of the "after-image," to put forward an intertextual reading of the Wordsworthian Imagination.[5]

Hartman nowhere offers an explicit reading of the Horse passage, but since he refers to it in a note as further illustration of what he means by the term "boundary image," the outlines of a Hartmanian reading can be surmised by applying the principles of his general interpretation.[6] It would go something like this. The drama that Wordsworth relates in *The Prelude* is the conflict between Imagination and Nature. "Imagination," here, must first of all be understood as a synonym for self, or spirit, or self-consciousness and not as the sympathetic imagination. The resolution of the conflict between self-consciousness and the external world occurs in certain key moments by means of the kind of blending found in the Horse passage, in which the visionary (the intuition of the next world) is bound very purposefully to the natural image (the encounter with a sleeping horse in moonlight). Thus, the momentary stasis of the halted traveler, matched in this case by the sight of the static horse, leads not to a dangerous fixation but to a moment of redemptive insight. Even though many readers will be familiar with the terms of this interpretation, let me expand as a way of providing context before returning to the passage in detail.

Wordsworth's dilemma, according to Hartman, is both historical and ethical. The poet of radical Protestant sensibility in a post-Enlightenment world—an environment in which Collins had expressed the conflict between "false themes and gentle minds"—Wordsworth could not resort directly to romance and visionary poetry, as had Spenser and Milton, but was caught between Imagination, on one hand, and Nature, on the other. Subject matter and style were intimately bound up with the question of poetic identity: to let Imagination run loose would sin against Wordsworth's natural reserve and produce the bad taste of the Gothic; imagination would overreach Nature and seek extreme, apocalyptic moments in which it could see itself, as it were, face to face. Yet there was danger on the other side as well. If the Imagination became too closely fixated on the natural image and on place, if it never emerged and understood its own autonomy, it ran the danger of premature death, which Hartman sees as the outcome in the parable of the Boy of Winander. While Gothic was not tenable, neither could Wordsworth become a realist like Crabbe, whose images of human life were not sufficiently veiled by imaginative redemption.[7]

Ultimately, the Imagination must not only come into full self-consciousness, as in the Simplon Pass apostrophe of *Prelude* 6, but must also reintegrate itself with Nature, not simply as an ethical and stylistic imperative, an avoidance of extremes, but as a necessary means to regeneration. The Imagination can be renewed only by going out of itself and interacting with external images, none better than those given by the continually shifting images and sounds of Nature as registered by eye and ear (with the ear given special preeminence as a counterforce to the potential tyranny of the eye). This dialectic between self and natural world creates a human middle space, poetry, in which neither is given precedence yet each is given its due. Once set in motion as a dialectic, then, Nature itself leads the Imagination beyond Nature, but only as a means of teaching it to respect natural limits, for the very fabric of sensibility, memory, and identity is woven out of the interplay between mind and nature. The focus on place and origin, essential to the health of the feelings, thus leads, not to a fundamentalist attachment and obsession, but to an expansion that respects place while going beyond it. Imagination thus naturally produces the sympathetic imagination as self-love expands outward in concentric circles to "love of man."

This complex of ideas rests on traditional religious and metaphysical assumptions. The dialectic presupposes (or posits) an underlying continuity, which

Hartman identifies in the idea of the "light of nature."[8] The light in nature is continuous with the light in man, both being manifestations of a divine light: inanimate, animal, and human are linked together by the larger creative spirit of which each is a part. Nature is that which heals the wound of alienated consciousness because it is perceived to be a source; yet in its more refined guise as Spirit, another version of source, it consoles by intimating that we have one foot in eternity.[9]

The image of the horse in MS. W exemplifies the ideal blend; in the poet's words, it is "an amphibious work of Nature's hand, / A borderer dwelling betwixt life and death." In this moonlight vision, the poet reads a gentle intimation of his fate in another world and yet remains in this one. Whatever suggestion there may be in the moonlit horse of night-mare or of Gothic (death-in-life, the living statue) is restrained, deflected, brought into balance by means of an opposite suggestion of a joyous epiphany, so that what is produced is a sublime whose terror has been effaced through its coalescence with the beautiful natural image. The horse as borderer is also a figure in miniature for the poem itself, poised between Nature and Imagination, as also for the poet, who stands in for humanity, poised between matter and spirit, a "mesocosm."[10]

Later criticism opened up avenues of approach that do not so much refute this reading of the relation of Imagination to Nature as revalue its terms. It is possible, for instance, to recognize the dynamics of the bordering we see in Wordsworth's Horse in Christopher Norris's exposition of aesthetic ideology as the "hypostatic union supposedly vouchsafed to poetic imagination by the language of metaphor and symbol, a language that not only transcends the distinction between subject and object (or mind and nature), but which also marks the point of intersection between word and world, time and eternity, the creaturely realm of causal necessity and the realm of free-willing autonomous spirit."[11] Such a "critique of idealism" brought to bear on early-nineteenth-century poetry asks corrosive questions about what may be meant by the word "Nature."[12] The issue is not whether such a thing as nature (oceans, mountains, etc.) exists outside of language, but what role the word "nature" plays as a signifier within a particular culture, or, further, which of its many denotations are filtered out when it becomes aestheticized within a particular network of significations. Nature in poetry, as in language generally, is unavoidably a cultural artifact. "Nature," in this line of thinking, is Culture's sign for what is noncultural, and as such it is in fact constituted by that (culture) which it is its function to deny. In Wordsworth's case, Nature, as the necessary and regenerating link to place and sentiment and tradition, as that which underwrites the continuity of the self and heals its inner division, appeared simply to ratify the current social order.[13]

Working within this radical shift in critical perspective, Mary Jacobus briefly reads the image of the sleeping horse in a chapter on the climactic Snowdon episode of *The Prelude* (see Appendix A for the text of 13.60–94).[14] Jacobus draws our attention to the way that an apparent metaphor — the vision on the mountain top "appeared to [him] / The perfect image of a mighty mind" — quickly becomes an analogy between kindred powers. Nature, so goes the claim, was the "express / Resemblance . . . made visible — a genuine counterpart / And brother" of the highest faculty of the human mind. Moreover, "Such minds are truly from the Deity, / For they are powers" ("Afterword," 106–7). Thus, it is not that the human mind knowingly projects its own dynamics onto nature but that nature itself has a mind of its own analogous to the human, and the source of both is divine.

An early draft of parts of this passage from Book 13 was discovered in MS. W together with roughly a hundred lines meant to illustrate this key notion of "analogy," the Horse passage being one of several "living pictures":

> Oft tracing this analogy betwixt
> The mind of man and Nature, doth the scene
> Which from the side of Snowdon I beheld
> Rise up before me, followed in turn
> By sundry others, whence I will select
> A portion, living pictures, to embody
> This pleasing argument.
>
> (Norton *Prelude*, 497)

Focusing on the word "analogy" from MS. W, Jacobus explains: "Analogy is a term that elides or erases metaphoricity by attempting to claim an actual or essential reality for what is figurative, and so rendering the fictions of the creating mind as if they were independently existing entities" ("Afterword," 267). The sleight-of-hand of the poetry, Jacobus observes, is that it posits a "naturalized analogy, or trope masquerading as essence" (291). In exposing the anthropomorphism that gives Nature a human mind, Jacobus offers a very close reading of both the completed Snowdon episode and the "living pictures" of MS. W by drawing upon two related systems of thought: deconstruction's analysis of the ungrounded nature of human language and psychoanalysis's hypothesis of the need for the ego to defend itself against death by inventing wishful fictions to interpose a little ease. Because Jacobus reads the Horse somewhat esoterically as an allegory of language, "literally a figure for figurality, 'all his functions silently sealed up'" (280), it is worthwhile laying out some of the assumptions on which such a reading is based.

If, for Wordsworth, the horse is a figure for the human borderer between this world and the next, and for poetry as the appropriate middle space, Jacobus reads "human" and "poetry" in terms of the special predicament of language. In this view, language offers us no path beyond itself to a transcendent vision of the next world because the vision is itself the creation of language and exists only there. The gap between the sensible and the intellectual, matter and symbol, is unbridgeable.[15] In her account, human language always has recourse to figures that express language itself, not the world. But if language (figuration) constitutes the human realm of culture and subjectivity, it also decenters individuals within that order, because the conditions that enable language (and self-consciousness) to operate, so the theories argue, are self-division, abstraction, and privation (the sign is structured by the absence of the referent).[16] The traditional counterpart to these notions is the distinction between the physical and the intellectual eye. Milton's blindness is a useful example. Privation of the senses is compensated for by an intensity of spiritual vision: "So much the rather thou Celestial Light / Shine inward" (*Paradise Lost*, 3.51–52).[17] The difference, of course, between the humanist and the antihumanist understanding of this structural privation is vast. In antihumanist discourse, this filling of the empty space with a reassuring content is no more than wish fulfillment, the ego's defense against the knowledge of impending dissolution. Metaphors, existing only in language, are not a foundation for metaphysical claims, hence the complex of ideas that makes up the "light of nature" are not a description of reality, merely a consoling trope.

Wordsworth's horse, which is meant to illustrate a moment of equilibrium between the natural, the human, and the divine, in Jacobus's reading becomes an emblem of the attempt to stabilize that which admits of no pause. In its state of suspended animation, the horse is a figure for language's abstraction from objects but also for the narrator's futile attempt to circumscribe language, to make it halt, to ground figures in "nature" when in fact their very existence is due to their being separate from nature. The doubleness of the horse, its amphibiousness, derives from the precarious nature of language as both home to humans and condition of their exile. The attempt to have it only one way, however, to posit the ground of language as stable rather than as constantly shifting as contexts and conventions change, is the purpose of Wordsworth's myth of nature. In grounding figuration by making it *analogous* to nature, the poet defends subjectivity against that which would undo its sense of its own centeredness. What is at stake, ultimately, is the stability of the autobiographical self which, through the narrative that is the poem, attempts to give significance to its own existence. Like the mind that is externalized by projecting its own reflection onto Nature, thus becoming an object of aesthetic contemplation, the horse is an externalized object of aesthetic reflection in which we can now read both the fear of death and the illusory calming of that fear.

Hartman's and Jacobus's reading are distinct and, indeed, opposed. Whereas Hartman explicates Wordsworth's text, Jacobus reads Wordsworth against his own intentions. The dispute, ultimately, is over fundamental beliefs, in this specific case about the nature of "Imagination." If, for Wordsworth, Imagination is a mode of revelation which gives insight into the invisible world, for Jacobus it is a narcissistic defense, and the figures the text provides (breach, abyss, mirror imagery) ("Afterword," 271ff.) tell us more about the narrator's psychological dynamics than they do about the constitution of the universe.

Nonetheless, we are not necessarily stranded at an impasse. There is a way the imagination works, and can be shown to work specifically in the Horse passage, that neither Hartman's nor Jacobus's strategies directly develops. In the humanist reading the Imagination establishes a relation to external objects, such as mountains, trees, streams, rocks, flowers, and, in this case, a horse.[18] For Jacobus, the relation to objects encodes an allegory of the psyche's internal fears and conflicts, which is to say, it is an allegory of "textuality," with the entire complex of notions which that word bears in poststructuralist thinking. Yet, for all their differences, we can see how an intertextual account of the imagination enables us to recognize poetry as itself "a borderer dwelling betwixt life and death." Whatever its relation to external objects, the poetry manifests relations between texts, and in this sense my view accords with the antihumanist understanding of "nature" as a textual construct. Yet, as will be seen, this view is not completely alien to what Wordsworth himself says, both in prose and in poetry, about the workings of the imagination. That is, when Wordsworth describes the relation between mind and nature he describes as well the relation between his and a prior text, and for this reason Hartman's account of Wordsworth remains suggestive.[19]

It is important to note that Jacobus brings into her argument another phrase from Wordsworth which recalls the description of the horse, but she treats it as a further example of her thesis. Her interpretation of the horse focuses on a specific line: the horse is amphibious, neither dead nor alive, because it is "literally a figure for figurality, 'all his functions silently sealed up'" ("Afterword," 280).

Jacobus adduces a line from Book 1 of *The Prelude* in which a similar phrasing is used, the passage in which the poet laments his crisis of inspiration, which is "a similar functional privation or blankness ('a more subtle selfishness, that now / Doth lock up my functions in blank reserve,' 1. 247–48)" (280–81). The question must then be asked: "What does Wordsworth's inability to get launched on his autobiographical poem have in common with a sleeping horse? The answer may well be a suspension of lived, empirical experience . . . paradoxically the very suspension enjoined by figurality" (281).

It is germane to Jacobus's approach to ask what these two passages have in common, and both are interpreted in similar terms as allegories of language. I am more intrigued by the differences between these passages and wonder how or why one got transferred, transported as it were, from one place to another. Further, what would an analysis of the two passages tell us about the workings of the imagination? To begin thinking through these issues, I shall quote at greater length the appropriate lines from Book 1:

> Humility and modest awe themselves
> Betray me, serving often for a cloak
> To a more subtle selfishness, that now
> *Doth lock up my functions in blank reserve,*
> That with a false activity beats off
> Simplicity and self-presented truth.
> (1805, 1.245–50, my emphasis)

This condition of frustration and near-despair, of feeling ambition without feeling concomitantly the power to act, at odds with oneself and acutely feeling *that*, is the famous antecedent to "this" in lines that follow shortly afterward: "Was it for this / That one, the fairest of all rivers, loved / To blend his murmurs with my nurse's song" (272f). And, of course, with this reflective turn to the sources of his early self, the poet finds his inspiration and theme. The functions that had been locked up are now, as sources of power, unlocked.

Perhaps the first thing one notices in reading these lines from Book 1 together with the Horse passage from MS. W are the different emotional valences. In one passage, the poet is empty, in the other, full. In one, he spins his wheels, in the other he is engaged. And most noticeably, in one it is the *poet's* functions that are sealed up, whereas in the other it is the horse's. More accurately, there is a slight verbal shift: in Book 1, the functions are "lock[ed]," whereas in MS. W they are "sealed." In any case, when applied to the poet, the valence is negative and signals the lack of imaginative and visionary power; when applied to the horse, however, the same phrase signals precisely a visionary power in the poet-observer, because the horse's suspended state becomes a kind of portal through which the imagination sees beyond the border of human life.[20]

But we can extend the relation further. Consciously or not, Wordsworth's imagination had recovered a line from another poet:

> So slow th' unprofitable Moments roll,
> *That lock up all the Functions of my soul;*
> That keep me from Myself; and still delay
> Life's instant business to a future day.
> (39–42; my emphasis)

This is Pope's *The First Epistle of the First Book of Horace, Imitated* (1738).[21] The emotional tenor of Pope's lines is quite close to that of Book 1, but by revising the key line (to read "Doth lock my functions up in blank reserve") and transporting the emotion directly into his own poem, Wordsworth has substituted himself for Pope. In MS. W, however, the word sequence is further from Pope and the emotional valence has been transformed altogether. Apparently, having domesticated Pope's line as his own, Wordsworth then simply revised *himself*.[22]

I am not interested, at the moment, in pursuing Wordsworth's relation to Pope, the implications of which for literary history and the ways literary history has been written I have addressed elsewhere.[23] Rather, I am interested, in a passage whose topic is the Imagination, in how the Imagination moves a line from one context to another, and here we can take our cues from Wordsworth's description of a similar movement in the Two-Part *Prelude* of 1799.

Importantly, Wordsworth gives us two versions of the relations of experience to memory and imagination: in the first, sense impressions are closely bound up with affections, and, in the second, they are dissociated from them and transferred to others. In the first, we are told of scenes that "did at length / Become habitually dear, and all / Their hues and forms were by invisible links / Allied to the affections" (Two-Part *Prelude*, First Part, 429–42). Yet there is also a countermovement. If imagination is nourished and inspired by memory, it is also the case that images cannot be strictly bound to a particular set of affections without diminishment. Imagination is also mobile; it is a horse that takes flight. Thus, only a hundred or so lines earlier in the Two-Part *Prelude*, at the conclusion of the Drowned Man episode, the narrator had told us:

I might advert
To numerous accidents in flood or field,
Quarry or moor, or 'mid the winter snows,
Distresses and disasters, tragic facts
Of rural history, that *impressed my mind*
With images to which in following years
Far other feelings were attached—with forms
That yet exist with independent life,
And, like their archetypes, know no decay.
(279–87; my emphasis)

What follows this, as illustration, are the famous "spots of time," each concerned, like the Drowned Man incident, with specters of death. Yet the imagination, proactive in its own defense, converts these images into sources of strength. Susan Wolfson comments that this reattachment of images to other feelings "not only revises, but re-verses the original impression" in turning landscapes of death and loss into archetypes of immortal life. Thus she speaks of an "immunized imagination," which aestheticizes loss by "shifting the genre from tragedy to romance, the idealizing discourse of 'purest poesy' " (Wolfson, 121, 124, 112).

Something of this process—original attachment followed by recontextualization—is captured in the Wordsworthian phenomenon Hartman has called the "after-image." In this process, the "mind not only recalls the past but also responds once more to what it has recalled. . . . There is the question of the poet's original recognition, and then of his insight as he tells, so to say, his story back to himself. The two do not coincide in all respects."[24] Hartman's discussion is detailed and nuanced, but for my own purposes I focus on the basic structure: the after-image can establish continuity with an earlier experience and thus act like the "renovating influence of nature" (*Wordsworth's Poetry*, 270), but it also may work to suggest "a possible discontinuity" (271). It is crucial to observe that this analysis of the after-image occurs as part of an exposition of the "prothalamic" imagination, "which brings together not only man and woman, but also myth and reality, human and divine, nature and human nature." This general drive toward unity and continuity, however, is not untroubled by what Hartman calls the "terror of discontinuity" (268). Yet, ultimately, in the example "Resolution and Independence," the "poem's high point comes not at the end but at the beginning, when the heart *is* renewed and enters the recollected image" (273), hence disarming and containing any real threat.

If we shift our focus, however, from a recollected image to a recollected chain of words, as in the case of the description of the horse in MS. W, what we have is an after-*text*. In this instance and at this level, however, rather than feeling terror at the possibility of a discontinuity in nature (a euphemism for death), it is the imagination itself that introduces discontinuity by transplanting a word-complex to another context and attaching to it far other feelings. Yet discontinuity at the level of an intertextual transposition is placed in the service of continuity at the level of theme. The halted observer perceives the horse as a borderer between two realms and thus also as the point of continuity between them. But the pegasus that speeds words from one context to another is a borderer between two texts; once we are aware of this movement it is the displacement that appears most salient, for the second text does not merely stencil the first. The creativity consists in significant difference. In some cases the transposition is effected by only a slight displacement; in others, very little trace of the original context remains. When we speak of something being "characteristically Wordsworthian," this almost instinctual power to make words his own no matter what the source, I would argue, is one of the things we mean.

An odd self-reflexivity, perhaps inevitable when we use language to talk about language, can be observed in Wordsworth's descriptions of the imagination. They simultaneously enact what they describe. An example is the final fate of Pope's phrase in the precincts of Snowdon. The Horse passage, as noted earlier, one of a series of "living pictures" intended to illustrate the workings of the imagination on Snowdon, was not included in either the 1805 or the 1850 versions of *The Prelude*, but remained in manuscript form. The word "function," however, one of the pivotal words from Pope's original phrase about mental functions, did find its way into the final Snowdon version:

—above all,
One *function* of such mind had Nature there
Exhibited by putting forth, and that
With circumstances most awful and sublime:
That domination which she oftentimes
Exerts upon the outward face of things,
So moulds them, and endues, abstracts, combines,
Or by abrupt and unhabitual influence

Doth make one object so impress itself
Upon all others, and pervades them so,
That even the grossest minds must see and hear,
And cannot chuse but feel.

(1805, 13.73–84)

I read this as a description of the workings of the poetic imagination, whose material must first of all be language. The word "function" itself, we can now see, was abstracted from its original context, molded, combined, endued, and subordinated to other objects by the domination of the very power that the poet describes.

What is true of poetic meditations on the workings of the imagination is true also of prose arguments, especially Wordsworth's discussion of imagination in the Preface to the 1815 edition of his poems, with its close analysis of the word "hang." This text lies behind de Man's focus on the use of "hang" in the Boy of Winander in "Time and History in Wordsworth," an essay that, in turn, influenced Jacobus's allegory of figure as suspension. Jonathan Arac quotes Hartman's phrase for a negatively capable criticism that delays closure, "suspensive discourse," linking Hartman to the Wordsworth "who made a signature of the word 'hang.'"[25] Indeed, the poet's focus on this one word as an illustration of the power of figurative language generally, with examples from Virgil, Shakespeare, and Milton, one would have thought is characteristically Wordsworthian. Yet it appears that a critical essay published anonymously in the *British Magazine* in the early 1760s lies behind Wordsworth's, just as observations by the French historian and critic Charles Rollin (1661–1741) provided a point of departure for the anonymous critic (see Appendixes B and C). The evidence suggests that the focus on the word "hang" in Virgil, Shakespeare, and Milton was an eighteenth-century commonplace and might even have still been recognized as such by some of Wordsworth's first readers. That now we think of the word "hang" as a Wordsworthian signature is an effect of the very power that Wordsworth analyzes.

In closing, I want to elicit one more illustration of the way that great poets naturalize in their text words and phrases from other poets, such that the alien words become part of a seamless fabric. My example is from Keats's *Hyperion.* The Titans have fallen, overcome by the emerging Olympian Gods. In council, only Oceanus understands that what has happened to them is a repetition of what they themselves did to "Chaos and blank Darkness" (2.207). He thus attempts to persuade the Titans they must acquiesce in an eternal law:

"We are such forest-trees, and our fair boughs
Have bred forth, not pale solitary doves,
But eagles golden-feather'd, who do tower
Above us in their beauty, and must reign
In right thereof; for 'tis eternal law
That first in beauty should be first in might;
Yea, by that law, another race may drive
Our conquerors to mourn as we do now."

(2.224–31)

I had read this poem and this passage—I have to admit one of my favorites in English poetry—on several occasions before it struck me like lightning out of a clear sky. That eternal law, "that first in beauty should be first in might," was too familiar. Where did it come from? It was Keats's transposition of the heroic ethic as stated by Homer's Sarpedon in Pope's translation: "The first in Valour, as the first in place." But this line had also been fused together with Pope's parody of Sarpedon in Clarissa's speech in *The Rape of the Lock:* "Behold the first in virtue as the first in face." In Keats's fusion, beauty had become the measure of heroic dominion. Poets, apparently, like the gods, need no other excuse.

Their speech is, at any rate, an "amphibious" speech in which gods describe their lives in words uttered by someone else—their language being all the more theirs for having been that of another, or others. In the linguistic bordering of intertextuality the words themselves may not reconcile the human to the natural or simply call attention to their own opaque figurality. Instead, speech emerges less as a communion and communication than as an intertextual connection that delivers up language as an after-image. Language, in its intertextual representation, does not express, much less echo. Instead, it emblemizes the ways in which speakers are themselves—borderers dwelling betwixt life and death—in both their perceptions and their language.

APPENDIX A

As recounted at the beginning of The Prelude, *Book 13 (1805), the narrator and a friend began climbing Mount Snowdon one night with the intention of seeing the sunrise from its top. A "dripping mist" (11) surrounded them as they climbed. The dramatic moment occurs when, near the top, with a flood of moonlight illuminating the clouds they have just stepped above, they find themselves on the shore of "a huge sea of mist" (43), the real sea now "Usurped upon as far as sight could reach" (51). At a distance, through "a blue chasm, a fracture in the vapour" (56), roared the voice of "waters, torrents, streams / Innumerable" (58–59):*

The universal spectacle throughout
Was shaped for admiration and delight,
Grand in itself alone, but in that breach
Through which the homeless voice of waters rose,
That dark deep thoroughfare, had Nature lodged
The soul, the imagination of the whole.

A meditation rose in me that night
Upon the lonely mountain when the scene
Had passed away, and it appeared to me
The perfect image of a mighty mind,
Of one that feeds upon infinity,
That is exalted by an under-presence,
The sense of God, or whatsoe'er is dim

Or vast in its own being—above all,
One function of such mind had Nature there
Exhibited by putting forth, and that
With circumstance most awful and sublime:
That domination which she oftentimes
Exerts upon the outward face of things,
So moulds them, and endues, abstracts, combines,
Or by abrupt and unhabitual influence
Doth make one object so impress itself
Upon all others, and pervades them so,
That even the grossest minds must see and hear,
And cannot chuse but feel. The power which these
Acknowledge when thus moved, which Nature thus
Thrusts forth upon the senses, is the express
Resemblance—in the fullness of its strength
Made visible—a genuine counterpart
And brother of the glorious faculty
Which higher minds bear with them as their own.
This is the very spirit in which they deal
With all objects of the universe:
They from their native selves can send abroad
Like transformation. . . .

(60–94)

APPENDIX B

The following is excerpted from an anonymous essay titled "On Poetry, As Distinguished from Other Writing," part of a series of essays which originally appeared in the British Magazine *between 1761 and 1763. They were attributed to Oliver Goldsmith and included in the 1801 edition of his* Miscellaneous Works, *subsequently reprinted throughout the nineteenth century. My text is a late-nineteenth-century edition of Goldsmith; the editor Cunningham disputes the attribution to Goldsmith but prints the group in a section called "Unacknowledged Essays." See* The Works of Oliver Goldsmith, *ed. Peter Cunningham, 4 vols. (New York: Harper & Bros., 1881), 3:342–44. In a* PMLA *article of 1924, Caroline F. Tupper argued that the essays were written by Smollett. Part of her evidence was Goldsmith's ridicule of the use of the word "hang" in English poetry simply because Rollin had made such a point of praising Virgil's use of* pendere.

There are certain words in every language particularly adapted to the poetical expression; some from the image or idea they convey to the imagination, and some from the effect they have upon the ear. The first are truly *figurative;* the others may be called *emphatical.* Rollin observes that Virgil has upon many occasions poeticized (if we may be allowed the expression) a whole sentence by means of the same word, which is *pendere.*

Ita meae, felix quondam pecus, ite capellae,
Non ego vos posthac, viridi projectus in antro,
Dumosa pendere procul de rupe videbo.

At ease reclin'd beneath the verdant shade,
No more shall I behold my happy flock
Aloft *hang* browsing on the tufted rock.

Here the word *pendere* wonderfully improves the landscape, and renders the whole passage beautifully picturesque. The same figurative verb we meet with in many different parts of the *Aeneid.*

Hi summo in fluctu *pendent,* his unda *dehiscens*
Terram inter fluctus aperit.

Those on the mountain billow *hung;* to those
The *yawning waves* the yellow sand disclose.

In this instance, the words *pendere* and *dehiscens, hung* and *yawning,* are equally poetical. Addison seems to have had this passage in his eye when he wrote his Hymn, which is inserted in the *Spectator:*

For though in dreadful whirls we *hung,*
High on the broken wave.

And another piece of a like nature, in the same collection:

Thy providence my life sustain'd,
And all my wants redress'd,
When in the silent womb I lay,
And *hung* upon the breast.

Shakespeare, in his admired description of Dover Cliff, uses the same expression:

——half-way down
Hangs one that gather samphire dreadful trade!

Nothing can be more beautiful than the following picture, in which Milton has introduced the same figurative tint:

——he, on his side,
Leaning half-rais'd, with looks of cordial love
Hung over her enamour'd.

We shall give one example more from Virgil, to show in what a variety of scenes it may appear with propriety and effect. In describing the progress of Dido's passion for Aeneas, the poet says,

Iliacos iterum demens audire labores
Exposcit, *pendet*que iterum narrantis ab ore.

The woes of Troy once more she begged to hear;
Once more the mournful tale employed his tongue,
While in fond rapture on his lips she *hung*.

The reader will perceive, in all these instances, that no other word could be substituted with equal energy; indeed, no other word could be used without degrading the sense and defacing the image.

APPENDIX C

The following is excerpted from Wordsworth's discussion of the Imagination in the Preface to the 1815 edition of his poems. In a footnote to this passage, Owen and Smyser cite Caroline F. Tupper ("Essays Erroneously Attributed to Goldsmith," PMLA *39 [1924]: 325–42) and note the parallels between Wordsworth's essay and the one I have excerpted in Appendix A. See* The Prose Works of William Wordsworth, *ed. W. J. B. Owen and Jane Worthington Smyser, 3 vols. (Oxford: Clarendon Press, 1974), 3: 42.*

Imagination, in the sense of the word as giving title to a class of poems, has no reference to images that are merely a faithful copy, existing in the mind, of absent external objects; but is a word of higher import, denoting operations of the mind upon these objects, and processes of creation or of composition, governed by certain fixed laws. I proceed to illustrate my meaning by instances. A parrot *hangs* from the wires of his cage by his beak or by his claws; or a monkey from the bough of a tree by his paws or his tail. Each creature does so literally and actually. In the first Eclogue of Virgil, the Shepherd, thinking of the time when he is to take leave from his farm, thus addresses his goats:

> Non ego vos posthac viridi projectus in antro
> Dumosa *pendere* procul de rupe videbo.

> half way up
> *Hangs* one who gathers samphire,

is the well-known expression of Shakespeare delineating an ordinary image upon the cliffs of Dover. In these two instances is a slight exertion of the faculty which I denominate imagination, in the use of one word: neither the goats nor the samphire-gatherer do literally hang, as does the parrot or the monkey; but presenting to the senses something of such an appearance, the mind in its activity, for its own gratification, contemplates them as hanging.

> As when far off at Sea a Fleet descried
> *Hangs* in the clouds, by equinoctial winds
> Close sailing from Bengala or the Isles
> Off Ternate or Tydore, whence Merchants bring
> Their spicy drugs; they on the trading flood
> Through the wide Ethiopian to the Cape
> Ply, stemming nightly toward the Pole: so seem'd
> Far off the flying Fiend.

Here is the full strength of the imagination involved in the word, *hangs*, and exerted upon the whole image: First, the fleet, an aggregate of many ships, is represented as one mighty person, whose track, we know and feel, is upon the waters; but, taking advantage of its appearance to the senses, the Poet dares to represent it as *hanging in the clouds*, both for the gratification of the mind in contemplating the image itself, and in reference to the motion and appearance of the sublime object to which it is compared.

Part III / Representation and Terror

Proleptic Histories

CHAPTER SEVEN

The New Historicism and the Work of Mourning

Alan Liu

Imagine that a creature—let us leave it nameless, ageless, even specieless—drowns. The rope it had been clinging to slips away as the creature begins its slow descent to the tidal shelf twelve fathoms down. Here, on the pale bottom sands, the rough sea is only a massive but gentle surge. The body rocks back and forth on the sands, one arm half raised and adrift. Planking rains down nearby, one iron-bound section pinning the arm to the sand. Time passes and the soft parts of the body lose their definition, swell and break open bloodlessly against the planking and sand. The body becomes no longer quite a body; it is a body/plank/sand assemblage. Fish pick at the flesh and graze the algae on the plank. They become fish/body/algae assemblages. Shellfish, small crabs, other bottom-feeders join the ensemble. Microorganisms are at work, too, churning the mass's internal structure and chemistry, fusing certain tissues more tightly, disassembling others and offering their elements up to the seawater as a subtle scent.

At the end of six weeks, the body lies cradled in an encrusted, rooted, intricate matrix linked by thin trails of atoms (borne along tidal currents and fish migration paths) to a host of static and motile assemblages elsewhere—the total aggregate gradually propagating outward like a network of veins across the larger body that is the ocean.

Nothing of the original creature has been lost: not an atom.

Such is a fable of the death of John Wordsworth — last seen clinging to a rope, not washed ashore until after six weeks — imagined from a point of view incapable of the perception of loss. However much this point of view resembles the vision of "something far more deeply interfused, / Whose dwelling is the light of setting suns, / And the round ocean" (96–98) in "Tintern Abbey," we know that it would have been unfathomable to William Wordsworth. For in this fable there never was loss requiring abundant recompense. ("Our loss is one which never can be made up," "we know what we have lost," "my loss is great, and irreparable," Wordsworth's letters of early 1805 chant.)[1] In the vision of the universe-as-assemblage no organisms die to be redeemed in a transcendentally organic One Life. There are only assemblages passing into other assemblages.

But *we* know how to fathom this point of view because we recognize in it the makings of our modernity — or, more accurately, postmodernity. Freud and Weber (who may stand here for the modern) saw the dawning of that point of view. For them, the relevant universe — mind or society, respectively — was not so much organism as an "economy" or "system." The system was normally a closed one (to generalize Weber's image: an "iron cage"), and thus homeostatic, retentive, lossless. Energies flowed from one mental faculty or social institution to another, at times cathecting in pathologies and reifications; but the systemic economy as a whole neither gained nor lost. Psychically or socially significant charges thus did not come unmediated from pure exteriority ("Freud was definitely and remarkably immune to the sublime moment," Thomas Weiskel comments in remarking our modern skepticism of infinitude).[2] Rather, such energies came from other zones of the system. And reciprocally, charges never disappeared; they just went from *here* to *there*. However repressed, reified, or otherwise dysfunctional the system became, in short, all its essential being remained, waiting to be unpacked by the analyst.

Or perhaps we would do better in interpreting our fable to follow the French *post*modernists in saying that such "being" in the system — constantly shuttled to and fro from assemblage to assemblage — is not being at all but "happening." Lyotard and Deleuze/Guattari are apropos here (my fable of the body/plank/sand assemblage is thus recognizably "rhizomatic" and its very form alludes to Lyotard's "A Postmodern Fable").[3] But for present purposes I will cite only Jean-

Luc Nancy's essay "Finite History." Characterizing postmodernity as the end to history he calls "finite history," Nancy writes:

> *Finitude* does not mean that we are noninfinite—like small, insignificant beings within a grand, universal, and continuous being—but it means that we are *infinitely* finite, infinitely exposed to our existence as a nonessence, infinitely exposed to the otherness of our own "being." . . . We begin and we end without beginning and ending: without having a beginning and an end that is *ours*, but having (or being) them only as others', and through others. . . .
>
> What results is that *we happen*. . . . We are not a "being" but a "happening."[4]

The "we happen" Nancy celebrates here, we recognize, is the very declaration by which postmodernism frees itself from both the older "I am" of divine and Cartesian identity and the newer "we are" of modernity. While modernity had previously dispersed the "I" of that "I am" into a plural "we" of mental and social faculties governed by parental or bureaucratic apparatuses, it nevertheless insisted on saying in place of "I am," "the *system* is." The systemic "we," in other words, retained a residually organic "being" identified with the very systematicity of system—with the premise that there *is* such a thing as bounded, self-conserving system. "*We*" are the system of mental and social regimes that create the hegemony of *a* mind or society. Postmodernism, on the other hand, completes the dismantling of the "I am" by then subtracting even the "are" from modernity's "we are" to leave only the finitely historical statement: "we happen." Sometimes we faculties and regimes happen to fall in with each other so as to seem *a* mind or society, that is, but sometimes we also happen to fall out so that mind or society deterritorializes. We are no longer a system whose ghost-in-the-machine is organic being; as the Borg might say, we are assemblage.[5]

And so from this infinitely finite perspective, John Wordsworth never "was," so how could he be lost? John Wordsworth was always a "we" or an assemblage whose boundaries overlapped constitutionally with that of other people, creatures, the sea itself. In becoming-sea and the creatures of that sea ("becoming animal, becoming woman, becoming intense," Deleuze/Guattari say in their mantra), he was still the happening or becoming he always was. He could have no end, because he also had no beginning.

"Organic and subjective our reading of Wordsworth once would have been,—'tis so no more; / We have submitted to a new control: / With the New Historicism a power is gone, which nothing can restore; / A deep distress hath humanized our

Soul. / Not for a moment could we now behold / A smiling sea and be what we have been: / The feeling of our loss will ne'er be old."[6]

This, I take it, is the fundamentally elegiac posture—not just about but *of* elegy—adopted by one of the most interesting critiques of the New Historicism in the romantic field. In 1993, Kevis Goodman, Clifton Spargo, and Leon Waldoff collaboratively addressed the topic "Wordsworth's 'Invisible Workmanship' and the Work of New Historicism" in a set of essays that took the New Historicism to task on grounds different from the now standard criticisms that it is neither positivistic enough as "history" nor textualist enough as "reading."[7] Conditioned by the antithesis of contextual and textual materials that has applied from the New Criticism through deconstruction, the standard criticisms have conformed to a fearful symmetry: either there is too much interpretive reading in New Historicist history (making it seem "metaphorical") or there is too much history in New Historicist reading (making it seem a vitiated deconstruction craving "reference"). In both cases, the debate has tended not to be very illuminating because it is at the level of first principles: the ships, as it were, pass in the night. By contrast, Goodman, Spargo, Waldoff, and other "post new historicists" (as they might be called) are willing to test the New Historicist premise that "historicism" is about the "reading of history" rather than either context or text in themselves; and that, therefore, advanced techniques of deconstructive interpretation can in principle be brought to bear on "absences" that are historically *there* (e.g., the nature of modern "debt" financing as determinedly *not* thematized in Wordsworth's "The Ruined Cottage"; the usurpative Napoleon *not* there in the Simplon Pass episode of *The Prelude*).[8] In the vocabulary of the New Historicism itself, what is there in a poem is precisely what is not there: all the history that has been displaced, erased, suppressed, elided, overlooked, overwritten, omitted, obscured, expunged, repudiated, excluded, annihilated, and denied.[9]

But having tested the principle, post new historicists find that the New Historicism comes up short even in its own terms. "Look at all we *lose* when we read in this manner" they object, voicing a plaint that a common thematization of drowned men allows me to pose as elegiac. (Goodman's essay centers on the Drowned Man episode in Book 5 of *The Prelude;* while Spargo's and Waldoff's essays focus on Wordsworth's "Elegiac Stanzas Suggested by a Picture of Peele Castle.") Look at all the historical matter, in other words, that the New Historicism itself displaces to concentrate on just the most dramatic displacements of history in literature—displacements on the scale of Napoleon or above.

What is lost? Each of the post-new-historicist essays I refer to has its own trajectory, so any generalization I can offer will be a compromise. But I believe we can understand the shared work of mourning that is their project by saying that all grieve for the loss of *personal* history. "Personal" here is not at all synonymous with "subjective." Indeed, far from trying to reclaim the "I am," Goodman, Spargo, and Waldoff hold a seat at the table for a concept as much the deconstruction as construction of the subject. We can call this concept, broadly, the pragmatics of subjectivity. It may well be that the subject is epistemologically and ontologically a white mythology, in other words, but then our essayists cannily look just *to one side* of the subject (as if just to the left or right of the blinding sun) to show that there exists a corona of subjectivity-effects not the same as public history but also not exactly nothing. The New Historicism, in other words, perhaps commits the fallacy of the excluded middle: the universe is not completely distributed between the nothingness of an illusory Subject (to be discounted) and the somethingness of Napoleonic history (to be recovered). Also happening is the history of intra- and interpersonal communication, relation, negotiation, and responsibility—a work of communicative action (as Habermas might put it) that not only cannot occur in solitude (in this sense, the personal is the antonym of subjectivity) but is the very means for converting the Subject from Being into a "being-*in*" the historical world. Thus Goodman looks to one side of the Subject to appreciate the personal "responsiveness" to history fostered by words that euphemistically—that is, pragmatically—allow us to cope, make, do, live in history. So, too, Spargo sights to one side of the Subject to underscore subjectivity's necessarily self-undermining, ethical openness to alterity. "The personal is no longer an extension of the poet's self-interest in the world—his harmonizing or totalizing self," he says, "but signifies the other and requires response and justice." And similarly, Waldoff looks past the Subject to glimpse the work of the subjectivity-effect he calls (with some analogy to Spargo on "alterity") the "transitional self."

Much is valid in such a post-new-historicist critique of the New Historicism. One can at this point only await the completion of these lines of thought to see what new expanses of history—perhaps a history of romantic privacy, everyday life, and ethics—will in fact be brought to the table to broaden the taste of the New Historicism for Napoleons. And much there is to question, too. Most urgent, I believe, is the way in which such critique—centered in this case specifically on "Wordsworth's 'Invisible Workmanship'"—participates indirectly in one of the major intellectual adventures of our time: the sudden rescoring of issues of labor in the postmarxist key of "practice." Somehow, it might be suggested, the romance of pragmatism that makes de Certeau's tricky "individual" walking around the city in a personal way one with the personalized subjects in the essays by Goodman, Spargo, and Waldoff, has seemed to justify literature as practical without thinking at all about that other evolution of labor in late-industrial economies: service (as in the Orwellian euphemism we so often hear today, "the service sector"). To prove that the practice of language is labor, perhaps, is now a hollow victory without also proving that the labor of words provides a service.

But I will here truncate my notice of the revisionary difference in such critique to observe, more fundamentally, that the post new historicists are also profoundly in concert with the New Historicism they criticize. What is common, I believe, and what positions them finally *with* the New Historicism as critics of the end of history, is an anxiety that may be called the fear of the loss of loss. After all, if the thematization of elegy in the essays by Goodman, Spargo, and Waldoff has allowed me to figure their project as the loss of the personal, that thematization should also prompt us to recognize that the New Historicism itself is all about—and of—loss. Both schools, in other words, rehearse loss. Let me rehearse again the dark brood of that method Marjorie Levinson calls "negative allegory": displacement, erasure, suppression, elision, overlooking, overwriting, omission, obscuration, expunging, repudiation, exclusion, annihilation, denial. Certainly there is a note of denunciation—even anger—in such criticism that views poetry as nothing but the loss of historical truth. But always also, I hazard, there comes a moment in the New Historicist denunciation when the critic's perception of lost history acknowledges that it has been strangely preempted by the perception of historical loss *in* the poetry itself—a moment, in other words, when the loss of history can no longer be spoken of as itself lost to the poet. In her "Elegiac Stanzas" essay, therefore, Levinson writes: the poem not only "consummates . . . displacement logic" but "turns around and *registers* what . . . has thereby [been] lost." "Far more profoundly and inclusively elegiac than we have guessed," she continues, "Elegiac Stanzas" is "*about* the loss of an order of referentiality . . . of a concept of external and independent otherness" (Levinson, 102; second emphasis mine).

This moment, when the critic of the loss of history suddenly sympathizes with the poet of the loss of history,[10] may be called the elegiac moment in the New Historicism—or, rather, the moment that opens the scene of elegy. In this moment of secret romantic ideology, all the critic's anger of denunciation turns into something else. It is incorporated within a critical work of mourning able to acknowledge that the poetry itself is a work of mourning and, as such, entitled to normative stages of displacement and repudiation on its way toward "registering" not just the loss of particular history but (and this is the deepest grief of the New Historicism) the fact that history considered universally *is* loss. History, as it were, is the perpetuation or retention of the process of loss. Thus, listen to the distinctively elegiac note that sounds the largest theses of history in romantic New Historicism: "All discourse may well be about loss," Levinson says in opening the final section of her "Elegiac Stanzas" essay, and continues: "Peele Castle is a reminder, indeed, the reification, of a *lost* Real" (128). And I have myself thrown ashes on the grave by saying: "History is the absence that is the very possibility of the 'here and now.' The reason poetic denial is ipso facto a realization of history . . . is that history is the very category of denial. It is history that says, 'This "is" but neither was nor will be.' Or in terms of social space: 'This is your place but was/is/shall be another's' " (Liu, 39).

In sum, what the essays I have referred to might teach us to see is that even more so than in the Renaissance field (which mourns "Elegiac Stanza's" "power [that] is gone" as the "subversive" marginality of literature) the New Historicism in the romantic field is primarily a form of elegy.[11]

What is the significance of such elegiasm? Let me close by recurring to the "lossless" assemblage-universe I began upon in order to map out—with the aid of Freud's "Mourning and Melancholia" piece—two antithetical, contemporary understandings of that universe. In Freud's terms, the French understanding of the postorganic/postsystemic world I previously sketched can be called "manic." At its best, French postmodern theory is about the joyous reinvention of the ethics, politics, and art of the closed world so that our "iron cage" will no longer *feel* so closed but instead radically open-ended, "free." "Freedom," Jean-Luc Nancy says, "shall be understood precisely as the proper character of the happening and exposure of existence. Not simply a way of being 'free' of causality or destiny, but a way of being *destined* to deal with them. . . . Freedom would mean: to have history, in its happening, as one's destiny" (Nancy, 157). Freedom in this acceptation, in other words, means learning how to be just, effective, and playful within the very interstices of contingency that constitute the assemblage-universe as an arbitrary system.

By contrast, New Historicism participates in what appears to be the major Anglo-American and Germanic understanding of postmodernity. It, too, dedicates itself to addressing the assemblage-universe. But its habit (matched by that of Jameson mourning the loss of "cognitive mapping" or Habermas the loss of "lifeworld") is the flip side of mania in Freud's schema: a mourning so existential as to be comparable to melancholia. "In what, now, does the work which mourning performs consist?" Freud asks, and then embarks upon the general theory of mourning (of which melancholia is the special case) in the following sentence: "Reality-testing has shown that the loved object no longer exists, and it proceeds to demand that all libido shall be withdrawn from its attachments to that object."[12] When the object is known to exist no longer, that is, *then* the proper work of mourning ensues. But the New Historicism cannot take it for granted that the loss of the object can be known, for "reality" itself is in this case the lost object and so cannot serve as the testing principle for its own loss. The project of verifying the "lostness" of the lost object, as a consequence, must be elevated from the status of a preliminary clause (as in Freud's sentence) and made the main work of New Historicist mourning.

Thus it is, we can conclude, that the most basic task of the New Historicism as a work of mourning is simply to verify the possibility of loss in an otherwise closed, lossless, posthistorical universe. The New Historicists say in essence, "we recognize that we live in a lossless world in which beneath every poetic denial the object denied can still be found, waiting to be unpacked by the analyst. But *even yet* we wish to believe that something significant is lost in the act of denial. For only if we conserve the possibility of real loss can we also hold the world open to the notion of real, and miraculous, gain. Thus shall we exaggerate the fiction of all-or-nothing, present-versus-absent history as an illusion saving the possibility that there can *be* absolute losses and absolute gains. This is the hope, the prophecy, of our elegy."

It remains to be seen whether the posture of mania or of mourning—the grand and abject poles, respectively, of the sublimity that postmodern theory has lately resumed—is the most ethical, political, and artistic stance to take in the face of the postmodern loss of loss.

Or less agonistically: we need not overdramatize the choice between these two postures because each draws secretly upon the other as its interior resource. Instructive in this regard is Lyotard's refusal to periodize the distinction between "regret" and "assay" in his "What Is Postmodernism?" piece. Modernism is that which expresses nostalgic "melancholia" in its sublime effort to present the "unpresentable" while postmodernism expresses "jubilation," Lyotard posits, but the "modern" versus "postmodern" pairing here is structural rather than diachronic: the two stances coexist in the same "condition" of postmodernity.[13] Moreover, they coexist not just on a global scale (the globe on which I crudely mapped a "French" sensibility alongside an "Anglo-American/Germanic" one) but locally: *within* the work of each theorizer of postmodernity. Thus, if the major key of such mourners of postmodernity as the New Historicists, Jameson, or Habermas is melancholia, their minor key is clearly a mania that keeps them skipping like weightless stones across vast reaches of historical material (thus the New Historicists study Napoleon *and* gypsies *and* family history *and* economics *and . . . and . . . and;* while Jameson studies postmodern architecture *and* video *and* painting *and* film *and* literature, etc.). And antithetically, if the major key of such maniacs of postmodernity as Lyotard is "jubilation," their minor key is clearly and keenly mourning—as in the paradigm of Auschwitz on the first page of Lyotard's *The Differend.*

To vary Lyotard's phrase, in short, it may be that melancholic "regret" and jubilant "assay" are the two faces of a single meditation on loss and history. Assay is haunted by regret; and regret finds itself open to assay—to a sublime effort to imagine the perdurance of loss. For us—here and now—it is loss that is the "unpresentable." "The nuance which distinguishes these two modes may be infinitesimal; they often coexist in the same piece, are almost indistinguishable; and yet they testify to a difference (*un différend*) on which the fate of thought depends and will depend for a long time, between regret and assay."[14]

CHAPTER EIGHT

Making Time for History

Wordsworth, the New Historicism, and the Apocalyptic Fallacy

Kevis Goodman

> ... gently hast thou told
> Thy message, which might in telling wound,
> And in performing end us.
>
> — ADAM TO MICHAEL, *Paradise Lost*

At the end of the fourth *Georgic*, Virgil rebukes himself for practicing the arts of "ignoble ease" (*studiis florentem ignobilis oti*) while the statesman, Octavian, is busy with the tasks of empire.[1] Like most modesty topoi, Virgil's apology is tinged with irony, as is the praise for Caesar. Yet few poets have remained free from questions about the worth of their labors, and as a genre the georgic has provided both occasion and outlet for vocational self-questioning. As other critics have recognized as well, Wordsworth is particularly vulnerable to this anxiety of indolence, ever asking himself a version of the question put to his leech-gatherer in "Resolution and Independence": "How is it that you live, and what is it that you do?" It is no coincidence, then, that Virgil's self reproach

This essay was first published in 1996, in conjunction with Alan Liu's accompanying "The New Historicism and the Work of Mourning," although both pieces had their genesis earlier, in a 1993 Modern Language Association panel. This article, here preserved essentially intact along with its original notes, took as its point of departure debates within the study of Wordsworth during the later 1980s and early 1990s. I have therefore appended a brief afterword, discussing the changes in the field, as well as the new directions in research that have been encouraged by the debate whose history is recorded herein.

haunts the first book of *The Prelude*, at once hopefully and defensively rendered in the form of an antonym to the phrase "*ignobilis oti*" from the *Georgics:*

> Meanwhile, my hope has been, that I might fetch
> Reproaches from my former years, whose power
> May spur me on, in manhood now mature,
> To honourable toil.
> (1799, 1.450–53; cf. 1805, 1.648–53; 1850, 1.621–26)[2]

Both directly and indirectly, an interest in work has also informed New Historicist readings of Wordsworth. There has been increased attention paid to the poetry's representation of physical labor, with the renewed popularity of the georgic as a related development within criticism. John Barrell's study of the pastoralization of georgic in eighteenth-century loco-descriptive verse, for example, had a direct impact on Marjorie Levinson's 1986 reading of Wordsworth "great period poems."[3] David Simpson brought to light the social and cultural pressures underlying Wordsworth's preoccupation with metaphors of property and labor, and Alan Liu, drawing in part from Kurt Heinzelman and Mark Shell, has sketched an "economy of lyric."[4] Moreover, this focus has shaded into concerns about poetry as a cultural production, poets as producers of culture, and poetry as a special form of historical action (or, depending on the perspective, inaction). Wordsworth's recent critics, in other words, have kept alive the poet's own double-edged question: "Is poetry honorable toil—that is, is it *honorable* and is it *toil?*" In doing so, as Liu has himself suggested in slightly different terms, they may embody a late-twentieth-century version of unease about "ignoble ease"—only now translated into the academy, and masking questions about the honor or productivity of the intellectual's labor.[5]

One answer that the New Historicism has given to questions about the poet's labor is now familiar. Liu comments that the "perfect primary text" for a New Historicist reading is "a text that on its surface [bears] the least possible affiliation with history in the everyday sense: a poem . . . as smooth of history as an effaced coin" (*Sense of History*, 637–38). The poem is therefore also an effacing coin, which "displaces," "occludes and disguises," or agonistically "denies" its own involvement in history, precisely and paradoxically when most engaged in ideological commitments. Thus the Romantic poem participates, wrote Jerome McGann with a deliberate pun, in " 'the Consciousness Industry'—a light industry . . . which the Romantics helped to found."[6] Where the Wanderer requests of the Pastor in *The Excursion*, "Give us, for our abstractions, solid facts" (*Exc.*, 5.637-38),[7] the New Historicism's Romantic poet produces, in return for solid facts, a great harvest of abstractions.

In the face of such erasures, the labor of the historical scholar has been restitutive as well as demystifying. He or she locates material omissions from the manifest surface of the poem, particularly those elided details that significantly shape the text because they are resumed at the level of image and metaphysics. Marjorie Levinson's statement of this Orphic project—where History is the lost Eurydice—is particularly vivid: "So smooth, sealed, and, in the language of 'Tintern Abbey,' *purified* a history does the poem develop, that history in the commoner sense . . . [has] no room to surface." She therefore advocates a criticism that seeks "to materialize a greatly idealized corpus; or, to locate the body in Wordsworth" (*Wordsworth's Great Period Poems*, 2, 12–13).

This critical act of reclamation, at least in its initial stages, frequently depended on the reversal or revision of the earlier terminology of Wordsworth studies. Reading Levinson and Liu together, one might be struck in particular by the reinterpretation of the dialectic between "apocalypse" and "akedah" first proposed by Geoffrey Hartman in 1964.[8] "Akedah," which in Hartman's work signaled a binding or tempering of consciousness by Nature, becomes associated with the distancing of socioeconomic and political history, as in Levinson's essay "Spiritual Economics" in "Michael."[9] And "apocalypse," particularly for Liu, becomes an encounter with historical reference: "Denial is the threshold of Wordsworth's most truly shocking act of Imagination: the sense of history. The true apocalypse will come when history crosses the zone of nature to occupy the self directly, when the sense of history and Imagination thus become one, and nature, the mediating figure, is no more" (*Sense of History*, 31). As Liu concludes, with answerable style, "The true apocalypse for Wordsworth is reference" (42).

Yet why should reference necessarily be apocalyptic—here or elsewhere in literature? There is, in much of the New Historicism, just such a bias, and in particular an assumption about the epiphanic structure of reference. This view emphasizes the all-or-nothing categories of presence and absence: if history is not to be denied, then it ought to be realized with its full dramatic or traumatic impact, untempered by the "mediating figure" of poetic language. It is true that in sophisticated arguments "denial" becomes a complex word of antithetical senses, so that "denial is also the strongest kind of engagement with history" (*Sense of History*, 35). Nevertheless, the New Historicism for the most part neglects the possibility of a history that is neither sharply represented nor denied.

Few studies thus far have really questioned the assumption that for the most part, except for the obviously topical pieces, Wordsworth's lyrics and lyrical narratives efface history. I want to do so, first by countering what I take to be the apocalyptic or epiphanic fallacy behind many historicist theories of poetic displacement. Then, in what follows, I intend something more than another critique or celebration of the New Historicism — both kinds of engagements already abound.[10] I take the New Historicist emphasis on Wordsworth's effacement, occlusion, and similar terms as an occasion to define an aspect of the aesthetic work of his poetry — one that is obscured by an emphasis on sublime history and apocalyptic reference.

One further introductory comment. At the end of the first *Georgic*, writing in the context of Roman civil war and disorder, Virgil imagined that "a time shall come when in those lands, as the farmer toils at the soil with crooked plough, he shall find javelins eaten up with rusty mould, or with his heavy hoe shall strike on empty helms, and marvel at the giant bones in the upturned graves" (1.493–97). To this image the Romantic New Historicism has responded with a characteristic reversal. Georgic, writes Liu, "is the form in which history turns into the background, the manure, for landscape"; "through georgic, Wordsworth is able, at least at first glance, to make the entire under-narrative of the Revolution sink into unbroken invisibility" (*Sense of History*, 18). My purpose is rather to ask what kinds of upturning, what cultivating labors of pen and verse, are best suited to make the body of the history not only visible but — more importantly — intelligible, lodged in the understandings of contemporary and later witnesses. While it may seem associative to move, as I do in this essay, between the theme of work and the issue of historicization, the question of how events become history necessarily entails questions about the work performed by acts of representation and about the operation and the limits of the aesthetic dimension in the literary transmission of historical event.

As a point of entry, let us return for a moment to Levinson's manifesto of her own practice: she seeks "to materialize a greatly idealized corpus; or, to locate the body in Wordsworth's poetry." Levinson is a very self-conscious writer, and one wonders how deliberate an allusion this is to *the* most famous account of the location and subsequent idealization of a submerged, material body: the drowned man of Esthwaite Water (1799, 1.258-87; cf. 1805, 5.450–81, 1850, 5.426–59). The historicist critic assumes, as it were, the active role of one of the "company" who sound the deceptively calm lake with grappling irons and long poles until the corpse rises to the surface. Wordsworth himself seems to ask us to read this episode as a meditation on historical experience: the 1799 version calls the lakeside incident one of many "tragic facts / Of rural history" (1.282–83). It may not be immediately recognizable as "history" to a readership accustomed to looking for the French Revolution or the institutions of State, Church, Nation; it represents a particular kind of a rural history which has received less emphasis so far, at least in the United States (one finds it in critics like Raymond Williams and John Barrell), an attempt to recover the lived experience of the countryside. Within Wordsworth's poetry, however, the story of the drowned man becomes the kind of local chronicle which looms large in later books of *The Excursion*—a work that is also dedicated to the location of bodies, only in a country churchyard.

Let us follow Wordsworth's (and Levinson's) suggestion that the drowned man episode of *The Prelude* enacts an encounter with historical event and the formation of a narrative for that history. I turn to the sequence first in its earlier version, just at the point where the poet tries to limit the suddenness and singularity of the corpse's apparition by "advert[ing]" to similar "numerous accidents" and "tragic facts / Of rural history." These, he says,

> impressed my mind
> With images to which in following years
> Far other feelings were attached—with forms
> That yet exist with independent life,
> And, like their archetypes, know no decay.
>
> (1799, 1.283–87)

According to the elusive epistemology of these lines, the facts of rural history leave their stamp on the mind as images, and to these images are later attached "feelings." Such later feelings are not named, but we do know that they are "far other" than traumatic (in other words, unrelated to what Wordsworth has just called "accidents in flood or field . . . distresses and disasters"). Moreover, we are told, it is *because* of the nontraumatic nature of the feelings that the original impressions continue to exist. Historical event in this passage is thus paradoxical: "tragic fact" itself may recede under subsequent layerings of what Wordsworth elsewhere calls a "tranquillizing spirit" (1805, 2.27), but at the same time these tranquil feelings cooperate with the "independent life" and longevity of the impressions left after witnessing such facts.

Wordsworth can posit that the empirical "facts / Of rural history" exist prior to the "forms" they later assume in mental life. However, for the reader of the scene, fact and feeling, trauma and tranquility, are always already intermingled. The experience is not twofold, chronologically or affectively. Like a twilight wash upon a Claudian landscape, the "far other feelings" have already worked over the scene and remain in all the elements that temper and calm what is at every moment a *potential* apocalypse, one that never quite overcomes all the impulses that seek to contain it, yet at the same time is never entirely removed by them. I should emphasize that by "readers" I do not only mean Wordsworth's audience, his public past or present, but all latecomers to the event, *including* the older Wordsworth himself, gazing across the gulf of time at a "passage of life" gone by.[11] The poet reads his own past state(s), standing as "two consciousnesses—conscious of myself, / And of some other being" (1805, 2.32–33). And in this attitude he resembles the historicist critic, bending down over the surface of past time. For where Wordsworth maintains that a "wide vacancy" distances without entirely separating his two selves, the critic (to quote Liu's modification of McGann's more extreme hermeneutic of suspicion) "opens up the interval between *then* and *now* . . . the epochal divide between self and other that is the aporetic ground . . . of historical understanding"—while also admitting that critical understanding depends on a degree of sympathy for the historical other: "Any critical method that holds the present and the past too immaculately apart for fear of cross contamination is not a possible method of critical understanding."[12] To introduce the perspective of the reader, in other words, is to raise the question of temporality and to disclose the historiographical situation implicit in the autobiographical one.

For the various readers, then, the facts are not accessible to experience without the layering of the "far other feelings," which is to say that they are available *through* the feelings.[13] Those feelings may seem equally remote, since Wordsworth's own reticence—expressed in the indefiniteness of "far other"—supplements the inherent intangibility of any feeling and the aporia between another's sensibility and our own. Yet we do meet the feelings in an immediate and particular way; they are detectable in fossil form, or rather their residual traces are in form itself, the passage's heightened awareness of the organizing power of language:

Twilight was coming on, yet through the gloom
I saw distinctly on the opposite shore,
Beneath a tree and close by the lake side,
A heap of garments, as if left by one

Who was there bathing. Half an hour I watched
And no one owned them; meanwhile the calm lake
Grew dark with all the shadows on its breast,
And now and then a leaping fish disturbed
The breathless stillness. The succeeding day
There came a company, and in their boat
Sounded with iron hooks and with long poles.
At length the dead man, 'mid that beauteous scene
Of trees and hills and water, bolt upright
Rose with his ghastly face. I might advert to
Numerous accidents in flood or field. . . .
(1799, 1.266–80)

Such formal consciousness, a sign that this passage has been worked over in the temporal process of "after-meditation" (1805, 3.648) and composition, includes most obviously a palpable literariness; several scholars have already commented on the allusion to *Othello* in lines 279–82, and it is important to recognize that the "facts" are never plain fact (whatever that would be) but "tragic fact," that is, already assimilated to the genre that includes *Othello.*[14] "Twilight was coming on," recalls Milton's Eden ("Now came still Evening on" [*Paradise Lost*, 4.598]), and behind Miltonic romance there lurks a pervading Spenserianism. Even before 1805, as Peter Manning has observed, one senses that this passage is about the role of "Books" (*Reading Romantics*, 98).

Allusiveness is a special case of the passage's awareness of form, of the reshaping that has occurred. There is also a design of a more colloquial but similarly distancing kind, an obliquity like the feature of the Lucy poems that Hartman has called "euphemism, not of the artificial kind, the substitution of a good word for a bad one, or the strewing of flowers on a corpse," but an "inbuilt commitment to avoid silence."[15] In the *Prelude* passage, even the most abrupt moment, the rising of the corpse, lacks its expected momentousness. The slowly dilating description of the pastoral scene ("mid that beauteous scene / Of trees and hills and water") interposes between the subject ("the dead man") and its verb ("bolt upright / Rose"), delaying an action that has already been postponed for twenty lines (277–79), and inserting a subtle periphrasis within the larger one that is the passage itself. "No one owned them" is a beneficent euphemism of this kind; we register the child's casual observation (oh—no one has claimed them) before the full understanding of its grim irony sets in (indeed, the owner is dead). So is "breathless stillness" — where the ominous interpretation of "breathless" (not breathing) is delayed at least for the space in which we pursue its different possible meanings. "Euphemism" in this sense cannot be understood simply as evasion or denial. For it is also the opposite: a form of aesthetic mediation that attempts to master the silencing effects of trauma on memory and speech — or, in terms of this passage, to counteract the potentially final pause at "Rose with his ghastly face." Such soft verbal irony *admits* the danger that it skirts — it admits it in part by skirting it — and thus requires the dialectical reading urged by Kenneth Burke in his discussion of the threat at the basis of beauty: "Let us remind ourselves . . . that implicit in the idea of protection there is the idea of something to be *protected against*."[16]

Wordsworth's decision in the 1805 *Prelude* to move the entire episode into the section devoted to "Books" is a recognition, a rendering explicit, of the earlier version's two latent concerns: the role of reading in the formation of a sense of the past and, less obviously, the relation between a willfully imposed calm and aesthetic form. I have suggested that in 1799 the tranquility attached to the memory of the event is detectable in the formal design of the scene; in 1805, the early exposure to literature is credited as the source of a later calm:

> At length, the dead man
> . . . .
> Rose with his ghastly face, a spectre shape —
> Of terror even. And yet no vulgar fear,
> Young as I was, a child not nine years old,
> Possessed me, for my inner eye had seen
> Such sights before among the shining streams
> Of fairyland, the forests of romance —
> Thence came a spirit hallowing what I saw
> With decoration and ideal grace,
> A dignity, a smoothness, like the works
> Of Grecian art and purest poesy.
>
> (1805, 5.470–81)

What had been attributed to the operation of memory (the attachment of "far other feelings" to "distresses and disasters") is now specifically the work of literature, which provides a prevenient aesthetic protection. As we have seen, this "hallowing spirit" — this smoothing and purifying — is precisely what is resisted by the New Historicism; in Levinson's words, "so smooth, sealed, and . . . *purified* a history does the poem develop that history in the commoner sense" has "no room to surface" (*Great Period Poems*, 2). One can share Levinson's and others' impatience with Wordsworth's smoothness, his peculiar "complacency" (1805, 8.75), yet still, recalling the textual background I have sketched, take seriously Wordsworth's claim to the contrary: history surfaces not only *in* but also *because* of an aesthetic medium that seals, sets some limit, to terror and makes representation possible. The New Historicist concern has been that aesthetic sealing or healing will be too effective and will eradicate all traces of the scar of history. But "history" as we know it, our "sense of history" in Liu's phrase, is a collection of scars left by a past we can only mark and remark, and in order to have scars there must be a degree of—incomplete—healing.

Let me clarify the issues behind what might seem merely a matter of emphasis. To bring together reference and apocalypse, as Liu so stunningly does, is to identify history as a form of trauma, both for the poet—for whom "history is heartstopping"—and for his readers ("We flinch before the topical" [*Sense of History*, 465, 35]). Hence, in spite of the historicist suspicion of psychoanalytic or related studies because the latter are not sufficiently culture-specific, and because they study the "self or mind" that historicism dismisses as a worn-out credo, we see an ironic but profound affinity between Liu's statement that "denial is the strongest engagement with history" and recent psychoanalytic elucidations of the nature of traumatic response. For the latter I cite Cathy Caruth's proposal that in trauma "the greatest confrontation with reality may also occur as an absolute numbing to it." "For history to be the history of trauma," Caruth continues, "means that it is referential precisely to the extent that it is not fully perceived as it occurs; or to put it somewhat differently, that a history can be grasped only in the very inaccessibility of its occurrence."[17]

But how far and with what consequences can one generalize, or adopt as models, such extremes? An apocalyptic encounter with reality, or trauma—defined by Freud as a sudden, excess influx of stimulation to the unprepared psyche from the external world—results *not* in comprehension, not in the ability to possess a "sense of history," but either in a numbed response to reality or in the involuntary return of the past.[18] There is, in other words, a danger in generalizing the traumatic potential of history to the extent that all historical experiences are seen to follow the pattern of traumatic ones (a position sometimes attributed to Caruth),[19] and there is a similar danger in asserting that reference is necessarily apocalyptic. Inaccessibility or opacity may indeed be a property of certain occurrences, and there is frequently an ethical imperative to admit that we cannot fit the past into our ready-made patterns of response, that such hasty narrative closures *are* frequently ideological. However, the historian cannot rest content with inaccessibility for at least two reasons: because of the problems of historical relativism that may ensue and because even a principled refusal of understanding may complicate the narrative transmission of such events.[20] The challenge to the interpreter becomes one of establishing intelligibility within limits, understanding without reduction or foreclosure.

Here, in the context of this essay, it is important to observe that *Wordsworth* wants to imagine the possibility of an experience that is recorded and grasped because it is not traumatic, because it does not possess its viewer, or reader, uncontrollably: "No vulgar fear possessed me." As his prose statements against the "torpor" of contemporary audiences accustomed to the "outrageous stimulation" of popular literature and numbed by "great national events" suggest, he is self-conscious about the gap between an empirical experience (whether of witnessing, at first hand, or of reading) and understanding.[21] His solution, however precarious, is to restore, or preserve through his own poetry, the element of time, the "preparedness" that Freud would later regard as critically elided in traumatic or apocalyptic encounters. The drowned man episode illustrates this strategy most evidently on the narrative level, where the experience of death is twofold, both in the 1805 version (prior sights "among the shining streams of fairyland, the forests of romance" anticipate the actual vision) and in 1799, when vision is followed by after-meditation. Wordsworthian euphemism, I believe, attempts the same effect on a more subtle level, its instinctive, at times ironic, obliquity extending the experience in time: it *does* refer, but gradually rather than apocalyptically.

It was the element of time which would later make the confrontation with external or internal reality a matter of psychic "work" for Freud. His notion of the "work of mourning," for example, consists of the difficult withdrawal of our attachments from an object that reality-testing has shown to be lost: "Normally, respect for reality gains the day," Freud comments, "Nevertheless its orders cannot be obeyed at once. They are carried out bit by bit, at great expense of energy." Elsewhere, the papers on technique make clear the limits of direct or sudden communication within the therapeutic process: "One must allow the patient *time* to become more conversant with this resistance with which he has become acquainted, to *work through* it."[22]

The peculiar aesthetic dimension of much of Wordsworth's poetry attempts to provide something very like the space of working-through. In fact, *The Excursion*'s turn to the georgic, to the Virgilian background as mediated through

Thomson, Cowper, and others, anticipates at the level of genre the later Freudian trope of "work." *The Excursion* imagines the verbal mediations that guide a response to history as a collective labor, and it renders the work of mourning not as a private affair, a lyric moment, but as a communal undertaking. The phrase "passages of life," *The Prelude*'s earlier epithet for the spots of time in which one "consciousness" must read the text of another, comes to describe the Pastor's churchyard narratives of rural history (*Exc.*, 7.294). Local storytelling and the transmission of tales between characters, which Walter Benjamin called "an artisan form of communication," become, in the language of the poem as a whole, a form of georgic husbandry.[23] "The mine of real life / Dig for us," requests the Wanderer (5.630–31), but that source is mined, that reality tested, with extreme care, and brought to light covered with layers of interpretation. The Pastor and the Wanderer are masters of gentle words or euphemism, and most readers, including this one, feel that they have mastered the art all too well. Yet whatever our irritation at the poem's "massive complacency"—as William Empson complained of another "Elegy, Written in a Country Churchyard"—we can see the notion of verbal labor that Wordsworth is proposing.[24] The Pastor attempts to close the wound of history, personal and national, that the melancholic Solitary has suffered, to combat the danger that the poem identifies as "uncomplaining apathy," or *insensibility* to history (2.206). Significantly, the attempt does not quite succeed, as to his credit Wordsworth recognizes, but the talk—the protracted "working through" of experience—continues.

In developing the idea of a nonevasive euphemism, I am mindful that it is not quite the right word, for its usual sense today is markedly pejorative. George Orwell's wonderful, derisive protest against the inflated euphemisms of "some comfortable English professor" defending totalitarianism seems appropriate to recall here: "A mass of Latin words falls upon the facts like soft snow, blurring the outlines and covering up the details."[25] But the term can be useful for the dangers it evokes, because in describing an obliquity of another kind, I am searching for a more complicated, dialectical understanding of this aspect of speech. One might visualize a spectrum marked at one extreme by euphemisms easily adapted for institutions of political repression and ideology. At the end of that spectrum, however, lies a different sort of "repression," caused by the rejection of language's capacity to delay what cannot be absorbed all at once.

Rejection of this aesthetic dimension is not directly advocated by the New Historicism, unless we say that its covert yearning for an unmediated vision of history works institutionally toward advocacy. It is fairer to say that historicism's power lies in demystification and that the rejection of aesthetic mediation is the negative side of an argument that fails to account for the "honorable toil" (along with the dishonorable kind) of what it demystifies. Yet to reserve room for such frequently inscrutable or "invisible workmanship" (1805, 1.353)—which not only "make[s] time for time," as in the Sephardic proverb, but makes time for history itself—is not necessarily to become an idealizing reader or a complicit and unselfconsciously "Romantic" one. Kenneth Burke, whom I cited earlier, cannot exactly be called a mystifying critic; Burke's analysis of the protective or therapeutic "comfort in beauty" grows out of a pragmatic sense of poetry as "*equipment for living*, as a ritualistic way of arming us to confront perplexities and risks."[26]

Of course, equipment operates in very different ways, and in practice (to return to the image I borrowed from the first *Georgic*) it is difficult to distinguish between formal mediations that bury history in nature or consciousness and those that provide the very ground for sustaining a historical past. What is needed, among other things, is a better history of style, alert to the politics and sociology, as well as the psychology, of literary technique. There are signs that historicism is beginning to include a new rhetorical emphasis and a sensitivity to aesthetic or linguistic action, revising an earlier tendency to treat the aesthetic as a synonym for the ideological. In Romantic studies more generally, there is more attention to "events of form" (Susan Wolfson's phrase) in their political field.[27] Liu, in his response to this essay (see "The New Historicism and the Work of Mourning," in this volume), would perform an act of incorporation whereby Wordsworth and his readers are included in a common—now New Historicist—project of mourning. However, until we know more about what constitutes that verbal work at any given time, just who (poet or critic) or what element in poetic or critical discourse keeps the history in imagination alive in the study of Wordsworth remains an open question.

Afterword, 2004

Almost ten years have passed since this essay's genesis. Ideology or historicist critique and Romantic aesthetics are simply no longer at the impasse that they seemed to have reached in the mid-1990s. Where the New Historicism of the time frequently represented itself as a renunciation of Romanticism for its supposedly dehistoricizing project, a more recent wave of scholarship has wondered if one is not at one's *most* Romantic when offering a historicist critique. As James

Chandler's *England in 1819* suggested to us, "'the return to history' itself unwittingly returns" to terms that emerge within Romanticism, like the discourse of dated specificity that Chandler illuminates.[28] Repetition, return, carefully constrained identification, "use"[29]—these relationships with our object of study have (for now) largely supplanted renunciation, at least in its more adversarial versions. Now, too, that the temperature around these debates has gone down, I see more clearly what Alan Liu himself notes in his companion essay to this one: the most sensitive New Historicist work paused, amid its denunciation, to acknowledge that it had been preempted by the poetry itself. As Liu's *Sense of History* had put it, such work often sought to know not only the interval of difference between itself and its object but also "the imprint of such impending division . . . *within* the other"—the text's own foreknowledge, as it were, in the form of its "internal distantiation" (457).

Although the New Historicist debate may now itself "be" history, it has driven and continues to drive new directions of research, some of which may be apparent in the preceding essay. In closing, I noted the (then) emerging attention to Romantic form's *own* historical self-consciousness; that trend has since been richly and variously developed in the work of Chandler and Wolfson, as well as in studies by Thomas Pfau, Marc Redfield, and others.[30] Moreover, "feeling," one of the main terms of this essay, has received new, more sympathetically engaged scrutiny, both in its physiological and its affective dimensions. We know much more, for instance, about the medical and scientific contexts for Wordsworth's claim that poetry is the "science of the feelings."[31] I now also see in this essay the embryonic form of concerns developed in my subsequent work, albeit with different emphases, especially the attempt to account for the history immanent in—and in some cases *only* accessible through—the pre- or extra-ideational field of sensation and affect. While this essay used the term "medium" (as in "aesthetic medium") intuitively, without particular forethought or research, I have since tried to identify both the specificity and the history of precisely that term, and to attend to poetry's newly peculiar place, during the "long" eighteenth century, as one *medium* (not just one form) among others, whose distinctive and proliferating modes of knowledge it found itself having to rival.[32]

One question that I asked in this essay—whose strong antecedents occur throughout the work of the scholar honored in this collection of essays—promises to remain central to the future as to the past, although answers must surely differ. Of *The Excursion*'s Wanderer, Wordsworth notoriously wrote: "Unoccupied by any sorrow of its own / His heart lay open to . . . / To sympathy with man" (*Exc*, 1.361–62, 364). Yet that economy of feeling is at root impossible, for how can the fully permeable or "open" heart remain unoccupied? Thus we still ask: What media of representation, what kinds of communication of the past, are best capable of keeping hearts and minds "open" enough for a nonreductive responsiveness, without becoming so invasive, or just so riveting, that the receptive mind closes down or, at worst, turns away—in Wordsworth's words—"to private interest dead and public care" (2.209)?

CHAPTER NINE

Sound Government, Polymorphic Bears

The Winter's Tale and Other Metamorphoses of Eye and Ear

Patricia Parker

> I am gone for ever. *Exit pursued by a bear.* . . .
> What . . . became of Antigonus, that carried hence the child? . . . . he was torn to pieces with a bear.
>
> — *The Winter's Tale*

> . . . sound, but not in government.
>
> — *A Midsummer Night's Dream*

In *A Midsummer Night's Dream,* Hippolyta comments on Quince's mispunctuated Prologue, that (like "a child on a recorder") he has produced "sound, but not in government" (5.1.124) — deforming the syntax of a message by joining what should not be joined. She thus calls attention to the government of sound, in a scene in which the aristocrats' ridicule of malapropping artisans simultaneously suggests sound government of other kinds. The moment recalls the equivocal "no sound jest" of *Titus Andronicus* (4.2.22–26), where "Horace" is heard promiscuously as "Whore-Ass"; and Hamlet's chastising of Rosencrantz and Guildenstern for attempting to "sound" him (as on a "recorder") by governing his "stoppes." In *A Midsummer Night's Dream,* where elided sounds confound even the discrete identities of I's and eyes (a confounding that modernizing editors attempt to correct by carefully differentiating their spellings), the most astute theorist of soundings beyond ocular proof is Bottom, whose bottomless dream suggests something too deep to be sounded: "The eye of man hath not heard, the ear of man hath not seen . . . what my dream was" (4.1.211–14).

Shakespeare was himself a notorious sound jester — as the "poison in jest" of *Hamlet* or the strumpet that appears nowhere to the eye in "The Moor! I know his trumpet" famously attest. What I want to foreground — not only in Shakespeare but in other (unmodernized) examples — is not just deliberate sound jesting but conflations made possible by unstable orthographies and variable sounds. Modern theories of textuality have focused on the excess of sound which written language cannot regulate. Geoffrey Hartman's readings of Wordsworth are famous for their art of overhearing and recognizing that ungovernable excess. In Shakespeare, such excess is repeatedly foregrounded. Since the field of ungoverned (or ungovernable) sounds is potentially unbounded, I restrict my examples here to the polymorphic "bear" and the ambiguous "borne," from a period in which even the modern "pun" would too anachronistically suggest the contrived combining of what was not yet discretely (or discreetly) separate.

As Margreta de Grazia reminds us, this is the sound that caused so much trouble for Dr. Johnson, whose complaint about Shakespeare's inability to resist such "fatal Cleopatras" is well known. Johnson found "bear" — with its homophone "bare" and its "phonetic approximations" "bier"and "barne" — such a problem that it drove the author of the *Dictionary* not only to give "the verb [i.e., to bear] two separate but hardly discrete or coherent main entries, one of which is followed by thirty-eight rather nebulous subsenses that attempt to distinguish different types of carrying, suffering, enduring, giving birth and yielding" but also to admit (in his entry on its first subsense) that "this word is used with such latitude that it is not exactly explained." In the period of Shakespeare's plays, attempts to sort the network of "bearing" into discretely separated senses were rendered even more difficult by the convergence in London of regional dialects and polyglot tongues, in a period in which multiple soundings could run together "bear," "barne," "bier," "bourne," and "born" (or "borne"), just as (despite nascent Elizabethan attempts at orthographic reform) there were no fixed orthographic differences between what we now spell "*bare* and *bear* or *born*, *borne*, and *bourne*."[1]

De Grazia's historical analysis of attempts to govern sound by discrete orthographies and other nascent neoclassical disciplines (not yet as dominant as they would become by the eighteenth century) takes as its focus the connections between the most notorious of all stage directions in Shakespeare — "Exit, pursued by a bear" — and the emphasis in *The Winter's Tale* on bearing of all kinds, from gestation and delivery (foregrounded in Leontes' suspicion that his pregnant wife Hermione is bearing Polixenes' "bastard") to the scene in which Antigonus (ordered by Leontes, in Sicily, to "bear" the newborn babe to "some remote and desert place," 2.3.174–75) abandons the child, or "barne," in Bohemia and is immediately devoured by a "bear." Building on an essay by Stephen Booth which explores connections between "bears, burdens, birth, boundaries, nakedness, and endurance" and within *The Winter's Tale* itself between this notorious "bear," the homophones of "bearing," "baring," "born," "borne," and boundary, or "bourne," and the elevation of these shepherds to the status of "gentlemen born" (spelled in the 1623 Folio "gentlemen borne"), De Grazia points out the extraordinary discursive nexus that makes the sudden appearance of the onstage "bear" a materializing of what she calls "the presiding word" of the entire play. This preoccupation with bearing of all kinds extends from Hermione's pregnancy and the "issue" of generative bearing both legitimate and bastard—included in the "Oracle from the uterine site of Delphos *[delphos,* "womb"]"—to the scene of "Exit, pursued by a bear," which calls sustained attention to the homophonic "bearing-cloth" found by the shepherds with the new-born(e) bairn or "barne" that Antigonus has "borne" from Sicilia to Bohemia. Echoing Booth's remarking of the reminders of this scene in the later elevation of these shepherds to the status of "gentlemen born(e)," De Grazia underlines the extension of this "presiding word" to the play's preoccupation with bearing as comportment or good "breeding," the term that adds its own generative or gestational metaphorics to the issue of gentle "bearing" in all of its polymorphic forms.[2]

Antigonus—whose own name means antibearing or birth—combines these multiple senses within the tragic, or winter half of the play, whose barrenness has been chronicled by Janet Adelman and others. Not only is he the figure who "carried hence" this child, or "barne," exposing her to death when he credits Leontes' accusation of Hermione's adultery or bastard bearing. He is also the "gentleman" devoured by a "bear" in the pivotal scene between "things dying" and "things new borne," the winter and spring, tragic and comic, halves of the play separated by the sixteen years of "Time" before the return of Perdita, the lost bairn herself. The scene of the devouring "bear" is thus the culmination of the earlier lines in which (as De Grazia remarks) "Antigonus proves true to his name in resolving to geld his daughters and himself if Hermione proves an adulteress" (2.1.146-48). In a plot in which it is paradoxically "the blessed shepherd's progeny rather than the accursed gentleman's that will flourish" and in which the raising of "Perdita's baseborn foster family into the ranks of her natural royal family" grafts "a bark of baser kind" onto a "bud of nobler race" (4.4.92–97), the transporting or bearing of initially impoverished shepherds to the status of "gentlemen borne" simultaneously joins high and low, "kings and clowns," in the kind of " 'mongrel tragi-comedy' Sidney criticized for its generic and social cross-breeding."[3]

Homophones multiply within *The Winter's Tale*, even beyond the bounds suggested by these rich analyses. Antigonus—whose name (like Antigone's) recalls Greek *gone*, generation, bearing, or birth but also the "gonad" of "*gonos*, generation, seed"—highlights not only the connection between generative bearing and what happens to him in the scene of the "bear" but also the emphasis on (the geldable) gonad that surfaces in Leontes' taunt that he does not have the manhood to "rule" his wife. "Gone" itself resonates in the final word spoken by Antigonus just before "Exit pursued by a Beare" ("I am gone for ever"), exploiting at once the Greek origins of his name (in a play filled with foreign-sounding names) and the English "gone" with which he exits from the play. This sense of "gone" for things dying rather than new born is sounded elsewhere, in the scene of Mamillius's death, when "The prince, your son, . . . is gone" (prompting Leontes' "How? Gone?") is clarified as "Is dead" (3.2.), and again when the Shepherd Son counsels his father that they "must to the King and show our strange sights" or "we are gone else" (4.4.818–20).

Bearing itself—in all of its overdetermined senses—simultaneously underwrites the combination of this play's gestational concerns with its emphasis on telling, tallying, and long-term investments so brilliantly charted by Stanley Cavell and others, particularly featured in the commercial atmosphere of the play's second half and grafted onto its romance plot of a "return" made more profitable by the passage of "Time." Tale-telling (or bearing tales) is directly connected with both kinds of increase in the ballad of the "usurer's wife . . . brought to bed of twenty money-bags at a burthen" (4.4.263–64), whose "credit" or credibility is testified to by the "midwife" Mistress Taleporter, deliverer or bearer of tales as well as prodigious tails. The ballad's reteller (and retailer) is Autolycus, "littered under Mercury" (4.3.25), the figure associated not only with marketing, stealing, message-bearing, and tale-telling but with bearing back from death, the role that helps explain why Hermione echoes his other familiar name. Usury itself was not only a form of "bastard" breeding but also part of the gestational lexicon of bearing through (and profiting from) the passage of "Time," whose Chorus in the play chronicles both the growth of Perdita and the gap of time in which the poor shepherds are ultimately "grown" from "very nothing" (4.2.39–40) to a wealthy estate, hosting a sheep-shearing whose "yield" cannot be calculated "without compters" (4.3.36).[4]

Gestational bearing in this play thus underwrites increase and returns of all kinds. But this polymorphic bearing in all of its generative complexity has not been part of the central debate over the choice of a "bear" for this notorious stage direction. This may suggest that it is still difficult for editors and critics either to think outside the trivializing model of the fatal Cleopatra, or the "merely" verbal that is a continuing part of the legacy of eighteenth-century editing, or to imagine that a generative verbal matrix might be an explanatory factor with regard to the choice of a "bear" rather than some other animal for this scene. Attempts to answer the question "Why a bear?" have varied from the association of the ursine with Arcadian settings and tragicomic plots, with rampant sexuality (in the bestiaries as well as the bear-baiting pits, or "Bear-garden," readily conflated with the adjacent public theaters), or with the Candlemas Bear as sign of the passage from winter to spring. But most editorial discussion has focused on a question that Stephen Orgel reminds us was never even felt to be a problem until the twentieth century—of whether it was a "real" bear, brought in from the nearby bear-baiting pits, or an actor dressed in a bear suit.[5] Attention has therefore been focused on other contemporary spectacles in which bears appear: *Locrine* (ca. 1590), the revised *Mucedorus* (1610), the polar bears of Jonson's *Masque of Oberon* (1611), and Jonson's 1622 *Masque of Augurs*, which featured John Urson and a troupe of dancing bears. But even here, as we shall see, the unrecognized soundings of this verbal matrix make clear that the either/or thinking that would cordon off a "real" bear from the "merely" verbal one has created a distractingly anachronistic cloven fiction. What I want to do, therefore, before returning to these contemporary analogues for the on-stage "bear" of *The Winter's Tale*, is to explore the kaleidoscopic cultural semantics of this discursive nexus, including the polyglot networks of sound and sense that already assimilated polymorphic bears with multiple forms of "bearing" in the period.

> They bore him bare fac'd on the Beer (Second Quarto of *Hamlet*)
> . . . might they not stopp a Beere-barrell (*Hamlet*, Folio; Q2, "Beare-barrell")

> A man borne vpon little legges, is alwayes a gentleman borne.
>
> —BEN JONSON, *Poetaster*

The homophones of bearing and born(e), so troublesome to Dr. Johnson, resonate throughout the Shakespeare canon, both before and after *The Winter's Tale*. *Julius Caesar* exploits the sounding of "barren," "bare," and "bear" when Antony describes Lepidus as a "barren-spirited fellow" who "bear[s]" honors "as the ass bears gold," in a scene that simultaneously invokes bear-baiting in Octavius's "we are at the stake / And bayed about with many enemies" (4.1.1–51). Gloucester compares his deformity to "an unlicked bear-whelp" in a soliloquy that combines the explicitly ursine with references to bearing as carrying, o'erbearing, and bearing as well as baring one's head (*3 Henry VI*, 3.2.153–71), a collocation continued in *Richard III* (3.1.128–31). Multiple homophonic crossings between bearing in the sense of transporting or carrying (including messages and tales) and bearing as breeding, comportment, forbearing, pregnancy, and birth make other connections our print-trained eyes (and modernized editions) too easily miss—including the elision of "bury" and bear when the Shepherd Son proceeds to "bury" what is left by the "Beare" who devours Antigonus, a collocation common in a period in which "beare" was not only "a brute beast that is baited with dogges" but a familiar spelling for the bier, or "cophine wherein a dead man is caried to his burial."[6] "Uncovered on the Beere, / Be borne to buriall in thy kindred's grave" in *Romeo and Juliet* anticipates the homophones sounded in the final scenes of *Richard II*, from the horse "borne to beare" (5.5.92) that carries the "conveyor" Bolingbroke to the bier (Quarto/Folio: "Beere") used to "beare" the dead king to the usurping king and the "buried fear" (5.6.30–31) that continues to be (re)borne, haunting this usurper even after the ostensible "buriall" of Richard. Bearing, burying, and "beere" (or bier) become in the process compounded with "conveyance" in all of its polymorphic senses, in histories whose "buried fear" continues to haunt the entire dramatic series, preoccupied with carriers, transporters, or "conveyors" of all kinds.[7]

In *Merry Wives of Windsor*—the comedy most closely connected not only to the dramatis personae of those histories but to their preoccupation with "conveyance" as well—bearing as conveying or carrying (including the bearing of messages that makes Mistress Quickly a "she-Mercury" or Falstaff a willing "porter") is part of a comedy of sexually suspected wives in which adultery itself is foregrounded as a bearing away, both a sexual bearing beyond patriarchal control and a potential birthing outside the patrilineal line, a combination underscored in Ford's anxious inquiry as to where his "buck basket" is being "conveyed"—to which the merry wives respond that he has nothing to do with what is "borne" (or "born") out of his house (3.4.50-51). As if to emphasize its preoccupation with multiple forms of bearing and breeding, *Merry Wives* begins with the ambiguous estate of the "gentleman borne," part of its comic plot of mobile transport in both social directions.

Bearing sexual burthens — or men — and giving birth to "barnes" was likewise already part of a widespread discursive network before the "bear" scene of *The Winter's Tale*, as was conveying, translating, bearing, or transporting, including to the status of "gentlemen borne." Serving as a "porter," or carrier (as the name of "Mistress Taleporter" suggests), carried equivocal dimensions lost to modern ears. Gordon Williams's *Dictionary of Sexual Language and Imagery in Shakespearean and Stuart Literature* defines "carry" in the period as "bearing a sexual burden," citing among other examples Middleton's *Changeling* ("I shall carry't well / Because I love the burthen"). But this kind of "carrying" was at the same time frequently compounded with "carriage," or bearing in other senses. In the Queen Mab speech of *Romeo and Juliet* ("when maids lie on their backs, / That presses them and learns them first to bear, / Making them women of good carriage," 1.4.92–94), "carriage" evokes both the bearing of a sexual burden and good breeding, comportment, or bearing (as when Constable Dull is described as "a man of good repute, carriage, bearing, and estimation" in *Love's Labor's Lost*, 1.1.268).

Bearing in its sexual as well as other polymorphic senses is exploited throughout the plays of Shakespeare, together with the homophonic "burthen," whose unmodernized orthography suggests both birthing and a burden to be borne. "Women are made to bear" is Petruchio's response when taunted by Katherine as a beast of burden ("Asses are made to bear, and so are you"), in lines whose "I will not burthen thee" (2.1.199–202) summons the connection with "birth" shared by the "usurer's wife" brought to bed of twenty money bags "at a burthen," by the "nativity" of *The Comedy of Errors* ("bore thee at a burthen two fair sons," 5.1.344) and by "a grievous burthen was thy birth to me" in *Richard III*. In *The Taming of the Shrew*, this bearing of "burthens" occurs just before the exchange on "tails" and "tales" in which Petruchio swears he is a "gentleman" to be "borne" by Kate herself (2.1.218). In *Much Ado about Nothing*, Margaret's "burden" as both "song" and generative bearing (3.4.43–46) is followed by "bearing," "barns," and children, or "bairns" (Folio: "If your husband have stables enough, you'll looke he shall lacke no barnes"), lines that come closer than any in Shakespeare to the "barne" or "bairn" and stables, or "barns," of *The Winter's Tale* (2.1.134–35).

The generative matrix of bearing in all of these overdetermined senses includes not only a woman's sexual bearing of a man and the gestational time before delivery or birth but also the combination of the sexual and the monetary in the discourse of usury itself, as an artificial simulacrum of "natural" bearing or breeding and a lender's forbearing of his money for the return to be gained by the passage of time through which an unpaid debt was "borne." In *As You Like It*, Touchstone's "I had rather bear with you than bear you. Yet I should bear no cross if I did bear you, for I think you have no money in your purse" (2.4.9–14) connects bearing as patient forbearance with what money also "bears." *Henry IV, Part 2* combines "Women are made to bear"—the familiar proverb of sexual and gestational bearing—with the Hostess's bearing of Falstaff's unpaid debt: "A hundred marks is a long one for a poor lone woman to bear, and I have borne, and borne, and borne" (2.1.29) Even the lines on Falstaff's death in *Henry V*—which we are used to seeing as Theobald's "babbled of green fields"—may instead (in its original "Table" of green fields) be a bawdy reference to the sexual "table-play" in which a woman was described as "bearing" a man, in lines whose "pen" invokes an unmistakably phallic reference. In this case, once again, an eighteenth-century emendation has long supplanted what in the earliest texts might be a resonance no longer heard.

Though foreign to post-Enlightenment editors, kaleidoscopic wordplay on porters, conveyors, and monetary along with sexual and other kinds of "bearing" was commonplace in the period of Shakespeare's plays. In Marlowe's *Doctor Faustus* (1588–92), a cuckolding servant says of his master's wife, "she's born to bear with me," combining bearing and "borne" with patient forebearing (2.3a.17). Dekker's *Northward Ho* (1605) describes a whore who has sexually carried or "borne her Country" as "borne for her Country" (3.1.83), exploiting the familiar sexual double entendre on "country" as well as the homophones "born" and "borne." Heywood's *Royall King* (1602–18) conflates carrying, bearing, and a burden to be borne with forbearing or patience and the double sense of "delivery" as both conveying and birthing, when the clown commissioned to deliver a lady's ring to her lover promises: "I shall bear this with as good will as you would beare him." Forbearance circulates as both sexual bearing and the bearing (or forbearing) of a debt in *Maroccus Exstaticus* (1595), in which a landlord is described as loving "a whoore as his life. For hee will forbear as long as shee will beare" (14), forbearing her debt as long as she will sexually "bear" him.

Even "gentlemen born"—in a period when "gentlemen" were increasingly not "born" (i.e., hereditary or natural) but "made" in the sense of artificially transported to that status—were subject to exploitation of the ambiguous "borne." Ben Jonson—though much less identified than Shakespeare with such fatal Cleopatras—rings just such homophonic changes in *Poetaster*, when Crispinus offers to show Chloe his (heraldic) "arms": "No, your legges doe sufficiently shew you are a gentleman borne . . . for a man borne vpon little legges, is alwayes a gentleman borne" (2.1). In a canon in which Hotspur responds "my horse, my horse," when his wife demands to know "what *carries* you away?" (*1 Henry IV*), it may be precisely attentiveness to such generative switchers that we need to acquire in order to be able to follow the connections between the notorious "bear" of *The Winter's Tale*, who pursues the "gentleman" who "carried hence the child" (5.2.59–60), and the impoverished shepherds, who are "made" by the "gold" they find with the "bearing cloth" of a "barne" and finally transported to the status of "gentlemen borne," in a plot that calls attention not only to forbearance through "Time" as yielding a more satisfying issue, increase, or return but also to the "credit" extended to all such "tales," including *The Winter's Tale* itself.

Though comedy has been particularly identified with such kaleidoscopic conflations, even Shakespeare's tragedies exploit this generative matrix, just as they frequently turn on what Kenneth Muir has called the "uncomic pun." Macbeth's early soliloquy ("If it were done, when 'tis done, then 'twere well / It were done quickly") compacts "bear," "borne," and "naked new-born (Folio: "New-borne") babe" into a few short lines (1.7.12–25), while its final scenes are haunted by the refrain "of woman born" (Folio: "borne": 5.7.3, 13; 5.8.13), even as they explicitly evoke bear-baiting in Macbeth's "They have tied me to a stake. I cannot fly, / But bear-like I must fight the course" (5.7.1–2) and his refusal to "be baited with the rabble's curse" (5.8.27–28).[8] Hamlet's "it were better my Mother had not born me" (in the "get thee to a nunnery" speech focused on Ophelia as a "breeder of sinners") appears as "borne me" in the Folio and Second Quarto. The Folio's "Beere-barrell" (1623) is alternately spelled "Beare-barrel" in the Second Quarto version of the Gravediggers' Scene, whose lines on Adam as the first "gentleman" born because he was the first to "bear arms" turn on the same combination of heraldic and body parts as Jonson's *Poetaster*. Ophelia's "They bore him bare fac'd on the Beer" (Q2; F: "Beere") compounds within a single line the familiar homophones of "bier," "bare," and "bearing" or carrying, its variable early spelling foregrounding connections unavailable to the eye in modernized editions. Even the combination of bearing, forbearing, and boundaries or bourns in "To be or not to be"—with its "bare bodkin," "fardels bear," "bear those ills we have," "bear the whips and scorns of time," and death itself as an "undiscovered country" from whose "bourn" no traveler returns—spells "bourn" as "borne" in both Second Quarto and Folio (I will not comment on the Folio's spelling "Must give us pawse").

The tragedy closest, however, to *The Winter's Tale*—which famously rewrites both it and the jealousy plot of *Othello*—is *King Lear*, which combines the "gone" of gonads and generative bearing (the Greek *gone* frequently conflated with *gyne*, "woman," as well as with "gonos, generation, seed") in the name of Goneril, its counterpart in this etymological sense to Antigonus. The generative *gone* (and *gonos*) sounded in Goneril is underscored in the terrifying scene in which Lear denounces her as a "degenerate bastard" (1.4.253) and places a curse on her very "organs of increase," the matrix or womb associated elsewhere in the play with the "mother": "Into her womb convey sterility, / Dry up in her the organs of increase" (1.4.278–79). The tragedy itself is intimately bound up with the issue of sexual generation and breeding (including the "vicious [female] place" of potentially bastard as well as degenerative begetting) from its opening scene, where the pairing of fathers and offspring (both natural and "unnatural") moves from the "bastard" Edmund to Lear's response to Cordelia ("Better thou / Hadst not been born than not t'have pleas'd me better," 1.1.233–34).

Generation, sexuality, and degenerative or "bastard" bearing in *Lear* are explicitly associated with Ursa Major, the Great Bear—the ursine figure invoked in the opening soliloquy of Edmund the Bastard, who connects its multiple plots of generation, forbearance, and suffering (ironically in "my nativity was under Ursa Major, so that it follows I am rough and lecherous," 1.2.111–14). This "bastard" born under "Ursa Major" is called "whoreson" in the play's opening lines (1.1.22–24), a term whose conflation (as son of a whore) with "Urson" (literally son of a bear) was commonplace in the period—sounded, for example, by Shakespeare's collaborator Fletcher in *Custom of the Country* (1619–23), where lines on a "game bear" ("play me ourly," 4.1) turn simultaneously on "(h)ourly/whorely" and ours/whoreson or urse.

"Bearing" in all of its senses sounds repeatedly throughout *Lear.* Sexual or generative bearing is joined by "forbearance" as both patience and doing without (1.1.162), by bearing with ("You must bear with me. / Pray you now forget, and forgive," 4.7.82–83); and by bearing as carrying as well as supporting. The tragedy ends with the ritual of bearing or carrying off the stage, Albany's "Bear him hence awhile" as Edmund is borne off stage (5.3.257) and his "Bear them from hence. Our present business / Is general woe" (5.3.318). But *King Lear* is, at the same time, filled with references to bear-baiting and "real" bears. Gloucester becomes (like Macbeth) a bear "tied to the stake" (3.7.53), tormented by Lear's "dog-hearted daughters" (4.3.45). Albany repeats the ursine figure in condemning these "degenerate" daughters for harming "A father, and a gracious aged man, / Whose reverence even the head-lugg'd bear would lick" (4.2.40–43), a condemnation to which Goneril responds by taunting him as a "Milk-liver'd man" who "bear'st a cheek for blows" (4.2.50–51). Bearing in the sense of suffering is explicitly yoked to the baited bear in Lear's "reason not the need!" and its "fool me not so much / To bear it tamely" (2.4.275–76). The night on the heath opens with the Gentleman's report on Lear's state ("This night, wherein the cub-drawn bear would couch," 3.1.12–14) and repeatedly calls attention to bearing as supporting or suffering, in the very scene whose "bear" and "sea" have long been acknowledged as reprised in the pivotal scene of "Exit, pursued by a bear" in *The Winter's Tale* ("Thou'dst shun a bear, / But if thy flight lay toward the roaring sea, / Thou'dst meet the bear i' th'mouth," 3.4.9–11).

In ways recalled in the gelding of a "purse" and the "burthen" of the "usurer's wife" in *The Winter's Tale*, the bearing identified with what *Measure for Measure* calls the "two usuries" (sexual and monetary) is compounded in *Lear* with this doubled sense of "breeding," in the new world of inflation and upwardly mobile social climbers, or "new men" [like Oswald], that Richard Halpern and others have argued is central to its plot.[9] The play begins with the "breeding" (1.1.9) of the bastard Edmund, in the double sense of "conceive" (12) and as bringing up at his father's "charge" (9), a combination of the sexual and the monetary repeated in the language with which this "bastard" describes his own conception ("My father compounded with my mother," 1.2.111). The compounding of monetary with generative, or sexual, bearing both here and in the song of the Fool in Act 2 ("fathers that bear bags / Shall see their children kind," 2.4.8–9)—conflating moneybags and gonads as " 'twas nothing to geld a codpiece of a purse" does in *The Winter's Tale*—is strengthened by the homophonic conflation of "dolors" (or "dollars") and "daughters" (2.4.47–55), in lines that combine both kinds of generative increase.

Usury, debt, and lending are stressed repeatedly in *Lear*—in the Fool's ironic prophecy ("When usurers tell their gold i' th' field, / And bawds and whores do churches build," 3.2.91–92); in Edgar's "Keep thy foot out of brothels, thy hand out of plackets, thy pen from lenders' books" (3.4.96–98); in Lear's "Thou ow'st the worm no silk, the beast no hide" and his "Off, off, you lendings!" in the scene on the heath. The double-meaning "use" of this same scene, evoked in the compounded senses of usury and sexual use in Lear's "Thou hotly lusts to use her," sounds in lines that go on to include the "furr'd gowns" of the "usurer" (4.6.163–65). But most haunting is the "use" made in this tragedy of "nothing" itself, the nothing or "O" that simultaneously summons the zero or cipher and what Hamlet calls the "nothing" that lies "between maids legs." In the opening act, when the Fool asks his master: "can you make no use of nothing, nuncle?" and Lear responds: "Why, no, boy, nothing can be made out of nothing," this "nothing" evokes the empty "O" that the Fool repeats a few lines later (in "now thou art an O without a figure," 1.4.189–90). But it also suggests the generative multiplying or "breeding" of nothing itself within *King Lear*, making it the Shakespearean tragedy of negative generation or increase, unfolding from Lear's response to Cordelia's "nothing" in the opening scene.

The combination of a female, sexual, or generative bearing with the "nothing" or "O" of such compounding is reprised at the beginning of *The Winter's Tale* itself, when the first appearance of Hermione's pregnant body on stage (sign of an increase and multiply that Leontes will read as the outward "note" of her suspect sexuality as the play's gestational plot proceeds) is accompanied by the "cipher," or nothing, that can "multiply" one into "many thousands more" (1.2.6–8). The potentially multiplying "nothing" of this opening is reflected in the play's tragic (or winter) half, the part that has been assimilated to the tragedy of *Lear*, culminating in the scene of the "bear" which so closely echoes the scene on the heath. Its terrifying increase and multiplication is reflected in Leontes' own paranoid imaginings of the dark place of begetting, the tragically proliferating "nothings" of his most paranoid speech. But in this rewriting of *Lear*—which moves from tragedy to comedy through the pivotal scene of the "bear"—the passage of "Time" ultimately yields a more fruitful issue or return.

> The Beer that had taken one of the chyldren . . . deuoured it not, but bare it in to his cauerne.
>
> — *Valentine and Orson*

As the "whoreson" Edmund's ironic invocation of Ursa Major, or the Great Bear, reminds us, the unstable spellings and proximate sounds that conflate "born," "borne," "barn(e)," and "bear" with "bare," "burial," "bier," "beer," and "gentleman borne" were joined by ursine names that were themselves part of this associational nexus in the period. Visual as well as verbal interconnections involving actual bears (and ursine connections) literally run riot, for example, in the famous portrait of Guillaume Juvénal des Oursins by Jean Fouquet (ca. 1460), which plays onomastically on the *oursins*, or "little bears," in the name of its subject. This visual as well as discursive network pervades almost every detail of the portrait (as Tom Conley has shown), from the tiny bears carrying his coat of arms and the fur of his clothing with its *ourlets*, or folds, to the huge "O," or "ursine mouth," of the ring at his right elbow—producing a visual rebus in which "there is so much identity of words and things that, in the wit of the image, Oursins begins to resemble the mammal of his own name."[10]

Such heraldic as well as Cratylic play had counterparts on the English side of the Channel, connected to both literary and historical figures. A "rampant bear chained to the ragged staff" (2 *Henry VI*, 5.1.203)—badge of the house of Warwick—appears both in Shakespeare's histories and visually in dedications or frontispieces to Golding's translation of Ovid's *Metamorphoses* (1567) and Whitney's *Choice of Emblems* (1586). The passage between an ursine name and multiple kinds of bearing forms the basis of Spenser's Legend of Courtesy in *The Faerie Queene*, where wordplay on burthens or *pésant* bearing ("Perdy thou *peasant* Knight, mightst rightly reed / Me then to be full base and euill *borne*, / If I would *beare* behinde a burden of such scorne," 6.3.31) is followed by the provision to "Sir Bruin" and his "barren" wife of a baby rescued from a "bear," in a legend preoccupied not only with generative bearing but also with gentle bearing, breeding, and comportment. Here, a keyword or set of related terms—which we have to train ourselves to hear and see—provides the matrix not just for local verbal play but for an entire narrative sequence, in a Legend of "Courtesy" that combines all of these with meditations on noble or gentle birth as well as other forms of bearing and breeding.[11]

Even more strikingly in relation to *The Winter's Tale*, these simultaneously homophonic, etymological, and polyglot interconnections appear in the very texts most often cited in twentieth-century discussions of whether or not the bear of "Exit, pursued by a bear" was "real" or play. The revised *Mucedorus* (1610)—routinely cited as a theatrical analogue for this notorious stage direction because of the scene in which Mouse enters crying "A bear, a bear, a bear!" (1.2.34)—describes the "white head" and "white belly" of this "bear" in ways that evoke as much a woman as a bear, forging a connection between "bear," naked or "bare," and the sexually suspect heroine of the play, in a play that literally bristles with such equivoques.[12] In Jonson's *Masque of Augurs* (1622)—cited because of its three "dancing Beares"—these "Beares" appear with their "Bear-ward" John Urson, whose name ("son of bear," or "Urse") participates in the same polyglot crossing between (Latin) "*urse*," (French) "*ours*," and English "whore-son," familiar from the lines on "Ursa major" in *Lear*, or the wordplay on "ourly," "whorely," and "game bear" in Fletcher. Jonson's masque even combines "Beares" described as "well bred" with "Gentlewomen borne" and Urson's dancing bears with the "beeres" of the alehouse sign they enact visually on stage, the conflation similarly sounded in the "Beere-barrell" and "Beare-barrell" of the early texts of *Hamlet*.

The polymorphic bearing and polyglot metamorphoses of sound that connect the "whoreson" born under "Ursa Major" in *Lear* with generative and other forms of bearing, or that generate in *The Masque of Augurs* connections between

"Urson," "Beares," "beeres," and bearing of other kinds, are likewise reflected in the nondramatic text most frequently used to gloss the suddenly appearing "bear" of *The Winter's Tale*—the popular romance *Valentine and Orson*, routinely cited both for the carrying away of Hermione's babe and for Antigonus's reminder that "Wolves and bears" have done "offices of pity" (2.3.186–88). The office of pity carried out by a "bear" in *Valentine and Orson* (the newborn twins of its title) has to do not only with the she-bear who carries away and raises "Orson," whose name derives from this ursine fostering, but with the refusal of this bear's whelps to "deuoure" him. But what has not been noticed is that *Valentine and Orson* is itself pervaded (in its own unmodernized spellings) by the same homophonic and variant orthographic connections between "bear," "born," and carried, or "borne," that traverse *The Winter's Tale.* The popular romance not only describes the pregnant mother who "bere" the twins in her womb and the "beare" or "beer" that carried, or "bare awaye," the Orson of its title. It figuratively turns the newly delivered mother herself into a pursuing bear, who "vpon bothe her fete & handes . . . wente after the beer in the forest."[13] The generative matrix connecting "bearing" with "bare" and "bear" thus appears in a text already closely associated with *The Winter's Tale*, whose own pregnant heroine (mother of Valentine and Orson) is, like Hermione, slanderously accused of adultery, in a plot of a separated but finally united family whose borne-away baby ultimately returns.

The enormously popular *Valentine and Orson* has been argued by critics to have influenced several Shakespeare plays before *The Winter's Tale*—motivating the choice of Valentine as the name for one of the lovers in *Two Gentlemen of Verona* and for Mercutio's brother in *Romeo and Juliet.* What is rarely mentioned, however, is the even more intriguing case of the "Valentine" and "Orsino" of *Twelfth Night*, the festival already connected with Candlemas and its bear. *Twelfth Night* is literally filled with references to bears, bear-baiting, and bearing of multiple kinds, as if the choice of the name Orsino (already linked critically to the noble Orsini) were emblematic of this play's own concerns with bearing, birth, and upwardly mobile transport to the status of the high born(e) as well as with the importance of a bearer or deliverer of messages to its plot.[14] Explicit attention is called to Orsino's name in the play's second scene, when the shipwrecked Viola (newly "delivered to the world," a line glossed by editors as "literally 'born' ") questions a captain described as "bred and born / Not three hours' travel from this place" (1.2.19–20), who tells her that Illyria is governed by a "duke" as "noble" in "nature as in name" (1.2.25). Orsino's name (Italian for "little bear" or the adjective "ursine" itself) would of course be appropriate to his "nature" if he were bearlike or might generate such a Cratylic connection, as in the portrait of des Ursins. But in the associational logic already familiar from other contemporary examples, his name would be also appropriate (as with the choice of "Sir Bruin" for Spenser's Legend of Courtesy) if he were noble or high born, the social status that makes Viola-Cesario's projected marriage to him not only a violation of class boundaries but an upward mobility not unlike that which Malvolio construes from the difference between those who are "borne great" (the Folio's spelling) and those who achieve greatness by some other means.

The ursine connotations of the name of Illyria's Orsino are joined by the references to bear-baiting in which this play abounds, in ways that once again recall the Bankside location of the sport to which Puritans like Malvolio objected as strenuously as to interludes and plays. Sir Andrew claims skill in "fencing, dancing, and bear-baiting" (1.3.76), in the scene immediately following the highlighting of Orsino's "nature" and "name." Fabian's "You know he brought me out o' favor with my lady about a bear-baiting here" prompts Sir Toby's "To anger him we'll have the bear again" (2.5.1–10). Olivia's "Have you not set mine honor at the stake / And baited it with . . . unmuzzled thoughts" (3.1.118–19) joins Orsino's vision of his "desires" as "fell and cruel hounds" that pursue him (1.1.18–22), in a speech that evokes both Actaeon and a baited bear. But it is Malvolio, who is simultaneously disapproving of such sports and ridiculed for his upwardly mobile aspirations, who is the play's most obviously baited bear—described as panting "as if a bear were at his heels" (3.4.249–50), subject of Fabian's "sportful malice" and the "sport royal" (3.2.172) of the trick with which Maria has "dogg'd" him (3.2.76–77), and ending the entire play with "I'll be reveng'd on the whole pack of you" (5.1.378).

Orsino's ursine name may even underwrite the multiple forms of bearing or delivery this comedy combines. As the disguised "Cesario" (the name she adopts when newly "delivered" to this world), Viola first intends to become a "eunuch" at the court of Orsino, a gelding suggested by her later reference to what she "lack(s) of a man" as well as a choice that recalls the *caesus*/cut of the name that in *Julius Caesar* generates the lines on "the most unkindest cut of all"). But as "Cesario, the County's man," she becomes instead a "nuncio," or bearer of messages, for Orsino, who calls Cesario his own "dissembling cub" (5.1.164–65). "Cesario" thus combines the ursine and the bearing or delivery of messages with a name suggestive of the "caesarian" delivery or birth that makes Macduff in *Macbeth* not "of woman born(e)," in a comedy filled not only with references to bear-baiting and to bearing as birthing (in its plot of twins "borne in an hour") but with proliferating sexual equivoques on gelding, from Sir Toby's "If thou hast not her i' th' end, call me Cut" (2.4.175) to Malvolio's famous construal of the letters "C-U-T" (2.5.86).

All of these ursine names-"Orsino," "Orson," "Urson," "Whoreson," and "des Oursins," together with "Ursula" and the pastoral "Orsacchio," or "Ursacchio," the "wild man" of Sannazaro's *Arcadia* (6.9; 10.29)—reflect, finally, the Latin matrix "Ursa Major," the Great Bear cited by Edmund the Bastard in *King Lear.* This Great Bear (familiar to students of a later period from Mallarmé's "Sonnet en -yx," whose "onyx" comes from this same ursine figure) was herself a pregnant and slandered mother, the Callisto whose story (familiar from Ovid's *Metamorphoses*) has already been acknowledged as reflected in *The Winter's Tale.*[15] In this pastoral or Arcadian story, Callisto is raped by Jove in Diana's form and tainted with the charge of "adultery" by the jealous Juno. Nine months later, she gives birth to Arcas, origin of the name Arcadia—a temporal emphasis ("Nine times the Moone full to the worlde had shewde hir horned face," 564) whose focus on the time of gestation itself has been acknowledged as echoed in the first scene in which the pregnant Hermione appears (1.2.1–3). In this Arcadian story, the newly delivered mother is first metamorphosed into a bear by the avenging Juno and then (when, unrecognized in ursine form and about to be killed by her grown son) transported with him to become Ursa Major and Minor, Great and Little Bear, what Golding's translation calls "neighbour starres about the Pole on hie," the constellation by the "Northern Pole," which, Juno complains, enshrines her "strumpet" rival's "whoredom" in the skies. The version of the story in Ovid's *Fasti*—whose seasonal festivals are recalled in the sheep-shearing festival of *The Winter's Tale*—ends with the transformed "Bear" (from *Arctos*) and the Little Bear or "Bear-Ward" ("Arctophylax"), who follows her in the constellations of the northern sky.[16]

Shakespearean references to the "bearard," or bear-ward, which protects this "bear" (as these constellations are recalled, in combination with the Warwick emblem of the baited bear, in *2 Henry VI*) demonstrate detailed familiarity with this story long before *The Winter's Tale.* Burton's *Anatomy of Melancholy*—treating of Callisto—would later observe that "an immodest woman is like a bear," identifying Ursa Major with a tainted female sexuality in particular. But the invocation of this "Great Bear" associated with an adulterous "whoredome" in *Othello* (2.1.14: "cast water on the burning Bear / And quench the guards of th'ever fixed Pole"), in the same scene as "The Moor! I know his trumpet" sounds the "strumpet" of the accusation against Desdemona—makes this figure part of both of the tragedies (*Othello* and *King Lear*) ultimately transformed in the romance that turns on the "bear" of its pivotal scene, between tragic and comic, winter and spring. The sexual taint on Hermione, accused by her own jealous spouse of adultery, is reiterated even in the scene of the "bear" itself, as the shepherd, taking up the abandoned child, or "barne," assumes it to be the product of "some stair-work, some trunk-work, some behind-door work" (3.3.71-72). As the story of a sexually tainted woman transformed first into a bear and then into an emblem of upward translation, this metamorphosed "bear" adumbrates the trajectory of Hermione herself, accused (like Desdemona) of adultery in the play's tragic or winter half but (unlike Desdemona) not finally killed, or gone, with no possibility of return, in a romance of metamorphoses that rewrites the tragedy of *Othello* as well as *Lear*.

Multiple details align this metamorphosed "Great Bear" with this famously metamorphic Shakespearean romance, whose plot (and final statue scene) depends on such Ovidian transformations, as well as the polymorphic forms of bearing within it. Arcas and his mother are intimately associated not only with Arcadia but also with Delphi, where they were memorialized in sculpture. The constellations of Great Bear and Little Bear are connected in Ovid's *Fasti* with Ceres' search for the raped Persephone, the analogue for mother and daughter, Hermione and Perdita, her lost child, or "barne," explicitly echoed in *The Winter's Tale*. Florizel's reference to the "transformations" that Jupiter and the other gods have taken on, "humbling their deities to love" (4.4.25–35), recalls metamorphoses like the one of which the raped Callisto was a victim, adding an edge to the disguised Florizel's protestations of innocent intentions in his pursuit of Perdita. Ovid reminds his readers that Callisto the bear was not only mother of Arcas but daughter of the Arcadian tyrant Lycaon, finally turned by Jove into a wolf. Lycaon (from Greek *lykos*, "wolf," ironically recalled in the name of "Autolycus" in the play's second half) stands at the opening of the *Metamorphoses* as provoker of the flood, the divine retribution repaired in time by Deucalion and Pyrrha, the other Ovidian metamorphosis invoked in *The Winter's Tale* (4.4.431), for the returning of the "stone" Hermione to life, in a return that reverses the tragedy set in motion by the "tyrant" Leontes, ruler of the traditionally Arcadian Sicily.

The transformation of Callisto and her child into the "Arctic," or Polar, constellations that guided storm-tossed mariners (like those in the "ship" that perishes on the seacoast of Bohemia in the scene of the devouring "bear") itself turns on the homophones of Greek *arctos* (or "bear") and the "arctic," or northern. The fixed "Polus," or North Star, may even be echoed in the name of *Pol*ixenes, ruler of the more northern Bohemia, in what is (surprisingly) the Arcadian half of *The Winter's Tale*, while Leontes suggests "Leo," the zodiacal sign of summer.[17] The story of this Arcadian "bear" and child thus chiastically couples Sicily with the Arcadian overtones of the more northern Bohemia ruled by Polixenes, introduced through the hinge-event of "Exit, pursued by a bear," when Antigonus (who has carried, or "borne," the "barne" across the distance from one realm to the other) is devoured by the bear and his place taken by shepherds. The pursuing bear's association with winter (the time of the storm when Antigonus is killed) may therefore come not only from the period of hibernation (from which the Candlemas Bear emerges to mark the transition to spring) but also from the long-standing association between *Arctos*, or "Bear," and the "Pole" from this well-known pastoral as well as ursine story.

Metamorphic echoes of the Great Bear—recalled in Shakespeare's earliest histories as well as the Bastard's speech on Ursa Major in *Lear* and the "burning Bear" of *Othello*—thus literally abound within *The Winter's Tale*, from the opening scenes of the pregnant Hermione to the metamorphic ending that concludes its pastoral, or Arcadian, second half. But even more strikingly for the interconnections between the Great Bear and Little Bear and the polymorphic verbal network that the scene of the "bear" reflects in its "new-born" bairn, or "barne," Golding's own translation of Ovid's Callisto story provides yet another contemporary instance of the homophonic nexus of associations between such bearing and the bear that is the burden of the story itself.[18] In Golding's Englishing, the Callisto who is first described as a virginal Arcadian huntress ("Sometimes a dart sometime a bow she used for to beare," 518), after nine months "bare a boy that Arcas men did call" (591), a child who is called by Golding a "barne" ("Was there, arrant strumpet thou, none other shift to finde / But that thou needes must be with barne?" 583–84), in lines where Juno, swearing that "neyther unto heaven nor hell this trespasse shalt thou beare" (586), transforms her into the "shape" of a "Beare" with "a wide deformed mouth." In other words, even the story of the "Beare" whose pregnancy is acknowledged as echoed in Hermione's pregnancy in *The Winter's Tale*—in the translation known to have been consulted by Shakespeare—exploits the association of bears with bearing of other kinds, connecting gestation, birth, and "barne" to the ursine form of a "bear," as the play itself does.

In a play that itself depends upon the ear—putting even its own Recognition Scene of Leontes and Perdita beyond the reach of the eye or ocular proof—sound thus exploits its own metamorphoses, performing the polymophic perversity of an ungovernable excess whose multiplication is beyond any arithmetic or counting. The "language itself," as Geoffrey Hartman puts it in his extraordinary reading of *Twelfth Night* (the play in which, as he remarks, "Malvolio is . . . baited like a bear" or the very "sport he objected to") "coins its metaphors and fertile exchanges beyond any calculus of loss and gain," as if "the treasury of words were always full." The "sensitive ear" that hears "Ill" and "liar/lyre" in the "Illyria" of that other Shakespearean staging sees (as Bottom might put it) that what Keats famously called the "poetical character" (which "has no self" or "character" but "is every thing and nothing") has its counterpart in "a language with a character of its own," in which (beyond any subsequent neoclassical attempts to discipline its "fatal Cleopatras") "the revels of language are never ended."[19]

CHAPTER TEN

The Other Scene of Travel

Wordsworth's "Musings Near Aquapendente"

Peter J. Manning

In the midst of the spots of time passage in Book 11 of the 1805 *Prelude*, Wordsworth laments:

> The days gone by
> Come back upon me from the dawn almost
> Of life: the hiding-places of my power
> Seem open; I approach, and then they close;
> I see by glimpses now; when age comes on
> May scarcely see at all. . . .
>
> (334–39)[1]

If diminished access to his childhood experience no longer seems an adequate explanation of Wordsworth's diminished poetic power after 1807, or 1814, or

This essay grew from talks delivered at the Harvard University Humanities Center, at the invitation of Ann Wierda Rowland and Sonia Hofkosh, the English Institute of the University of Copenhagen, and the 2003 convention of the North American Society for the Study of Romanticism, on a panel organized by Nicola Trott. An earlier version, "Home Thoughts from Abroad: Wordsworth's 'Musings Near Aquapendente,'" appeared in *Angles on the English-Speaking World*, n.s., 3 (2003): 93–111; I am grateful to the editor, Lene Østermark-Johansen, for permission to publish this developed argument. Arkady Plotnitsky will recognize his contributions to its reframing.

wherever one sets the date of his decline, and that decline itself now seems less certain than it once did, these lines nonetheless point to the problem of discovering new *material* faced by a poet determined, to borrow Eliot's insistence on the indispensability of the historical sense, to "continue to be a poet beyond his twenty-fifth year," and Wordsworth's publishing career spanned more than sixty years.[2] The tours of Scotland that Wordsworth undertook in 1803, 1831, and 1833, and through Europe in 1820 and 1837, might be understood as the means of putting himself in the way of new sights and sensations or, when going over ground traversed earlier, provocative differences on which to reflect. Each resulted in a substantial body of new poems.

The Wordsworth who traveled through Italy in 1837 was sixty-seven years old and had been a public figure for decades, two obvious and related facts to explore. According to the recollections of his traveling companion, Henry Crabb Robinson, Wordsworth "repeatedly said of this journey, 'It is too late.' 'I have matter for volumes', he said once, 'had I but youth to work it up.' "[3] It had been twenty years since Coleridge declared in the *Biographia Literaria* that Wordsworth's poems had "for nearly twenty years well-nigh *engrossed* criticism, as the main, if not the only, *butt* of review, magazine, pamphlets, poem and paragraph."[4] By 1837 the *Biographia* itself was merely an entry in a public debate over Wordsworth's merits which continued for another twenty years, lit up by Francis Jeffrey's attacks in the *Edinburgh Review*, John Wilson's alternations of praise and mockery in *Blackwood's*, parodies by John Hamilton Reynolds and others, and Hazlitt's condemnation of his egotism. Wordsworth had seen himself contrasted to Scott as the morbid introvert to the healthy extrovert and to Byron as the rural simpleton compared to the man of the world. By 1837, moreover, Wordsworth had outlived his contemporaries, and the next generation as well: Byron, Keats, and Shelley were all long gone. Wordsworth's 1835 "Extempore Effusion upon the Death of James Hogg" explicitly marks the passing of an era, reflecting the poet's sense of his own frailty and the anxious need to define his place "among the English Poets after [his] death."[5]

"Musings Near Aquapendente," subtitled "April, 1837," purports to be a spontaneous rumination on Wordsworth's visit to the waterfall and the town named for it on the road between Siena and Rome. Wordsworth placed it first among "Memorials of a Tour in Italy, 1837," a section of his last published separate volume, *Poems, Chiefly of Early and Late Years* (1842). Crabb Robinson thought it "perhaps the most beautiful" of the "Memorials" (*Memoirs*, 329), and those who have learned to read Wordsworth through Geoffrey Hartman will recognize some characteristically Wordsworthian topoi in the opening:

Yon snow-white torrent-fall, plumb down it drops
Yet ever hangs or seems to hang in air,
Lulling the leisure of that high perched town,
Aquapendente, in her lofty site
Its neighbour and its namesake — town, and flood
Forth flashing out of its own gloomy chasm
Bright sunbeams — the fresh verdure of this lawn
Strewn with grey rocks, and on the horizon's verge,
O'er intervenient waste, through glimmering haze,
Unquestionably kenned, that cone-shaped hill
With fractured summit, no indifferent sight
To travellers, from such comforts as are thine,
Bleak Radicofani! escaped with joy —
These are before me; and the varied scene
May well suffice, till noon-tide's sultry heat
Relax, to fix and satisfy the mind
Passive yet pleased.[6]

(10–26)

The waterfall might well have been expected to trigger "the engulfing solipsism of Imagination," as Hartman writes of the "might of waters" invoked in Wordsworth's encounter with the blind beggar in Book 7 of *The Prelude*.[7] And a waterfall named "Aquapendente" will have recalled Wordsworth's delicate criticism in the 1815 Preface on the imaginative force of Virgil's *pendere* in the first Eclogue and the equivalent power of the usages of the English verb "hang" in Shakespeare and Milton:[8] If the flood, flash, fracture, rocks, and chasm suggest various apocalyptic moments in *The Prelude*, the temptation to the sublime is declined in favor of a leisurely narrative impulse that soon subsides into a meditative pause. "Musings," as a form, recalls the deliberately low key "Lines" of "Lines written a few miles above Tintern Abbey," a poem that also includes a date in its title, as a signal of its fidelity to experience.[9] Unlike "Tintern Abbey," composed within days of Wordsworth's return visit to the Wye, "Musings Near Aquapendente" was not written until 1841, when Wordsworth had long since returned to England (see *PW*, 3:490).[10] The delayed composition is typical, but the date is significant. Stephen Gill observes that in "Musings Near Aquapendente," "Wordsworth's strongest poetic strategies operate once again in what is his last of many poems of friendship and his last substantial elegy."[11] These terms provide an approach to "Musings," and the friend to whom Gill points is Walter Scott, the subject of lines 88–98:

Utter thanks, my Soul!
Tempered with awe, and sweetened by compassion
For them who in the shades of sorrow dwell,
That I—so near the term to human life
Appointed by man's common heritage,
Frail as the frailest, one withal (if that
Deserve a thought) but little known to fame—
Am free to rove where Nature's loveliest looks,
Art's noblest relics, history's rich bequests,
Failed to reanimate and but feebly cheered
The whole world's Darling. . . .

It does not seem too crude to paraphrase this passage as "Scott is dead, but thank God I'm alive," a sentiment that struck me as so brutally self-regarding that I could not get it out of my head. This essay is an attempt to understand the lines by working through their contexts and their function; it is therefore part biographical, part literary historical, and part critical. As the terminus of Wordsworth's representations of Scott, "Musings" needs to be situated within the long arc of their friendship, an act that in turn provokes the question of why Wordsworth's poetic representations of Scott occur only as that friendship approached its end with the death of Scott in 1832. This inquiry leads in turn to questions about the uses of friendship and the nature of Wordsworthian strength, and second, to the *places* of travel writing. Though ostensibly a poem of travel, I want to suggest that "Musings" is much more what Michael Millgate has called a testamentary act, a poem in which Wordsworth deliberately positioned himself against his rivals for literary reputation, and in so doing, I want also to suggest, found in the representation of him by others an urgent inspiration for new work.[12]

Scott and Wordsworth learned of each other in the autumn of 1800 through John Stoddart, who praised the *Lyrical Ballads* and *Christabel* to Scott and then Scott to Wordsworth and Coleridge.[13] On September 17, 1803, William and Dorothy, touring Scotland, paid a surprise visit to Scott, a visit so warmly received that it extended until the twenty-third and founded their relationship. Scott recited the unfinished *Lay of the Last Minstrel*, leading Wordsworth to declare that "the clear picturesque descriptions, and the easy glowing energy of so much of the verse, greatly delighted me" (Johnson, 1:213). On returning to Grasmere Wordsworth sent Scott, at his request, a sonnet he had composed during their visit, signing his letter: "Your sincere Friend, for such I will call myself, though slow to use a word of such solemn meaning to anyone."[14] As Gill nicely observes, this open affection contrasts with the coolness he had shown to Thomas De Quincey just three months before: "My friendship it is not in my power to give: this is a gift which no man can make, it is not in our own power: a sound and healthy friendship is the growth of time and circumstance" (Gill, *Life*, 216; *Early Years*, 400). In January 1805 Wordsworth sent Scott "Yarrow Unvisited," hoping that the stanzas "for the subject at least, will give you some pleasure. I wrote them, not without a view of pleasing you, soon after our return from Scotland" (*Early Years*, 530).

By March 1805 Wordsworth had received the published *Lay of the Last Minstrel* sent him by Scott, and he wrote to say that "high as our expectations were, I have the pleasure to say that the Poem has surpassed them much. We think you have completely attained your object; the Book is throughout interesting and entertaining, and the picture of manners as lively as possible" (*Early Years*, 553). The hint that "your object" might be different from Wordsworth's own became explicit when he received Scott's next narrative poem in 1808: "Thank you for Marmion which I have read with lively pleasure—I think your end has been attained; that it is not in every respect the end which I should wish you to propose to yourself, you will be well aware from what you know of my notions of composition, both as to matter and manner" (*Middle Years*, 264). One might find such frankness the criticism of an honest friend; one might find it ungenerous, especially when Wordsworth continues by noting that he has "heard that in the world" *Marmion* is not "as well liked as the Lay" and concludes by remarking that he has been misquoted:

> in the notes you have quoted two lines of mine from memory [from "Yarrow Unvisited"], and your memory admirable as it is, has here failed you. The passage stands with you
>
> The Swans in (or on) *sweet* St. Mary's lake—
>
> The proper reading is—
>
> The *Swan* on *still* St Mary's lake
>
> I mention this in order that the erratum may be corrected in a future edition.[15]

Wordsworth devotes as much space in his letter to observing a single-line misquotation in a note (canto 2, n. 3, xxxviii) as he does to Scott's 377-page poem, fails even to acknowledge Scott's graciousness in quoting "my friend Mr. Wordsworth's lines," and while complaining that Scott has been insufficiently attentive to the particulars of his verse and demanding a correction, cannot even trouble to quote Scott correctly—"in (or on)"; Scott wrote "on."

The gap between the two men *as poets* had been apparent from the beginning. Lockhart, recalling Wordsworth's conversation, writes of his first meeting with Scott:

> The impression on Mr Wordsworth's mind was, that on the whole he attached much less importance to his literary labours or reputation than to his bodily sports, exercises, and social amusements; and yet he spoke of his profession as if he had already given up almost all hope of rising by it; and some allusion being made to its profits, observed that "he was sure he could, if he chose, get more money than he should ever wish to have from the booksellers."
>
> This confidence in his own literary resources appeared to Mr Wordsworth remarkable — the more so, from the careless way in which its expression dropt from him.[16]

To Wordsworth, in his thirties inwardly convinced of his poetical merit but with his reputation still to establish, Scott's man-of-the-world ease and unabashed focus on the financial aspects of his poetry must have been particularly surprising.

The distinction between Wordsworth's concern for his art and Scott's forthright professionalism did not estrange the two men. In August 1805 Scott came to the Lakes and climbed Helvellyn with Wordsworth and Humphry Davy. The Wordsworths spent the winter of 1806–7 at Coleorton, the home of Sir George Beaumont; in April 1807 they met Scott in London and he returned with them to Coleorton in May. In July the Wordsworths visited Bolton Abbey, and by the end of the year Wordsworth was at work on *The White Doe of Rylstone*, based on a legend of the Abbey told in Thomas Whitaker's *History and Antiquities of the Deanery of Craven* (1805). The Border setting of this episode from the great Rising in the North of 1569 would alone have suggested that Wordsworth, disappointed by the returns of *Poems, in Two Volumes* the year before, was seeking to follow in the popularity of Scott's narratives, even had Whitaker not himself made the connection: "Had the milk-white doe performed her mysterious pilgrimage from Ettrick Forest to the precincts of Dryburgh or Melrose, the elegant and ingenious editor of the 'Border Minstrelsy' would have wrought it into a beautiful story."[17] Scott, hearing of the project from Southey, proffered Wordsworth some historical information about the Norton family, the protagonists of *The White Doe*, which Wordsworth firmly rejected: "Thank you for the interesting particulars about the Nortons: I shall like much to see them for their own sakes; but so far from being serviceable to my Poem they would stand in the way of it; as I have followed (as I was in duty bound to do) the traditionary and common historic records—Therefore I shall say in this case, a plague upon this industrious Antiquarianism that has put my fine story to confusion—" (*Middle Years*, 237).

After such a clear demarcation of poetic principles, it is perhaps not surprising that for the next fifteen years or so the exchanges between Scott and Wordsworth were largely confined to occasional meetings in London, though Scott claimed in 1807 to have made Francis Jeffrey "admire the song of Lord Clifford's Minstrel, which I like exceedingly myself,"[18] and Wordsworth permitted him to include "Tintern Abbey" in his 1810 collection, *English Minstrelsy* (Johnson, 308). Scott anonymously reviewed both himself and Wordsworth in "The Living Poets of Great Britain" in the *Edinburgh Annual Register for 1808*, which also appeared in 1810. There he declared that "a better heart, a purer and more manly source of honourable and virtuous sentiment beats not, we will say it boldly, within Britain," but he characterized Wordsworth as "hitherto an unsuccessful competitor for poetical fame" and ascribed his lack of popularity to his seclusion, comparing him in a pointed simile to "a person accustomed to navigate a small boat upon a narrow lake, to whom, if he possess an active imagination, the indentures of the shore, which hardly strike the passing stranger, acquire the importance of creeks, bays, and promontories."[19] In so doing his assessment converges with that expressed by Francis Jeffrey in his review of *Poems, in Two Volumes* in the *Edinburgh Review*.

In Scott's review the relationship between Wordsworth and Scott shifts from the biographical to the public, and the citation of Jeffrey seals the shift in this discussion. Scott is surprisingly absent from Wordsworth's poetry through 1815. Their conjunction is sharp in the November 1814 issue of the *Edinburgh Review*, which notoriously begins with Francis Jeffrey's unsigned review of *The Excursion:* "This will never do." Over the course of thirty pages Jeffrey accuses the poem of "bear[ing] no doubt the stamp of the author's heart and fancy; but unfortunately not half so visibly as that of his peculiar system." As the review proceeds Jeffrey deepens Wordsworth's "peculiarity" into the symptoms of an incurable disease, a stubborn refusal to adapt, caused by "long habits of seclusion, and an excessive ambition of originality." The poem is characterized as "a tissue of moral and devotional ravings," the product of "moral and religious enthusiasm . . . dangerous inspirers of poetry." Dismissing Wordsworth as "fantastic, obscure, and affected," he repeatedly excoriates his "wretched and provoking *perversity* [my italics] of taste and judgment."[20]

Less well known to Wordsworthians is that in the same issue of the *Edinburgh Review* Jeffrey also noticed Scott's *Waverley*.[21] Juxtaposing the opening sentence of this favorable review with the condemnation of Wordsworth brings Jeffrey's principles into focus. "It is wonderful," Jeffrey begins, "what genius and adherence to nature will do." Genius, the term that in contemporary critical discourse usually licenses transgression, here remains firmly subordinated to nature, as Jeffrey clarifies in his second paragraph: "The secret of this success, we take it, is merely that the author is a person of genius; and that he has, notwithstanding, had virtue enough to be true to nature throughout, and to content himself, even in the marvellous parts of his story, with copying from actual existences, rather than from the phantasms of his own imagination." Scott's excellence proceeds from his character, from the integrity to resist imagination and remain content with copying the actual.

Throughout his review Jeffrey praises Scott for what he terms a "faithful and animated picture of the manners and state of society that prevailed in this northern part of the island, in the earlier part of the century." He insists repeatedly on "the perfect accuracy of the picture" Scott has drawn. The emphasis on ocular fidelity connects with the second article in the volume, which Jeffrey as editor presumably deliberately placed immediately following the review of *The Excursion*, a discussion of the claims of the Cassegrainian Telescope, which renders explicit the standards of exact observation and empirical truth that underlie the endorsement of Scott. Jeffrey particularly lauds the "extraordinary felicity . . . with which all the inferior agents in the story are represented." Even those who lack firsthand knowledge of "the traits of Scottish national character in the lower ranks," he argues, will appreciate the justice of the portrayal: "It requires only a general knowledge of human nature, to feel that they must be faithful copies from known originals." The attribution of objectivity signals the coincidence of the codes of the author with those of his critic: the truth is simply what *feels* right. Both *Waverley* and Jeffrey's review appeared anonymously, an anonymity that may be read as indicating the common-sense consensus against which Jeffrey read Wordsworth's name as betraying "a puerile ambition of singularity" (Woof, 404). His perversion was his introversion.

The contrast between healthy, extroverted Scott and pathologized, introverted Wordsworth became commonplace in critical discourse.[22] In the three-part review of *The Excursion*, which Wordsworth read as it appeared in the *Examiner* from August to October 1814, Hazlitt observed of Wordsworth that "all other interests are absorbed in the deeper interest of his own thoughts" and that his "poems in general are the history of a refined and contemplative mind, conversant only with itself and nature." Solitude in nature becomes morbid in Hazlitt's succeeding generalization: "All country-people hate each other."[23] In the lecture "On the Living Poets," with which Hazlitt concluded his *Lectures on the English Poets* in 1818, he remarked that Scott "describes that which is most easily and generally understood with more vivacity and effect than anyone else. . . . He never obtrudes himself on your notice to prevent your seeing the subject. What passes in the poem, passes much as it would have done in reality. The author has little or nothing to with it." If this seems like faint praise, the contrast with Wordsworth, whom he characterizes as "the reverse of Walter Scott in his defects and excellencies," throws it into relief: "His poetry is not external, but internal . . . he furnishes it from his own mind, and is his own subject. . . . He tolerates only what he himself creates. . . . His egotism is in some respects a madness."[24] Hazlitt reprinted a reduced version of his *Examiner* review in the *Round Table* in 1817, and he returned to Wordsworth and Scott in *The Spirit of the Age* in 1825. By that time Scott's novels had eclipsed his metrical romances, with justice, Hazlitt averred: Scott, he contended, lacked the "power in true poetry that lifts the mind from the ground of reality to a higher sphere. . . . He does not soar above and look down upon his subject, imparting his own lofty views and feelings to his descriptions of nature" (Maclean, 225–26). If this criticism suggests a contrast with Wordsworth, Wordsworth is treated essentially as before: "We do not think our author has any very cordial sympathy with Shakespear. How should he? Shakespear was the least of an egotist of any body in the world." The chapter concludes with warning Wordsworth of the danger "of becoming the God of his own idolatry!" (258, 261).

The distinctions the reviewers drew were dramatized when Scott visited the Lakes in August 1825, when three days of festivities honored Scott and George Canning, the Foreign Secretary. Lockhart's account, in letters to his wife, Scott's daughter, of the first encounter between the two men in ten years is at once comic and awful:

> Wordsworth is old and pompous, and fine, and absurdly arrogant beyond conception—evidently thinks Canning and Scott together not worth his thumb. . . . We with Wordsworth and his daughter went to Keswick,—he spouting his own verses very grandly all the way. . . . This I remark once for all, that during these rides, etc. the Unknown was continually quoting Wordsworth's Poetry and Wordsworth *ditto*, but that the great Laker never uttered one syllable by which it might have been intimated to a stranger that your Papa had ever written a line either of verse or prose since he was born. (Grierson, 9:207 n. 2, 211 n.1)

By their next meeting bankruptcy had fallen on Scott, followed by overwork, illness, and a stroke.[25] News of a seizure in 1830 drew from Wordsworth a direct avowal: "Dear Sir Walter! I love that Man, though I can scarcely be said to have lived with him at all; but I have known him for nearly 30 years."[26] Scott's doctors advised him to winter in Italy, and in August 1831 he wrote urging Wordsworth to fulfill a promise of many years' standing to visit, "adding that if I did not come soon to see him it might be too late" (*Later Years*, 421). Wordsworth was not in much better health; his eyes were so inflamed that he had to postpone the journey "for nearly 3 weeks" (435), and even protected by a green eye-shade and accompanied by Dora he had to delay the journey once begun (434). They arrived on September 19, just five days before Scott's departure. He found Scott "a good deal changed" (441); the gravely ill poet took his visitors to Newark Castle, and two days later wrote a few stanzas in Dora's album, misspelling his own name, and telling her that "I should not have done anything of this kind but for your Father's sake: they are probably the last verses I shall ever write" (*PW*, 3:526).

Wordsworth was shaken, but his emotion turned him to his own poetry. The tour that had begun with the visit to Scott produced the "Poems Composed during a Tour in Scotland, and on the English Border, in the Autumn of 1831," which make up the first section of *Yarrow Revisited*, his successful volume of 1835, his first new volume in many years.[27] And the specter of Scott, as Gill astutely notes, drove Wordsworth to put "in order past poetry, so that, should he be afflicted like Scott, fair-copy manuscripts would be ready for the press" (Gill, *Life*, 372). In June 1832 he published a further, four-volume *Collected Works*.

Before Scott left for Italy Wordsworth had sent him "Yarrow Revisited," memorializing their visit to Newark Castle and closing the series that had begun when he sent him "Yarrow Unvisited" in 1805, and a sonnet, "On the Departure of Sir Walter Scott from Abbotsford, for Naples." "Yarrow Revisited" is too familiar to need quoting, but the sonnet is less well known and deserves attention:

A trouble, not of clouds, or weeping rain,
Nor of the setting sun's pathetic light
Engendered, hangs o'er Eildon's triple height:
Spirits of Power, assembled there, complain
For kindred Power departing from their sight:
While Tweed, best pleased in chanting a blithe strain,
Saddens his voice again, and yet again.

Lift up your hearts, ye Mourners! For the might
Of the whole world's good wishes with him goes:
Blessings and prayers in nobler retinue
Than sceptred King or laurelled Conqueror knows,
Follow this wondrous Potentate. Be true,
Ye winds of ocean, and the midland sea,
Wafting your Charge to soft Parthenope![28]

As "Mourners" (8) suggests, the poem is a proleptic elegy for Scott. At Abbotsford Scott had talked to Wordsworth "a good deal about the singularity that Fielding and Smollett had both been driven abroad by declining health, and never returned" (Lockhart, 7:309–10). The premonition was perhaps heightened by the already proverbial phrase "See Naples and die"—a phrase silenced by Wordsworth's reference to the city rather by its classical name, Parthenope. The poem adheres to the scene Wordsworth saw as the two men came back from Newark Castle: "On our return in the afternoon we had to cross the Tweed directly opposite Abbotsford. The wheels of our carriage grated upon the pebbles in the bed of the stream, that there flows somewhat rapidly; a rich but sad light of rather a purple than a golden hue was spread over the Eildon hills at that moment; and, thinking it probable that it might be the last time Sir Walter would cross the stream, I was not a little moved, and expressed some of my feelings in the sonnet" (*PW,* 3:526). But the light is also that which Wordsworth had specified in the "Essay upon Epitaphs" appended to *The Excursion* as appropriate to the mode: "The character of a deceased Friend or beloved Kinsman is not seen, no—nor ought to be seen, otherwise than as a Tree through a tender haze or a luminous mist, that spiritualizes and beautifies it; that takes away indeed, but only to the end that the parts which are not abstracted may appear more dignified and lovely, may impress and affect the more."

Placing Scott at the center of the sonnet, Wordsworth casts the action as "Spirits of Power, assembled there, complain[ing] / For kindred Power departing from their sight" (4–5) rather than as the exercise of his own imaginative powers: the Wordsworthian "I" is missing from the poem.[29] The elimination of himself is the correlative of the imagining of Scott as already deceased; the double disappearance enables an act of generosity that forgets all Wordsworth's condescension to Scott's poetic practice and envy of his success.[30] The unremarkable conventionality of the language marks Wordsworth's achievement of the impersonality he had praised in that essay:

> The first requisite, then, in an Epitaph is, that it should speak, in a tone which shall sink into the heart, the general language of humanity as connected with the subject of Death. . . . The perfection of this species of composition . . . will be found in a due proportion of the common or universal feeling of humanity to sensations excited by a distinct and clear conception, conveyed to the Reader's mind, of the Individual, whose death is deplored and whose memory is to be preserved; at least of his character as, after death, it appeared to those who loved him and lament his loss. . . . It is truth hallowed by love—the joint offspring of the worth of the Dead and the affections of the Living![31]

Though not strictly an epitaph, because neither inscribed on a gravestone nor exploiting the fiction that it is, the impersonality marks the poem as a representative gesture, speaking "the whole world's good wishes" rather than Wordsworth *in propria persona.* This public quality makes it appropriate that in early December 1831 Wordsworth sent the poem to Alaric Watts for publication in the *Literary Souvenir.* Despite his dismaying experience with *The Keepsake* in 1829, Wordsworth turned to the annual to disseminate his anticipatory elegy for Scott.[32] It was published on page 1 of the *Literary Souvenir* for 1833 not long after Scott's death on September 21, 1832 (*Later Years,* 462, and n. 5): Wordsworth, whom Watts had praised in the 1832 *Souvenir,* was thus enabled to appear almost immediately as Scott's elegist and so to shape the narrative of their relationship. The poem's power to fix Wordsworth as Scott's deeply grieving friend was further magnified when Lockhart used it in the *Memoirs*—to which I will return—to close his chapter on Scott's last night at Abbotsford before the futile trip to Italy, where it occupies a page by itself (Lockhart, 7:311).

The "Extempore Effusion upon the Death of James Hogg" is the next in this series of tributes to Scott. Reading in November 1835 of the death of James Hogg, Wordsworth was moved within the half hour to compose the elegy that opens by twinning Hogg with Scott:

> When first, descending from the moorlands,
> I saw the Stream of Yarrow glide
> Along a bare and open valley,
> The Ettrick Shepherd was my guide.
>
> When last along its banks I wandered,
> Through groves that had begun to shed
> Their golden leaves upon the pathways,
> My steps the border minstrel led.

> The mighty Minstrel breathes no longer,
> Mid mouldering ruins low he lies;
> And death upon the braes of Yarrow,
> Has closed the Shepherd-poet's eyes.[33]

Together with Scott and Hogg the "Effusion" memorializes the deaths of Coleridge, Lamb, Crabbe, and (from 1836) Felicia Hemans, losses that provoke an urgent question:

> Yet I, whose lids from infant slumbers
> Were earlier raised, remain to hear
> A timid voice, that asks in whispers,
> "Who next will drop and disappear?"

If the deaths of his juniors led Wordsworth to look toward his own death, they also intensified the need to define his place before his voice too was silenced, as the uncharacteristically immediate composition corroborates. Hogg was not a personal friend, and if his death was the occasion for Wordsworth to release feelings about those to whom he had been close, it was equally an occasion publicly to fix an era. Despite his repeated declaration that "I do not like to publish . . . in a newspaper, nor in any periodical . . . , for with any of these I have carefully abstained from connecting myself," Wordsworth sent the "Effusion" to the paper in which he had read of Hogg's death, the *Newcastle Journal*, to which he had earlier canceled his subscription.[34] The verses appeared in the December 5 issue, under a heading that makes clear that the poem effectively converted the mourning the poem narrates into a celebration of the poet: "The following exquisite Verses, which need no comment at our hands, have been transmitted to us by one of the most distinguished of England's Bards — one of her best and most loyal subjects — the poet Wordsworth. We feel highly flattered by the compliment thus paid to us by our kind-hearted and excellent friend" (*Last Poems*, 305).

By the time *Yarrow Revisited*, beginning with the poem of that name immediately followed by the sonnet "On the Departure of Sir Walter Scott," appeared in April 1835, Scott had been dead for almost three years. The hopes expressed for Scott's recovery had been deceived, but placed in Wordsworth's most successful publication in many years the poem set for good the image of an enduring friendship between Wordsworth and the loved author whom, as Wordsworth had earlier acknowledged, "I can scarcely be said to have lived with . . . at all."

Scott was not the only figure with whom Wordsworth found himself linked in contemporary critical discourse: the triangulation of Scott, Byron, and Wordsworth was commonplace. Hazlitt begins his essay on Byron in *The Spirit of the Age* by marking Scott and Byron as "afford[ing] a complete contrast to each other, in their poetry, in their prose, in their politics, in their tempers, no two men can be more unlike" (Maclean, 235). The opposition between Byronic self-centredness and spleen and Scott's self-effacing "truth and nature," between a poet who "chiefly thinks how he shall display his own power" (235) and one with whom "the veil of egotism is rent" (236), resonates when, two chapters further on, Hazlitt specifies Wordsworth's "solitary musing" (255) and implies—what he had excoriated in his review of *The Excursion* in the *Examiner*—his egotism (258). Think about the effect on Wordsworth through the years of such double portraits as Hazlitt's:

> Lord Byron we have called, according to the old proverb, "the spoiled child of fortune." Mr. Wordsworth might plead, in mitigation of some peculiarities, that he is "the spoiled child of disappointment." We are convinced, if he had been early a popular poet, he would have borne his honors meekly, and would have been a person of great *bonhomie* and frankness of disposition. But the sense of injustice and of undeserved ridicule sours the temper and narrows the views. To have produced works of genius, and to find them neglected or treated with scorn, is one of the heaviest trials of human patience. (260)

These contrasts between his own popularity and that of writers whom he linked as exemplifying the merely fashionable acquired a new force in the 1830s. In 1830 Thomas Moore published his *Letters and Journals of Lord Byron* in two splendid quarto volumes, dedicating them to Scott. The controversy the biography ignited only added to the success of the enterprise. Murray then republished the work as the first six volumes of the great seventeen-volume edition of 1834—*The Works of Lord Byron: With His Letters and Journals, and His Life, by Thomas Moore*—works that he had found too risky to publish in Byron's lifetime were now absorbed into a canonical text. Then, in 1837, came Lockhart's seven-volume *Memoirs of the Life of Sir Walter Scott, Bart.*, a moving, detailed, and highly influential study of Scott's character, his circumstances, and the development of his career.[35]

Wordsworth's turn to Scott in "Musings Near Aquapendente" has Lockhart as its stimulus: Wordsworth and Henry Crabb Robinson were reading the biography as they traveled in Italy in 1837.[36] Though his distaste softened as he read the later volumes, Crabb Robinson repeated the disdain for Scott's concern with popular success repeatedly sounded by Wordsworth: "I found the book, what

Wordsworth declared it to be, a degradation of the literary character of our countryman. Walter Scott was a trader in poetry, the size of his poem being adapted to that of the building it was written to pay for" (*HCR*, 2:534). Carlyle's extraordinary 1838 review of Lockhart's portrait of Scott, a hero undone by his earthly ambition, became the *locus classicus* of this view: "Surely, were not man a fool always, one might say there was something eminently distracted in this, *end* as it would, of a Walter Scott writing daily with the ardour of a steam-engine, that he might make 15,000£ a-year, and buy upholstery with it."[37]

Here, then, was a tangle of motives underlying the treatment of Scott in "Musings Near Aquapendente." If Wordsworth thought Lockhart's frankness degraded "the literary character of our countryman," his views of Scott's poetry were consistently critical, from his condescension to *The Lay of the Last Minstrel* in 1805 to his conversation in 1844: "He does not consider that it any way goes below the surface of things . . . it is altogether superficial" (Hayden, 381–82), or, more tersely, as remembered by Aubrey de Vere, he spoke of Scott's poetry "with contempt" (Peacock, 340). If the lines on Scott were intended to counter Lockhart's portrait of his father-in-law, Wordsworth's assessment of the poetry, and its subordination to commercial interests, was even more severe. Praising Scott in "Musings," Wordsworth associated himself with a far more popular author, given new dignity by his struggle against adversity, by reasserting the story of their friendship already narrated in "Yarrow Revisited."

"Musings Near Aquapendente" is the first poem in "Memorials of a Tour in Italy, 1837." The sequence is preceded by a brief dedicatory poem to Robinson which opens the sequence in the register of friendship, but the verso observes of the omission of any mention of the Italian Lakes: "Neither of these lakes, nor of Venice, is there any notice in these Poems, chiefly because I have touched upon them elsewhere. See, in particular, 'Descriptive Sketches,' 'Memorials of a Tour on the Continent in 1820,' and a sonnet upon the extinction of the Venetian Republic" (96). This note, like the printing of *Poems, Chiefly of Early and Late Years* with a supplementary title page that places the new collection as volume 7 of *The Poetical Works of William Wordsworth*, reminds the reader of the accumulating oeuvre of the poet and reveals the rhetorical pose inherent in Wordsworth's subsequent self-description as "one withal . . . but little known to fame."

The purposes underlying that pose become clearer if we consider that if the European tour poems recall another poet it is Byron rather than Scott. "Nature's loveliest looks / Art's noblest relics, history's rich bequests" sounds like a synopsis of Cantos 3 and 4 of *Childe Harold's Pilgrimage.* This is no accidental connection: I propose that the tour poems are a deliberate anti-*Childe Harold,* that in them the poet who had been steadily criticized for his seclusion in the Lakes set out to show that he could be as cosmopolitan as Byron. Incorporating lines that he had written for *Michael* in 1800 ("Onward thence . . . border bards"), Wordsworth stubbornly displayed himself at the start of the poem as still the poet of the Lakes, for whom Italy serves to renew his ties to "my own Fairfield . . . old companionship . . . Seat Sandal" (47–52), while now exploring "Pisa's Campo Santo" in the best Byronic manner. Juxtapose these lines, for example, with Byron's descriptions of the Colosseum or of St. Peter's dome in the Fourth Canto of *Childe Harold's Pilgrimage:*

—Oh what a spectacle at every turn
The Place unfolds, from pavement skinned with moss,
Or grass-grown spaces, where the heaviest foot
Provokes no echoes, but must softly tread;
Where solitude with Silence paired stops short
Of Desolation, and to Ruin's scythe
Decay submits not.

(192–98)

In the Byronic manner, but with a crucial difference: where Byron was libertine, Wordsworth is pious; where Byron was Titanic, Wordsworth is modest:

If one—while tossed, as was my lot to be,
In a frail bark urged by two slender oars
Over waves rough and deep, that, when they broke,
Dashed their white foam against the palace walls
Of Genoa the superb—should there be led
To meditate upon his own appointed tasks,
However humble in themselves, with thoughts
Raised and sustained by memory of Him
Who oftentimes within those narrow bounds
Rocked on the surge, there tried his spirit's strength
And grasp of purpose, long ere sailed his ship
To lay a new world open.

(119–30)

Behind these lines lies a famous episode from Moore's *Life* of Byron:

> Toward the latter end of June, as we have seen in one of the preceding letters [June 27, 1816], Lord Byron, accompanied by his friend Shelley, made a tour in his boat round the Lake. . . . In the squall off Meillerie, which he mentions, their danger was considerable. In the expectation, every moment, of being obliged to swim for his life, Lord Byron had already thrown off his coat, and, as Shelley was no swimmer, insisted upon endeavouring, by some means, to save him. This offer, however, Shelley positively refused; and seating himself quietly upon a locker, and grasping the rings at each end firmly in his hands, declared his determination to go down in that position.

To Byron's account Moore subjoins in a note Shelley's:

> I felt, in this near prospect of death (says Mr. Shelley), a mixture of sensations. Among which terror entered, though but subordinately. My feelings would have been less painful, had I been alone; but I knew that my companion would have attempted to save me, and I was overcome with humiliation, when I thought that his life might have been risked to preserve mine. When we arrived at St. Gingoux, the inhabitants, who stood on the shore, unaccustomed to see a vessel as frail as ours, and fearing to venture at all on such a sea, exchanged looks of wonder and congratulation with our boatmen, who, as well as ourselves, were pleased to set foot on shore.[38]

That this episode stands behind Wordsworth's lines becomes indisputable in the Fenwick note on the passage:

> We took boat near the light-house at the point of the right horn of the bay, which makes a sort of natural port for Genoa, but the wind was high & the waves long and rough, so that I did not feel quite recompensed by the view of the city, splendid as it was, for the danger apparently incurred. The boatman (I had only one) encouraged me, saying we were quite safe, but I was not a little glad when we gained the shore, tho' Shelley and Byron—one of them at least who seemed to have courted agitation from every quarter—would have probably rejoiced in such a situation, more than once I believe were they both in extreme danger even on the Lake of Geneva. Every man however has his fears of some kind or other; &, no doubt, they had theirs—of all men whom I have ever known Coleridge had the most of passive courage in bodily peril, but no one was so easily cowed when moral firmness was required in miscellaneous conversation or in the daily intercourse of social life.[39]

The Fenwick notes appeared for the first time in the 1857 edition of Wordsworth, brought out by his executors in order to assert a fresh copyright. The notes constitute "Wordsworth's last great act of imaginative self-assessment," as Stephen Gill rightly concludes, and were integral to the edition.[40] In this instance they confirm that what purports to be merely a biographical incident from 1837 is Wordsworth's multilayered resituating of himself in literary history. Byron's practical courage and Shelley's speculative calm—and in the notes, Coleridge's lack of moral firmness—yield to Wordsworth's account of his own (ostensibly) humble meditations, and if the capital letter in "Him" colors the scene with echoes of Christ walking upon the waters, so much more strongly is the comparison enforced between piety and radical "agitation."

The treatment of Scott unfolds within the same self-validating pattern. Wordsworth follows his imaginative transport from Italy back to the Lake District by asking "who that travels far / To feed his mind with watchful eyes could share / Or wish to share it (54–56)?" If this query exposes his gesture to charges of provincialism, Wordsworth rebuts them by invoking Scott:

> —One there surely was,
> "The Wizard of the North," with anxious hope
> Brought to this genial climate, when disease
> Preyed upon body and mind—yet not the less
> Had his sunk eye kindled at those dear words
> That spake of bards and minstrels; and his spirit
> Had flown with mine to old Helvellyn's brow,
> Where once together, in his day of strength,
> We stood rejoicing, as if earth were free
> From sorrow, like the sky above our heads.
> (56–65)

The maneuver of legitimating his poem by incorporating Scott's approval is reinforced by the Fenwick note: "His, Sir W. Scott's, eye *did* in fact kindle at them for the lines 'places forsaken now' & the two that follow were adopted from a Poem of mine which nearly 40 years ago was in part read to him and he never forgot them" (Curtis, 69). Instead of the polarity of the healthy, extroverted Scott and the pathologized, introverted Wordsworth developed by Jeffrey and Hazlitt, instead of his own condescension to Scott's art, Wordsworth gives us himself and Scott standing together atop the mountain associated with Wordsworth, the mountain where Haydon placed Wordsworth in his famous portrait of the same year as the publication of *Poems, Chiefly of Early and Late Years.*[41]

"Musings" continues:

Still, in more than ear-deep seats,
Survives for me, and cannot but survive
The tone of voice which wedded borrowed words
To sadness not their own, when, with faint smile
Forced by intent to take from speech its edge,
He said, "When I am there, although 'tis fair.
'Twill be another Yarrow."

(71–77)

At the conclusion of "Tintern Abbey" Wordsworth composes his ideal epitaphic vision of himself by forecasting how his sister is to remember him. A similar act of ventriloquism obtains here, only instead of his younger sister, it is a celebrated poet who immortalizes Wordsworth's poetry: "These words were quoted to me from 'Yarrow Unvisited,' by Sir Walter Scott when I visited him at Abbotsford, a day or two before his departure for Italy," runs the note in *Poems, Chiefly of Early and Late Years* (147). Absent is vexation at Scott's misquotation of "Yarrow Unvisited" in *The Lay of the Last Minstrel;* absent is any hint that such misquotation "betray[ed] his own uncritical principles of composition," as Wordsworth had declared in 1827 (see n. 14). If the quotation attests to Scott's tactful minimizing of his doubts that Italy would restore him, and his generosity to Wordsworth, a generosity repaid by Wordsworth's brief revival of Scott's voice, its deployment here also suggests Wordsworth's covert self-endorsement.

"Musings" concludes with an anticipation of Wordsworth's visit to Rome, trenching ever more directly on the territory of the Fourth Canto of *Childe Harold's Pilgrimage*, but Wordsworth's Rome is not that of the butchered gladiator, of Nemesis and the revenges of history, or of the sculpture gallery, but of "Christian Traditions!" (291). The vision of Saints Peter and Paul in the "Mamertine prison" (305) rises to an affirmation of the need of "religious faith" (337) in a secular "chilled age" (325), a reiteration of the arguments of the maligned *Excursion.* "Let us now / Rise, and to-morrow greet magnificent Rome" (371–72).

Such a conclusion is a commonplace in pastoral, and it particularly echoes Milton's *Lycidas*.[42] Just as Milton's poem is less a personal lament for Edward King than Milton's meditation on his poetic vocation, so is "Musings Near Aquapendente" less a straightforward poem of friendship than an apologia for Wordsworth's career. More persuasive than Wordsworth's pretenses of frailty, indifference to fame, and humility are the lines that introduce the episode in Genoa harbor: "Who would keep / Power must resolve to cleave to it through life, / Else it deserts him, surely as he lives" (115–17). The devotion to power justifies the accusations of egotism that Hazlitt had affixed to Wordsworth decades earlier, but Power here is not Byronic commanding presence. Having outlived his contemporaries, Wordsworth seized the opportunity to shape literary history in his terms.

By the 1840s the inner "fluxes and refluxes of the mind," as the Preface to *Lyrical Ballads* specifies the territory of poems such as "Tintern Abbey" and *The Prelude*, had been filled with the representations of him by others. Wordsworth's "musings" are no longer the form of solitude, as his critics had insisted, but a theater filled by the rival actors and authors of the previous decades—Scott, Hazlitt, Byron, Shelley, Jeffrey—in a performance that he scripted and directed. The outer became the inner, to be rebroadcast publicly by the new poem. Wordsworth's private censure of Scott's poetry may be the envy of a fastidious craftsman for the greater success, in remuneration and reputation, of a less demanding writer. Yet the private pique drove the seventy-year-old poet to renewed creation, and such striking images as that of the survival, "in more than ear-deep seats," of Scott's transmission of his own words. The phrase recalls the "thoughts that do often lie too deep for tears" at the conclusion of the Intimations Ode, the poem that continued to close every one of Wordsworth's collections.[43] Its intensified inwardness points to the place of "Musings Near Aquapendente," which is less a record of the tour in Italy than of Wordsworth's stocktaking of English literary fame: the imaginative return to England at the start of the poem is a telltale gesture.

Still alive, Wordsworth could not have a Moore or a Lockhart to establish his reputation (he was enraged when De Quincey put forward an unauthorized account of the Wordsworth household in *Tait's Edinburgh Magazine* in 1834–40), and he was determined to control his depiction. Even as he continued to write, Wordsworth became his own biographical subject, as if he were already past, in every way except for the anxious energy expended on his public self-construction. "Musings" again summons Chiabrera, whose Epitaphs he had translated and who figures prominently in the "Essays on Epitaphs" associated with *The Excursion.* At Savona, city of his birth, Wordsworth sought but failed to find any of his epitaphs: "not a stone, / Mural or level with the trodden floor, / In Church or Chapel" (236–38). "Yet," Wordsworth writes,

> in his page the records of that *worth*
> Survive, uninjured;—glory then to *words*,
> Honour to word-preserving Arts
>
> (248–50; italics added)[44]

For those who look, Wordsworth's page blazons his own name.

"Imaginative self-assessment," as Gill terms it, was for Wordsworth inseparable from his differential assessment of others: in "Musings Near Aquapendente" he is at once his own elegiac subject and the chronicler of his times, re-presenting his earlier works and ensuring his place for posterity. Travel functions in the poem less as the record of an encounter with the foreign and the opportunity for new experience than as a trope for meditative distance. The mediation of Wordsworth's narrative of his experience in Genoa harbor by Moore's *Life* of Byron might be taken as exemplary of the general mediation of fresh experience by the familiar: Wordsworth's tour of Italy was prepared for by a lifetime's reading. How little physical relocation mattered to Wordsworth may be seen in his placing, in the edition of 1845, "The Pillar of Trajan" as the last of the "Memorials of a Tour in Italy, 1837," a poem written more than a decade before Wordsworth had ever visited Italy and first published in 1827, which drew its vivid representation of the column from Joseph Forsyth's *Remarks on Antiquities, Arts, and Letters during an Excursion in Italy*.[45] The placement gives the sequence a satisfying symmetry: as in "Musings near Aquapendente" Wordsworth's imagination returns from Italy to England, so in *The Pillar of Trajan* the poet,

> Borne by the Muse from rills in shepherds' ears
> Murmuring but one smooth story for all years
> . . . gladly commune[s] with the mind and heart
> Of him who survives by classic art.
>
> (23–26) (*PW*, 230)

The easy movement between different geographical settings reduces the particularity of locale and centers the poems on Wordsworth's preoccupations rather than on place. The Wordsworth of 1841, more secure of his stature than in earlier years, nine years past Scott's death, and four years removed from an Italy colored by annoyance at Lockhart's biography of Scott, could recollect Scott in a tranquillity untroubled except by his recurrent anxiety over his own comparative literary stature. Neither apocalyptically annihilating place, nor celebrating it in the delighted surprises of much travel-writing about the warm South, "Musings Near Aquapendente" shows that for Wordsworth the place that chiefly counts is his in the pantheon.

CHAPTER ELEVEN

Writing Criticism

Art, Transcendence, and History

Donald G. Marshall

Over many years, I have been among the numerous beneficiaries of Geoffrey Hartman's generous collegiality. His ideas have proven so stimulating in my thinking and teaching that honoring him is equally a means of intellectual gain to myself. In Heidegger's suggestive paranomasia, *danken* and *denken* are twinned.

Out of Hartman's rich corpus, I have decided to take up the themes indicated by my title. The word "transcendence" is a deliberate provocation. Throughout the course of Western culture, poetry has been called on to justify itself. The charge against it has been that it corrupts its audience, stirring their passions, offending good morals, and committing sacrilege against religious truths. Poetry was not accused of being either an escape from the earthly or a means of access to the transcendent. The poet might fly from heaven to earth and range freely within the zodiac of his own wit, but the consequence of delivering a golden world was to "make the too much loved earth more lovely."[1] Whether from a Platonic or Christian perspective, poetry was the enemy of the disciplines needed to withdraw our minds from care for material things and turn them to a realm beyond the flux of our experience.[2] The defense of poetry in Aristotle and the rhetorical tradition, brilliantly traced by Wesley Trimpi and his student Kathy

Eden,[3] claimed, on the contrary, that the constructions of art fitted us for more intelligent and effective action in the human world. That tradition shows no interest in transcendent experience, refusing to waste time debating whether there even is such a thing.

It seems to me that the notion that art might be able to stand apart from the historical life of human beings emerged in the eighteenth century. Paradoxically, it emerged both as the expression of Enlightenment thinking and as a reaction against that thinking. Enlightenment meant that intellectuals assumed the immense responsibility of improving the conditions of actual human life. Deprivation and suffering were removed from the moral and religious sphere and treated as practical problems to be solved through the exercise of reason. Solving them in turn required throwing off the authority of tradition and dissolving the self-evidence of existing social, political, and economic arrangements. In this courageous program of progress toward the promise of the future, intellectuals drew near to the spirit of modern science expressed forcefully, though diversely, by Bacon and Descartes. But in this cultural reconstruction, the position of art became problematic. One could fall back on an older rhetoric and assert art's civilizing function to tame the passions, polish the manners, and provide a sphere for harmless social interaction separated from the dangerous conflicts inherent in religion, politics, and moneymaking. Such an approach implied not taking art very seriously and cooly purging it of any elements that threatened to overflow its delimited function. At best, art could serve as a socially acceptable expressive intensification of bodily life and hence a useful safety valve or, more ambitiously, as the epitome of the free human activity critical reform aimed to make widely accessible and hence as the goal that legitimated reform.

The proliferation of treatises on aesthetics during the eighteenth century testifies to a double difficulty. On the one hand, since art could not supply knowledge that measured up to the emerging standard of science, the concept of imitation, which had previously given art its claim to be taken seriously, became untenable. On the other hand, art remained highly prized, so a new theoretical legitimation for it needed to be found. On this matter as on many others it is Kant who most penetratingly articulates both the problem and its solution within the perspective of Enlightenment philosophy. I certainly do not mean to suggest that Kant sees art negatively, as a cultural remainder he must somehow fit into the architectonic of his thought. On the contrary, the *Critique of Judgment*, as Ernst Cassirer has convincingly argued,[4] is motivated by the positive discovery of a third kind of a priori, one different from those of pure and practical reason.

Indeed, in order to grasp this third a priori, we must withdraw ourselves from the intensely human interests that ordinarily drive us to know and to act. This suspension cannot legitimate itself on cognitive or practical grounds. Though Kant did not intend or foresee it, his characterization of art opens the possibility of the questions formulated by Hans-Georg Gadamer, "Is there still a time and place for art in an age where social unrest and the discomfort with our social life in an anonymous mass society is felt from all sides and where the demand for rediscovering or reestablishing true solidarities is advanced over and over again? Is it not an escape when one claims art or poetry to still be an integral part of human being?"[5]

The most widespread answer to this question starts from the conviction that "literary texts have always been, more or less, products of their historical, social, political, and economic environments."[6] This claim may take on a positive tone if the artwork is seen as articulating a historical milieu's values and beliefs in a way that clarifies its audience's self-understanding and calls them to their responsibilities. But in recent scholarship, the claim takes a more suspicious turn. The scholar who adopts it intends to unmask the work's inauthenticity and concealment of the disturbing realities it refuses to acknowledge.[7] In both cases, the critical measure to be applied to the work is whether it resists or cooperates with the forces of progress leading to human liberation.[8] Where the first step is to take the work of art as the product of its environment, and the second step is to measure it against what is progressive in that environment, it is a short third step to hold that the artist is obliged to validate this claim by transforming it into an active program. I borrow again Gadamer's formulation: "Must not all literature be now *littérature engagée?* And like all committed literature quickly become outdated?" ("Silent," 73).

Stated in so condensed and bald a fashion, this line of thought too easily shows itself to be questionable. I must appeal to the conscience of every reader to acknowledge how legitimately strong is its hold on us, not only because we desire freedom and justice but also because we desire that poetry should play a manifest role in achieving them. I call to witness only Keats, who would wish to be carried "on the viewless wings of Poesy" far from this place "where men sit and hear each other groan" ("Nightingale," 33, 24) and yet in *Hyperion* imagines the youthful Apollo gazing into the face of Mnemosyne and reading there the knowledge of suffering and change that enables him to "Die into life" (3.130).[9] Historicist ways of thinking are so deeply rooted in us that we can scarcely imagine a criticism that refuses to situate a poem in its historical context.[10]

And yet, after the collapse of utopian schemes for remaking human life, the conviction is unavoidable that there is something wrong in this line of thought. What is wrong lies in the word "product." A poem is not a product of its time. Indeed, a poem is not a product in any sense at all.[11] It is not an artifact, and that means it cannot belong to the sphere of use and consumption. This thesis seems even less tenable than the claim that a poem is a product. Are not poems obviously made by poets so that they may be read with pleasure by other human beings? In the *Republic*, Plato reproaches tragedies for being unreliably crafted for unregulated use and consumption. This invites Aristotle's reply that tragedy-making is an activity that can be regulated by principles derived from the nature of the object produced by that art. An endless stream of poetic manuals tried to make good this claim. But the failure throughout the centuries of every effort to turn the structural analysis of successful poems into a reliable prescription for creating them carries a warning we can scarcely ignore.

The collapse of neoclassical poetics ended the project of making poems the product of conscious art and left the field to the notion that they emerge from some unspecifiably elusive creative process. But the conception of the poem as product was recuperated by transposing the theme of making into the realm of history. The notion that history is made is often attributed to Vico—and indeed, he marvels "that the philosophers should have bent all their energies to the study of the world of nature, which, since God made it, He alone knows; and that they should have neglected the study of the world of nations, or civil world, which, since men had made it, men could come to know."[12] But Vico's claim is obviously false. Everyone sees at once that we do not understand history at all and find it constantly unintelligible. That is why the historian falls back on recording sheer fact. Vico cannot maintain his claim coherently. He is forced to invoke both geometry and Providence to make his claim intelligible (104, pars. 348–49). It may be that geometry "constructs the world of quantity out of its elements, . . . creating it for itself," but geometric construction is entirely different from historical narration. Vico has to postulate that the intelligible order of history rests on its governance by Providence, and he presupposes that the "common sense" he uses to grasp this order is itself "taught by divine providence." But this evidently abandons the claim that human beings "made" history. In fact, the historian cannot achieve the closure of subject and object available to mathematics and theology. As Gadamer asks, "Is not the fact that consciousness is historically conditioned inevitably an insuperable barrier to its reaching perfect fulfillment in historical knowledge?"[13]

Vico is too early and too remote from the centers of the development of modern science to grasp that the contrast he draws between history and nature is completely mistaken. The core of the scientific project is to "make" nature, to subject it to human processes of control and production. Nature as conceived by science is in principle completely intelligible. The Enlightenment perspective on history was much more realistic than Vico's in its conviction that history was fundamentally unintelligible, the record of inexplicable errors and blunders. If it had any coherence and meaning, they were the product of conspiracies, of the deliberate manipulation of ignorant masses by cunning and self-interested parties. History was unreason or it was reason as cunning. The point, then, was to eliminate superstition and ignorance or—and basically it comes to the same thing—to bring the conspiracy of history-makers into the open, into the public sphere where all those qualified by intelligence, that is, certified with the credentials of reason, could join the open conspiracy of shaping the course of events. This is what Kant means by "the public."[14]

Developing his thinking alongside the massive application of science to the natural world which constituted the heroic age of nineteenth-century engineering, Marx carried through the Enlightenment idea that history is not a product but should be. But hard realism requires an admission that history does not exhibit the conspiracies postulated, so that even when kings and priests are overthrown, events still get out of hand, and the attempt to identify conspirators who can be blamed results in arbitrary executions. Hence it becomes necessary to presuppose a conspiracy that is a secret from the conspirators themselves. This doubled conspiracy is "ideology." Ideology cannot be liquidated by sheer reason but only by raising the proletariat into consciousness and hence into the status of a shaping force. As in the scientific domination of nature, the aim is to convert the seemingly autonomous and alien processes of history into a conscious product.

It is Karl Popper who shows decisively that this project is futile and indeed self-contradictory,[15] and events have confirmed his view. The lesson I draw is that art and history cannot be related in this way, namely, under the rubric of "product." Neither our concept of art nor of history is to be regulated by the completeness attained in artifacts, a completeness that puts them at our disposal. We must seek some other relation, and this conclusion leads me back to Kant in a way that may diverge from what I think is a common view of him, namely, that he conceives the artwork in an ahistorical way. Certainly, the emphasis of the first half of the *Critique of Judgment* falls on the work of art as the content of perception. While the artwork has come to stand there enduringly through a productive process, it is also freed from the instrumental and utilitarian sphere of purposive action, which is saturated with care for ourselves. And correlatively, the perceiver is freed as well. In that sense, the experience of art may be said to "transcend" its circumstances. Such a transcendence is no leap into an idealist void. Because the aesthetic judgment in which the work of art is experienced is a reflective judgment, it implicates the actual exercise of our faculties in a way that enables us, as nothing else can, to sense our own life. Reflective judgments legitimately enable us to intuit a whole in an experience that does not go beyond our finite, discursive nature.[16] These judgments, in which we discover purposiveness or design, whether in nature or in an artwork, bring us a new conception both of the self and of nature. We feel a purposive whole and cannot help feeling it, but we cannot explain it. We thus encounter the boundaries of our human capacities and, by locating these boundaries, discover what we are. We can thus experience the poem as a whole without conceiving it as a realized artifact and without adopting an idealist conception of meaning. This felt wholeness of life cannot be specified conceptually. Its coherence does not belong to natural law or to human will freely fixed on a moral purpose. Feeling this sort of wholeness consequently enhances our mind's power to encompass the most variegated experiences while maintaining the freedom of our perceiving minds. To say that a poem transcends historical circumstances does not mean that the poem flies away from concrete life, leaving it behind, but that it falls upon concrete life, deflecting it with a blow that is historical in the sense that its ramifications are unpredictable and endless. A poem is not a product extruded from or in the course of historical process. Rather, it attains its relation to history in our response to it. The being of the artwork "lies in its issuing a challenge which it expects to be met," namely, the challenge of making it "the focal point of recognition and understanding."[17] The blow (Heidegger's *Stoss*) the work delivers, however, is not assault and battery. It requires a certain generosity in us to rise to the challenge, but thinking that is held in relation to a poem is also borne up by it, actively to validate it as a promise. Responding to the work's self-presentation means that "we take the construction of the work upon ourselves as a task" ("Relevance," 28). We go beyond "mere sensory registration" to take the work as true (29; Gadamer is making explicit the two meanings of the German *wahrnehmen*). The identity and unity of the work lie in this hermeneutic response, not in any classical ideal of harmony as a property of the work. This activity is an "indeterminate anticipation of sense," and consequently the work can never be appropriated "for knowledge and understanding in all its meaning" (33). In the work, sense is "secured and sheltered" "so that it does not run away or escape from us," but this sense remains bound to "the sheer fact of the work's existence," and consequently it "destroys all presumption that we can make sense of it all" (34).

This line of thought seems to me confirmed by Wordsworth's *Prelude.* This work can hardly be subsumed under classic conceptions of unity; it is not a "well-made" artifact. It is available now in three separate versions, and what is more, Wordsworth never in his lifetime brought it to any definitive text or supervised its printing. The content of the poem is, if possible, even more indeterminate. It presents neither a coherent topical nor a chronological organization. It shuttles across the web of the poet's experience, building up the layered palimpsest of memory. Its texture is variegated, punctuated by dramatic "spots of time," yet also encompassing discursive passages that modern criticism glosses over. Even the spots of time are not definitive articulations of meaning. Their function is to bring memories to stand in their facticity so that they can be read and reread as the poet articulates later experience and dramatically different feelings in relation to them. The poem is already an interpretation, a responsive anticipation of the wholeness of a life that cannot be grasped in conceptual or practical, purposive terms. This certainly does not imply an abandonment of the claims of knowledge or of responsibility but rather the poem presents the poet to himself in the only way possible.

I believe this line of thought is also confirmed in Derek Walcott's *Omeros*,[18] which has been described as a poem in which the poet speaks out of a people to a people. It might therefore seem to stand at the opposite pole from Wordsworth's focus on his own life, though I think that contrast does not adequately appreciate the validity of Wordsworth's claim to be a representative man. Nevertheless, Walcott's poem perhaps makes it easier to reflect on the way a poem's being embedded in local history in no way restricts the claim it makes on every reader. Walcott takes up the responsibility and the opportunity to name a world hitherto unrecorded. The words in which that world comes to stand already overlay both the lost language of the native Aruacs and the African languages torn from the black fishermen's ancestors on the Middle Passage. But the evocation or recalling of Homer is equally displaced from the English the poet speaks, which is further displaced by French and a range of other languages and dialects, by the Dantean terza rima of his meter, and by the very name "Omeros," drawn from a Greek language he does not know. The polyvocal, by no means broken language of the poem—along with the layering of scenes (Boston, Santa Lucia, Africa, London) and the layering of times (present and precolonial Santa Lucia, seventeenth-century colonial wars, precolonial Africa, the poet's childhood and adulthood, and the Trojan War that suffuses the poem but is never explicit) — certainly could not be described as effecting an unproblematic synthesis. The poem is not offered as a souvenir for tourists. The reader is challenged to follow out the poet's own movement:

> "O-meros," she laughed. "That's what we call him in Greek,"
> stroking the small bust with its boxer's broken nose,
> and I thought of Seven Seas sitting near the reek
>
> of drying fishnets, listening to the shallows' noise.
> I said: "Homer and Virg are New England farmers,
> and the winged horse guards their gas-station, you're right."
>
> I felt the foam head watching as I stroked an arm, as
> cold as its marble, then the shoulders in winter light
> in the studio attic. I said, "Omeros,"
>
> and *O* was the conch-shell's invocation, *mer* was
> both mother and sea in our Antillean patois,
> *os*, a grey bone, and the white surf as it crashes
>
> and spreads its sibilant collar on a lace shore.
> Omeros was the crunch of dry leaves, and the washes
> that echoed from a cave-mouth when the tide has ebbed.
>
> The name stayed in my mouth.
>
> (1.2.3:14)

Naming is the most salient case of the poet's labor of finding the right word and making the place for it. In naming the world, even for the first time, the writer writes it into a language that is at home for everyone. "Thus poetic language stands out as the highest fulfillment of that revealing (*deloun*) which is the achievement of all speech," Gadamer says.[19] "Our fundamental experience as beings subject to time is that all things escape us" ("Truth," 114). But in the poem, the word "stands written," so that it "summons up what is 'there' so that it is palpably near" (113). Thus, "When we grow up in a language, the world is brought close to us and comes to acquire a certain stability" (114). It would be a strange misunderstanding to think that Walcott's poem seeks its validation by directing us to visit Santa Lucia or to see for ourselves the landscape it speaks about. Its truth "consists in creating a 'hold upon nearness' " (113), which "is not a romantic theory, but a straightforward description of the fact that" the language of this poem "by being there bears witness" (115).

Though I am speaking the language of Gadamer, I think what I am saying is consistent with Hartman's great essay "Toward Literary History."[20] Hartman evokes Aristotle's assertion that "poetry, therefore, is more philosophical and more significant than history, for poetry is more concerned with the universal."[21] What "the universal" (*to katholou*) means becomes clear in chapter 17, where Aristotle urges the poet first to get a "general view" (*to katholou*) of the play's plot before filling in episodes (1455b3). It is not easy to connect this to what Aristotle says elsewhere about "the universal," for here he is talking about form, not as mechanically imposed but as arising out of the poem's substance, the subject matter it presents. What Aristotle's famous dictum appears to mean is that a plot will repay the sort of attention that is focused on making sense out of experience better than mere matter of fact will do because a plot is coherent and can therefore stand there as an abiding object of contemplation. This position seems to me entirely consistent with Kant's conception of reflective judgment as interpreted above. What Hartman goes on to consider is the possibility of form that can inhere in or perhaps constitute the poet's understanding of his or her historical situation, including the situation of literature itself and its existent forms. To return to Gadamer's language, in the formed work sense is "secured and sheltered" but remains so bound to the work that it "destroys all presumption that we can make sense of it all" ("Relevance," 34).

More recently, Hartman poises this possibility more polemically between the consumerist erosion of situated content and the dangerous counterpoise of identity politics. Hartman cites John Dewey to the effect that the tension is not between an abstract, idealist universality and the density of lived historical experience but between a local and therefore well-reasoned judgment and the vulnerability to bunk, hokum, and "undiscriminating sentiment and belief" consequent on the homelessness of those compelled by rapid transportation and communication "to live as members of an extensive and mainly unseen society."[22] To react to this obliteration by erecting an identity preserved negatively through the refusal to answer to another would, Hartman judges, be fatal. For refusing to answer to another is refusing to answer for oneself.

This rather long reflection on art and history leads to the question of criticism, for just as the place of poetry has become questionable in our time, so has the place of criticism, and this has become an increasingly prominent theme of

Hartman's work. We can say at once that the critic is pulled in contrary directions, and being thus pulled implies an unwillingness to dismiss any of them as illegitimate.[23] It is not easy to say exactly when the critic's role began to be defined within emerging mass media and the marketing of art, but that situation is already fully evident in Poe.[24] The critic may comment on a book in detail, but readers may take such comments as at best mere backing for the real point, namely, the final recommendation to buy and read or not; or, at worst, simply as a way to fill space, their true function being to provide an alibi for the juxtaposed advertising. The critic may be assigned a more useful role in helping us sift through an excess of information to find the few items we really want or need to know. But the critic can also assume a certain autonomy not only in independent essays but also in exchanges about books in which the exchange itself rather than the book becomes the focus of the reader's interest. In this world of media and marketing the critic is squeezed into steadily narrower limits, must speak about what is contemporary, must not expect the audience to know anything in particular, must use the most common language. Speed is of the essence: neither the subject discussed nor the critic's own writing attains durability, for this kind of writing is written to be read by him who runs.

In sharp contrast, the critic is also drawn toward the world of scholarship, particularly insofar as he is drawn into the university. The scholar aims at historical depth and exact learning. There is no sharp division here; T. S. Eliot's brief and pungent criticism of Donne rested on the scholarship of H. J. C. Grierson's edition, but Grierson's introduction had already laid out the patterns of Donne's poetry in a way that opened the text for a modern reader. Nevertheless, the scholar pays a price for the historical perspective, since scholarship implies a time scale that is almost never helpful in the short-range decisions that constitute the texture of everyday life. The movements of culture the scholar speaks of ring like fate: we can do nothing about them and can only participate in them by a sort of well-informed pathos. It is true that the broadly informed mind may be guarded against fashions and transitory alarms, but the scholar's role as sage may easily collapse into that of paralyzed bystander or, worse yet, dogmatic conservative.

A third role is that of the expert. This role is not, I think, fully recognized, but it seems to me dominant in the contemporary academy. The loosely used term "theory" points in this direction. Expertise is different from scholarship. The contemporary theorist attains distance from and mastery over a body of material not by appeal to the "common reader" or by the mediations of historical erudition but by the application of method. What the expert is expert in is some systematic scheme of analysis: psychoanalysis, for instance, or Marxism. What marks the expert as expert is jargon, a language that testifies to specialization and, by redescribing a subject matter from an autonomous standpoint, claims to generate insights that are valid yet could not have been attained by common sense.

The critic's role as expert has proven particularly vulnerable in recent years. It is easy for experts to put at a disadvantage whoever does not understand their jargon or cannot follow the intricacies of their method. But the expert's role is not legitimated by expertise but by a willingness to put that expertise at someone's service.[25] This commitment to service is complicated by the fact that in the human sciences expertise invariably takes the form of critique and thus of invalidating what the person served posits as goals and assumes as common knowledge. The expert finds his legitimation in discovering hidden interests or bringing to light a secret logic that connects actions with evil consequences in a way that attributes self-deception or concealed motives to agents who disclaim those consequences as unintended. But an expertise that asks people to act against their own best judgment is in a difficult situation. When critics, regarding themselves as experts, step forward to apply the analytic tools they use in literary study to the "reading" of social phenomena and the criticism of culture, the fruits of expertise are dangerously exposed to the judgment of the common man—or perhaps I should say woman, since, as Jonathan Swift reminds us, it was a Thracian woman who laughed when Thales, busy gazing at the stars, was betrayed by his lower parts into a ditch.

I doubt Hartman would claim that he has safely negotiated these contrary pulls; he might only claim modestly that he has acknowledged all of them and more. I want, however, to return to the relation I asserted between art and history. What corresponds for the critic to the moment of "transcendence" is, I believe, reading. Hartman has long been concerned with the fate of reading in an era that has little time to go beyond information retrieval and processing.[26] But reading is threatened more intimately by academic work, as Hartman suggests in his essay "History Writing as Answerable Style."[27] For, "as interpretability becomes more important than historicity," the art object threatens to collapse, on the one hand, into a mere object of the interpreting mind and, on the other, into a mere chaos of interpretations (105). Hartman has seemed to some to argue elsewhere for just this "indeterminacy" of meaning, but I would claim that they misunderstand. He does not mean a mere Dionysian revel in which the work is ripped limb from limb and scattered among the celebrants. Rather, indeterminacy was supposed to stand for responsive thinking, a thinking that did not consume the work or dispose of it but contrived to hold it before the mind. In this earlier essay, Hartman objects that "ontic stubbornness . . . is hardly sufficient to characterize the reserve of art, which should be a reservoir of resonances rather than a mystifying void" (105). Ethnomethodology shows that every utterance or act implicates an infinity of assumptions, that is, of actualized interpretations. But in ordinary life, interpretation is used up very quickly. Paradoxically, it is the poems that are most closed, that most definitely "stand there," that produce endless interpretation. The more open the text, the less there is to say about it—or at least, the less there is to say that matters.

The critic's preeminent function is located precisely here, where, as scripture says, "He that has ears to hear, let him hear." Hartman admits engagingly that when he reads literature, "I stumble about, sometimes hedonistically, in that word-world; I let myself be ambushed by sense or sensation and forget the drive toward a single, all-conquering truth; and I unravel the text only as it is simultaneously rethreaded on the spool of commentary" (*Prophecies*, 207). His ear has been resistant to seeing "through texts rather than with them" (208). Here, I would claim, is where history takes place. In recent years, we have heard often and in many phrasings about the political responsibility of the critic. But surely this is the specific political responsibility of the critic, namely, to help other readers give ear to what it is essential for them to hear in the literature that speaks—or rather that whispers, barely audibly, to them. As Gadamer observes, in an era when the poets may be falling silent, the critic has a special responsibility to be all ears ("Silent," 81).

An equivalent way of stating this is to say that the critic's function is to make a judgment—not in the judicial sense, as though passing sentence on a work, but in Kant's sense, where the critic attains the right distance and the right angle from which to see what the work really is, its *qualitas*, and then to present, to be a witness to that *qualitas* in his own statement, in our presence. The means for achieving the right distance and the right angle correspond to the varied claims I have noted on the critic. The obligation to develop a taste requires that the critic put himself in the presence of a wide range of literary works so that judgment is comparative, infused by memory's power to gather intertexts spontaneously. History creates its own peculiar distance, which does not push away but holds near, and the scholar's judgment is a capacity to speak out of the tradition for which he has assumed an uncompelled responsibility. The alienating effects of expertise seem to me more questionable, but they may also have their place. As Gadamer argues, the expert has his own responsibility: to anticipate the results of scientific findings; to hold to what his expertise has actually learned and asserts even against "the pressure of interests and the expectations of the public," including other experts; and finally, to keep in view "the deep solidarities underlying all norms of human life" even against the claims of specialization, difference, and disputed cases ("Expert," 191–92). While it is certainly difficult to keep these claims fully activated in judgment, Hartman has stated convincingly what judgment means "in historical or literary-critical discourse," and it is with his words that I wish to close: "to change history into memory: to make a case for what should be remembered, and how it should be remembered. This responsibility," he adds, "converts every judgment into a judgment on the person who makes it" (*Prophecies*, 148).

Part IV / Audible Scenes

Ecologies of Reading

CHAPTER TWELVE

Gentle Hearts and Hands

Reading Wordsworth after Geoffrey Hartman

J. Douglas Kneale

The title of this chapter contains an example of one of Geoffrey Hartman's favorite rhetorical figures: the phrase "Reading . . . after Geoffrey Hartman" can itself be read as what Quintilian calls prolepsis, a figure of prediction.[1] Yet how can we speak of reading "after" Geoffrey Hartman when he is still very much with us? Or does the proleptic suggestion in my title contain a muted epitaphic gesture, in the way that the closing lines of Wordsworth's "Solitary Reaper" do: "The music in my heart I bore, / Long after it was heard no more"?[2] "After," in its temporal sense, implies belatedness but also the sense of "after-effect," or of "aftering" itself, which Hartman would associate with a "westering" impulse.[3] I would not, perhaps, go so far as to suggest that prolepsis and epitaph necessarily evoke each other, though virtually any leaping ahead in Wordsworth contains implicitly a hint of final thoughts.

This essay was originally written for a conference entitled "Culture and Critical Form: Reading after Geoffrey Hartman," sponsored by the Centre for Research in Philosophy and Literature, University of Warwick, May 1993. I am grateful to Peter Larkin for organizing the conference and for his comments on my paper, which inflects the general conference title for specific purposes.

I prefer, therefore, to construe the title along stylistic and methodological lines: "Reading . . . after Geoffrey Hartman" I take to mean interpreting according to, or in the manner of. "Use every man after his desert, and who should 'scape whipping? Use them after your own honor and dignity," Hamlet says.[4] But here too we are faced with a problem: if reading after implies writing in the manner of, then indeed our burden is great, now the name of Hartman is laid upon us. He is a hard act to follow, and who comes after must needs do so with a consciousness of self raised to critical, if not apocalyptic, pitch. Let me, then, present what Wordsworth might call an "after-thought," the title he gives to the final sonnet in his "River Duddon" sequence: "I see what was, and is, and will abide; / Still glides the Stream, and shall for ever glide; / The Form remains, the Function never dies" (*PW,* 3:261).

Well, what are the "form and function" of reading after Geoffrey Hartman? According to him, criticism is getting harder to do, "yet more and more people are doing it," he writes.[5] Long before the manufacturers of athletic shoes got into the market, Hartman was saying to critics: "Just do it." "The best apology for criticism (as for literature)," he writes in *Criticism in the Wilderness,* "is doing it; and, at present, reading it closely."[6] But what is it that we do when we read? And what sort of apology, what defense of criticism, can close reading offer us today? A larger question that remains implicit here is the status of theory after Hartman. Like other discourses, and as a discourse of the other, theory has its own intentional structure—that is, it exists as a theory *of* something, if only of theory itself. For this reason there is always something precarious about theory to the extent that it derives its language or method from other fields—literature, psychology, linguistics, or philosophy, to name a few. Since these disciplines tend to protect their own language and procedures, defending against another's appropriation of them, theory will always be, as Paul de Man said, in crisis.[7] While at present the crisis is not life-threatening—on the contrary, it appears to be self-sustaining—one cannot help wondering about the long-term prognosis. Theory has had a relatively short life, and the prospect of its endurance is a legitimate concern. Even if it survives the numerous attacks from different quarters, it is clear that theory will inevitably adapt, or mutate, in response to its cultural and intellectual environment.

Yet no matter how critical reading changes, some "Form remains," as Wordsworth puts it. What Paul Klee said about his art applies to poetic interpretation, too: close reading, like drawing, sometimes means taking a line for a walk. With Hartman, however, the critical path often leads through a wilderness in which interpretation itself becomes risky: regardless of which text by Hartman we consider, the "mournful iteration" of reading is something that is not to be repeated.[8] Each essay, each performance stages its own hermeneutical drama, full of suspense and riddling questions, reflexive or metatheatrical awareness, and even comic relief; yet each also contains a through-line of plot or progress, ultimately the "progress of poesy" or of criticism itself. Nevertheless, while each performance by Hartman is unique and therefore not reiterable, even by himself, there are certain habits or recurrent conventions that govern the encounter between Hartman and a text. We expect local illumination, or *explication de texte*, to be sure; but also a setting of both text and commentary in the larger orbit of comparative literary history. "Nothing in language is alien to me," Hartman has written, "not even Heidegger's German."[9] No field of discourse, either classical commonplace or contemporary cliché, is ruled out. We become witnesses to a habit of reading in which "the question of style is also a question of method."[10] Now, certainly since the advent of poststructuralism, but even earlier in some of Hartman's writings, reading has been taken as the proper subject of literary criticism just as writing has been declared the proper subject of literature. What we call "reading" nowadays refers not to the way that we encounter texts, nor to the way that texts address us, but to the way that they talk about themselves—that is, how they repeat their own figurality or how they thematize, again and again, their own *difference*. In this view, whose heyday has passed but whose aftereffects are still being felt, textuality is expressed in terms of otherness, displacement, repetition, and *mise en abyme*.

But this is not the language of Geoffrey Hartman. For despite his close identification with deconstruction and the Yale School of criticism, Hartman has never been dogmatic in his experimenting with poststructuralism, never truly an adherent. It was not that he touched, but did not lift, the hem of deconstruction's tunic; rather, he has preferred to play the field and to enjoy the many pleasures of the text and the chase of interpretation itself. Hartman had to invent his own system or be enslaved by another's. Yet "system" is hardly the right word, since Hartman rarely stands still (at one point he characterizes his own method as "intertextual leaping") long enough for his mode to become modish or imitative of a fixed procedure.[11] In *Saving the Text*, for example, he maintains that his criticism is "a counterstatement to Derrida"—"not a refutation," he says, "but rather a different turn in how to state the matter" of literary representation. "A restored theory of representation," he continues, "should acknowledge the deconstructionist challenge as necessary and timely, if somewhat self-involved—

that is, only occasionally reflective of analogies to its own project in religious writing and especially in literary writing."[12] There were, however, many features of poststructuralism and deconstruction that attracted Hartman: greater interpretive freedom for commentary and the commentator, validation of a creative critical style, and, perhaps above all, the necessity of theory itself. Though Hartman's interest in theory predates the rise of poststructuralism — even his earliest works reveal theoretical preoccupations — there is no doubt that the ascent of theory as a discipline was felt by Hartman as both necessary and liberating in the history of criticism.[13]

But let me back up historically to consider a particular aspect of literary commentary that responds to Hartman's work on the history of critical style. I repeat the question that he himself asked in his "Short Discourse on Method" in 1954: What is Hartman's approach?

> What is his approach? Whenever a critic of literature is discussed, this question tends to preface all the rest. More than any other it rings in the student's ears the first weeks at graduate school. I could not understand it then, and still cannot. Approach? Either one has the truth about a poem or one does not. Approach? Just as a thousand misunderstandings will not alter in the least the possibility of a correct understanding, so a thousand varied approaches cannot negate uniqueness of meaning.
>
> Then I began to eat of the tree of knowledge, so that my eyes were multiplied, and where I had seen but a single *text* I now perceived the formidable legion of variant, if not discordant, *interpretations.* The philologist and the philosopher, the sociologist, the humanist, the various historians — of ideas, of literature, of politics, and of economics — the psychoanalyst and the empirical psychologist, the theologian and the lay Jewish and Christian critics, the more orthodox and the less orthodox — all had their "approach," believed themselves in possession of the truth, demanded a hearing, quarreled suavely or with verbal spittle, and insisted that even when the text did not quite fit, their analysis clarified a truth dimly perceived in the original.[14]

While I find this theoretically precocious for 1954, I am all the more impressed by the presence of certain concerns that would be deepened and elaborated throughout Hartman's oeuvre. The love of the art of interpreting is one. The awareness of competing approaches is another. The stylistic wit — "quarreled suavely or with verbal spittle" (in which the ear picks up a subtle chiasmus in the *s* and *v* consonants) — is a third. Even the etiology of what Hartman would later call his "superiority complex vis-à-vis other critics, and [his] inferiority complex vis-à-vis art" is evident here.[15] There is the sense, as we now read this before-text in the after-light of interpretation, that much of what was to follow in Hartman's career is contained here. Of course, our own historical and interpretive perspective, like that of the boy in the stolen boat in Wordsworth's *Prelude*, who rows with his back to the fore and his eye on the aft, allows us to confer or to reconfigure meaning retroactively. Yet there can be no mistaking certain interests of Hartman's which begin here and continue through his most recent work. Take, for example, his following comments on how critics in the 1950s were being "forced to consider literature as more than an organic creation, a social pastime, a religious trope, an emotional outlet, a flower of civilization, more even than an exemplary stage for ideal probabilities":

> Literature was being recognized as a moral force in its own right, an institution with its own laws, and incipiently, a distinctive form of knowledge. The recognition meant labor, hard labor. The criticism of Voltaire and the classical writers, relying on an instinctive sense of decorum, as on the free and common consent of a class of gentleman readers, seemed to have perished like Atlantis. In its stead appeared the work of the owl-eyed philologist or historiographer with broad sympathies, the professional scholar with his "field," and the unpredictable responses of a profane crowd of enthusiasts, journalists, and college students. (*UV*, x)

These remarks, cast in the past tense but in fact prophetically forward-looking, turned out to have their fulfillment in both the immediate and the long term. Three years after Hartman published these thoughts on literature as "an institution with its own laws," Northrop Frye published his *Anatomy of Criticism;* and, perhaps more relevantly, almost forty years later, the loss of "an instinctive sense of decorum" in letters and the disappearance of "the free and common consent of a class of gentleman readers" are still active concerns for Hartman. The opposition between what he calls the "gentlemanly" or "friendship style" of criticism, on the one hand, and the technical, abstract strivings of theory, on the other, is one of the themes of his 1991 book *Minor Prophecies*, in which he seeks "to understand what happened to English criticism in the period of roughly 1920 to 1950, when a 'teatotaling' style developed in academic circles":

> Now what happened is that, in a sense, nothing happened. An order of discourse strove hard to remain a discourse of order. . . . In adopting this demeanor English commentators followed an ingrained tradition. They took no solace from the notion of a science or a theory of literature: that was the Continental way, leading from

> Dilthey to Lukács, and then increasingly to reflections inspired by Marxism and structuralism. The English classical writer, even when the stakes were high, wished to please rather than teach, and to remind rather than instruct. This critical tradition, keeping its distance from sacred but also from learned commentary, sought to purify the reader's taste and the national language, and so addressed itself to peers or friends — in short, to a class of equally cultured people.[16]

It is significant and surely not accidental that Hartman's prose here emulates the very classical balance that he describes — "to please rather than teach, and to remind rather than instruct."[17] Such balance has the effect of tempering the wild side of theory with the groundedness of literary history, while at the same time kick-starting interpretation through the self-awareness of theory. In its chronic form, this grammar can become a "wavering balance," as Wordsworth might say,[18] but when the treatment is nimble or acute, as it is with Hartman, it acquires the sure-footed power of paradox: the foreignness of theory, when wedded to the goodly universe of gentlemanly discourse, becomes what Hartman calls "a strange conversation" (*Minor Prophecies*, 89). Yet it is a conversation in which the critic is no longer, like Wordsworth's poet, "a man speaking to men,"[19] but rather a "compiler" of "heterogeneous stories or types of discourse" whose relation is "antiphonal" (89). The individual voice trades off against the voice of familiar society — neither in complete harmony nor in absolute discord with it, but rather in a "concourse wild" *(Prelude*, 5.378) or "strange conversation" which is always responsive to the call of the text.

Given Hartman's long-standing interest in the boundaries between literature and criticism — and, indeed, his efforts to renegotiate those boundaries — it is perhaps not surprising that the stylistic (and sometimes more than stylistic) phenomenon of "gentlemanliness" that Hartman describes in criticism also obtains in the poetry of the same period. In 1962 the English poet and critic Alfred Alvarez edited an anthology entitled *The New Poetry*, which included works by Anne Sexton, Sylvia Plath, Ted Hughes, Thom Gunn, Philip Larkin, and others.[20] What is most interesting about this anthology is the introductory essay by Alvarez, first published in *Commentary* in 1961.[21] It is immediately apparent how its concerns complement Hartman's. Just as Hartman wished "to understand what happened to English criticism in the period of roughly 1920 to 1950" (*Minor Prophecies*, 60), Alvarez claims that he is "simply attempting to give [his] idea of what, that really matters, has happened to poetry in England during the last decade [i.e., the fifties]" (*New Poetry*, 17). Alvarez's essay, entitled "The New

Poetry or Beyond the Gentility Principle," traces the development of English poetry from the 1920s to the 1950s, with its series of what he calls "negative feedbacks," or stylistic reversals, which

> work, in their different ways, to preserve the idea that life in England goes on much as it always has, give or take a few minor changes in the class system. The upper-middle class, or Tory, ideal—presented in its pure crystalline form by John Betjeman—may have given way to the predominantly lower-middle class, or Labour, ideal of the Movement and the Angries, but the concept of gentility still reigns supreme. And gentility is a belief that life is always more or less orderly, people always more or less polite, their emotions and habits more or less decent and more or less controllable; that God, in short, is more or less good.
>
> It is a stance which is becoming increasingly precarious to maintain. (25)

Calling for "a new seriousness" in poetry which, "like Coleridge's Imagination, would reconcile 'a more than usual state of emotion with more than usual order' " (28, 32), Alvarez concludes: "My own feeling is that a good deal of poetic talent exists in England at the moment. But whether or not it will come to anything largely depends not on the machinations of any literary racket but on the degree to which the poets can remain immune to the disease so often found in English culture: gentility" (32).

Hartman's focus on criticism, and Alvarez's on poetry, certainly supplement each other, though Hartman does not go so far as to call a genteel or gentlemanly style in criticism diseased. Yet both critics point to the "precariousness" of a style—critical or poetic, it makes no difference—pitched on the assumption of an audience of peers. Alvarez even suggests that British poets who spend at least some of their formative years in America have "the creative advantage of being three thousand miles away from the fog of English gentility." Such poets are, Alvarez argues, "less open to pressures which would flatten both their intelligence and the sharp violence of their experience into a socially more acceptable middle style."[22] For Hartman, however, the precariousness is worth maintaining, for there is in his work the sense of ambivalence toward both theoretical strangeness and conversational "tea-totaling" as critical extremes that would aspire to be norms. "Without contraries is no progression." Despite his quarrel with the smug or overly formal style of English criticism, Hartman still shows a muted appreciation of it, and certainly an ability to conform to it if he wishes. But for Hartman, this style is to theory what Beulah was to Jerusalem for Blake: a resting-place from the culture wars of eternity. The "middle flight," disdained by Milton as by all the Romantics, is also passed over by Hartman in his quest for what he calls "an alternative form of reflective speech to set against the seduction of a sentimental and dominant mode" (*Minor Prophecies*, 88).

Thus, if there is a tradition of "gentility" in criticism there is also gentleness in literature, a blessing in the gentle breeze of poetry. The convention of the "gentle reader," for example, which Wordsworth adapts in his poem "Simon Lee," is only one instance of how the topos of gentleness, understood variously as social class, aesthetic category, and literary style, develops into questions of genre and intertext.[23] One poem that touches on the cognate concerns of gentleness and genre is Wordsworth's "Nutting" (*PW*, 2:211–12), begun in late 1798 and published in *Lyrical Ballads* in 1800 and, as Wordsworth said in his note to Isabella Fenwick, "intended as part of a poem on my own life, but struck out as not being wanted there."[24] Precisely why "Nutting" was not "wanted" or needed in *The Prelude* we cannot say; like other manuscript fragments, such as the powerful *ekphrasis* of the horse standing on three legs in MS. W, the text "Nutting"—perhaps with the exception of its last three lines, which I consider later—could easily have been included with other childhood episodes in Book 1 or, indeed, in any of a number of other places in *The Prelude*.[25] It surely qualifies as a "spot of time," though to say so does not advance interpretation much. The poem has generally been read as a quest-romance, although the point of the quest—its aim and object—remains puzzling.[26] A boy goes out one day to gather hazelnuts, but comes back instead with a burden of guilt for having violated nature. The violation motif, common to a number of episodes in Book 1 of *The Prelude*, as Hartman has shown, also recalls statements by Wordsworth in *Home at Grasmere*:

Nothing at that time
So welcome, no temptation half so dear
As that which urged me to a daring feat.
Deep pools, tall trees, black chasms and dizzy crags
And tottering towers—I loved to stand and read
Their looks forbidding, read and disobey,
Sometimes in act, and evermore in thought.[27]

What is striking about this passage is the way that the topos of the book of nature is assimilated to the text of literary history. Exactly whom does the poet "read and disobey," nature or poetry? In this "forest of romance" (*Prelude*, 5.455) trees begin to stand in for precursors; we find ourselves in the enchanted grove where personification, or prosopopoeia, becomes literalized as animation. As interpreters it is easy for us to lose our way, especially when Wordsworth covers his tracks so cleverly that he throws us almost completely off the scent. It is not that Wordsworth is a "chameleon" poet, constantly altering his appearance, but rather that he has the power to absorb and transform his influences so thoroughly—yet so gently—that he appears "natural." One result of such transformative power is what Harold Bloom has called "apophrades," the intertextual effect in which precursors begin to sound like their descendants.[28] I was struck by such a phenomenon some years ago in a passage from Roland Barthes's *Empire of Signs*, in which Barthes attempts to describe the essence of the Japanese haiku. I quote this brief excerpt, not for its insight into the haiku but for its purely gratuitous allusion: In the haiku, "meaning is only a flash, a slash of light: *When the light of sense goes out, but with a flash that has revealed the invisible world*, Shakespeare wrote; but the haiku's flash illumines, reveals nothing."[29] It is an astonishing and wonderful error for Barthes to hear Shakespeare when in fact he is quoting Wordsworth; yet it is an interpretive after-effect I have myself experienced and continue to marvel at, all the more because of the way that, in this mini–literary history, Shakespeare displaces Milton. For a period in the 1970s and eighties, after the publication of Bloom's *Anxiety of Influence*, a number of critics productively labored under the impression that Milton was the alpha and omega of Wordsworthian influence, that Shakespeare belonged, as Bloom himself said, "to the giant age before the flood" (*Anxiety*, 11), and that really the only conversation worth listening in on was the dialogue between Milton and the Romantics. Bloom has since increasingly expanded his focus, however, and other readers have also liberated themselves from what now appears as an unnecessarily restrictive concentration on one instance of a more general theory of poetry. Hartman, of course, was one of those who were uncomfortable with the system, as shown when he wrote in 1980 that the emphasis on the presence of the Miltonic voice in Wordsworth occluded another, deeper voice: "It seems to me that Wordsworth approaches Shakespeare *through* Milton. The overt presence, Milton's, may be the less dangerous one: it is possible that the real block, or the poet defended against because of the power of his word . . . is Shakespeare."[30] Intuitively, this seems right to me, although we cannot stop here; we need to open up intertextual perspectives on Wordsworth that take us back through both Milton and Shakespeare to even earlier hintertexts.[31]

It is tempting, therefore, to read Wordsworth's "Nutting" as an allegory of intertextuality in which Wordsworth, "fearless of a rival," sallies forth to a bower of bliss which he sullies through a "strength / Of usurpation" (*Prelude*, 6.599–

600). At first, these "fresh woods" seem to present themselves in a Miltonic mode, as so many of Wordsworth's poems do. We have, for example, the sallying forth that echoes Milton's *Areopagitica:* "I cannot praise a fugitive and cloistered virtue, unexercised and unbreathed, that never sallies out and sees her adversary, but slinks out of the race where that immortal garland is to be run for, not without dust and heat."[32] The boy who journeys to the "dear nook," "O'er pathless rocks, / Through beds of matted fern, and tangled thickets, / Forcing [his] way," resembles, as critics have noted, Satan on his quest through Chaos;[33] and Wordsworth's description of the "virgin scene," "where not a broken bough / Drooped with its withered leaves, ungracious sign / Of devastation," clearly echoes Eve's temptation scene and Adam's response in Book 9 of *Paradise Lost.* At the same time, however, the middle section of the poem, with its evocation of a pastoral, fairy world, "Where fairy water-breaks do murmur on / For ever," and mossy stones lie "scattered like a flock of sheep," contains Shakespearean overtones: Lear and the flowers ("beneath the trees I sate / Among the flowers, and with the flowers I played"); the Sonnets (echoed in the "wealth of kings"); and both *Richard III* and *Hamlet* in the modulation of "sallied" (in the 1800 version) into "Deformed and sullied."[34] In the performance of his own intertextuality, the poet of "Nutting" becomes "a Figure quaint, / Tricked out in proud disguise of cast-off weeds." A trick is a trope, in Renaissance rhetoric, and "cast-off weeds" are also second-hand words. "The trick of that voice I do well remember," Gloucester says of Lear (4.6.105). A Shakespearean voice coexists with a Miltonic rhetoric; the boy enters both the world before the Fall—the opposite image of which is Wordsworth's "Adam, yet in Paradise / Though fallen from bliss" (*Prelude*, 8.659–60)—and also what Wordsworth elsewhere calls "the wild woods / Of Arden" (8.138–39).

The parallelism of the Miltonic and Wordsworthian scenes (sylvan or virgin, as the case may be) implies that this episode hinges on a "before-and-after" structure. Even though at least one early reader could "make neither head nor tail of it," there is very little middle to this text: out of a total of fifty-six lines, only two deal with the central action, that is, nutting itself.[35] I do not mean to suggest that "Nutting" is about nothing, but that rather it is about the nutting that is not there and, of course, the nutting that is:

> Then up I rose,
> And dragged to earth both branch and bough, with crash
> And merciless ravage. . . .
>
> (43–45)[36]

The poem thus displaces its nominal subject; it is all preamble and dénouement, like preface and essay supplementary, surrounding a transitory action, the motion of a muscle. What the poem delights in is the before- and after-vacancy, which turns out to be pure affect: "eagerness," "boyish hope," "suppression of the heart," "wise restraint / Voluptuous," "temper," "expectation," "sweet mood"—all these terms describing the before moment; and "present feelings," "Exult[ation]," "sense of pain," and "gentleness of heart" afterward. A heavy load of affect is poised precariously on a slim fulcrum, keeping both text and reader off balance, as they strive to find a footing in "Nutting." Recall the perilous balance mandated by the Preface to *Lyrical Ballads*, in which Wordsworth says that the "feeling" developed in his poetry "gives importance to the action and situation, and not the action and situation to the feeling" (*Prose*, 1:129).

But what a daring imbalance "Nutting" achieves! It mixes stasis with action, a contemplative mood with a violent act, and "apocalypse" with "akedah."[37] Though the sexual allegory of the poem remains understated, it is still arguably the most overt example of eroticism in Wordsworth's poetry, and it has never been satisfactorily interpreted, partly because its very obviousness seems to obviate interpretation.[38] Yet the lingering of the boy, his "sweet reluctant amorous delay," hints at perverse or fetishistic fantasies. Lingering, as Freud argued in his *Three Essays on the Theory of Sexuality*, is a perversion if the sexual activity "linger[s] over the intermediate relations to the sexual object which should normally be traversed rapidly on the path towards the final sexual aim."[39] "I play the loiterer," Wordsworth says elsewhere (*Prelude*, 3.582); but it is precisely this character of suspense or hesitation, one that is, for a moment, almost "stupidly good," that defines the poise of a text that is nearly all forepleasure and afterglow. The lingering of the boy is significant, moreover, for its relation to what Freud calls "deferred action," or *Nachträglichkeit*, the way that early, often traumatic experiences are reworked at a later date.[40] Here, expectation sits in the air while echoes of Milton play all around, recalling his defense of "why our sage and serious poet Spenser . . . describing true temperance under the person of Guyon, brings him in with his palmer through the cave of Mammon and the bower of earthly bliss, that he might see and know, and yet abstain" (Milton, 728–29). The boy's delay, described as "wise restraint / Voluptuous," borrows a Miltonic syntax to drive the emotion toward the sensuous and the passionate, confirming that this lingering "restraint" is indeed pleasurable. Seeing and knowing and yet abstaining, however, are precisely the imaginative processes that are usurped in "Nutting," as if the boy's act were also a trespass against Shakespeare, Milton, and their visionary company. In both word and deed, Wordsworth passes them "unalarmed" (Prospectus, *PW*, 5:4).

The poem concludes, not with a customary Wordsworthian benediction, but an admonishment:

Then, dearest Maiden, move along these shades
In gentleness of heart; with gentle hand
Touch — for there is a spirit in the woods.

An earlier draft of this conclusion foregrounds the poem's ethical and didactic emphasis on instruction:

Then dearest maiden if I have not now
The skill to teach thee think I pray of him
The ragged boy & let his parting look
Instruct thee how to move along these shades
In gentleness of heart. — With gentle hand
Touch, for there is a spirit in the woods.[41]

The poem is a Romantic exemplum, but an exemplum whose provenance is covered o'er, like "beds of matted fern, and tangled thickets." The "spirit in the woods" reminds us at once of the topos of the *genius loci*, or presiding spirit of place, which has been definitively treated by Hartman.[42] Wordsworth overdetermines this sense when he admonishes the "Maiden" to "move along these shades / In gentleness of heart." The word "shades" is itself haunted, inhabited by a multiple semantic presence that invokes both the locus of the "shady nook" and the return of the intertextual undead. This episode, after all, belongs to "One of those heavenly days that cannot die." Yet who speaks this touching final admonition? Is it automatically assumed to be the boy, now matured into a man, having put away his childish pastimes? I suggest that the final three lines of the poem convey obliquely the voice of an epitaph, a warning to the living to tread softly, to touch gently: as Shakespeare says, "Curst be he that moves my bones." The abruptness of the turn from narrative to coda, with its imperative rhetoric, also suggests a shift of perspective, as though someone or something else were speaking the injunction. There is the feel of self-reference, as if the demonstrative in the phrase "these shades" pointed to the speaker himself or included him in a company of shades.[43] To say this is to imply that "Nutting" is related not only to the genre of epitaph but also to nature-inscription, with its typical address to the reader: "*Siste, viator*" — one of the epigraphs that Hartman chose for his book

Wordsworth's Poetry (1). Yet while implicitly acknowledging this tradition, "Nutting" revises the convention of the "halted traveler," in Hartman's great conceit, advising the maiden instead to move, or move along. Repeating her own stopping by woods, however, the poem itself halts, hesitates, and lingers before it resumes its way. If the boy is Hartman's classic "halted traveler," the Maiden also stops and starts, saying to genre, as Rosalind says to Jaques, "Farewell, Monsieur Traveller!" (*As You Like It*, 4.1.32). What is more, in its concern with touching a tree, the poem also recalls and reverses a biblical prohibition: "Nor shall ye touch it, lest ye die."[44] Touching is not forbidden in Wordsworth, as long as it is done with "gentle" hearts and hands.[45]

Politically as well as poetically, the early Wordsworth always had the common touch. But here he appears to be attempting a style that is common and gentle at the same time. We should note that Wordsworth's interest in ghostly trees is by no means limited to "Nutting" but is part of a larger trope of a nature-consciousness in his poetry. Consider his later poem "The Haunted Tree," which centers on the image of a talking oak:

> As if (so Grecian shepherds would have deemed)
> The Hamadryad, pent within, bewailed
> Some bitter wrong. Nor is it unbelieved,
> By ruder fancy, that a troubled ghost
> Haunts the old trunk; lamenting deeds of which
> The flowery ground is conscious.
>
> (*PW*, 2:291)

"The yew-tree had its ghost," Wordsworth writes in *The Prelude* (8.379); and in almost self-parodying fashion, demonstrating an awareness of both topos and style, he writes in *Home at Grasmere* that "this grove / Is haunted—by what ghost? a gentle Spirit / Of memory faithful to the call of love" (75). As with Wordsworth's other "Yew-trees" (*PW*, 2:209–10), in whose shade Hartman and Michael Riffaterre have met in friendly disputation, fancy, or "Phantasy," invests the tree with a ghostliness that is consciously poetic.[46]

The connection between trees and poetry is as old as trees themselves. From the etymological link in the word "*liber*," meaning "the inner bark of a tree" but also by extension a book, woods and words have gone together, often in specifically amorous contexts, as when the souls of Virgil's lovers end up in the form of a myrtle or erotic poetry is carved or hung on tree trunks, as it is in Shakespeare.[47] The same topos is present, in a disguised way, in Wordsworth, and may help us understand the sexual content of "Nutting." That is, insofar as this poem imagines a spirit in the *wood*, in the wounded tree itself, we begin to hear classical and Renaissance precedents beyond those of Shakespeare and Milton. Whose woods these are we think we know, or we are tempted to find out. What other spirits are there, not trapped in epitaphic stone, but speaking from out trunk or timber? Does Wordsworth's tree have a name? And can we retrace a path from Wordsworth's hazel through Ariel's pine to Daphne's laurel?[48]

"Nutting" is Wordsworth's *Golden Bough*, a manifestation of the "pagan" (or Druidic) Wordsworth that Coleridge found so intriguing or of the "animism" that R. D. Havens explored in Wordsworth more than half a century ago.[49] Frazer has much to tell us about primitive forms of tree worship and totemism which might bear on a reading of the poem's coda and which might also, from our late-twentieth-century ecological, or "green," perspective, uncover the atavistic connections between tree-hugging and tree worship, whether seen in Eve's "low reverence done" to the tree of knowledge in *Paradise Lost* (9.835) or in such Wordsworthian settings as his Maypole celebrations and his comparison of Loughrigg Tarn to the sacred Lake Nemi or *Speculum Dianae* (the very scene with which Frazer, in an *ekphrasis* of J. M. W. Turner's painting, opens *The Golden Bough*).[50] "There's a Tree, of many, one." But equally we might turn to John Evelyn's *Sylva, or A Discourse of Forest-Trees* (1664), which we know that Wordsworth read while yet a schoolboy at Hawkshead and which contains in its lengthy "Historical Account of the Sacredness and Use of Standing Groves" a discussion of the belief that trees contain the souls of the departed. Citing examples from Euripides, Ovid, and Tasso of sacred or animated groves—"like that which *Rinaldo* saw in the enchanted *Forest* [of *Gerusalemme Liberata*, Canto 18.34–38]"—Evelyn writes: "And that every great *Tree* included a certain tutelar *Genius* or *Nymph* living and dying with it, the *Poets* are full."[51]

Still, if we wish to follow the trajectory of "Nutting" "from ritual to romance," from text to poem, we might begin where we are and work backward. The tradition survives as late as Robert Frost, whose 1942 volume *A Witness Tree* opens with a poem entitled "Beech," containing the following lines: "One tree, by being deeply wounded, / Has been impressed as Witness Tree / And made commit to memory / My proof of being not unbounded."[52] But in the eighteenth century, when the topos reaches Wordsworth, it is "too late for the fond believing lyre": like Keats's Psyche or Milton's postnativity oracles, haunted trees are dumb. Cowper's poem "Yardley Oak," to which Hartman has pointed as an example of the tradition of the "oracular" tree, with connections to Wordsworth's poem "Yew-Trees," uses only a faded after-image of the convention.[53] Addressing the oak, Cowper says that there was a time when trees may have spoken, but that time is past:

> Oh couldst thou speak,
> As in Dodona once thy kindred trees
> Oracular, I would not curious ask
> The future. . . .[54]

Not expecting that "trees shall speak again" (49), Cowper stands in for the voice of nature:

> But since, although well qualified by age
> To teach, no spirit dwells in thee, nor voice
> May be expected from thee . . .
> . . . .
> I will perform
> Myself the oracle, and will discourse
> In my own ear such matter as I may.
> ("Yardley Oak," 137–39, 141–43)

"Pardon," Keats asks of Psyche, "that thy secrets should be sung / Even into thine own soft-conched ear." "Let me be thy choir," he continues, "thy shrine, thy grove, thy oracle" (*Poems*, 275, 276).

The obvious classical source, one that Wordsworth would have known well in 1798 and even better after 1823–24, when he translated it, is the Polydorus episode from Book 3 of *The Aeneid*.[55] Aeneas, recounting his adventures after Troy, describes his landing at the Thracian Fields, where he immediately seeks to offer up a sacrifice. "Studious to deck the Altar with green shoots," Wordsworth's translation reads, Aeneas begins pulling up trees, only to find that they drip blood. Again he plucks the trees, "And from the bark blood trickled as before." On the third attempt, "a mournful groan was sent / And a voice follow'd, uttering this lament":

> "Torment me not, Aeneas. Why this pain
> Given to a buried Man? O cease, refrain,
> And spare thy pious hands this guilty stain!"
> (*PW*, 4:337–38)

"Then, dearest Maiden," Wordsworth writes in his own voice in "Nutting," "with gentle hand / Touch—for there is a spirit in the woods." Wordsworth's "gentle hand" recalls Virgil's "*pius manus*," the pious or dutiful hand defiling a tree that gives off both blood and voice.[56]

It seems clear, on stylistic grounds, that when Wordsworth translated the Polydorus episode of *The Aeneid*, he had in mind Spenser's reworking of it in the first book of *The Faerie Queene*, Canto 2, in which Fradubio is the spirit imprisoned in a tree.[57] Here we have the introduction of a maiden of sorts (Duessa), for whom the Redcrosse Knight tries to make a garland. But when he breaks off a bough, it bleeds, and "a piteous yelling voyce [is] heard, / Crying, O spare with guilty hands to teare / My tender sides in this rough rynd embard" (1.2.31). "Guilty hands" are impious hands, as they are in Book 6 of *The Prelude*, where Nature admonishes a group of "riotous men" (6.425): "Stay, stay your sacrilegious hands. . . . Your impious work forbear!" (6.430, 433).[58] To heal the wound in the tree's bark, Redcrosse applies fresh clay, even as Aeneas undertakes to "bestowth / A second burial, and fresh mould upthrow" (*PW*, 4:338). With Wordsworth, however, there is no such recompense, only "a sense of pain" felt by the poet as he "beheld / The silent trees, and saw the intruding sky" (*PW*, 2:212). In a sudden, guilty reversal, Wordsworth the intruder becomes intruded upon, while talking trees are reduced to "mute dialogue" (*Prelude*, 2.268). Both blood and voice are gone, though a phantom pain remains; and Wordsworth survives to caution and protect.

It is a curious topos, this intersection of blood and voice in nature, though we begin to suspect its attraction for Wordsworth has something to do with the epitaphic tradition, with hearing or reading the text of a buried self. In Genesis 4.10, the Lord says to the murderer Cain, "The voice of thy brother's blood crieth unto me from the ground." In the *Inferno*, Canto 13, Dante encounters the souls of suicides, transformed into trees whose leaves are perpetually eaten by the harpies as punishment for their self-murder.[59] When, at Virgil's urging (followed by his reference to his own Polydorus episode in *The Aeneid* [*Inferno*, 13.48]), Dante breaks off a branch from a thornbush, it too exudes speech and blood, or "*parole e sangue*," a phrase that Leo Spitzer in 1942 saw as a version of the rhetorical figure of hendiadys.[60] Dante's speaking, bleeding plants, Spitzer says, are monstrous for their being unnatural hybrids of a "vegetal body" in which "human consciousness survives unabated" (84). In Wordsworth too, "the flowery ground is conscious." Like its earlier and later counterparts, this motif of *parole e sangue* literalizes what Hartman, in a different context, has called "words and wounds" (*Saving the Text*, 118–57). A speaking, bleeding tree is at once a classical and a Gothic motif; it mediates its traditions in a way that Wordsworth's poem

"The Danish Boy," for example, does not. In "Nutting" there are troubled deeds done in nature, and though these feats have a certain classical authority, they are transformed in Wordsworth from the higher strains of epic and romance to the "gentle hand" of folklore and ballad. "Nutting" begins, we should note, with the half-line "It seems a day," echoing the conventional ballad formula "It is," as Hartman has shown with respect to other Wordsworthian texts,[61] yet even the modulation of "It is" into "It seems" introduces interpretive uncertainties. Seems, Maiden? Nay, it is. Yet the seeming aspect is right for such a haunted place, with its unsureness, its hesitation; even the motif of disguise ("a Figure quaint, / Tricked out in proud disguise") fits the ghostly pattern.

So far, these intertextual filaments are tantalizing but tenuous; and certainly, to add Ovid, Tasso, and even Freud as further precedents or analogues is to make more ado about "Nutting" than has been made before.[62] I do not wish to have Wordsworth's allegory of intertextuality become bogged down in that most ungentle activity of "carrion-eating," as Bloom has characterized source-hunting,[63] though further excursions into these dark woods might be defensible on the grounds that, as Bloom himself has said, "criticism is the art of knowing the hidden roads that go from poem to poem" (*Anxiety*, 96). Let me therefore suggest one last source before returning to my larger argument. There is one hintertext in particular that, on both historical and stylistic grounds, helps to illuminate this unbloody, mute topos of voice and blood in "Nutting." It is Ariosto's *Orlando Furioso*, Canto 6.26–56, in which Rogero ties his hippogryph to a myrtle that suddenly speaks, identifying itself as Astolpho and recounting how the witch Alcina had transformed him into the tree (48–51).[64] Astolpho is given a magic horn by Logistilla, and when he blows it, everyone panics (cantos 15.14–15 and 22.20–22). Now, *Orlando Furioso* is not actually present in the final text of "Nutting," but we recall how well Wordsworth knew his Ariosto from his Cambridge days, through his European tour in 1790, where a copy of *Orlando Furioso* was his "companion," to his translation of *Orlando Furioso* in 1802 and his letter in 1805 stating that he has been translating Ariosto "at the rate nearly of 100 lines a day."[65] More convincing than this circumstantial evidence, however, is a remarkable passage in the earlier, discarded version of the poem, dating from the summer of 1798. This version begins:

> Ah! what a crash was that! with gentle hand
> Touch these fair hazels — My beloved Friend!
> Though 'tis a sight invisible to thee

> From such rude intercourse the woods all shrink
> As at the blowing of Astolpho's horn.
>
> (*PW*, 2:504–5)

The source is unmistakable, though commentary generally has not noted it.[66] Yet why did Wordsworth remove this allusion? Was it, like the poem as a whole in relation to *The Prelude*, "struck out as not being wanted there"? I move that this discarded passage be entered as evidence against Wordsworth in the charge of covering his tracks. This poem "Nutting," so natural and Wordsworthian on the surface, belies a depth of artifice and imitation that amazes the reader. A deceptively simple poet, with an avowedly common style, supremely uses art to hide art. His method is egotistically sublime: start with a topos, a genre, or a literary formula and then so radically transform it that it becomes unrecognizable except in traces, phrases, overtones. Make your style no style. "Nutting" will come of nothing.[67]

Yet Wordsworth's covering of his tracks—his removal of names, quotations, or specific references (though not of their resonant after-effects)—should move the interpreter to reflect on what repressions or evasions haunt his or her own style, beyond those echoes in criticism that we call footnotes. If Wordsworth has been "found out," as Thackeray might say, what should the aftermath be? I return to Hamlet: "Use every man after his desert, and who should 'scape whipping?" The covering of one's tracks, however, need not be an act of bad faith, especially if it is done under the sign of gentility. By removing name or reference, does Wordsworth mean, as Hartman would say, "to please rather than teach, and to remind rather than instruct"? Would allusion or quotation, in this poem, somehow be ungentle? And if so, does Wordsworth's common-gentle style therefore not amount to a naturally classical Romanticism?

I have suggested that the topos of the "gentle hand," and its correspondent "gentleness of heart," is a question of style, though it is clearly more than that. The "dearest Maiden" apostrophized at the end of "Nutting" takes the place of the older convention of the gentle reader, in this case a reader of nature inscriptions, and her "Touch," admonished by the poet to be gentle, suggests an interpretive as well as a physical gesture. The first rule of interpretation, like that of medicine, ought to be to do no harm: the "gentle hand" of the reader or critic should offer no "rude intercourse" with texts, or at least it should be prepared to smooth that rough touch with a tender kiss. If such interpretive handling seeks to redeem the "gentle sin" of reading, however, it does not do so without a lingering sense of responsibility, as seen in Wordsworth's manuscript disclaimer, in reference to the "mutilated bower," that "hand of mine / Wrought not this ruin — I am guiltless here" (*PW,* 2:505). The heroic axe that would destroy the sacred wood has been metamorphosed into the gentler "nutting-crook" (7), yet the boy who wields it, as Hartman has noted, quoting from Wordsworth's prefatory essay to *The Borderers* (*Prose,* 1: 77), "is not unlike 'the Orlando of Ariosto, the Cardenio of Cervantes, who lays waste the groves that would shelter him'" (*Wordsworth's Poetry,* 74; cf. Hagstrum, 95).[68] Wordsworth's "silent trees" (53) "g[i]ve up / Their quiet being" (47–48), and in their mute and epitaphic witness the poet reads the ruined text of his own undoing, the romance of a shade. "Heroic argument" (*Prelude,* 3.184), whether interpretive or literary, is called into question; it becomes a theme that Wordsworth wishes "to touch / With hand however weak, but in the main / It lies far hidden from the reach of words" (3.185–87). "In the main," *à la main:* Wordsworth's motivated sequence of "touch . . . hand . . . main . . . [and] reach" reconstitutes the cautionary topoi of "Nutting." Though he may turn "to some gentle place / Within the groves of Chivalry" (1.170–71) in search of a theme, Wordsworth recasts rather than refuses the notion of reading as romance and defers or deflects action into before- and after-meditation.

But the before-and-after structure of "Nutting" does not tell the whole story, for it omits the "hereafter" coda, the posthumous warning to the maiden to touch gently in the future. This is a proleptic gesture, for although the caveat is expressed in the present moment — "Then, dearest Maiden, move along these shades / In gentleness of heart; with gentle hand / Touch — for there is a spirit in the woods" — it seeks to prevent a repetition of violence; it instructs us how to read from now on. The *liber naturae,* or book of nature, will become a text before which we shall stand and read, read and *not* disobey. Reading after is where we begin. This prolepsis marks a reversal of the earlier version — although the history of composition is quite tangled — in which the Maiden is the one who ravages the tree, is deemed "An enemy of nature" and is invited to forego her behavior, "half cruel in its eagerness," and "sink into a dream / Of gentle thoughts."[69] "She is gentil that dooth gentil deedes." Switching the maiden from the beginning of the manuscript version, where she is the aggressor, to the end of the poem, where she is merely forewarned against offering such violence, constitutes another form of deferred action, a *nachträglich* revision that displaces the central act of the poem from one agent to another, from the present to the past, and then finally to the future. Instead of announcing to the Maiden, "*Siste, viator,*" that is, "stand still," the moral tag seems to declare, "*Desiste*": "O cease, refrain, / And spare thy pious hands this guilty stain!" The epitaphic voice chastens and moves the reader, as if to say: Go, and do not sin again.

This kind of discourse, if it is not "gentlemanly," might instead be called "maidenly": depending for its effect on a gentleness of heart and hand, it transforms classical, medieval, and Renaissance topoi into a poetic version of Hartman's "friendship style," in which severe injunction is tempered into "dearest" conversation. Correspondingly, the argument for interpretive touch as a figure for reading or hearing the text of literary history prompts reflection on one's relation to critical tradition, not least what it means to read Wordsworth after "gentle-hearted" Geoffrey Hartman. My style, I believe, amounts to more than homage, though it is also that, and it depends partly for its effect on an encounter of spirit and letter in both Wordsworth and Hartman. Like Wordsworth's Poet, the critic, "gentle creature as he is" (*Prelude*, 1.135), fears to profane with unworthy hand the "frail shrine" of words, yet is hardly content with touching and not lifting. Decorum is always so precarious. The equilibrium of "Nutting"—its suspension of action and its digression into thought—necessarily gives the reader pause. Literary conventions, recognized only in their mutilated form, stand as broken signposts on a forest path leading from classic to Romantic. What starts out as a schoolboy excursion takes us deep into Wordsworth territory, toward that intersection of prolepsis and epitaph with which I began, where a voice crying in the wilderness falls hauntingly on gentle ears and bids us greet the spirit in its words.

CHAPTER THIRTEEN

"Reading After"

The Anxiety of the Writing Subject

Lucy Newlyn

Roland Barthes claimed that "the birth of the reader must be at the cost of the death of the author."[1] But in light of more recent critical theory, it is clear that romantic ideas of authority and creative reciprocity go on defending the writing-subject from extinction while granting the reader new rights and freedoms. Take, for instance, "reading after" (as distinct from "reading since") Geoffrey Hartman. While covertly evoking the figure of echo, this activity connotes a range of possible relations between writing and interpretation. If "after" plays on hierarchical as well as chronological priority, then reading is imitative creation; voice answered in its own spirit, yet "with a sound but half its own."[2] But the transformative potential within echo allows reading to move into a position normally occupied by writing itself.[3] This metathesis can imply that antecedent voice is muffled by later sounds—or, more generously, that later sounds become vocal on their own account.

The conditions for so equivocal a reading of echo are nowhere more propitious than in the work of Hartman himself. "Reading after," as here encouraged, is emphatically not a parasitic activity; but neither does it submit to the eclipse of originating voice. In seeking an equality between writing and interpretation, it seeks the only viable alternative there is to a dialogue with the past;

for although critics may answer the texts they read, no ongoing exchange is possible. As Jacques Derrida puts it, "The absence of the sender, the addressor, from the marks he abandons, which are cut off from him and continue to produce effects beyond his presence and . . . beyond his life itself, this absence . . . belongs to the structure of all writing."[4] Criticism is an imaginary dialogue with an absent other, who does not speak when spoken to, but with whom the illusion of communion must be preserved, if voice is to be prolonged. Hartman looks to give this other presence, by engaging it in conversation — by "staying it with words."[5] And the importance of reciprocity is underlined, in metaphors that have distinctly romantic resonance: "The critic explicitly acknowledges his dependence on prior words that make his words a kind of answer," Hartman says. "He calls to other texts 'That they might answer him.' "[6] Just as the romantic subject interprets nature as a book, whose spiritual meaning it half-perceives and half-creates,[7] so, in Hartman's criticism, the reading-subject enters into a colloquy with writing, which "by giving makes it ask."[8] Something of what Jerome McGann has called "Romantic Ideology" is carried over here, even as it is given new validity by Hartman's far from submissive critical procedures.[9] And this earlier value system is mediated, not just by Wordsworthian echoes and allusions, but through a transactional model of reading, implicitly underwritten by romantic theism.

Is "reading after Geoffrey Hartman" implicated in a similar bind? Some of these essays consider Hartman's call "to answer earlier and other texts responsibly." This fact alone, it might be argued, conditions the kind of interpretation that is brought to bear on those earlier and other texts, some of which are Hartman's own, others of which have been modified by his criticism. In this context, "reading after" Hartman becomes "reading through" or "reading with" Hartman, both of them essentially discipular activities. It can even become "reading for" Hartman, since responses to his texts may be tributes, as well as tributaries. My own prose, for example, plays with the figures of calling and answering, voice and echo — Wordsworthian metaphors for the mind's communion with nature, which Hartman uses repeatedly.[10] They have since been amplified by Douglas Atkins and Donald Marshall, both of them concerned to map Hartman's interpretative practice onto Wordsworthian epistemology.[11] I am reminded of the hexameters in which Coleridge pays homage to Wordsworth:

> This be the meed, that thy song creates a thousand-fold echo!
> Each with a different tone, complete or in musical fragments —
> All have welcomed thy voice, and receive and retain and prolong it!
>
> ("Ad Vilmum Axiologum," I.5–6)

Not only is eternal vocality conferred on Wordsworth (and, separately, on Hartman) by the reader-writers who receive and retain their words, but a mingling of Wordsworth and Hartman is achieved in the reverberating chain itself. The act of "prolonging" voice thus performs a cohesive function — in bridging past and present and in assembling a fraternity of readers whose corporate ethos depends on prior authority. Moreover, the privileges of authority are shared equally, between author and critic, so that Hartman's symbiotic ideal is enacted in the process of reception.

Readers become "responsible" only by testing tradition. But they also belong to a community in which it is hoped that voice will answer voice, and this community has perennial recourse to the bonding and binding power of influence. The attempt to maintain an equilibrium between past and present can be construed as a defense against the anxiety that voice will be altogether silenced — that the critic will follow the author to his grave. And the strength of this defense may be measured by the amount of immediacy conferred on the past, in asking it to speak. So, at the risk of appearing to have murderous thoughts or of endowing Geoffrey Hartman with the questionable shape of a ghost, I would suggest that his presence is reassuring: it implies that although writing is earlier and other, it does answer its readers when called upon to do so. This thought may well encourage us to read echoically — that is, to reinvest hermeneutics with some of its ancient hermetic status,[12] by becoming the transmitters of an authority that precedes us. I want to argue that, in doing so, we enter a collaboration to protect the writing-subject from mortality; but that, far from being a special case of compliance on our part, this is evidence of a will-to-power which reflects on our own survival as readers.

Whom might we be conspiring to defend, then, in "reading after Geoffrey Hartman"? Not Hartman in person, except insofar as he literalizes what is usually hidden from view, but rather the notion of an identity which *finds itself in binding the present to the past, and which can be confirmed in writing.* This notion goes back a long way further than the romantics; but at the end of the eighteenth century it played an important part in reconciling two quite different systems of aesthetic value. On the one hand, there still survived the neoclassical assumption that authority is tradition — an assumption nearly epitomized in the claim made by one writer, that "Vastly less Invention and Judgment is required to make a good Original than a fine Imitation."[13] On the other hand, there existed a new and urgent pressure to be innovative — to produce what Edward Young called "original composition." "What glory to come near, what glory to reach, what glory (presumptuous thought!) to surpass our predecessors!": so Young had written in 1759.[14] By the turn of the century, the cult of originality had gathered momentum, and "invention" was widely regarded as a prerequisite for genius. Moreover, since no less was at stake than the author's claim to ownership of his own ideas, originality had acquired commercial value in a capitalist culture. This fact is humorously exposed by Blake, in one of his annotations to the *Works* of Joshua Reynolds: "When a Man talks of Acquiring Invention, & of learning how to produce Original Conceptions, he must be expected to be call'd a Fool by Men of Understanding. But such a Hired Knave cares not for the Few. His eye is on the Many, or rather the Money."[15]

The tension between tradition and individual talent has its parallels in the political arena, where (again) expanding individualism puts the status of past authority under question. In the immediate wake of the French Revolution, the merits of precedent were hotly debated by Burke and Paine, who represent the alternative extremes of conservative respect and radical revisionism. "A spirit of innovation is generally the result of a selfish temper and confined views," Burke writes, in his *Reflections:* "People will not look forward to posterity, who never look backward to their ancestors."[16] And he goes on to justify hereditary monarchy according to a patrilineal model of inherited wealth, backed up by organic notions of continuity:

> The people of England well know, that the idea of inheritance furnishes a sure principle of conservation, and a sure principle of transmission, without at all excluding the principle of improvement. Whatever advantages are obtained by a state proceeding on these maxims, are locked fast as in a sort of family settlement; grasped in a kind of mortmain for ever. By a constitutional policy, working after the pattern of nature, we receive, we hold, we transmit our government and our privileges, in the same manner in which we enjoy and transmit our property and our lives. (119–20)

Paine, however, in *The Rights of Man*, exposes the arbitrary illogic of deference to past authority: "The fact is, that portions of antiquity, by proving everything, establish nothing. It is authority against authority all the way."[17]

This debate between Burke and Paine is suggestive of two altrnative models of canon-formation, which have their reverberations both in romantic writing, and in current critical positions. It can be argued that poetric authority is received, retained, and prolonged in the same way that "we receive, we hold, we transmit . . . our property and our lives" according to the Burkean model. But equally the analogy of inherited wealth and power can be rejected, and we can seek to revise the established line of descent by challenging its patriarchal basis. There is, undeniably, a close connection between political and literary constitutions; and yet the equations I have just suggested are overly straightforward. Whereas in the political arena ideological factions are clearly demarcated, in the domain of poetics it is harder to distinguish democratic from elitist ideals. Harold Bloom's model of influence is a case in point: poetic authority is here "locked fast as in a sort of family settlement, grasped in a kind of mortmain for ever"; but poets have to fight for their rightful inheritance by dislodging the claims of their fathers,[18] and in doing so they give expression to what Christopher Norris has called a "dissident tradition."[19] It would be specious to label this model either Burkean or Paineite: the themes of inheritance and patricide, here closely interwoven, confirm elements of both.

A similar blurring of boundaries is apparent in romantic writing, wherever the acquisition and transmission of poetic power are figured in terms of connectiveness. These figures can be politicized with equal validity in both reactionary and progressive terms. Coleridge, for instance, believed that "The truly great / Have all one age, and from one visible space / Shed influence" ("To William Wordsworth," 50–52). The products of genius are valued not just for themselves, but because they "make audible a linked lay of Truth / Of Truth profound a sweet continuous lay" (58–59). Wordsworth, likewise, envisages a line of poets "each with each / Connected in the mighty scheme of truth" (1805 *Prelude*, 7.301–2). And Shelley describes "that great poem, which all poets, like the co-operating thought of one great mind, have built up since the beginning of the world."[20] Despite their very different political perspectives, then, these writers all share a notion of authority which is both continuous and synchronic. Their overriding concern is with the preservation of poetic spirit and with defeating the curse of time.

That something akin to these romantic notions of connective authority should survive into the twentieth century is a measure of their success in mediating between the spirit of collaboration and of competition. They flatter individuals with respect to their original contribution, while assuring them of their place in a lasting community of equals. But their survival is also corroboration of Michel Foucault's claim that the "author function" satisfies an abiding need in our culture, and persists in a variety of shapes, long after the author has been pronounced dead.[21] Foucault himself uses the term "writing-subject" as a neutral alternative to "author," attempting to divest writing of genius and canonicity. But he leaves room for identity in the noun "subject," and this is bound to reawaken some of the old romantic associations.

To take account of this stubborn humanist continuity—stubborn, because it has resisted the attempts of poststructuralism to shift it—a term is needed for the "writing-reading subject" who negotiates an intermediate position between polarities, and by acknowledging the claims of both, protects one role from extinction by the other. In the absence of such a term, both reader-response theory and the practice of "reading after" perform the function I have described; but their success in doing so does not mean that the vulnerabilities attaching to the subject are magically dispelled. Every now and again, there surfaces the anxiety that this twin-subject, looking before and after, is really a divided subject,[22] whose loyalties are torn—in which case, "after" really is "after." No amount of continuity between voices can do away with death, or the belatedness it incurs.

To assuage this anxiety, romantic defenses are brought actively into play; indeed, it becomes difficult to separate anxiety from defense. Resistance to the idea that the fate of writing is dependent on the fate of reading appears strongest among critics whose special concern it is that writers are also readers. Thus, the "anxiety of influence," as formulated by Bloom, works in one direction only: it is an anxiety of *being influenced*, which broods over the self's diminished status, in relation to the past. "A poem," Bloom says, "is a poet's melancholy at his lack of priority" (*Anxiety*, 96). He goes so far as to concede a connection between this melancholy and the fear of mortality, when he claims that a poet must accept failure as "the first of many little deaths which prophesy a final and total extinction."[23] But the failure he mentions is a failure of *priority*. Nothing is said of an anxiety pressing from the opposite direction: of a subject who imagines what is to come as a usurpation of power. Writers can in his view be allowed to achieve greatness only by becoming antagonistic readers; but they themselves are somehow granted immunity from future threats—for the ephebe-as-son is always-already "belated" in relation to his precursor, and the precursor-as-patriarch cannot afford to appear insecure.

It goes without saying that this cosy domestic arrangement turns its back on more global threats, such as the one posed by a Derridean reading of the written. ("The situation of the scriber," Derrida says, "is fundamentally the same as that of the reader." Its "essential drifting" is "due to writing as an iterative structure cut off from all responsibility . . . writing orphaned, and separated at birth from the assistance of its father" ["Signature Event Context," 316]). But even remaining within the family romance, could Bloom's model not be adapted so that it works in two directions? As well as an anxiety of influence, there is, surely, an "anxiety of reception." And this becomes especially pressing at the point where the writing-subject displaces past authority through antithetical reading,[24] for it is here that the subject recognizes the threat that reading poses for writing, and therefore its own instability.

As developed and qualified by Hartman, Bloom's model of belatedness loses its strictly oedipal implications and becomes a more liberal testing-ground for creative freedom. The emphasis is on Kantian recuperation in the face of sublimity,[25] not on psychic sickness acquiring poetic strength. "If there were no precursor he would have to be invented," says Hartman. "The imagination needs a blocking-agent to raise itself, or not to fall into solipsism. We become great, Kierkegaard said, in proportion to striven-with greatness" (*FR*, 49). He still works along the temporal axis established by Bloom, but he gives influence a beneficent emphasis, using metaphors of interchange to suggest writer-reader reciprocity: "Without a greatness prior to our own there may be nothing to *respond* to. There may be no *dialogue*, let alone *dialectic*" (*FR*, 123). Writing is assured of its place in a continuing chain, while reading is welcomed into an exchange nurtured by difference.

Bloom relies on patriarchal stability to socialize self-preservation — to prevent the family romance from degenerating into a Darwinian struggle for existence (flip the coin, and it is Oedipus, not Laius, who dies at the crossroads).[26] Hartman, on the other hand, resists Freudian determinism, and allays the fear of random selectivity, by allowing writers to be more than their compulsions — by restoring to them their citizenship in culture. Readers are made *responsible*, as though entering a contract with writers, and this keeps at bay the fear that subsequent words might remain deaf to prior words or might drown them altogether. A further threat is insured against by accentuating indeterminacy. As Umberto Eco has established, there is a making open which is really a making closed: acts of invasive or appropriate interpretation can be preempted, by increasing the reader's cognition of agency, and therefore answerability.[27] Thus, Hartman's model of influence placates the writing-subject in a more reassuring (because socially cohesive) fashion than Bloom's, but it can still be analyzed as both anxiety and defense.

In the title essay from *The Fate of Reading*, Hartman laments that technology has limited the horizon of reading, by teaching it techniques which, in obedience to ideologies of performance and production, are far from liberating. Writing appears "productive, activist, material," and reading "passive, accumulative, retrograde" — a relation which, like Barthes, Hartman dismisses as "the most recalcitrant of bourgeois idealisms" (272). He thus envisages the possibility that one side of a cooperative dialogue might be paralyzed under certain conditions; and although this is voiced as a fear for reading, the obverse repercussions are thinly disguised. There is a sense in which what is really at stake, here, is the fate of *writing;* and not just because technology poses a special kind of threat to the hegemony of the author, but because we lack a way of envisaging how reading can move from its secondary role without taking on the characteristics of writing. Even the most strenuous efforts to reimagine the reader fall in with the prevailing ideology Hartman describes. The division Barthes proposes, between subservient, or "readerly," texts on the one hand, and proactive, or "writerly," texts on the other, is a case in point ("Death of the Author," 168–69). Barthes makes explicit a conundrum which Hartman poses also, in the exhilarating thought that "literary criticism is now crossing over into literature" (*CW,* 213).

There is, I suspect, a tendency for writing to be the protected and reading the protector, even where equity is attentively sought. But criticism, when it celebrates its difference from that on which it depends, asserts the right to be more than "supplementary";[28] and it is here that the anxious writing-subject might find a contract at once tempting and insufficient to safeguard its continuing existence. Even if the author can be honored by the critic, this cannot be guaranteed; and the critic can exact no equivalent promises from the dead. A contract would need some supplementary magic, along the lines proposed by Shelley, to make the idea of authorship continuous and shared (eternal and one), and thus to ward off death altogether (see note 20, above).

This is where Hartman's dependence on romantic authority comes into play, for he summons the past at the point where his own systems of reassurance begin to break down. Expressing reservations about semiotics, for instance, he uses a prior system of belief to defamiliarize and bring under question current values. Turning from enlightenment to enchantment, he utters a spell to guard the spirit of writing from ephemerality. "Though a text is discontinuously woven of many strands or codes," he says, "there is magic in the web" (*FR,* 254). It is this "magic" which prevents the conclusions drawn correctly by semioticians from settling into reductive rules and which allows wishfulness its part in the experience of reading. As Hartman puts it, "The sense of an informing spirit, however limited and conditioned, outwitting those limits and conditions, is what holds us. To exorcise this spirit is to make the web inefficacious" (254). I am reminded of the closing lines in Wordsworth's poem, "Nutting," where the poet asks his sister to "move along these shades / In gentleness of heart; with gentle hand / Touch — for there is a Spirit in the woods" (52–54). These words, something between admonishment and a blessing, are powerless to protect the bower of hazel whose "quiet being" has been "deformed and sullied" by "merciless ravage" (42–45, passim). They are uttered as a healing and self-forgiving spell, whose frailty is moving, because it invites us to suspend our post-Enlightenment faith in a world where oracles are dumb and spirits long since fled.

"Nutting" reminds its readers of their obligations to Nature, to the spirit of place they are in danger of forgetting, and as such it exemplifies what Jonathan Bate has recently called "Romantic Ecology."[29] But its figurative potential also opens the way for less explicit kinds of ideological closure. As an account of writing, heavily determined by its associations with violation, it reveals a fear about the disfiguring potential of language as acute as Shelley's.[30] This allegorization is invited by the poem's self-reflexive structure and by a framing device that underlines the gap between experiential past and textual present.[31] However, the *duality* of the writing subject—who is reading, but perhaps "misreading" his earlier self—allows the admonishment to apply in two directions at once: to his own writing, which threatens to invade or colonize what is "other"; and to reading, which replicates this threat, in respect of the written materials it seeks to master.

Is the "gentle maid," whose respect for enchanted nature the poet implicitly trusts, inscribed in his poem as a figure for the reader? If so, she could be said to reinforce Wordsworth's ecological principles in a way that applies not only to nature itself, but to the poem he has written: "Move along these shades / In gentleness of heart; with gentle hand / Touch."[32] And so the allegory, undoing closure as it goes,[33] passes into terrain that is recognizable as Hartman's own. Writing is prey to the random appropriations of readers, just as nature yields itself up to marauding boys or is abused as textual material by writers. Reading, too, is subject ot ideological exploitation by materialist culture. But there is a spirit in the woods, and magic in the web: to respect this *genius loci* demands an ecology of writing which is also an ecology of reading.[34]

"Criticism," Hartman claims, "is the secular aspect of commentary: it seeks to settle or unsettle values by recovering, through the comparative method, historically diverse forms and transformations, and it does not authorize itself by leaning on a sacred text."[35] And yet there are points where Hartman is open to the charge of self-authorization: for does he not lean on prior texts, especially Wordsworth's, to protect writing from sacrilege by an alien culture? For this reason, his work has come under heavy fire as an example of the perpetuation of

"Romantic Ideology" through what Jerome McGann terms "an uncritical absorption in Romanticism's own self-representations" (1). I am tempted to elaborate McGann's case, if only as a disclaimer to Jonathan Bate's recent argument, that "romantic ecology" places Wordsworth at a distance from left/right appropriations, and thus unsettles the Marxian characterization of romanticism as conservative (*Romantic Ecology*, 8–9).

Bate neglects the ways in which romantic ideology protects some of its most cherished beliefs by appealing to ideas he identifies as "ecological." He also reduces the complexity of ideology itself, by overlooking its sometimes conflicting strains of thought. There is, for instance, a clear intersection between Wordsworth's conservationist politics of reading and his resistance to the encroachments of urban culture: he preserves poetry from invasion by hostile readers, as though it too were presided over by a spirit of place, a "genius" with inviolable rights. Conversely, though, he follows Rousseau in seeking to reassure the writing-subject of its validity as a socially connected being and in making reading into a social contract.[36] The conservative and the progressive strains of romanticism exist alongside each other in Wordsworth's thinking; and I have suggested that both have their echoes in Hartman's critical practice.

The question McGann raises is not simply one of political alignments, but of the fossilization of a belief-system that may well contain assorted elements and appear jumbled according to both contemporary and current judgments of what is or is not "conservative." His charge remains a powerful one. To rest the case there, however, would be to appear ready to accept the wider presuppositions of his thesis: namely, that the preservation of ideology is counterhistorical; that ideas belonging to one century can be conducted into another along a sympathetic current, and that in the process they acquire not only homogeneity but the false status of truths. Instead, it seems important to ask questions based on a quite different set of premises: Why is it *Wordsworth's* poetry that Hartman repeatedly turns to? And what purposes, specific to his mode of criticism, are thereby served? To approach these questions, as Douglas Atkins and Donald Marshall have done, is to give the congruence between Wordsworth and Hartman a distinctively historical meaning. For it is to understand "reading after" as a critical act, involving processes of selection and self-definition. It is, furthermore, to recognize a mode of interpretation (Atkins calls it "negative hermeneutics")[37] which is flexible enough to remain unenthralled.

What, then, are the distinctive features of Hartman's method of commentary, and what causes him to turn to Wordsworth, rather than to other available models, for his theory of writing/reading? Marshall has ventured the suggestion that "Wordsworth is characteristically the poet of ghostly middles" (*UnRW*, x); but middles in general are suspect for Hartman, because they are places where opposites either confront each other or coalesce, and the latter, if applied to the meeting place of writing and reading subjects, connotes a kind of death. It is, indeed, a wariness about middles that differentiates Hartman's ideal of a co-authorship between writer and reader from its blander manifestations in reception theory. Wolfgang Iser, following Roman Ingarden, proposes that "the literary work cannot be completely identical with the text, or with the realization of the text, but in fact must lie half-way between the two."[38] So exact a symmetry, even in the virtual dimension, is less palatable to Hartman than formulations of a dialectical kind.

Nor does he subscribe to the "fusion of horizons" propounded by Hans Georg Gadamer,[39] whose hermeneutic definition of dialogue is in most other respects extremely close to his own. Is this perhaps because the status of subjectivity is brought radically under question in Gadamer's model of writing/reading? Language, for Gadamer, is like a game in which the players lose consciousness of themselves as players, by being caught up in the to-and-fro movement which is the focus of their concentration: "The individual self, including his activity and his understanding of himself, is taken up into a higher determination that is the really decisive factor." This forgetfulness of self is experienced not as loss, but rather as "the free buoyancy of an elevation above oneself."[40] And in the same way, understanding a text involves understanding oneself in a kind of dialogue—but "the real event of understanding," for Gadamer, "goes far beyond what we ourselves can become aware of" (58). Hartman's idea of reading, however playful, holds back from what Gadamer calls "ecstatic self-forgetting" (55). In giving a dialectical emphasis to the game being played, it builds loss and recuperation of self into the process of understanding. Thus, although the reader can experience being a reflective player in the game as well as being assimilated into the game, these two experiences oscillate. It is the oscillation that constitutes a dialogue within the self.

In their different ways, then, Iser's and Gadamer's models of reading both succeed in ironing out the friction between author and reader: the first, by having them meet each other exactly half-way, in a kind of diplomatic compromise; the second, by moving the reconciliation of opposites onto a transcendental plane. In so doing, they threaten the basis of dialogue itself. Wordworth's epistemology, by contrast, adapts itself readily to Hartman's theory of reading, and this is because its "middles" are genuinely "ghostly": places of fearful recognition, not of comfortable assimilation. While Wordsworth seeks to establish a myth of reciprocity between nature and mind, he betrays his apprehension that mind might be eclipsed by nature or that nature might become the prey of mind.[41] A balancing act can be (and is) theoretically posited, but in practice power oscillates uneasily between these subject-object poles, each wary of the other's status. And this tension translates itself into Hartman's theory of writing/reading, not coincidentally or anachronistically, but because it is crucial to the critical endeavor in which he is engaged. At the point where the rival claims of reading and writing jostle for supremacy, he too posits a plane where reconciliation might occur, only to resist its neatness. Acknowledging the necessary distance from such a plane which praxis incurs, he uses distance itself to celebrate the freedom of critical procedures that are "creative" insofar as they are dialectical.

His adaptation of hermeneutics (we can call it "Hartmaneutics") thus takes on a hybrid character, propelling itself forward, like Coleridge's water-insect, by alternate pulses of attraction and resistance to the threat of assimilation.[42] Or, to adapt a Wordsworthian analogy, it resembles an amphibious creature: stone turning into sea-beast, sea-beast turning back into stone, never resting at the theoretical meridian, where the two "unite and coalesce."[43] This oscillatory movement comes about because of the strength with which Hartman acknowledges a *desire* in the reading/writing subject, which manifests itself as a will-to-power: the desire that critics might be authors, or even (like Satan) authors of themselves.[44] And this acknowledgment of desire places a double burden of anxiety on the critical/creative activity in which he is engaged. The critic as writing-subject must exercise vigilance, to prevent the act of interpretation from sliding into repetition and thereby dying its own death. Yet the critic's desire for authorship is founded on envying identification, and this draws the hermeneutic activity in a contrary direction. For there is a need to preserve intact the author with whom the critic identifies his desires, and to preserve that author as the subject of desire, not as its object. The *spirit* of authorship must be preserved if both sides of the dialogue are to be kept alive.

In respect of the threat of extinction, then, author and critic are complicit, in Hartman's writing, even where they appear to be at odds. But there is a sense in which, to use Paul de Man's terminology, the critic remains "blind" to an insight which the author discloses. It is as though the hunger to be an author surmounts the critic's recognition of the author's contingent status—even (or perhaps especially) in those places where naked dependency is most apparent. With Hartman, this defensiveness is considerably less noticeable than with Bloom, but it can nonetheless be discerned. In the closing pages of the essay, "Self, Time, and History," Hartman famously interprets a poem suggestive of the relationship between writing and reading. He detects a parallel between Wordsworth's Boy of Winander, who makes nature echo responsively, and the reflective man standing over the boy's grave. The man, like the boy, is "calling a voice out of silence" (*FR*, 289), and this resemblance suggests by extension a reader on the horizon, who will ponder the poet's inscription: "Time stretches through this reader into a potentially infinite series of echoes. It is the reader who makes the verse responsive, however inward or buried its sounds: he also calls a voice out of silence" (*FR*, 291). The echo structure here discerned moves in one direction only—from boy to poet to reader, and then on, implicitly, into a future of readers—so that a bridge is built between two activities separated by time, without collapsing together the roles of writing and reading. What is elided in the process is the circularity of the poem's logic; for once the allegory of reading has gone thus far, can we not turn back to the earlier part of the poem and construe it too in figurative terms? If so, Nature is a silent other, from whom the boy elicits responses, just as the poet hopes to awaken in his readers a joyous confirmation of his vocal power (compare Coleridge's "Ad Vilmum Axiologum," quoted above).

It was Keats who imagined the moment when "this warm scribe, my hand, is in the grave" ("The Fall of Hyperion," 1.18). Wordsworth's figuration of hands as instruments of voice (see "The Boy of Winander," 7–10) is on one level more consoling: it makes the poet a musician, not just a scriptor, and it imagines an afterlife for poetic utterance in a concert of echoes, "redoubled and redoubled: concourse wild of mirth and jocund din" (15–16). But if the colloquy between boy and owls is a figure for poetry and its reception, some of its features are disconcerting. The owls, instead of obediently hooting back to the boy, make a cacophony of noises that sound uncannily human. Nor are they always responsive to his call. "Pauses of deep silence" sometimes "mock his skill," and these moments of resistance or blankness acknowledge the ephemerality of voice, its inability to guarantee response (17–20). The pattern of Wordsworth's later poem "To Joanna" is here anticipated, then, but with a difference. The owls have the power to alienate through mimicry, just as Joanna's laughter becomes amplified by echo into a "loud uproar" of derision, tossed from one mountain peak to the other, and causing her to seek shelter "from some object of her fear" ("To Joanna," 54–76). In "The Boy of Winander," though, the pauses of silence, as much as the echoes themselves, are imagined as a form of mockery—as if, for one whose vocation is imitation, the ultimate fear is a parody which does not speak, a parody of the expectation that there will be answers.

The poem collects itself by allowing tranquility to remind the boy of the otherness of a world he has attempted to control. It is the unmediated voice of mountain torrents, not of anthropomorphized owls, that is "carried far into his heart," and it is a visible scene, not a choral accompaniment, that "enters unawares into his mind" (Boy of Winander," 21–23). Sublimity is registered subliminally: the emphasis falls on "unawares," since at dusk the contours of landscape are darkly visible. In this crepuscular atmosphere, the boy's mind merges with the "bosom of the steady lake," into which the solemn imagery both "enters" and is quietly received (23–26). The boy is thus recalled from an anxiety about his reception to his own receptive (indeed maternal) powers; he becomes, if you like, a reader *instead* of a writer — a reader who is responsive to the poetry of place. But this recuperation of self through otherness is only momentarily consoling, for the poem moves abruptly into inscription — a bare stating of the facts of the boy's death — followed by lines in which the silence of the owls is echoed by the muteness of the traveler, looking at the grave in which the boy lies.

What we are left with is an act of commemoration which the traveler commits to silence, not a calling out from silence of poetic voice. Hartman's reading has elided the poet's anxiety of reception, which centers on the fate of writing, as it passes under the mute (and perhaps, by transposition, deaf) gaze of future readers.[45] In so doing he has produced a myth of reciprocity between author and reader which is at once deeply Wordsworthian and resistant to the more troubling implications of Wordsworth's poem. This comes to seem an important elision, especially in light of the death the poem mourns; for as its textual history reminds us, the Boy of Winander is a surrogate for none other than the poet himself, in whose person this passage was originally narrated.[46] It is a poem whose central activity dramatizes "reading after" in ambivalent ways; and in which the confused identity of the dead person scarcely conceals the writing-subject's fears. Hartman has honored both its echoic and its elegiac structure, but he has held at bay its anxiety, and resurrected its dead.

Might this affirmative reading of "The Boy of Winander" be a special case of what Bloom calls "apophrades" — that is, a "swerve" that makes Hartman more Wordsworthian than Wordsworth, thus guaranteeing that the dead will return?[47] If so, it is at one and the same time a trope of complicity and of self-authorization in its most literal sense — for it ensures that the spirit of authorship is continuous and shared, eternal and one. And in this way it is paradigmatic of the kind of "reading after" which I discussed at the beginning of this paper, where voice and echo do not much compete as accommodate. Indeed, Hartman's filling out of silence with voice registers how important it is, not just for his understanding of Wordsworth, but also for his own writing, that voice should be answered and thus prolonged. He writes, in his poem, "Aubade": "The cock wakes the dawn / Scarlet as the coxcomb on its head: / But I wake the voice of the cock / In the barn of the dead."[48] Whose voice is it, though, that is being awakened? All reading, not just "negative hermeneutics," registers a disturbance in subject-object relations, such that the reading-subject is in two places at once or does not know where precisely it is sited. As Georges Poulet puts it, "Whatever I think is part of my mental world. And yet here I am thinking a thought which manifestly belongs to another mental world, which is being thought in me as though I did not exist. . . . Whenever I read, I mentally pronounce an *I*, and yet the *I* which I pronounce is not myself."[49] And this disturbance is increased, with all its attendant anxieties about the disappearance of the subject, wherever identifications are particularly strong—as, in Hartman's case, with Wordsworth. It is at this point that the notion of "commentary" is required to separate itself off from servile repetition, and yet it is also here that the critic is in danger of becoming what he beholds.

But Poulet's observations can also be applied to the *writing* subject, insofar as it fears, imagines, and prefigures its own readers. And this is everywhere in evidence in a poet who seemed "Two consciousnesses—conscious of [him]self, / And of some other being" (1805 *Prelude*, 2.32–33). Hartman is perhaps at his most "Wordsworthian" in his salvaging of this double bind as an enabling critical tool. For the ability to be *in two minds*—or as he puts it, "to undo thought and resist certain kinds of assertion"—is one he prizes highly (*UnRW*, xxix). With its reflexive writing subject, its separating and conflating of past and present selves, its recuperative treatment of gain in loss, Wordsworth's poetry offers a reflection of, but also *on*, Hartman's own procedures—as though he were himself the "other being" of whom Wordsworth writes.[50] Indeed, the quality of Wordsworth's poetry, as it is given to us by Hartman, is the quality of the hermeneutic act as it unfolds itself to itself. This may be why, in "The Boy of Winander," we can understand both the boy calling and the owls answering (or hesitating to answer) as acts of interpretation, each of them equally applicable to reading and writing.[51] They evidence a movement to and fro, between self and other, that is constitutive of hermeneutic consciousness.

Before my argument vanishes altogether in a maze of mirrors, it is worth pursuing one further reflection. If we approach Wordsworth in this hermeneutic spirit, are we making the critic the double of the poet or the poet the double of the critic? To formulate this question is to return to the vexed issue of ideology and its perpetuation through mimetic commentary. We are now in a position to ask whether romantic ideology really does transmit itself in the way McGann describes—that is, through an "uncritical absorption" in romanticism's own "self-representations"—and if so, whether this means, to repeat the question Gadamer puts to Habermas, do we "understand" only when we "see through pretexts or unmask false pretensions"? (*Philosophical Heremeneutics*, 32). Surely not, Gadamer would answer, because while "the real power of hermeneutic consciousness is our ability to see what is questionable" (13), "authority is not always wrong" (33). A purely ideological critique, by setting itself up as the accuser of prejudice, becomes itself complicit in a prejudicial act. Hermeneutics, by contrast, subjects *all* modes of reflection to reflection. As Gadamer puts it, the act of understanding "allows the foreign to become one's own, not by destroying it critically or reproducing it uncritically, but by explicating it within one's own horizons with one's own concepts and thus giving it new validity" (94). Continuity cannot therefore be manufactured by a kind of genetic cloning across the centuries, nor is it a question of submission on the part of blind or lazy readers to established truths. It can be encouraged, with varying degrees of critical purchase and freedom, by criticism. But this involves a complex network of elective affinities, in which what is at stake is the preservation of the writing-subject itself, as an identity with a history and a future.

And if at times critical purchase appears to be lost—if, that is, "negative hermeneutics" moves into hermeticism, honoring texts as though they contained sacred and hidden truths—this should not be dismissed as culpable recidivism. Instead, it asks to be considered as a defense-mechanism the reading-writing subject adopts, to maintain temporary balance in a precarious situation; for the critic is a *divided* subject, required to be both players at once in the "game" of interpretation, who registers with anxiety the sense that "identity" is no sooner won but lost. As Hartman himself acknowledges, "Things get crossed up in this jittery situation. It should be the interpreter who unfolds the text. But the book begins to question the questioner, its *qui vive* challenges him to prove he's not a ghost. What is he then?" (*FR*, 19).

CHAPTER FOURTEEN

Daring to Go Wrong

Leslie Brisman

Perhaps all the more remarkable because hyperbole is so uncharacteristic of Geoffrey Hartman's elegance, one sentence from his "Struggle for the Text" seems to stand out from so many outstanding struggles, before and since, and to invite extended brooding:

> While midrash must be viewed as a type of discourse with its own rules and historical development, and while we cannot assume that its only function was exegetical, little is more important today than to remind secular literary studies of the richness and subtlety of those strange rabbinic conversations which have been disdained for so long in favor of more objective and systematized modes of reading.[1]

From what temporal perspective and from what set of values can he judge that "little is more important today"? Writing some fifteen years after Hartman's directive, I wonder if his "today" is my own. In one especially happy sense it may not be. If the need to call attention to midrash seems less urgent now than then, the difference may be attributed, in good measure, to Hartman's own work. Both in biblical studies and in literary criticism generally, we have become far more aware of the gray area between elucidation and invention, exegesis and midrash.

Hartman himself, fifteen years before the midrash piece, had teased us with the thought that if interpretation is like a football game, and one must find a hole and run through, there remains the question of whether the hole is found or made: "But first you may have to induce that opening. The Rabbis used the technical word *patach* ('he opened') for interpretation,"[2] and no one has done more remarkable work in opening up specific texts and alerting us to the various ways in which openings might be "induced." In another sense, Hartman's "today" is very much our own, and "secular literary studies," grown poor with the vast expenditure of effort to discover historical meanings, stands all the more in need of the reminder "of the richness and subtlety of those strange rabbinic conversations."

In what follows, I would like to brood on the special significance of designating midrash "those strange rabbinic conversations" and consider in turn three modes of conversation: the conversation that one biblical text has with its precursors, the recounted conversation that becomes the medium of opening the text, and the conversation that an allusive literary text carries on with its biblical addressee. I have chosen two passages from the New Testament in which the role of midrash seems especially problematic.

Hate Your Enemies

To a significantly greater extent than its parallel passage in Luke, Matthew's Sermon on the Mount seems to be carrying on a conversation with Mosaic law. It is conversation in the sense that fragments of Torah are brought in to speak, and then Jesus, with the turn "But I say unto you," speaks not just to his immediate circle of auditors or the Gospel's readers but also, as it were, back to the old text. The series culminates in the new law of love:

> Ye have heard that it hath been said, Thou shalt love thy neighbour, and hate thine enemy. But I say unto you, Love your enemies, bless them that curse you, do good to them that hate you, and pray for them which despitefully use you, and persecute you; That ye may be the children of your Father which is in heaven: for he maketh his sun to rise on the evil and on the good, and sendeth rain on the just and on the unjust. For if ye love them which love you, what reward have ye? do not even the publicans the same? and if ye salute your brethren only, what do ye more than others? do not even the publicans so? Be ye therefore perfect, even as your Father which is in heaven is perfect. (Matt. 5:43–48)[3]

Countless commentators have noticed that "love thy neighbour" is Leviticus 19:18 but that there is no text in Hebrew Scripture that reads, in so many words, "and hate thine enemy." There are, to be sure, verses that one could single out as being spoken in the spirit of "hate thine enemy," such as the promise that God will be good to His obedient people but "put all these curses upon thine enemies, and on them that hate thee, which persecuted thee" (Deut. 30:7). But for every such verse, there may be another enjoining that hatred or vengeance be left to God. Deuteronomy specifies, "Thou shalt not abhor an Edomite; for he is thy brother: thou shalt not abhor an Egyptian; because thou wast a stranger in his land" (23:7). And these injunctions against ethnic hatred seem generalized into principles of individual conduct, for which the specific ethnic example is but an example: Thus, "Love ye therefore the stranger: for ye were strangers in the land of Egypt" (10:19) does not appear to be founding the love of strangers on a tit-for-tat basis, demanding tolerance of Egyptians strangers but allowing incivility to others.

One conclusion that could be drawn from such consideration of relevant passages of Hebrew Scripture is that "Hate thine enemy" is intended neither as indirect quotation nor as a summary view of Old Law but as tautology, the plain sense of things. In this subtle criticism by association, the injunction "Love thy neighbor" loses the authority of Mosaic law and becomes part of the pedestrian dichotomy, "Love those you love, hate those you hate." Like Wallace Stevens's poet-speaker at the end of *The Auroras of Autumn*, Jesus would be mildly protesting, "There's nothing there to roll / On the expressive tongue, the finding fang." Since "enemy" appears to be no more than "the one one hates," "neighbor" appears to be no less than "the one one loves"; the force of a counterintuitive, or rather counterinstinctual injunction, "Love (treat fairly) those you may not particularly feel drawn to," is weakened. In its place comes the real counterintuitive principle worth the difficult formulation it receives. In this interpretation, it is as though Jesus heeded Stevens's further injunction,

> Now, solemnize the secretive syllables.
> . . . .
> Read to the congregation, for today
> And for tomorrow, this extremity.[4]

As the new rabbi, Jesus has a more interesting new text. The "extremity" "Love thine enemy" has at least spiced up the religious rhetoric, gaining for the new tongue something tastier than the pablum of tautology or what appears, looking back, to have been little else.

It may be appropriate to designate such a reading no midrash on Leviticus 19 but something we might label an anti-midrashic or even anti-literary exegesis. I like to think of Jesus reading Hartman's article on Jeremiah and heeding his lure to interpretation: "It is a matter of witnessing, of the individual stepping forward and confessing, of taking the chance of being profane."[5] But in a strange way, what characterizes the reading of "Hate thy enemy" as though it were more definition than injunction is precisely that it takes no chances, it reduces the risk of interpretation. And the essence of midrash, as Hartman has so formidably set it forth, lies in its risk. Before launching into his own midrash on Jacob struggling with the angel, a midrash that dares to rearrange a bit of the text, he preludes his reading with this apotropaic gesture: "The only virtue I can claim for the literary study of the Bible is . . . that while it can hardly be more imaginative than the masters of old, *it can dare to go wrong*. Let me try" ("Struggle," 9). If the playful element in midrash constitutes its daring, perhaps we can say of the reading that reduces "Hate thine enemy" to "Hate those you hate" that it lacks daring; it cannot go wrong.

What other options are there? If we think of Hartman's daring to go wrong as especially characteristic of what he terms "literary study," we might oppose *literary* to *historical* and single out, as the opposition, the reading that would interpret "Hate thine enemy" as the slogan or characteristic sentiment of a particular group. In such a reading, there is still something of an assault on the Hebrew Scriptures' injunction, "Love your neighbor," but instead of reducing the authority of scripture by association with the purely tautological, there is the reduction that comes by association of the authority of scripture with the authority of an unquestionably local pronouncement. The support for such historicism comes in part from Josephus, but most especially from the Dead Sea Scrolls. According to the rule of the Essene Community, members are enjoined "to love all the sons of light, each according to his lot among the council of God, but to hate all the sons of darkness, each according to his guilt in the vengeance of God."[6] The reductiveness of such an allusion might work one of two ways. First, the injunction to hate everyone not of the sect makes "Love your neighbor" seem as local, as sectarian as "Love all the sons of light." Though the Essenes themselves may have been a relatively insignificant splinter group, a self-isolating community without power directly to affect the Jews at large, the pasting together of pieces of Leviticus and Essene exclusionism makes the Torah's notion of chosenness seem as parochial as the sect's.

A second way in which the allusion might work depends on the translation of the difficult Hebrew phrase about hating all the Sons of Darkness *ish kiashmato binekamat El*—either "each according to his guilt [deserving] God's vengeance" or "each according to his guilt in [the time of] God's vengeance.[7] The second, temporal distinction acknowledges but curbs the desire to hate the Other. I am reminded of a devout acquaintance who used to pepper his religious conversation with repeated salutations of "my friend." When I teasingly inquired how I could be such a good friend, given that I shared none of his beliefs, he replied that he could love me well enough now, while the world endured; there would be plenty of time to hate me and mine at the Second Coming. On a national level, "Love now, hate later" may be less frivolous than politic a solution, perhaps even a reasonable basis for peace negotiations among ethnic enemies; but for anyone who insists on remembering that "love your neighbour" comes from the same verse in Leviticus that enjoins us not to bear a grudge, there is the alternative of translating the second half of the Essene command as hatred proportional to guilt. Such is that thing enskied and sainted, the morality of Shakespeare's Isabella:

> I have a brother is condemned to die.
> I do beseech you, let it be his fault,
> And not my brother.
> (*Measure for Measure*, 2.1.34–36)

One can never condemn the man, the whole man, by this logic, since any person is more than a particular deed. To keep due proportion, one would have to condemn just the behavior deserving God's vengeance and have mercy on the doer of the deed.

I am aware that I have perhaps gone too far in considering the fragment of Qumran text as text, when the whole effort of those who would cite it is to give Jesus's allusion a historical rather than a textual basis. Perhaps the real dare behind Hartman's "dare to go wrong" is the concomitant dare to linger on the words. Consider Isabella, once again, at one of her most daring moves:

> *Angelo:* Your brother is a forfeit of the law,
> And you but waste your words.
> *Isabella.* Alas, alas!
> Why, all the souls that were were forfeit once;
> And He that might the vantage best have took
> Found out the remedy.
> (2.1.71–75)

Forfeiture, whether forfeiture to the law of Vienna or to the law of God, seals things shut. But lingering on "forfeit," Isabella opens the text, in the mode of the rabbinic *patach.* The Son of God might have passed easily from love of angel to hatred of man, when man first proved less than angel and sealed his doom. But—as though himself inventing or, more precisely, discovering the remedy—the Son opened the seal, found out the remedy, and passed from love of neighbor to the preeminent love of enemy—if man, in the time of or in consideration of the vengeance of God, may be called God's enemy. Much stronger than a mere theological reminder of God's grace, her "found out" suggests an act of originality on the son's part, a midrashic moment of daring that could, if only he would, be imitated by God's viceroy. Daring to go wrong may turn out to mean daring to do right.

All the readings of "Hate thine enemy" considered so far are involved in some form of diminishment of the old law in order to make room for the new. Whether "Hate thine enemy" means something as local as "Hate those outside your particular religious community" or something as unquestionable as "Hate evildoers"—as God does, for example, in Psalm 5.5, were it necessary to seek textual authority for something so near tautology—in either case the effect is to distance the Leviticus teaching from the new, more substantive one introduced in the Sermon on the Mount. There remains, however, one mode of interpreting "Hate thine enemy" which works to diminish the difference between old law and new. It does so by singling out the meaning of the turn on the old law in the turn itself—in the elegance, the professionalism, of such a turn. For any of the arts, the critic's need (or the need of the artist as self-critic) to find something distinctive and praiseworthy about a particular performance vies with the artist's need to establish or reaffirm competence. I am always astonished to hear a musician discriminate the nuances of an interpretation of a piano sonata, for example, when to me, as an amateur pianist, the overwhelmingly impressive phenomenon is (or ninety-nine one-hundredths of it is) the pianist's success in *not* having introduced something new—wrong notes.

Now teaching—at least teaching in the humanities—is a performative art about which we generally feel more relaxed concerning the components of getting it right and daring to go wrong. Yet the Bible's models of scenes of instruction are at least as much involved with the authentication of the teacher as they are with the demonstration that he is getting it new—or nuanced—in an interesting way. Thus, the very heart of the Sinai revelation may be the remarkable depiction, "Moses spake, and God answered him with a voice" (Exod. 19:19). For one magnificent moment, equally awesome if the answering *kol* is translated "voice" or "thunder," what matters is not the content of the revelation but the authentication of Moses as teacher. It is worth remembering that the seal of authentication, the verse specifying that the people "believed the Lord, and his servant Moses" (14:31) actually occurs not at Sinai but at the Red Sea, where Moses does not speak at all. The King James Bible, like its predecessors, renders the verse "believed . . . Moses" rather than, as most modern translations, including the Revised Standard Version, have it: "believed . . . in Moses." The new Jewish Publication Society translation reads "had faith in . . . Moses," which clarifies what might otherwise be mistaken for an equivocation: To believe Moses did not mean to believe in anything specific that Moses said; he did not speak at the sea, and it did not matter what he spoke at Sinai; what matters is not whether he asked "What is the first commandment?" or "What do you look like?" or even (more wrongheaded, from a Hebrew Bible perspective) "What do I need to do to get into the Kingdom of Heaven?" What matters is simply that he spoke with God and that Exodus 19 authenticates Moses as prophet.

For the Sermon on the Mount to be interpreted likewise as a passage concerning, preeminently, the authentication of its prophet, Jesus would have to impress his auditors not with some "strange point and new" (to borrow a Satanic locution)[8] but with the familiar, traditional nature of his homiletics. Thus, the purpose of adding to the familiar Leviticus tag "Thou shalt love thy neighbour" the unfamiliar "and hate thine enemy" might be to demonstrate that the new teaching to follow ("But I say unto you . . .") is actually closer to the authentic text, or is more authentically derivable from the old text, than the straw man "Hate thine enemy." This "authentication argument" is advanced by H. W. Basser in a series of articles that purport to hear behind the turn on "Love thy neighbor" a midrashic technique of playful punning. To illustrate the *sort* of thing he has in mind, Basser cites, for example, Midrash Rabba on Esther 3:9, where Hamaan asks the king, "Let it be written that they may be destroyed" (*leabdam*) — and the midrash proceeds to fill in a magnificent conversation between Moses and Elijah in which the Jewish people are saved by prayer because, though the decree against them has already been written and sealed, it has been sealed in clay, not in blood (*lo bidam*). The midrash "dares to go wrong," to point the text as it could not possibly be pointed, to make its splendid argument for prayer and repentance even when the evil decree seems about to prevail. Basser then proposes that the Sermon on the Mount puns in an equally playful, midrashic way, on *rea*, Hebrew for neighbor, by pointing the text to read *ra'akha*, which he would like to translate "your enemy." The sermon would thus have Jesus engaging in a silent demonstration of his midrashic technique: Do not read "Love your neighbor (*re'akha*)" but "Love your enemy (*ra'ekha*)."[9]

I find myself haunted by the question of whether or not Basser is Hartman's true heir, "daring to go wrong," inventing a midrashic conversation with the Leviticus text in which it reads "neighbor" where the new teacher (Jesus? Basser?) reads "enemy." Despite Basser's protestations, Jastrow's *Dictionary* does not sanction a reading of "enemy" for *ra*. *Ish ra* (an evil man) is common enough in rabbinic Hebrew, where *ra* is an adjective; and the Hebrew Bible has several examples of *ra* as a noun meaning "the evil one." Not surprisingly, most of these come from Proverbs, where there is much general talk about the ways of the evil. Basser's "daring" consists in leaping from firm ground "*Ra* (evil person) most certainly exists as a noun in the singular equally as in the plural," to *ra'akha* as "('one who is evil to you') which cannot mean anything other than an enemy" ("Midrashic Form," 151).

Basser rises to what I would call true Hartmanian playfulness in a footnote that proposes a cross-language pun: "If the statement was originally thought to be cast in Aramaic, the switch from *havrakh* to *havlakh* is the basis of the midrash. The semantic equivalence of the liquids resh and lamed is completely attested in this period as Jastrow notes in his Dictionary, p. 685. However, it seems [to] me that the verse would have been believed to have been quoted in Hebrew even if everything else was considered to have been in Aramaic" (151–52 n.). Despite the straight-faced last sentence, the footnote as a whole may be less important as scholarship than as sheer exuberance. Now *havlakha* could mean "your injury," or "your ruin," or perhaps, by a similarly daring leap, "your enemy"—who else would be your ruination? But it is madness to take a further leap, as may seem to be implied by such paronomasia, from love of the one who injures me to love of the injury. Yet near allied to such madness is a genuine insight into the miraculous working of the Matthew text. Whether or not Basser is correct about *ra'akha* or *havlakakha* meaning "your enemy," the argument that Jesus goes on to make leaps over questions of personal injury to God's overriding mercy. The Hebrew Bible does indeed seem to be stuck with the theological problem that may be summed up by one of the instances of *ra* as "evil one": Proverbs 11:21 assures us, *lo yinakeh ra*, that "the evil [man] will not go unpunished." It is against such insistence on reward and punishment that the Sermon on the Mount takes the broader view: Love your enemies "that ye may be the children of your Father which is in heaven: for he maketh his sun to rise on the evil and on the good, and sendeth rain on the just and on the unjust." What "daring to go wrong" has revealed is a theology that leaps over personal reckoning—both one person's reckoning of the injuries done to him and God's personal reckoning of each person's account—and dares to imagine, for a moment, a Lord of universal grace.

In our weaker moments, we prefer a God who keeps tally, who rewards the workers in the vineyard all day more than those who have come at day's end, and who, in any case, will make sure that those who do not work in the vineyard at all get their just recompense. Alas, too much theological gibberish, including perhaps the whole invention of heaven and hell, has come to serve that weaker impulse for separating the chosen from the rejected, good from evil, and all degrees of in-betweenness. The most daring moment in Matthew's sermon may therefore come in the pseudo-logic of comparison of man's ways and God's. "For if you love them which love you, what reward have ye? do not even the publicans the same?" Ostensibly arguing for a love that transcends strict reckoning (loving those who love one, "according to the bond"), verse 46 in fact intimates a deconstruction of the whole theology of reward and punishment. The following verse dares to take the argument further, and makes of the difference between the hearers of the sermon and those who try to stand still at Sinai a figure for the largest possible difference between Hebrew Scripture and New Testament: "And if ye salute your brethren only, what do ye more than others? do not even the publicans so?" At stake is not a question of manners (to how large a circle of acquaintance am I obliged to say "hello"?) but the very notion of a chosen people, for whom, to the exclusion of others, a member of the select group inquires after and prays for peace. *Lidrosh shalom* can mean "to inquire into [someone's] health"—something as neutral as "How are you?" But it can also mean to pray for peace: "May He Who makes peace in the high heavens make peace over us and over all Israel."[10] Peace—and the desire for peace—does not have to be imagined as great but limited, for us but not for them. And so our pericope concludes by returning to Leviticus 19 with a renewed sense of what was there all along, the teleology of holiness: "Be ye therefore perfect [teleioi], even as your Father which is in heaven is perfect." *Kedoshim tihiyu*, "Ye shall be holy!" Leviticus 19:1 proclaims, "for I the Lord your God am holy." Perhaps little is more important today than to remind secular literary studies of the conversation between the privileging and universalizing desiderata.

Pick up the Crumbs

If, behind the spirit of midrashic engagement with a text is *drishat shalom*, seeking peace with the enemy I am to love, perhaps I should name a critical enemy against whom Hartmanian daring would help me contend. Northrop Frye might do, for the surety of his schemata defied all midrashic inquiry, or at least all others' inquiry, into the free play of the text. But since I owe Frye both the honor due a teacher and the honor due the dead, let me single out instead Meir Sternberg, whose *Poetics of Biblical Narrative* proceeds, page after relentless page, with absolute conviction. Surely it is of him that Luke wrote, "There was a certain rich man, which was clothed in purple and fine linen, and fared sumptuously every day" (16:19), and though my students have, from time to time, complained about the tedium of watching him feed so sumptuously every day, I do confess a desire "to be fed with the crumbs which fell from the rich man's table."

The rich man's smugness might be represented by the conviction that those who disagree are "extremists," and "short of such extremes, biblical narrative is virtually impossible to counterread."[11] I pit, against Sternberg's surety about just where the narrator and his Jacob stand, Hartman's gracious sense of the interpreter as counterreader: "It is the privilege of a literary interpreter to revive this uncomfortable perspective, though not in order to slander Jacob. Rather, once again, to reveal the *mahanaim* situation, the doubleness and duplicity out of which Jacob must always emerge" ("Struggle," 14). Sternberg, analyzing the story of Dinah, finds no doubleness on the narrator's part. While Jacob equivocates, Sternberg sees his sons acting resolutely with ultimately valorized religious fervor. One might have thought that Jacob's curse of Simeon and Levi in Genesis 49:6–7 would give Sternberg pause, especially since Sternberg, disdaining the documentary hypothesis, assumes that the narrator in 49 is the same as the narrator of 34. But he maintains his sense of surety about the narrator at Jacob's expense, and imagines the narrator "summon[ing] his omniscient authority to undermine the reliability of Jacob's late version" (*Biblical Narrative*, 453). Ultimately, the refusal to consider that the narrator sides with Jacob's fury against the brothers is the refusal to brook any question of the rectitude and chosenness of the Children of Israel.

Let us turn to a second New Testament pericope where "daring to go wrong" may lead to further question of or clarification about chosenness:

> And from thence he arose, and went into the borders of Tyre and Sidon, and entered into an house, and would have no man know it: but he could not be hid. For a certain woman, whose young daughter had an unclean spirit, heard of him, and came and fell at his feet: the woman was a Greek, a Syrophoenician by nation; and she besought him that he would cast forth the devil out of her daughter. But Jesus said unto her, Let the children first be filled: for it is not meet to take the children's bread, and to cast it unto the dogs. And she answered and said unto him, Yes, Lord:

> yet the dogs under the table eat of the children's crumbs. and he said unto her, For this saying go thy way; the devil is gone out of thy daughter. (Mark 7:24–29)

Whether or not we would identify the way the woman opens Jesus's text as midrashic, this is clearly a passage about daring to get it wrong—and a passage about conversation: the woman gains the cure she seeks not because of her faith but because of her *saying*. Though Matthew normalizes the encounter and has Jesus say, "O woman, great is thy faith: be it unto thee even as thou wilt" (15:28), in Mark the woman is commended for her *logon*, a term that elsewhere can refer to the Gospel itself. It is curious that, among various scholars who wish to insist that this is a faith story anyway, despite the absence of reference in the text to the woman's faith, the most honest in pursuit of the faith reading needs to confess that "Markan faith has little to do with beliefs about Jesus. . . . The focus of faith in Mark is 'trust that a request will be granted.' "[12] This seems to me to come perilously close to the old joke about the person being baptized by full immersion, who repeated the phrase "I believe!" until required to specify *what* he believed: "I believe you two is try'n to drown me." The joke, like the exegesis, serve to point all the more insistently back to the *logon*, and with it the midrashic interest in verbal exchange.

As in the Sermon on the Mount, midrashic reading here could be contrasted with historical interpretation. The latter can take several forms. Those who see the story as being about Jesus' mission to the Gentiles may believe that such a mission is both the origin and end of the pericope; the story arose out of the need to justify a broad-based missionary effort on the part of an early Christian community. One variation on such reading (strangely circling back to an origin in a *logon*) supposes that Jesus' answer was, preveniently, a proverb in need of refutation. People were saying, "It is not meet to take the children's bread, and to cast it unto the dogs," and those in favor of casting the bread of salvation as widely as possible sought a narrative representation of their sense of mission. "Those who supported Christian mission among pagans created the story as a narrated polemic against tendencies to prevent the uncircumcised pagans from becoming full members of the Christian community."[13] If we can recognize something of the old, recalcitrant historicizing tendency even in this formulation based on an imagined preexistence of a nasty proverb, perhaps we could distinguish as a mode of New Historicism the reading that supposes the children/dog distinction to have an economic basis in the rich/poor and city/country dichotomies that we have always with us. Thus Gerd Theissen redeems the original Jesus proverb as something worthy of the defender of the poor and offers this explication: "First let the poor people in the Jewish rural areas be satisfied. For it is not good to take poor people's food and throw it to the rich Gentiles in the cities."[14]

Let us step off the supposed terra firma of historical ground and "dare to go wrong." Were we to follow the lead of Basser's Aramaic speculations, we might imagine Jesus and the Syrophoenician woman brooding together over the saying given to us in Mark 10:14: "Suffer the little children to come unto me, and forbid them not: for of such is the kingdom of Heaven," or even its Matthean version, "Except ye be converted, and become as little children, ye shall not enter into the kingdom of heaven" (18:3). Our midrash might then make the following playful substitution: Do not read *kirivyah*—like a child—but *kilivyah*—a little dog. ("The semantic equivalence of the resh and lamed is completely attested.")

But of course midrash does not have to depend on the crumbs of paronomasic imagination. What matters here is that a focus on crumbs, on the bread of life imagined to be a limited commodity, leads to an insight as one passes from vehicle to tenor and confronts the plenty of God's grace. There is no reason to think of Gentiles being fed with "crumbs" from the Jews' table because one does not have to be called to a specific place at a table with limited seating. That was the point, Deuteronomy tells us, of the manna episode, "that he might make thee know that man doth not live by bread only, but by every word that proceedeth out of the mouth of the Lord doth man live" (8:3). Not loaves but logia, and available not in limited baskets but generally, like manna, all over the land.

Who "dares to go wrong"? Various explicators of our pericope have pointed to the daring of Jesus as teacher, venturing out of home turf, or the daring of the non-Jewish supplicant, who approaches the rabbi, and just when he wanted to be alone. But the daring of such acts is as nought beside the risky presentation, by Jesus in our pericope, of Jesus, by the author of our pericope, saying something so ostensibly offensive to Jew and Gentile alike. Talking about figurative children when there is a sick child to be attended to seems like a strange rudeness. And calling any woman a bitch is risky behavior—risking the reader's displeasure should she or he not stay to see the misprision corrected. But this is not a mere question of politeness. At stake is the age-old doctrine of chosenness, crummiest of theological markers. The risk is that Jesus will appear to be reinforcing the us/them dichotomy even while making allowance for this woman as an exception to the rule or as representative of all who are allowed to approach the table later and eat of the crumbs. The risk is that Jesus' saying, "Let the children first be filled," will appear to validate such firstness.

And so he has the first *logon* in this remarkable exchange, but not the best. The woman's answer appears to be modestly accepting the denomination of "dog" and arguing merely for some status, however diminutive, in the house of the Lord. But miraculously, she picks up his idiom in a way that utterly destroys that vain proton, "let the children *first* be filled." There is, to be sure, a historical "firstness" to the mission to the Jews; but though they were served first, dogs and children eat at the same time. Daring most to go wrong, she gets it right.

We may call the exchange between Jesus and the Syrophoenician woman what Hartman calls the exchange between Jacob and the angel, a "struggle for the text." Many a reader of the Genesis scene has regarded the wrestling as an occasion to right the wrongs Jacob has committed against Esau, as though Jacob suddenly stopped being a thief and suddenly had the proton, the birthright, divinely granted him. Yet, as Hartman points out, "no redactorial revision, no appeal to his fated role in a providential drama, can remove the suspicion that he is cunning rather than noble—in short, a trickster" ("Struggle," 7). But so is our Syrophoenician woman. Her pericope is likewise about crossing borders, about wanting to be alone, about wrestling with God—and about reversing the positions of supplicant and bestower of blessing. She gets what she ostensibly wanted, a cure for her daughter; he gets what he seemingly did not know he wanted, a cure for his chosenness.

I am aware, as I close this meditation on midrashic "literariness," how deeply I myself am involved, beyond my literary interests, in the cure this passage would make; for I believe with all my heart that chosenness is a disease from which Judaism can and must be redeemed, though it takes no Gospel of Mark to exorcize the demon. Yet I am aware, too, of how dangerous it is to imagine Christianity trumping Judaism in this regard, all the more so because neither faith has, at least in its dominant movements, freed itself from the doctrine of the chosen people. Within our pericope, we should acknowledge that the Syrophoenician woman does not "trump" Jesus—or better, if one is borrowing the metaphor from cards—she plays anew an ancient trick. As Hartman puts it, in a rare extension of his midrashic imagination to New Testament turf, "By setting one Testament's realism against another's spiritualism I do not mean that there are no figures but only *realia* in Hebrew Scripture. Nor do I suggest that the Christian process of spiritualizing is successful: it, too, may be a divine theft, a possessive move that *appropriates* a prior and sacred text."[15] She may be a Syrophoenician, but she is a Jacob too. If she steals the show, she does so in a manner that makes general, and generally available, the struggle with and blessing from the text.

Reason Not the Need

I close with a glance at another "divine theft," this one a slight, mischievous gesture, more lark than larceny, in the lesser works of Swinburne. On March 10, 1881, the poet wrote his mother about little Bertie Mason, the child of Watts's sister, who had come with his mother, aunt, and uncle to live with Swinburne at The Pines:

> I quite understand how (as you say) "a mother loves those words" which warn us against offending one of the little ones—but to me the divinest of all divine words and thoughts is that "of such is the kingdom of heaven." I am very sure it is so here on earth—where nothing—except age in its brightest beauty of goodness and sweetness and kindness—is so adorable as a little child is. At the same time—to be practical and candid—I must admit that it is a noisy quarter of Paradise which is occasionally occupied when I am (so to speak) admitted to it by my little Bertie.[16]

I do not think we should stretch the meaning of "midrashic" to include play on the double sense of "divine." If Swinburne's letter seems far from midrashic conversation, we should acknowledge how far it is, really, from any sort of conversation in the ordinary sense of people talking to rather than at each other. Swinburne is praising "the divinest of all divine words," not because he has come a jot closer to "the religious faith of his youth"—what Lady Jane wished to see—but because he has fallen in love with the "divinest" little boy. The letters at cross-purposes might resemble an exchange a hundred years later in which a gay son raved about the loveliest angel, and his mother thought of some being down from heaven rather than down at the gym.

On the other hand, Lady Jane was no fool and certainly was not blind to her son's sexual proclivities. When she protested to Watts that "the love of, and the appreciation of innocent childhood is good and *wholesome*,"[17] she meant to acknowledge rather than obscure the difference between pederasty and innocent affection for a small child. All the same, the fact remains that those overly concerned about Swinburne's attachment saw to it that Bertie was whisked away for some months, during the first of which the poet composed his series *A Dark Month*.

One of these poems, section 9, "goes wrong" in something like the ordinary, moral sense with which one might regard a pederast at the schoolyard fence:

As a poor man hungering stands with insatiate eyes and hands
Void of bread
Right in sight of men that feast while his famine with no least
Crumb is fed,
Here across the garden-wall can I hear strange children call,
Watch them play,
From the windowed seat above, whence the goodlier child I love
Is away.[18]

To be fair, we should acknowledge that the poor man here is "void of bread" not because he is sexually deprived but because the particular child with whom he is so taken is not among the group. The poem may raise a soupçon of voyeurism, but only to contrast with a gentle touch the likeness (to borrow a Swinburne term) of the *deus abscondus* with the likeness of the incarnate god:

Here the sights we saw together moved his fancy like a feather
To and fro,
Now to wonder, and thereafter to the sunny storm of laughter
Loud and low—
Sights engraven on storied pages where man's tale of seven swift ages
All was told—
Seen of eyes yet bright from heaven—for the lips that laughed were seven
Sweet years old.

He is thinking of reading Lamb's *Tales of Shakespeare* to the seven-year-old Bertie, and he risks depicting his own "insatiate eyes" in the opening line only as a foil to the essence of his vision, the "eyes yet bright from heaven" in the penultimate line. Trailing clouds of glory does he come (and the "yet" in that penultimate line holds on to a redemptive false surmise of eternal presence) from God who, we might say, so to speak, is his home.

One does not need the story of Lazarus and the rich man, or any other allusion, to make sense of the common stuff of the emotions in section 9. But something richer, and I think riskier, transpires in section 12:

Child, were you kinless and lonely—
Dear, were you kin to me—
My love were compassionate only
Or such as it needs would be.

But eyes of father and mother
  Like sunlight shed on you shine:
What need you have heed of another
  Such new strange love as is mine?

It is not meet if unruly
  Hands take of the children's bread
And cast it to dogs; but truly
  The dogs after all would be fed.

On crumbs from the children's table
  That crumble, dropped from above,
My heart feeds, fed with unstable
  Loose waifs of a child's light love.

Though love in your heart were brittle
  As glass that breaks with a touch,
You haply would lend him a little
  Who surely would give you much.

Like the pericope of the Syrophoenician woman, this poem plays with a rich ambiguity about being or dispensing bread. As the bread of life, Jesus *is* salvation, though in the exchange about whether there is enough for children and dogs, the question is about the cure, the grace, he gives out. Bertie, or Bertie's affection, is the bread of which the poet would partake, and as an honorary uncle he knows that his share could be no more than occasional crumbs. Yet since the subject here is a seven-year-old child, hands that are not the child's own place him here or there, in a position or in no position to dispense favors. What could it possibly mean for unruly hands to "take of the children's bread / And cast it to dogs?" Even if the thought crossed one's mind of abducting the child and bringing him back to The Pines, that would be casting the child, not bread given to the child, to the panting dog. The ambiguous genitive, "children's bread," mirrors the ambiguity in the tenor for which it stands, "children's love." Who "owns" the love of children, the children who are loved or the children who love? If we could entertain for a moment the notion of the poem as a midrash on "children's love," we might see it as involved, like the Markan pericope, with an astonishing correction in the question it asks.

We begin with a question of "free love," of the difference between affection that wells up in spontaneous response to a child's joy (joy in life, joy in an early literary experience, joy in the presence of someone playing with him). Strangely, riskily, the opening stanza collapses the difference between parents' love, the love parents "owe" their offspring, and agape, the love we owe those who have no one else to love them. Either of these could be called "compassionate only," a term perhaps not insulting to parents' love if one thinks of *compassion* in a root sense of "feeling with or suffering with another." But there is something daring, something outrageous, in collapsing what Blake calls "storgous appetite craving" (another ambiguous genitive) and the relative coldness of foster care, only to contrast the two with the freer (unrequired, but also free to come and go) love of the unattached. Behind the freely asked question, "What need you have heed of another / Such new strange love as is mine?" one hears the urgent plea of Lear, "O reason not the need!"(2.4.263).

In her biography of Swinburne, Jean Overton Fuller singles out this "new strange love" as the one place where Swinburne exhibits any "recognition of the abnormal nature of his passion."[19] Perhaps so. But by saying no more, she may throw away the real strangeness of this phrase, its capacity to be at once so allusive and so elusive, so particular, if one thinks of pedophilia as "strange," and so general, if one thinks of avuncular love, and indeed all love, inasmuch as that love transcends reason and duty, as strange and true and divine. Strangest of all is that stanza two seems to define love as that attraction beyond need, only to give way in stanza three to the shocking realism ("to be practical and candid," as Swinburne wrote in the not so practical and by no means so candid letter to his mother cited above) that "truly / The dogs after all would be fed." Does *would* here signify "desire" (I, Swinburne, and for that matter, all humans, even all literal dogs would like a bit of affection)? Or is there not a second, riskier, nastier compulsion that acknowledges just what the first two stanzas ignored, that we have emotional *needs*? The poet dares to go wrong, to intimate the terribly "wrong" reading in which someone who has not provoked an affection in return demands something, emotional or physical, in fulfillment of a basic biological need. This hint, this slight, dark shadow of rape, propels us back from physical need to the metaphysics of love. If "would be fed" has a shadow of the ominous about it, all shadow is dispelled in the fourth stanza's happy statement of fulfillment, "my heart feeds." Its presentness is a reminder that though no literal dog can survive on crumbs, the heart does survive on crumbs of affection, whether the dispenser of those crumbs is present or absent. The remarkable phrase, "loose waifs of a child's light love" may connote something like clouds—light, loose, wandering objects or affections. But consider also what the *Oxford English Dic-*

tionary lists as a technical definition of waif, "a piece of property which is found ownerless, and which, if unclaimed within a fixed period after due notice given, falls to the lord of the manor." Swinburne, back at The Pines, stakes the emotional claim of the lord of the manor — not because he, with Watts, has taken The Pines, but because every human being is to the manor born, a dog if not a child, entitled to some crumbs of love.

Daring to go wrong in raising the specter of pedophilia in a poem really about agape in its widest application, Swinburne gets it right. In the last stanza, we might say that Swinburne as midrashist returns to Luke's version of the great sermon and reminds Bertie and us all, "Lend, hoping for nothing again." Those who lend a little love find that their reward shall be great, not in a heaven elsewhere but in the one they help create, on this earth, for themselves and others. He then risks one last "wrong" implication: "Though love in your heart were brittle / As glass that breaks with a touch" makes no allusion to a revelatory shattering, after which we will see face to face; but it does remind us of a barrier between avuncular and pedophilic love, a barrier that could be crossed "with a touch." He dares to bring it up, or I dare to bring it up, only to remind us how much this is *not* a poem about "strange love" in the debased sense of *strange*. The midrashist in Swinburne leaves us with a meditation on the absent Bertie that is also a meditation on an absent text. You have heard it said, "Love your neighbor." But I say unto you, recalling Deuteronomy 10:19, Love ye therefore the stranger in your midst — and the stranger, in this dark month of May, however long May last, not in your midst.

CHAPTER FIFTEEN

Rachel When from the Lord

J. Hillis Miller

Many reasons to admire Geoffrey Hartman's work come to mind. His style is distinctive and witty, with much pointed wordplay. He is extremely learned. This means both an impressive range of authors discussed with authority, and, along with that, an impressive ability to assimilate and evaluate previous work on a given topic. An example is the remarkable recapitulation of previous Wordsworth scholarship in Hartman's magisterial *Wordsworth's Poetry*. All Hartman's work conveys a love of literature and of literary tradition (especially the trajectory that leads from Milton to Wordsworth and then down to our own day). This love is infectious and responsible. Hartman is not the creature of any critical or theoretical school. He is primarily a reader of most unusual sharpness. He was one of the first critics in the United States to make use of phenomenology in literary criticism. I remember the excitement, the feeling of opening horizons, with which I read his first book, *The Unmediated Vision*, when it fell more or less by accident into my hands.

I want, however, to single out two additional features of Hartman's work which I have always especially admired. One is his uncanny ability to identify in a given text the crux, the passage that is most problematic, the one on which the meaning of the whole turns. The other is his clear recognition of what is lost, culturally and personally, if some form of religious or metaphysical grounding is not regained, beyond its putting in question just those cruxes he has an almost infallible gift for noticing. Hartman notices, that is, just those passages that most challenge or put in question his own commitments. He knows what is at stake in these texts and takes lightly neither the challenges to religious or metaphysical belief in those crucial passages nor the consequences of not finding some way to recuperate that belief. A famous example is the poetic gesture ascribed by Hartman to Wordsworth, in *Wordsworth's Poetry*. This gesture he calls the "refusal of apocalypse." Another example, however, has abided with me ever since I first read the essay in *Beyond Formalism* entitled "False Themes and Gentle Minds." This wide-ranging essay culminates in a majestic formula about Wordsworth: "Wordsworth's animism, his consciousness of a consciousness in nature, is the last noble superstition of a demythologized mind. All nature-spirits are dissolved by him except the spirit of Nature" (296). This assertion is then generalized, in a culminating phrase, as a characteristic of "Romanticism" generally from Milton through Collins to Wordsworth, Bürger, Coleridge, Scott, and Keats: "The emergence of the gentle out of the haunted mind" (297).

Deciding how to pay homage to Hartman's work has not been easy, since I cannot hope to match his tact and insight. An episode in Marcel Proust's *À la recherche du temps perdu*, however, raises some of the issues that have remained central in all Hartman's work. This passage, too, deals with false themes and gentle minds. The episode I have chosen also has biblical echoes that are a quiet background for Hartman's own work.

Each episode in Proust's great work is a separate and to some degree detachable anecdote, episode, or little narrative. Each episode has its own singularity, so it is particularly difficult to make thematic generalizations about Proust's work as a whole. A given episode is a bead strung on the potentially endless sequence of such units, some short, some long, that make up the *Recherche*. The sequence is potentially endless because the number of episodes is virtually limitless and will moreover be extended as long as Marcel is still alive and has new experiences, that is, as long as the gap between the Marcel writing and the Marcel written still exists. That gap is the definition of still being alive. The sequence is also potentially endless because each episode can be dilated interminably, or new ones interpolated. As Mark Calkins has shown in a brilliant dissertation on Proust, dilation and delay are the chief characteristics of Proust's narration.[1] Both features can be defined as a putting off or holding off of death, as Sheherazade in the *Arabian Nights*, so frequently referred to in the *Recherche*, can avoid execution only as long as she goes on telling stories.

The episode I shall discuss can be quickly summarized.[2] Marcel and his aristocratic friend Robert de Saint-Loup make a visit to a suburb of Paris where Robert keeps the mistress, Rachel, whom he deeply loves and who causes him much jealous suffering. Robert wants Marcel to meet Rachel and to admire her sensitivity and beauty. It is a splendid early spring day. The shabby little village is crowded with pear and cherry trees in bloom. Marcel waits to admire these while Robert goes to fetch his mistress. When he sees her Marcel instantly recognizes her to be "Rachel when from the lord," a prostitute he had last seen, much earlier in the novel, in a house of assignation he used to frequent (F, 1:565ff.; E, 1:619 ff.). She was a person anyone was able to buy for twenty francs. Now Robert showers expensive presents on her in order to keep in her good favor. He is prepared to sacrifice everything to his infatuation. Marcel reflects on this discrepancy, hiding from Saint-Loup the real history of the woman the latter so loves by pretending to be moved by the beauty of the pear trees in bloom. All three then take the train back to Paris, where they dine together and where Rachel causes Robert great anguish by making eyes at a waiter.

Though neither Marcel nor the reader knows it at this point, Rachel is a gifted actress. When Marcel sees her on the stage he comes to understand somewhat why Saint-Loup has become infatuated with her and "the nature of the illusion of which Saint-Loup was the victim" (F, 2:472; E, 2:177). Seen close up she is nothing much, a thin freckled face, but seen at a distance, on the stage, as Saint-Loup had first seen her, she is transformed into someone radiant and fathomlessly mysterious. Seeing her first this way, Saint-Loup "had asked himself how he might approach her, how get to know her, a whole miraculous world had opened up in his imagination — the world in which she lived — from which emanated an exquisite radiance but into which he could never penetrate [*en lui s'était ouvert tout un domaine merveilleux — celui où elle vivait — d'où émanaient des radiations délicieuses mais où il ne pourrait pénétrer*]" (F, 2:472; E, 2:178).

No more than that happens in this sequence. The genius, however, is in the detail, both in the detail of Marcel's reflections and in the detail of the language he uses to describe Rachel and the scene in which he now again meets her. The passage has to do with the passion of erotic desire, what Marcel calls "the general malady called love [*l'affection générale appelée amour*]" (F, 2:454; E, 2:158), its creative power, its ability to project behind the face of the beloved a fictitious person: "There was really nothing that interested, that could excite him except what his mistress wanted, what she was going to do, what was going on, discernible at most in fleeting changes of expression [*par des expressions fugitives*], in the narrow expanse of her face and behind her privileged brow" (F, 2:454; E, 2:158). Marcel's name for this power is "imagination." His terminology throughout the passage has to do with value, the relative "worth" of the two Rachels, the cheap twenty-franc prostitute, "nothing more nor less than a little whore [*simple petite grue*]" (F, 459; E, 164), that Marcel knows, and the glorious, radiant, unattainable woman, sensitive, intelligent, and tender, to whom Robert de Saint-Loup gives a necklace costing thirty thousand francs and who seems worth all the world to him. The two valuations follow from the way Rachel's "little scrap of a face" has been approached initially:

> I realised then how much a human imagination can put behind a little scrap of a face [*un petit morceau de visage*], such as this woman's was, if it is the imagination that has come to know it first, and conversely into what wretched elements, crudely material and utterly valueless [*en quels misérables éléments matériels et dénués de toute valeur*], something that had been the inspiration of countless dreams might be decomposed if, on the contrary, it had been perceived in the opposite manner, by the most casual and trivial acquaintance. (F, 2:457; E, 2:161)

This citation anticipates a great passage much later in the *Recherche* when Marcel, in Venice, suddenly sees that beautiful place he so loves, the Venice of Ruskin, "decomposed" into a worthless heap of stones, something also crudely material and utterly valueless (F, 4:231; E, 3:667). This present passage, like the later one and like countless other passages in the *Recherche*, seems to oppose a mystified view, generated by passion and leading to a performative "reading into" of trivial signs, in this case Rachel's face, to the demystified view that sees the signs as no more than crudely material, not valid signs for anything, that sees them truly as what they are. Here the two views are not the innocent Marcel as against the Marcel who has learned from experience ("Then I thought . . . ; later I came to learn"), but two simultaneous perspectives by different persons on the same object, or rather person. That Saint-Loup's infatuation with Rachel is a performative "reading into," expressed in his language about her intelligence and sensitivity, is reinforced throughout the passage.

Saint-Loup's misreading starts when he makes the big mistake of "imagining her as a mysterious being, interesting to know, difficult to seize and to hold [*un être inconnu, curieux à connaître, difficile à saisir, à garder*]" (F, 2:457; E, 2:161). This is a surface/depth error, the assumption that there must be something hidden and secret behind a visible superficies taken as a sign. Proust has Marcel compare this more than once to the projection of a deity behind an icon, altar, or veil. Rachel's remarks are, in Robert's view, "quite Pythian" (F, 2:455; E, 2:159), that is, as if said by an oracle through whom the God Apollo speaks. Her personality seems, says Marcel of Robert's sense of her, as "mysteriously enshrined as in a tabernacle" (F, 2:456; E, 2:160). She, or rather what he can see of her, especially her face, is "the object that occupied incessantly his toiling imagination, whom he felt that he would never really know, as to whom he asked himself what could be her secret self, behind the veil of eyes and flesh [*derrière le voile des regards et de la chair*]" (F, 2:E, 2:160).

So far so good. The passage seems unequivocally to set Saint-Loup's projection into an imaginary void behind Rachel's eyes and face, a sanctum of inaccessible complexities like those the religious believer imagines behind the icons of his god, something of infinite worth, against Marcel's disillusioned recognition of what is really there, just so much female flesh with nothing mysterious behind it, flesh that can be bought for twenty francs. Things are not quite so simple here, however, as a more complete and scrupulous reading will show and as the reader will not be surprised to learn. Let me look a little more closely at the "rhetoric," in the sense of tropological integument, in the passage.

The reader may begin by reflecting that Marcel is not exactly a disinterested spectator of Rachel. He is hardly able to see her dispassionately as just what she is. He has displayed much homosocial affection for Saint-Loup, for example, when he visits him at his army barracks at Doncières. Saint-Loup turns out ultimately, toward the end of this immense novel, to be homosexual or bisexual. He betrays his wife, Gilberte, Marcel's first great love, in homosexual liaisons. Marcel's affection for Saint-Loup is the chief place in the novel where Marcel Proust's presumed homosexuality surfaces most overtly, as opposed to its covert exposure in the way, for example, all Marcel's beloveds have transposed male names: Gilberte, Albertine, Andrée, not to speak of the overt and obsessive treatment of the theme of homosexuality in "Sodom and Gomorrah" and elsewhere as something the supposedly straight Marcel witnesses as a recorder of the mores of his pre–World War I French society. *À la recherche du temps perdu* is one of the first great novels about the role of homosexuality in modern bourgeois European culture. A curious scene adjacent to the one I am reading shows the amazed (and still innocent)[3] Marcel witnessing Saint-Loup's beating of a man who accosts him on the street, apparently, the reader can guess, with an invitation to a homosexual tryst. Marcel has every reason to be jealous of his friend Saint-Loup's extravagant love for Rachel.

The sequence I am reading begins with Marcel's ecstatic admiration of the fruit trees in bloom in the shabby suburb, cherry and pear trees, especially pear. The latter were a symbol in the Middle Ages, as Proust may conceivably have known, of lust, as in Chaucer's tale of January and May, *The Franklin's Tale.* These trees are personified in Marcel's descriptions, first as women, then, rather unexpectedly, as men, and finally as angels, whereas the "clusters of young lilacs," "light and pliant in their fresh mauve frocks [*souples et légères, dans leurs fraîche toilette mauve*]" (F, 2:455; E, 2:159) are straightforwardly maidens. The pear and cherry trees in the little gardens are first personified as "newcomers, arrived overnight [*nouvelles venues arrivées de la veille*], whose beautiful white garments [*les belles robes blanches*] could be seen through the railings along the garden paths" (F, 2:455; E, 2:159). By the next page, however, one particularly beautiful pear tree alone in a meadow is personified as possibly male. At least that is the choice made by the translators: "There had nevertheless arisen, punctual at the trysting place like all its band of brothers [*comme toute la bande de ses compagnons*], a great white pear-tree which waved smilingly in the sun's face" (F, 2:455; E, 2:160). Finally, as they leave the little suburb Marcel sees yet another pear tree, this time personifying it as an angel. All angels, the reader will remember, are masculine, messengers of the Lord: "We cut across the village. Its houses were sordid. But by each of the most wretched, of those that looked as though they had been scorched and branded by a rain of brimstone, a mysterious traveller [*un mystérieux voyageur*] halting for a day in the accursed city, a resplendent angel stood erect, stretching over it the dazzling protection of his widespread wings of innocence: it was a pear tree in blossom" (F, 2:459; E, 2:163).

What justifies all my close attention to Marcel's prosopopoeias? Are they anything more than examples of Marcel's "poetic" way of seeing things and embellishing them with extravagant language that need not be taken all that seriously or interrogated deeply? The passage just quoted gives the clue in its transformation of the little suburb into Sodom and Gomorrah, destroyed by God in Genesis 19 by a rain of fire and brimstone, though Lot is saved because he has welcomed two mysterious strangers, actually angels, into his house, offering them hospitality. The reader will remember that Lot's wife was turned to a pillar of salt when she, Orpheus-like, disobeyed the angelic prohibition and turned to look back at the home city she was fleeing with Lot in obedience to the angels' warning. Jacques Derrida, in an admirable recent seminar on hospitality, has "read" in detail the marvelous episode of Lot's hospitality to the disguised angels.

The whole episode in Proust I am reading is permeated by biblical references, allusions, and echoes. Rachel, after all, is not just any name. It suggests that Rachel is Jewish, as Marcel tells us she is. She is also a Dreyfusard. She weeps to think of Dreyfus's suffering in his prison cell on Devil's Island (F, 2:462; E, 2:167). Rachel was the name of that one of Jacob's wives he most loved. Jacob served Rachel's father, Laban, for seven years in order to earn the right to marry her. Jacob is at first fooled by Laban into marrying her elder sister, Leah, just as Robert de Saint-Loup is fooled into thinking his Rachel is something she is not: "And it came to pass in the morning, behold, it was Leah: and he [Jacob] said to Laban, What is this thou hast done unto me? Did I not serve with thee for Rachel? Wherefore then hast thou beguiled me?" (Gen. 29:25). Laban then gives Joseph Rachel also as wife, though he has to serve Laban yet another seven years to earn her. Those Old Testament patriarchs were unashamedly polyandrous, polygamist, and even in a certain sense incestuous, as in Jacob's simultaneous marriage to two sisters. In early nineteenth-century England under the Church of England, it was still illegal to marry one's deceased wife's sister, much less legal of course to marry them both at once.[4] While Leah was bearing Jacob four sons, Rachel was at first barren. She finally conceived: "And God remembered Rachel, and God harkened to her, and opened her womb. And she conceived and bare a son" (30:22–3). Rachel is a distant type of the Virgin Mary. Her womb was miraculously opened by God, just as God impregnated the Virgin Mary, or rather the Holy Ghost did in the form of a dove, accompanied by the angel Gabriel as messenger of the Annunciation. The Annunciation was a miraculous performative utterance if there ever was one: "And the angel said unto her, Fear not, Mary: for thou hast found favor with God. And, behold, thou shalt conceive in thy womb, and bring forth a son, and shalt call his name Jesus," to which Mary answered, in a self-fashioning speech act in response to his speech act: "Behold the handmaid of the Lord" (Luke 1:30–31, 38). Rachel's first son was Joseph. Joseph was not Jacob's male heir that counted most in the long genealogy that leads through the house of David down to Jesus himself. The genealogy of Jesus at the beginning of Matthew lists "Judas" as the son of Jacob who established the line. Presumably this is the fourth son of Leah, "Judah" in the Old Testament.

Joseph, nevertheless, with his coat of many colors (Gen. 37), receives much attention in Genesis. Joseph is of course also the name of Mary's husband, cuckolded before their marriage by God, or rather by the Holy Ghost in the form of a dove. "Josef, c'était le pigéon," Joyce has Stephen Dedalus in *Ulysses* imagine Mary saying in explanation to her husband of her pregnancy. All the names of Jacob's sons by his various wives are "motivated." The names' meanings are called attention to in the text of Genesis. Rachel calls her firstborn "Joseph," meaning "Adding." The name is a magic proleptic indicating her hope to add still more sons now that she has proved not barren: "And she called his name Joseph; and said, The Lord shall add to me another son" (30:24).

This whole tangled background is imported into the reader's understanding of Saint-Loup's relations to his mistress by way of the name that Proust chose to give her, just as Jacob's wives gave their sons symbolic names. Proust could, after all, have called Saint-Loup's mistress anything he liked, in the sovereign exercise of that godlike privilege of naming his creatures that is the writer's prerogative, one aspect of his magic performative power: "I name thee 'Rachel.' "[5] This power is disquietingly revealed when the reader discovers from the drafts that Robert de Saint-Loup was at first called "Montargis." What was his real name? the reader naively asks.

Why, then, is Rachel called by Marcel "Rachel when from the Lord [*Rachel quand du Seigneur]*"? That does not have a biblical precedent, at least not in so many words, though the unapprised reader may think it refers to the way God finally harkened to Rachel's prayers and opened her womb, so that she conceived and bore Joseph. The reference, however, as that earlier episode in the brothel reveals, is actually to the first words of the most famous aria in a nineteenth-century opera by Joseph (or Jacques François Fromental Élie) Halévy (1799–1862) , *La juive* (1835), with a libretto by Eugène Scribe, still performed in Proust's day, though rarely heard now. (The only recording I could find of this aria was made by Enrico Caruso in September 14, 1920, almost at the end of his career, though I have heard on Public Radio part of a more recent recording of the whole opera.) The heroine of the opera bears the biblical name "Rachel," with all its connotations. Joseph Halévy, member of a prominent nineteenth-century Jewish family (Daniel Halévy was Marcel Proust's friend in his youth), may have been attracted to Scribe's libretto because the heroine bears the name of the biblical Joseph's mother.

It is easy to see why the opera is little performed these days, though it is included in Ernest Newman's *More Stories of Famous Operas* of 1943.[6] *La Juive* treats the sensitive subject of antisemitism and is outrageously melodramatic, to say the least. The action takes place in Constance in 1414 and dramatizes the persecution of the Jews by a certain Cardinal de Brogni and the authorities of the

Holy Roman Empire. Rachel and her father, Eleazar, a rich goldsmith, are condemned to death because Rachel has become the beloved of a Gentile, Leopold, prince of the empire. She lies to save Leopold. Rachel, however, is not really a Jewess, daughter of Eleazar. She is the lost daughter of Cardinal de Brogni. That daughter the Jews had saved years before from a fire that had burned Brogni's palace in Rome to the ground and killed his mistress. Eleazar and Rachel, having refused to save themselves by abjuring the Jewish faith, are led up the scaffold to be plunged in a cauldron of boiling water in the public square of Constance. (I kid you not!) As Rachel mounts the scaffold first, Eleazar whispers to the cardinal that Rachel, at that moment being pushed into the cauldron, is really Brogni's lost daughter. Eleazar then goes triumphantly to his own death by the same hideous means of execution. You see what I mean by melodramatic!

The opera's most famous aria, "Rachel quand du Seigneur," is sung at the end of the fourth act by Eleazar as he meditates on the conflict between his desire to save his beloved adopted daughter and his hatred of Christians. He is unwilling to abjure his faith even to save his foster daughter. Apparently the aria is not by Scribe but by Adolphe Nourrit, the leading French tenor of the period. Nourrit persuaded Halévy that a dramatic climax was needed for the fourth act and is said to have supplied the words for the famous aria that resulted:

> Rachel! quand du Seigneur la grâce tutélaire
> À mes tremblantes mains confia ton berceau,
> J'avais à ton bonheur voué ma vie entière.
> O Rachel! . . . et c'est moi qui te livre au bourreau![7]

At first Eleazar decides to save Rachel, but when he hears the cries of hatred from the crowd outside he determines to sacrifice both her and himself to their faith. Proust's allusion to this celebrated aria from *La Juive* carries one more reference to the theme of antisemitism associated with the Dreyfus case, a central motif in all this part of the *Recherche.* It associates Rachel, the twenty-franc prostitute, with the heroic Rachel of Halévy's opera. Though Marcel never actually sleeps with Rachel, the madame, in that early episode, repeatedly offers her to him and goes along with Marcel's witty name for her, though not understanding it. To call the whore Rachel a gift from God is a savagely ironic fashion of naming the way she is offered to him and to all comers by the procuress. Moreover, just as the Rachel of the opera is not what she seems, not the Jewish daughter of the hated Eleazar but actually the daughter of a cardinal of the Church, so Proust's Rachel is transformed from the lowly prostitute to the beloved mistress of the aristocrat Robert de Saint-Loup: "In this woman I recognised instantaneously 'Rachel when from the Lord,' she who, but a few years since (women change their situation so rapidly in that world, when they do change) used to say to the procuress [*la maquerelle*]: 'Tomorrow evening, then, if you want me for someone, you'll send round for me, won't you?' " (F, 2:456; E, 2:160).

I have mentioned the way the power of naming, whether by Marcel Proust himself when he named his characters or by Jacob's wives when they named their sons, exemplifies one salient performative utterance: "I name thee . . . so and so." Marcel's spontaneous witty allusive invention of the sobriquet "Rachel when from the Lord," metonym for the aria and for the whole opera, is a striking example within the novel itself of naming as a sovereign speech act making or remaking the one who is named. The reader of J. L. Austin's *How to Do Things with Words* will remember Austin's use of the figure of christening to name what is happening in his invention of a new nomenclature for speech acts: performative, constative, illocutionary, behabitive, and so on.[8]

Yet one more reference functions powerfully in the complex integument of displacement woven in the episode of Marcel's meeting Saint-Loup's mistress. This is an allusion to perhaps the most famous prostitute of all, certainly the most famous in biblical and Christian tradition, Mary Magdalene. The invocation of Mary Magdalene is the telos toward which all the personifications of the pear trees have been tending. When Marcel recognizes that the mistress Saint-Loup has invested with so much mystery and with infinite value is no more than "Rachel when from the Lord," he is greatly moved: "It was not 'Rachel when from the Lord,' who seemed to me of little significance, it was the power of the human imagination, the illusion on which were based the pains of love [*les douleurs de l'amour*], that I found very great" (F, 2:458; E, 2:162–3). In order to hide the true source of his emotion from Robert, Marcel turns to the pear and cheery trees, "so that he might think it was their beauty that had touched me. And it did touch me in somewhat the same way; it also brought close to me things of the kind which we not only see with our eyes but feel also in our hearts [*ces choses qu'on ne voit pas qu'avec ses yeux, mais qu'on sent dans son coeur*]" (F, 2:458; E, 2:163). The distinction here is between the clear and distinct, but cold, knowledge that comes from seeing and that other kind of nonknowing knowledge that is generated by passion, "knowledge" that we "feel also in our hearts." The examples here are Saint-Loup's creation of a Rachel who does not exist and Marcel's transformation, through metaphor's performative power, of the pear trees into angels. Just as Saint-Loup had been mistaken about Rachel, so had Marcel been mistaken about the pear trees.

These two similar mistakes, however, mistakes though they be, nevertheless, according to a paradigm explored elsewhere later in the *Recherche* and which I have elsewhere discussed,[9] give the mistaken, mystified one access to a realm of beauty that is lost in a past that never was. Nevertheless, it is treasured as a "memory," a memory without memory and hoped for in a future that always remains future, the "recompense which we strive to earn." All works of the imagination, love, music, literature, art, however illusory in fetishizing this or that embodiment of beauty, give us a glimpse of this lost paradise, or rather these lost paradises, since they are multiple and incommensurate, each in its own separate and sequestered place in the capacious realm of the imagination. This multiple and unattainable beauty is equally allegorized through catachreses in the illusions of love and in the fictitious, factitious creations of poetry. The passage is of great beauty, though it describes a speech act that both is "felicitous" and is at the same time seen as a mistake. It is a false theme asserted by a gentle mind:

> In likening those trees that I had seen in the garden to strange deities, had I not been mistaken like Magdalene when, in another garden, on a day whose anniversary was soon to come [Easter], she saw a human form and "supposed it was the gardener." Treasurers of our memories of the golden age, keepers of the promise that reality is not what we suppose [*garants de la promesse que la réalité n'est pas ce qu'on croit*], that the splendor of poetry, the wonderful radiance of innocence may shine in it and may be the recompense which we strive to earn, were they not, these great white creatures miraculously [*merveilleusement*] bowed over that shade so propitious for rest, for angling or for reading, were they not rather angels [*n'était-ce plûtot des anges*]? (F, 2:458–9; E, 2:163).

The reference is to that moving episode in the Gospel according to St. John (20:11–18) in which Mary Magdalene, the sinner whom Jesus cured of her devils and whom he loved, comes to the tomb of the crucified Jesus and finds the sepulcher empty and guarded by two angels in white. She then mistakes the risen Jesus standing in the garden for the gardener. When Jesus speaks to her she suddenly recognizes him and hails him as "Master":

> She turned herself back, and saw Jesus standing, and knew not that it was Jesus. Jesus saith unto her, Woman, why weepest thou? whom seekest thou? She, supposing him to be the gardener, saith unto him, Sir, if thou have borne him hence, tell

> me where thou hast laid him, and I will take him away. Jesus said unto her, Mary. She turned herself, and saith unto him, Rabboni, which is to say, Master. Jesus saith unto her, Touch me not; for I am not yet ascended to my Father; but go to my brethren, and say unto them, I ascend unto my Father, and your Father; and to my God, and your God. Mary Magdalene came and told the disciplines that she had seen the Lord, and that he had spoken these things unto her. (20:14–18)

Mary Magdalene first turns away from the empty sepulcher and then turns again when she recognizes the gardener as Jesus. These turnings mime the reversals of conversion and of spiritual insight. Each of these turnings is a trope (that is what trope means: turning), a redefinition of meanings by performative language, as when Jesus salutes Mary by her name, and she names him "Master." The turnings mime also the reversals of Marcel's evaluation of his transformation of the pear trees into angels, Saint-Loup's transformation of Rachel into a person of infinite worth. First he says the pear trees were just pear trees, not angels at all, just as Rachel was really "Rachel when from the Lord," but then he says they were really angels, Rachel really Robert's Rachel, just as the gardener turned out to be Jesus.

Jesus' "Touch me not [*Noli me tangere*]" contrasts strikingly with another episode a few verses further on, also recorded only in John, the story of "Doubting Thomas." Thomas Didymus (meaning "Thomas the twin"), was invited by Jesus to touch the nail holes in risen Jesus' hands and to thrust his hand in the wound in Jesus' side. Thomas apparently does not actually touch Jesus but believes on the strength of Jesus' words. The risen Christ is both tangible and intangible, embodied and disembodied, like a ghost or apparition: "But he [Thomas Didymus] said unto them. Except I shall see in his hands the print of the nails, and put my finger into the print of the nails, and thrust my hand into his side, I will not believe. . . . Then said he to Thomas, Reach hither thy finger, and behold my hands; and reach hither they hand, and thrust it into my side: and be not faithless, but believing. And Thomas answered and said unto him, My Lord and my God. Jesus saith unto him, Thomas, because thou hast seen me, thou hast believed: blessed are they that have not seen, and yet have believed" (John 20:25, 27–29). Seeing is believing, but the truest faith is to believe without seeing. Faith is precisely that: belief in things unseen. The passage in Proust, when it is put back in its biblical context, is a passionate celebration of the human imagination for its power to reach a hidden truth, accessible not to reason but to performative speech acts. This is exemplified not only in Marcel's transformation of the pear trees into angels but even in Saint-Loup's transformation of "Rachel when from the Lord" into his beloved mistress.

As anyone who has traced the evolution and permutations down through the centuries of the legends of Mary Magdalene knows, Mary Magdalene has been the focus of an activity of "imagination" as intense as that Saint-Loup lavished on Rachel. As opposed to the Virgin Mary, Mary Magdalene was a sinner, a repentant prostitute, therefore someone with whom mere mortal sinners could more easily identify themselves. Moreover, without sound scriptural authority, Christians early and late have conflated the various Marys in the gospels and made them into a single Mary (though not in the Eastern Church, where each Mary has a separate saint's day). Believers have then invented a whole circumstantial life story for Mary Magdalene, exemplified saliently and most familiarly in the version of her life in Jacobus de Voragine's *The Golden Legend: Readings on the Saints.*[10] A "legend" means, etymologically, something to read, but also an act of reading. There are, however, many other versions besides the *Legenda Aurea* one, versions both literary and graphic, including even an apocryphal version that has Mary Magdalene the mother of a daughter, Sarah, fathered by Jesus, who became the originating mother of the line of Merovingian kings when Mary Magdalene and Sarah fled Palestine for Marseilles.[11]

The transformation of Mary Magdalene into a Christian saint parallels the transformation of Rachel into Saint-Loup's beloved and exemplifies the same power of the linguistic imagination. This transformation was inaugurated by Jesus when he forgave Mary Magdalene her sins, substituting, as Hegel has said in a powerful passage in his early theological writings, Christian love for Judaic law and thereby inaugurating the new religion as the canceling and at the same time the sublation or sublimation of the old, its *Aufhebung.* Magdalene was an in-between or threshold figure, poised between the old dispensation and the new.[12]

The opposition in the episode of Marcel's meeting Saint-Loup's mistress and seeing that she is "Rachel when from the Lord" is not between Saint-Loup's "imagination" of a Rachel who is not there and Marcel's clear seeing of what is there but between two forms of imagination that are nevertheless versions of the same power, fueled by emotion and acting through performative positings. "The immobility of that thin face, like that of a sheet of paper subjected to the colossal pressure of two atmospheres, seemed to me to be held in equilibrium by two infinites which converged on her without meeting, for she held them apart. Looking at her, Robert and I, we did not both see her from the same side of the mystery [*nous ne la voyions pas du même côté du mystère*]" (F, 2:458; E, 2, 162).

Marcel here ends by endorsing the belief that Rachel is a mystery, as thin as a sheet of paper (inscribed perhaps with words or graphic signs to be read, though Marcel does not say so), but nevertheless remaining impenetrable, unfathomable, unknowable, whatever infinite imaginative pressure from either side is put on it. She is therefore open to the two radically different and infinitely powerful acts of imagination, one performed by Saint-Loup, one by Marcel. These end by balancing in an equilibrium that is equally ignorant on both sides of what Rachel "really is."

The signals of Marcel's performative power are all those allusions and references that make the episode a complex allegory in which nothing is just itself but is also a sign that stands for something else, evidence that "reality is not what we suppose," as Rachel is for Marcel the biblical Rachel, but also the heroine of Halévy's play, and also Mary Magdalene, and, also, Lot's wife, just as the pear trees are turned into girls, then into men, then into angels, and then into the particular angels that guarded Christ's tomb after the Resurrection, all by sovereign speech acts.

Behind Marcel's performative positings, registered in the text of his narration, stands Marcel Proust, the narrator's maker and the ultimate source, in lordly self-effacement, of all these metaphorical or allegorical transpositions, effected by acts of language. *À la recherche du temps perdu* may seem to many readers to be a fictitious autobiography obeying the conventions of realism. If this is so, the figures Marcel uses would be mere embroidery, fanciful metaphors brought in to make the realist narrative more vivid and to demonstrate Marcel's psychology, his "poetic" gifts. On the contrary, this episode, like the *Recherche* in general, is allegorical through and through. It names one thing by means of another, demonstrating that "reality is not what we suppose." The meaning of the *Recherche* depends on the tropes, or turnings, that make pear trees into angels, Rachel the whore into "Rachel when from the Lord" in Halévy's opera, and then into Robert's mysterious, unfathomable beloved, a deep enigma.

Of what is the *Rercherche* an allegory? The episode, like the *Recherche* "as a whole," is an allegory of allegory, that is, of the activity whereby impassioned language posits transformations, turns trees into angels, whores into mysterious beloveds of infinite worth. This activity resists cognition, since it is a performative positing. The act of trying to understand this positing and to express that understanding in words repeats the enigmatic, unknowable event that is the object of anxious interrogation. These new positings, positings on positings, such as my words about Proust, following Proust's words about Marcel's words about his own and Saint-Loup's words about Rachel, are ways of doing things with words rather than the constative expression of achieved knowledge. They exemplify the incompatibility between knowing through or by words and doing things with words. This incompatibility is perpetually demonstrated by what I call, in another speech act, "speech acts in literature."[13] To "call" is to name. Naming is an initiatory performative utterance, a "calling." That calling is based or grounded on nothing but the call from the other that impassions me. This call is mediated, in this case, by a text or embodied in a text. This call I respond to in another calling, in this case my remarks about one episode in *À la recherche du temps perdu*. These remarks, in turn, are a demand for a further response for which I, in the end, as the one who has responded and makes the further demand, must take responsibility.

CHAPTER SIXTEEN

An Interview with Geoffrey Hartman

Cathy Caruth

Geoffrey Hartman's career extends from his pioneering early work on Wordsworth to his more recent writing on video testimony. His recent work has emphasized a possible continuity in this career: an exploration of the intricate relation between what he calls "literary knowledge" and the various forms of traumatic loss. I interviewed him in the fall of 1994 on his early and ongoing work with Wordsworth, the implications of this work for understanding literary ways of knowing, and the relation this might have to the kind of knowing and testifying provided by video testimony.

Traumatic Impasse an Poetic Knowledge

CC: I'm interested in the implications, for an understanding of poetry, or literature in general, of your comment that your literary critical work has always had a "concern for absences or intermittences of consciousness, for the ambiguous status of accidents in mental life, for the ghosting of the subject."[1] The most obvious place to illustrate this early and ongoing interest in absences and intermittences would be your repeated readings of *The Prelude*, and particularly the paradigmatic episode of the Boy of Winander. You note that, in *The Prelude*, which you call the first account of developmental psychology in our era, this particular episode surprisingly describes an impasse in development, and you go on to ask, in regard to it, "What is the relation of memory to loss, to loss of control perhaps, even to trauma? What kind of knowledge is poetry?"[2] You seem to be speaking almost paradoxically, linking impasse and knowledge, trauma and poetry. I'd like you to comment on the kind of impasse we find in Wordsworth, and how it is related specifically to poetic knowledge.

GH: Trauma is generally defined as an experience that is not experienced, that resists or escapes consciousness. In *The Unmediated Vision* I already mentioned a more mystical notion, that of Meister Eckhart's *Unerkennendes Erkennen*, an unknowing knowing. The context there was a necessary, whether deliberate or natural, anti-self-consciousness. And certainly from the beginning I've been interested in how to define a specifically *literary* knowlege, which can reveal without full consciousness or systematic analysis. Again, thinking back to *The Unmediated Vision*, its last chapter, called "The New Perseus," focused on the figure of the Medusa. It speculated that as we move from the romantics into the modern period, there is an attempt to see things unaided, to catch a reality on the quick. I noticed in modern authors a certain inner distancing or coldness, or an attempt to achieve a coldness despite the nearness to, the apparent nearness to, reality. I associated this coldness, leaning on the Greek myth, with Perseus's shield, which guarded him from the petrifying glance of the Medusa, and speculated that tradition functioned as this shield. It managed to provide obliquity, or representational modes that had an inbuilt obliquity. But absent these traditional decorums, the poet had to go against the real with the unshielded eye or the unshielded senses. This seemed to increase the risk and potential of trauma.

Then, in the Wordsworth book, I posited certain fixations, in particular what I called the spot syndrome, or the obsession with particular places, an obsession which came to the poet often unexpectedly and in ordinary circumstances: "And there's a tree, of many one." I understood the emphasis on oneness, on singularity rather than unity, as being part of the same complex, and which played a role in the drama of individuation.

CC: So the spot syndrome was linked with that perceptual confrontation, or that unmediated vision.

GH: Yes, and I was interested in how Wordsworth drew his stories and fictions out of his fascination with particular places. These highly charged images, I tried to show how the poet unblocked them, how he developed them. Many of them were ocular. Visuality was dominant within his sensory organization; and something, call it nature, call it an economic principle within sensory organization, pitted the other senses against the eye. Symbolic process, I said, was related to this undoing of images.

CC: Are you saying that the image was at first a block that had to be unblocked?

GH: Yes. Or a fixation.

CC: And that Wordsworth's poetry had to do with unblocking the eye?

GH: Yes. It wasn't necessarily that they were always the same images, let's say primal images or primal scene images. But whatever the psychic etiology, that structure was there, and Wordsworth talked quite openly about the dominance of the eye. He confessed he had passed through a period of "picturesque" composition and later felt that this was related to a stage of obsessive visuality. But there are many other important statements in Wordsworth on the development of visuality and nature's counterpointing of visuality, and how his development as a poet has to do with that.

CC: So visuality here is not something that immediately produces some kind of development, but presents itself as an impasse to development, or potentially so.

GH: Yes. But as I also said, there is something abstract about visuality, in distinction from individual images. So you can fall in love with the visual, whereas you can't fall in love with obsessive images which overpower you or which you can't get rid of.

CC: The distinction then is between perception as a whole mode and the shock of an individual perception.

GH: That's right. In Wordsworth, the movement from charged individual image to visuality is parallel to the movement from specific and haunting places to Nature. Nature is his most generous concept. I try to connect this evolution with a tension in the history of religion centering on epiphanic places. Bethel, for instance, the place where Jacob lies down and has the dream of angels ascending and descending, is nothing but a stone. Yet here are the gates of Heaven! It is what Mircea Eliade calls an *omphalos:* the umbilical and nether point of the earth. But there is another issue that you and I have talked about in relation to trauma:

how almost any place — and that's part of the accidentality of revelation — can be revelatory or charged or have something of a traumatic effect through deferred action. So, on the one hand, you have the omphalos, the umbilicus of the world. On the other hand, it's merely tree or stone; the seminal episode of *The Ruined Cottage* is the poet seeing four bare walls that remain, and a broken pane of glass glittering in the moonlight.

CC: So, as with visuality, the place can have, on the one hand, a traumatic, blocking effect, yet on the other this traumatic effect is intimately tied up with the possibility of poetic writing, or poetic development. In the Boy of Winander episode, for example, as you point out, there is at once impasse and promise of development: the first paragraph describing a boy who creates an instrument with his two hands to blow "mimic hootings to the silent owls" and who is suddenly confronted with the nonresponse of the owls, a "lengthened pause," and a "gentle shock of mild surprise." In the second verse paragraph, the boy is said to have died in youth, and the poet stands "Mute, looking at the grave in which he lies." How are "pause" and "shock" linked to development here?

GH: This is one of the most intriguing episodes in Wordsworth. It is in part autobiographical, as we know from the manuscripts. The impasse, to describe it very briefly, is that the first verse-paragraph leads one to expect that the boy should grow into maturity and perhaps become a poet. The imagination of the boy is being prepared through a dissonace: the owls do not respond, or respond as they will. Within the context of experience of responsiveness, something is not symmetrical, and this prepares for the future, develops the boy's consciousness of a world that is independent of him. Remember the lengthened pause, which meets the boy's best skill: it is part of the dissonance, because it makes him reflective, and it anticipates a further lengthening, until the final pause is mortality or death — more precisely the philosophical mind that looks at death. So that while horizontally death is foreshadowed, you expect from the first verse-paragraph that in the second the poet would say, "I was that boy." Instead the boy dies, and you have the poet as survivor looking at the boy's grave.

CC: So you're saying that normally one would understand the moment of absence in the first verse-paragraph as preparing the boy for some kind of self-consciousness and, ultimately, though at a greater temporal distance, his death. But in this case the death comes before self-consciousness emerges. Could one say, then, that the impasse for the poet, the traumatic moment in the developmental scheme, is not the death as such, but the fact that the death comes at the wrong time?

GH: Yes, the death is untimely, but not only the death. Wordsworth adds an argumentative frame to the Boy of Winander episode when he inserts it into Book 5 of *The Prelude.* He argues that we cannot totally prepare the developing psyche, the young person, for what befalls. That would be, he claims, engineering the psyche. Natural development is much freer and depends on accident. And accident is always defined as something you cannot prepare for. In that sense development is always both propadeutic and exceeds formal training. So that trauma is related to development by excess as well as lack. Yet Wordsworth's great myth in *The Prelude* remains: that there could be development—a "growth of the poet's mind"—without psychic wounds, that the psyche could be "from all internal injury exempt."

CC: But what is the relation between lack and excess in this accident?

GH: Keeping strictly to the passage, the failure of response may have linked itself, in the mind of the poet, to a thought of death. This intuition is then literalized, by prophetic extension, as in the Lucy poems. A failure of response anticipates—by the extremest reach of Wordsworth's imagination—that there would be no more nature. That if the human mind does not live fully, responsively, within nature, or nature does not respond to us, then the end result, projected forward, is apocalyptic. The death is like a hyperbole of this moment, a hyperbolic act of an imagination that leaps down not up, taking off from a simple failure of response. Should this failure of response accelerate, then we will have no habitat, no mutuality of nature and the human mind. At this point you transcend the development of the individual, you get a more cosmic model, you speed up time, and that's apocalypse.

So that the moment of excess is not only in the wild hooting of the owls when it comes, but in the imagination itself, which reacts to both failure of response and an "ecstatic" correlative of death, that piercing of the skin of the psyche when the natural scene "enter[s] unawares into [the boy's] mind."

CC: Yet the impasse is, in a sense, passed through: at the end of the episode you do not simply have a death but a poet who is looking at, reflecting upon, this death (and writing the poem). The problem that arises, then, is the way that poetic and exemplary moment is characterized: even though it is a poetic moment, it is also a moment of muteness (which peculiarly does not seem to be completely opposed to poetic writing). And this brings back the problem of how development, here, is not simply dialectical, taking the negative and making a positive. You say specifically about that mute moment, "we sense that the poet is looking as well into himself, that he is a *posthumous* figure, he stands towards a prior stage of life, as a reader, a quasi-epitaphic reader . . . the poet's stance emerges as a haunting issue."[3] If the poem is in some sense about poetic knowing, how can it be mute, how is the muteness poetic, or what is the link between muteness and poetry?

GH: Let me bring in the reader, at this point. The theme of time—of its flow—brings us to the reader, just as in Milton's *Lycidas.* Milton foresees what he calls "lucky words": "I should utter something in honor of Lycidas, and so in the future, I hope someone will write my epitaph, and make the passerby [who could be the reader] turn and be struck by what has been said about me." This fast-forwarding of imagination is what I mean by a posthumous stance in Wordsworth and it includes an adumbration of the reader. Wordsworth allows you to move from the poet looking at the grave of the boy to the reader reading the poet, an image of speechless and perhaps epitaphic reading. The problem is then: how do mute speech and (self)reading relate?

We go from muteness to muteness, even if it is a muteness described in words. That is, the Boy of Winander—and this is one reason why we feel that the episode was meant to be paradigmatic of human development, and that the death came too soon—is shown at the point where speech is still mimicry. He is not shown speaking, he makes a pastoral pipe with his hands, but this is not speech. He doesn't mimic speech, he mimics the owls, nature's sounds. And so you expect the question to be: how do you go from that stage to mature poetic speech. Yet *The Prelude* records the growth of the poet's mind, not of speech itself. You are given the pre-mature moment, then the mature moment, but the mature moment is like the pre-mature moment because the pause is lengthened, and you are shown a silent poet. Now what does it mean to be a silent poet? Speech is not theorized in Wordsworth as an agency in the growth of the (poetic) mind.

CC: It's almost as if the poem moved from what is called the "preverbal" or the "preverbal trauma"—trauma before it can even enter as a verbal construct—to muteness, and the paradoxical poetic development, at least in this episode, is the link between this preverbal or "shocking" perception and muteness. And the difficulty that you're trying to get at is to say that *that* somehow is linked to poetic insight.

GH: The impasse is not dialectized, as you correctly say. We go from one form of muteness to another form of muteness, yet Wordsworth *speaks* again and again about muteness. About mute insenate things. He doesn't simply want to speak *for* them. It's not an orphic perspective. There is, perhaps, something potentially orphic in the first verse paragraph, but even if it is orphic, nature won't cooperate. It's not really orphic, then, not a myth that animates nature, not a Rilkean myth of internalizing nature or making it invisible, not a Blakean transformation either, not a metamorphosis or anthropomorphizing of any kind. The mute insensate things remain mute and insensate. *But they're brought live into human perception and they play a part, like the mother does.* Mute dialogues with nature exist, as between child and mother. The muteness is not always negative: it can be, at times, the shadow cast by ecstasy.

CC: Maybe one way to restate the question would be to look at something else you say about silence. You say that the entire episode, even it is based in part on failure of response, is framed, I would say paradoxically, as an address. Your words are specifically, "his address to Winander claims a sufficient foundation in humanity by being an aversio as well as an exclamation. That is, by using a turntale, in Putnam's words, to invoke a preternatural or mute witness."[4] So in the classical case there is a witness, a mute witness, the fields of Winander, the cliffs of Winander. I want to ask: is there a link between the failure of response that the boy experiences, then the muteness of the poet, and the poem's frame of address — an address that implies a response?

GH: Yes, but I would phrase it differently. The address to the cliffs and islands of Winander evokes a lasting or apparently lasting presence, and this presence recurs at the end of the Boy of Winander episode with the Lady, the Church, also a kind of monitory shape. You really have three figures: the cliffs and islands, the poet himself at the grave, and finally the Church, watching over the children among whom the Boy of Winander lies.

CC: They're all witnesses.

GH: Monitory shapes. One is tempted to say "witness," and "witness" is certainly appropriate to the forms of nature evoked at the beginning of the episode because of the formal force of the apostrophe. I am always reminded of Coleridge's marvelous phrase in his lines after hearing Wordsworth recite the poem on his own life, "The dread watchtower of man's absolute self." It's close to that, almost an eternity-figure, a figure for conscience, a super-ego. The beginning of the episode, the apostrophe to the cliffs and islands of Winander, puts human development within a quasi-eternal frame.

CC: Because the cliffs are eternal?

GH: Yes — the danger of apocalypse, of Nature (familiar nature) disappearing, is distanced here. There is lastingness, the sense of not only watchful but enduring presences. Which sense is instilled in the Boy from Nature. Instilled in Wordsworth also, from nature, and it becomes an instinctive article of faith. That something endures. That something is immortal or universal. It is not in the case of the Boy of Winander quite what Coleridge felt: Coleridge's special emphasis is on anxiety, the dread watchtower. That's not in Wordsworth, but it goes along the same lines, along the same emotional spectrum, though it has more of a consolation, an assurance that nature will *not* be no more. And it has the effect of affirming, in that sense witnessing, the boy's experience. It does not deny the Boy, it does not say, hey little titch, you think you're important. So the entire tonality of the experience is different from Coleridge's watchtower at this moment, it's more like the other presences, the stars rising and setting. That has always intrigued me, "rising or setting." You remember those are the lines that follow the apostrophe. You get a sense of vast cyclical movement: it doesn't matter whether they're rising or setting, or setting and rising. They're always going to be there. The setting is not a death; rising or setting, they will be there. It is a perpetual background which does not negate or threaten but affirms the individual life. If you wish, bears witness to it in fact. And the reason why it can do this, other than some kind of grand sentimental projection, has to do with Wordsworth's peculiar, non-Coleridgean *Angst*, always kept in check by that sense of permanent presences. Wordsworth's fear is that if the human mind separates, divorces itself from nature, and we invest our imagination elsewhere, then and only then is there danger of the fading of nature. In other words, precisely the ego, the psyche, is not ghosted in Wordsworth by nature, as it must be ghosted by the supernatural. Yet Wordsworth sees that if, because of industrialization and a turning away from a Nature ethos, nature is neglected, then the situation will drastically change. But here he remains within the faith that human life is not ghosted but affirmed by nature.

CC: Yet you speak elsewhere, as I said, of the poet's stance as a "haunting" issue . . . Wouldn't your emphasis now on the "affirmation" by nature be interpreted as overlooking that haunting aspect?

GH: One cannot forget that the child is haunted by Nature, and the death of the Boy of Winander could express this ghosting in the form of a "return to nature." The balance here between affirmative and negative is a "natural" one, and the reader recognizes that, and does not wish to intervene concerning what in the poet's brooding is, at once, mortality *and* an intimation of immortality: the promise, cut short, of a communion with Nature which approaches ecstasy.

The poet looking at the grave, and framed by these other witness figures, does not stress the ghosting of human life, does not stress mortification. Mortality is there but not mortification. So it works against trauma, I would say. Look, everything works against trauma in Wordsworth, yet the basis of trauma is there. "A gentle shock of mild surprise." Now really!

The muteness of the poet in the episode also raises more generally the question of the muteness in poetic speech. For his standing there "mute" is a kind of fading—counterpointed by his "full half-hour" steadfastness. I explore parallels in "Words and Wounds" and the essay on Christopher Smart in *The Fate of Reading.*[5] We avoid, evade, muteness, but it's always there. We speak, but under certain conditions, as if we were allowed to speak only when fulfilling these conditions, and so euphemic modes are produced. The muteness indicates that there's something that is too difficult to utter. The way to get past that difficulty, however you conceive of the monitors, the dread you have to get past, however you conceive of it, or whatever Freudian understanding you may give to it, involves euphemism in the strong sense. Even irony may be euphemistic. Irony, the boast of the modern poet, remains within the euphemic mode (though the modern poet would say I'm "destroying euphemism").[6] It's not satire's mad laughter—satire breaks through the euphemic. It is not cursing. In other words, there is a mode of breaking through and I'm assuming that there was trauma, shock, something dreadful or ecstatic. You know that there exists a pathology of speech, in which the person speaks only by cursing. And I say there is also a mode of speech in which the person talks only in terms of blessings. We arrange ourselves between these two extremes.

Pausal Style

CC: That brings me to the second point I wanted to raise. The general argument you're making here, and in a number of different places, concerns poetic style, which you refer to as "pausal style," and again it appears to suggest a paradoxical link between something that interrupts and something that continues. You mention specifically that at the very moment of the turn to an ordinary style, or conversational language, there's a pressure on conversation, something that remains missed and impossible.

GH: I do say that, I feel there is a tension which I'm not sure how it is resolvable, between the development, almost the genesis, in terms of the history of poetry—or the converstional style, and the pressure of imagination, which is more traumatic, interruptive, transcendental. And I think it is part of Wordsworth's gift to contain each within each. There are points, however, where you feel that the suturing will give way.

CC: My impression was nontheless that it's still the conversational style that's saving poetry. You say that poetry is mortal and that Wordsworth assured the continuity of great poetry by a revolution of style. And it seems that you were saying that the conversation, or ordinary language, the conversational style, saves poetry, but only in relation to this interruptive or pausal awareness.

GH: Yes. It's *Wordsworth's* conversational style that saves it. Not conversation, because conversational style, insofar as it comes out of the epistolary mode, or middle style, is an achievement of the late seventeenth and eighteenth centuries, and falls into habits of what Wordsworth called "poetic diction." That is, it elevates itself despite itself, and isn't really genuinely conversational. It's familiar in the sense that the author tries to speak to the audience as equal to equal, but in fact when we read the epistles, any of the epistles, whether Pope's poetic epistles or Chesterfield's letters, we face an artificial tone and diction. But Wordsworth, as certain notorious lyrics show—think of "The Idiot Boy"—would rather have bathos than an artificially elevated diction.

CC: Does this conversational style found something that would be linked to modern poetry?

GH: I would think yes. The main line of modern poetry develops that link. And in Ashbery, the casualness can become excessive. The more excessive it becomes, the more you feel an internal pressure that is being evaded.

CC: So this so-called ordinary style in Wordsworth is shadowed by that pausal sensitivity.

GH: Always.

CC: Could that be a modern sensitivity: that the ordinary is inextricably bound to the pausal or interruptive?

GH: I wonder. Possibly. But trauma is not modern. You don't need a theory of trauma to "experience" trauma. And in terms of a historical schematism I have only one firm idea, namely, that what I call the Eastern epiphantic style, visible in the Great Odes and neoclassicism, has trauma directly inscribed into it. By epiphanic style I mean a style with sharp turns, of which the apostrophe at the beginning of the Boy of Winander is a faint echo. And by Eastern I mean the moment in the Ancient Mariner (written in the older style) when "at one stride comes the dark." That abruptness is inscribed in the older style. But it's not in Wordsworth: "A *gentle* shock of *mild* surprise." Instead we have a sense of continuity or achievement of something much, much milder, not that you ever lose the sense of the pressure of what that mildness is in function of, but the Wordsworthian poetic turn, let's not talk about revolution for a moment, creates a conversational poetic style that subsumes the epiphanic style. So that he does not go from, he doesn't jump from nature into the supernatural. There is no dream vision, almost none in him. Eastern is not just a geographical category, although it has something to do with the "at one stride comes the dark." Imaginatively, if there's no twilight, then you are already in the zone of trauma.

CC: I wonder if your interest in, on the one hand, the relation between imaginative pressure and this interruptive mode, which you're also trying to see in the relation to style, and on the other hand ordinary conversational style, has something to do with a more general notion of modern writing. When trauma theory emerges as a modern theoretical mode of writing, after all, it emerges as something within ordinary life.

GH: That is true. Theory as a mode of discourse is anticonversational and links up with the pressure of trauma. I would prefer to focus here on literary knowledge: how literature is a mode of experience. In the nonpathological course of events, the "unclaimed experience," as you call it, can only be reclaimed by literary knowledge.[7]

CC: When you speak about this literary knowledge in your essay on trauma studies and literature, you suggest that trauma studies allow us to read the relationship of words and wounds without medical or political reductionism, and you say specifically that figurative or poetic language is linked to trauma.[8] Could you expand on that a bit, because there seems to be a kind of a paradox: normally one would think of trauma as the absencing of the possibility of speech, but you link it inherently to figurative language.

GH: I've always been intrigued by certain basic literary forms, and the riddle is one of them. I suggest that all poetic language partakes of the riddle form, with its surplus of signifiers. An answer is evoked, but can you get to the answer? If you could get there, the signifiers would become redundant and fall away. But in poetry you can't get to the answer. So the signifiers keep pointing to what is missing. Or mute. There's too little that is referred to, if you want to use that scheme, and too much that is suggested. But I've not been able to develop fully the poetry-riddle relation. I'm not a systematic thinker. I began this line of speculation in "The Voice of the Shuttle,"[9] where muteness and trauma are at the center, Philomela's tongue having been cut out. "The voice of the shuttle" is, you remember, a phrase cited in Aristotle's *Poetics*. It refers to, we think, the Philomela story: how her shuttle weaves a garment that restores her voice. But the compactness itself of the phrase is riddling, and I try to describe that structure as, basically, overspecified ends ("voice" and "shuttle") and something in the middle that is muted or left out. And I suggest that all figurative language has these overspecified ends, as if the middle were cut out. It is the cutting out that's important.

CC: Yes, and cutting, rather than erasing, which is relevant.

GH: Yes, we glimpse figuration as a counterforce. My essay, however, stops short at one point, and I've never been able to extend it. I speculate that the very structure of figurative language, if it has these overspecified ends and an absent middle—which interpretation can fill in—also holds for narration. But I don't show it by a narratological analysis. I simply suggest that in the Oedipus story you can glimpse an extension from figurative language to narrative structure. Insofar as the Oedipus story converges on incest, persons do not have enough space for development. Incest violates developmental space. It collapses the plot of life. I try to bring that structure together with the overspecified ends and the middle that is lost.

CC: Are you saying that figurative or poetic language is linked in some way to "trauma," or the kind of muteness you've been interested in all along? If we think of muteness through the Boy of Winander, then language wouldn't be so much trying to get at some kind of experience which is ever-receding, but at a failure of experience. Because the muteness, the muteness of the Boy, is a failure of response, you said. So is that a way of saying that figurativeness is referential because the referent itself has to do with failure? In other words, you suggest that the figuration uncannily intensifies the referent, and I am asking if that is because the referent for you has always been, insofar as you are Wordsworthian, a failure of response in some way, or linked to untimely speech?

GH: That is a far-reaching thought, and I touch on a "mimetic" strengthening of the referent in "I. A. Richards and the Dream of Communication."[10] Yet I'm not sure I want to give the referent that specific a content. Because in poetry it is not entirely empirical or historical. The fact that figuration, moreover, uncannily intensifies the (deferred) referent, indicates a desire (however frustrated) for "timely utterance"—even for prophetic or ecstatic speech. But I accept everything you say about untimelessness. Trauma is certainly linked to the untimely. In the basic theory of trauma, derived from Freud, you weren't prepared (hence also a certain anxiety). And it is doubtful that you could be prepared for either shell-shock or experience shock. Wordsworth's argument is, Nature does everything to prepare you, to make you immune, or to gentle the shock. He doesn't say there is no shock, or surprise, but that nature aims at a growth of the mind which can absorb or overcome shock.

Video Testimony and the Place of Modern Memory

CC: We have been talking about Wordsworth's revolution in style, and its way of communicating (without succumbing to) shock. Do you think that there is another, similar revolution of style, after the momentous events in this century that we have passed through? In your recent work, you have begun to focus on the video testimony project in the Fortunoff Holocaust Video Archives at Yale, which you helped found, and in which individuals are filmed telling their stories, in relatively undirected fashion, to trained interviewers. In recent years, you have talked about these videos as providing a means of communicating or witnessing an event that is difficult to represent adequately by other means—for example, in the seemingly realistic medium of mainstream movies, which, as you suggest, become less realistic, or more surrealistic, the more realistically they attempt to portray visual detail.[11] Would you say, then, that the video testimonies also represent a revolution in style for communicating this kind of event?

GH: Yes, but see for yourself! They are effective as an antidote, within technology, within the era of mechanical reproduction, to the glossy super-realism of the media. They are audiovisual and yet do not privilege the ocular or assault the eye. I have suggested that they avoid the contagion of "secondary trauma"—that they allow the sensitive mind space for reflection, even if there is shock.

CC: You have talked about the effacement of an earlier type of recollection marked by memory places. I'm curious if that reflective moment in Wordsworth, which you look at in the Boy of Winander as paradigmatic, is linked in any way, through the problems of muteness and speaking that it raises, to later questions you come up against, in regard to contemporary attempts to remember.

GH: They are linked. The reflective moment must be at the center of this. By "must be," I mean for me, when I compare what interested me in Wordsworth and what I'm interested in now—the role that video testimony can play in remembrance. My focus, on the one hand, on the individual as individual and his memory processes, and on the other hand, on what can be called public memory,[12] how a public knows or could know about events, is linked to an increasingly besieged and competitive condition that many have talked about. A condition in which our mind is actually blocked, rather than encouraged, prevented from developing mentally, experientially, by our very virtuosity in reconstructing technically what occurred. Max Frisch said that technology was the knack of so arranging the world that we didn't have to experience it. You have a surplus of simulacra, technically transmitted, but subtler mediations are elided, so one is never quite released from this surround of simulacra. The question therefore arises, What happens to reflection in this increasingly ocular situation?

There is a relation between that and my understanding of Wordsworth, or Wordsworth's self-understanding, since he talks prophetically, toward the beginning of the Industrial Revolution, about the increasing pressure of external stimuli, which act on the mind like a drug that causes dependence. He mentions specifically journalism, urbanization, and (still a part of journalism), "wretched and frantic novels," where the word "novel" contains the word "news." These things converge to besiege the mind and deprive it of the moment of reflection. There is no mind without a pastoral space, and this is disappearing. The pastoral and the utopian may be close, but the pastoral is not quite the utopian because, in Wordsworth at least, it is within time. It may be an imagined place, but it occurs within time. One does have space within time, for reflection, one must have. Where else is mind?

And here of course the psychological dimension comes in, and this fascinated me, because it pointed also to what I had observed in the history of religion: that revelation is always linked to specific place. These places can be given a national or nationalistic interpretation. It may be that the revelation, in order to fire up the community beyond the individual who has it, needs to be substantiated by evidential detail, such as the idea of specific place. And it has to be an earth-place; it doesn't work as well if it's a place in the air. To have a revelation it has to be associated with a specific place, even if you don't know anymore where that place is. And of course, as in modern Israel or Islam, people still claim Moriah is here, no, Moriah is over there, and so on. To locate Moriah, you actually need two things, name and place. You need those specifics; you need place names, if you wish. And a certain storied detail.

Now I was made conscious of the arbitrariness of this, why this place and not another. Time is also in question, but the time is always needy, a time of urgency, a time of crisis, and hence the pressure of apocalyptic thoughts. Yet why should it be this place rather than another, since the revealing force, call it God, could manifest itself anywhere?

There is, then, a fertile tension between the potential universality of the message of revelation and the accidentality and invididuality of place and person, of the bearer and the location. In Wordsworth's case, and this is part of his originality, place become memory-place: spots of time, spots in and creative of a temporal consciousness. That is, the reflective moment is introduced in all its dimensions. And there is recovery. For the recovery to be effective, salutary, it has to be associated with place. It cannot be simply a feeling. There are feelings without place in Wordsworth, but he is not satisfied with those, he wants to follow them to a surreptitious source. "Where shall I seek the origin?" Where the fountain from which this feeling or this specific thought came? But clearly it is impossible to envisage an origin without thinking of emplacement. So the recovery, the retrieval process, insofar as it can be called healing or therapeutic, involves the notion of place, the image of a power place.

I do not know how much of this, in Wordsworth or in my own thinking, is related to a need for thought to be situated, and safely situated. For the power place keeps working the memory, as if it were the pulse which allows that stream, the stream of consciousness, to continue, so it's not that there is only — in Wordsworth — a desire to rest. The reflective moment is not just a moment of pastoral safety and rest but *one where you can be equal to your experience.*

Implicit in much I have done is a meditation on place and its relation to memory and identify (individual rather than collective). It wasn't the study of Wordsworth that led me to study the Holocaust. There is a clear separation between these two subjects. But once I had engaged with questions the Holocaust raised for me — how do I take this into consciousness, what can I do about it, is this in any way thinkable, is it representable — once I had gone along that path, my interest in Wordsworth's understanding of the memory process did come in. I sensed a loss of memory place, of the Wordsworthian memory place, after the Holocaust and after entering an era of mechanical reproduction. While the places of Jewish existence destroyed in the Holocaust are remembered, they cannot be as dynamic in the individual consciousness as the Wordsworthian memory places. Alas, they are severed, or fixed, or nostalgic. And in relation to the Wordsworthian perspective of a memory not hindered by shock, I think there is always a question in my mind how future generations can be brought to remember the Holocaust without secondary trauma. I don't underestimate defenses, of course, and don't claim that everybody is all that sensitive. My move is not a protectionist move. It's more a question of how trauma can work creatively rather than destructively in one's life.

CC: It's the opposite of protectionism because in your argument, a violent imposition often ends up numbing the psyche, so that in fact by making it less violent one paradoxically allows for more of a shock.

GH: It is, as you say, precisely the question of how sensitivity can be maintained, and how sensory overload, leading to numbing, leading to feelings of impotence, can be avoided. Or as in some Holocaust studies—to feelings of mystery and enigma, which I do not value. I do not reject all feelings of mystery, but I don't want them to become protectionist, only protective. I want to see as clearly as possible, and yet preserve the reflective moment sufficiently so that something creative comes about. In terms of future generations especially, the dialectic there may be very complex, because for them what must be overcome is not only numbness but also indifference.

CC: So the question of representation that we're looking at now concerns not only the nature of the different events that are represented, that is, the Holocaust as opposed to whatever it was that was traumatic before (or after), but specifically the possibility for modes of representation to prevent, rather than create, indifference.

GH: Yes, I agree with that wholeheartedly. There really is something at once terrible and hypnotic in contemporary representations of violence, in their directness and detail.

CC: Curiously, then, the less direct mode of the video testimony would seem, in your view, to permit more of a sense of events to enter, without the hypnotic or numbing quality of direct visual representation. I am wondering if this would help us understand what you meant when you said, in one essay, that your concern with video testimony has to do with the ethical aspect of representation;[13] what would be ethical in this mode of representation would be, paradoxically, how it gives less directly to sight, or raises questions about what it means to see, and what the relation is between seeing and knowing.

GH: That is correct. If it is sufficient to describe the ethical as something that leads to questions, rather than to decisive action. Moreover, the "hypnosis" in literature and art *tests* us ethically. I would have to add that, being an intellectual, it's hard for me to conceive of the ethical as possible without reflection.

CC: I'm not sure that bringing questioning into it, or reflection, actually opposes itself to action.

GH: In Wordsworth this is quite clear in the Boy of Winander episode. He saw the activity within contemplation. He breaks down the dichotomy between action and reflection, action and contemplation. Not succumbing to the hypnosis replays this issue of reflective answering, of pushing back against what comes from outside. I come back to the Wordsworthian insistence on a creative response to what is given. Again, to qualify, the Holocaust is not only the type or general instance of a violent historical event, but there are very specific features of it which make video testimony an important agent, an instrument, I would have to say, of memory.

CC: In this light, what are the continuities and differences between the romantic texts that you've worked on and the speech-texts of video testimony?

GH: What one finds occasionally in Wordsworth is something like natural metaphor. I think of a fragment from the time of writing his first great poem, *The Ruined Cottage*. Margaret is abandoned, her husband having sold himself into the army because he couldn't bear seeing his children and wife starve. In the fragment Margaret says about the baker's wagon that used to stop, but now goes by because the baker knows there's no business there: "That wagon does not care for us." She doesn't want to say, "The baker doesn't care," she therefore says the wagon doesn't. That's what Anna Deavere Smith calls "naturally figurative speech." A vernacular vigor in the speech of ordinary people.[14] And this you also have in the speech of the witnesses, many of whom, in the United States, are not especially literate. Because coming to America the survivors became displaced persons, separated from their culture, whose education was interrupted and who, after the war, did not always have the means to take up their education again. They had to live in a strange land, they had to learn a new language. . . . So in America many of the survivors are not people who could write it down. But their speech nevertheless has a certain eloquence. It has the pathos and vigor of the ordinary people Wordsworth tries to evoke in *Lyrical Ballads.*

CC: You have also talked about the "mute eloquence" of the survivors' gestures. The muteness in the gestures suggests that there is a resistance to the telling of these stories beyond the question of skill in writing or speaking, a difficulty linked to the problem of memory and memory places that you mentioned above. I wonder if some of your thinking about the video archive in terms of what it makes possible in the relation between sight and the sound of the words—or the natural eloquence of the speech and the mute eloquence of the gestures—suggests a way of creating a place of memory.[15]

GH: I'd have to repeat first of all that something has happened to memory places, because it's difficult to think of the camps as being such memory places, although obviously they are fixed in the imagination of the survivors. The older *lieux de mémoire*, the memory places the survivor has left behind, were the traditional ones of home or native region. Yet we find it very difficult to get specific information when we try to question survivors about the time before the camps. It is so far in the past, and, it may be too painful to recall. But the camps—they are not like a Wordsworthian memory place, although there is something sinister or dark about Wordsworth's spot of time.

I like your formulation that the archive itself creates a place of memory. But let me talk of what is in the archive—the stories. And let me also separate these stories from memory place for the moment, although I think the traditional story is often focused by a memory place. I have to say two things. We call the survivor testimonies "stories," but I'm uneasy with that word. I say "story," because it's the most common word. I don't want to say "tale," which is too close to fiction, and "narrative" I find cold. The testimony is not a story with narrative desire. On the few occasions when I have found a story told with suspense of picaresque gusto, for instance, the Schlomo Perl story filmed as *Europa, Europa,* I begin to doubt. It is, in any case, very untypical. The testimonies are not stories about overcoming obstacles by cunning or other qualities, so that you could survive. Accident played a much greater role in survival, as did physical strength or having a trade needed in the camps, than powers of intellect, discernment, intuition, and so on.

Secondly, you don't have suspense, and for a very simple reason. The *univers concentrationnaire* in which the inmates lived blinded them to the future. There was no future. "Tomorrow" became, for most, a horizon beyond which mind could not stretch. Everything had to be concentrated on the sheer attempt, this moment, and the next, and the next, to keep alive. So that an element which is essential to story-telling, foreshadowing, keeping things in suspense, until you know how to resolve them—that dimension, in the consciousness of the survivor, was rarely there. Yet allowing the survivor *now* to tell something like a story, even though it doesn't have strong properties of suspense or narrative desire, restores what had been taken away. It restores a power of communicating with the future or toward the future, a future most clearly indicated by interviewers themselves and this mode of communication (the video testimony) which can speak to the generation after, including their own sons and daughters. It is retrieval in that sense, it is recuperated in that sense. In other words, the capacity of telling a story, even though it doesn't have the characteristic of a fictional story, restores to the survivor who tells it this capacity to imagine a future, a transgenerational effect coming from his own act of telling.

CC: But how then is what isn't narratively experienced communicated? And does this have something specific to do with the visual mode of the video?

GH: What you call the mute element is to some extent in the broken language, in its poetry. But always in what might be called the reembodiment of the survivors. I mean by that their gestures, the ensemble of their gestures. Allowing them to be represented by the medium is a very important effect of the medium. It makes more sense against the background of deprivation. Because another thing survivors were deprived of, deliberately of course, was their body. Its ordinary, human fullness. That is not speech. Given the historical background of the deprivation, this is an important dimension, quite apart from the semiotics of gestures, which fall into the area of speech.

CC: What about the way in which the survivor faces the camera and seems in that sense to create a kind of address? You have spoken about video testimony as activating a willingness to listen, of a person being made into an addressee of a conversation. You say in speaking about the video testimonies:

> While survivor testimony elicits its own kind of dialogue, it is only partly a dialogue with us. Survivors face not only a living audience, or now accept that audience rather than insisting on the intransitive character of their experience. They also face

> family members and friends who perished. It is the witnesses who undertake that descent to the dead. They address the living frontally. Often using warnings and admonishments they also speak for the dead, or in their name. This has its dangers. To go down may be easy, but to come up again, that is the hard task. "I am not among the living, but no one notices it," Charlotte Delbo wrote. So they remember the dead, that they too were in the house of the dead, yet they are not back here, but truly instructing us. ("Learning from Survivors," 139)

This takes us back to the question of response, lack of response, and address. One of the things that you're bringing forward from your earlier work, and for me specifically from the Boy of Winander episode, is the relation between a moment of reflection and an address, an address that is not simply aimed at the living. Here, in the testimonies, you have an address that is directed not only to the living but also to the dead. That is something that you remarked on in talking about the Wordsworth poem: you said the apostrophe as a figure of speech comes from an apostrophe to the dead.

GH: Yes, to define that mode of address is essential. We're talking about a structure. In the classical apostrophe, you turn to the dead in order to summon their help. You swear by them. But it is not that you're asking for their help, necessarily, it is that you have to represent them. At least that's true of the camp survivor. I would put it this way, perhaps. You, the survivor, are alive, they are dead, but you have to speak in some way with the voice of the dead. Obversely, while in the camp, you were in a universe of death, but still there was something alive in you. In both cases there is a chiasmic relation between the survivor and his past self as camp inmate. The survivor, part of him is still with the dead, whether he uses the figure of address or not. For the camp inmate, and that's part of the obligation of the witness, to face it—even though he was dead or as if dead there were still moments of extraordinary life.

Interrupted Pastoral

CC: I want to close with a question about your own life. In describing your passage out of Europe, when you were a boy, you talk about the love that you had for the English countryside, how distant you felt from everything, and the love of nature you had then: "I felt at home in the gentle countryside of Buckinghamshire."[16] You didn't experience your experience as a constant shock at that time. And I was struck by something that you say at the end of your introduction to *Holocaust Remembrance*, about your more present situation as an academic, where you are on the way to a lecture during the fall:

> It is mid-October. In New England the leaves have turned. One or two begin to float in the crisp air. Further north many maples have already shed half their gold, a hectic treasure for the children. I see them in the large frontyard of an old house, running and shouting, five of them, all sizes. A woman is raking the leaves, or trying to. The children, romping around, undo her work; she cuffs them with the rake, as tolerantly as a kitten a perplexing ball or comatose object. The pile of raked leaves grows, and the children invent a new game. They collapse into the pile, spreading out deliciously, while the woman—mother, housekeeper—abets their game, and covers them with the still fragrant, light leaves. At first giggles and squeaks, then, as the tumulus rises to a respectable height, total silence. But only for a minute. For, as if on signal, all emerge simultaneously from the leafy tomb, jumping out, laughing, resurrected to the mock surprise of the one who is raking and who patiently begins again.
>
> I am on my way to give a lecture on the Holocaust, when I come across the pastoral scene. What am I doing, I ask myself. How can I talk about such matters, here? I cannot reconcile scenes like this with others I know about.
>
> In a fleeting montage I see or dream I see the green, cursed fields at Auschwitz. A cold calm has settled on them. The blood does not cry from the ground. Yet no place, no wood, meadow, sylvan scene will now be the same.[17]

For me this scene resonated, the moment I read it, with the Boy of Winander, the silence of the children linking up somehow with your own going off to a Holocaust lecture. The pastoral scene has a pause in it here, too. There's something about the movement from that earlier pastoral scene of you in England, to this moment of you as a lecturer on the Holocaust, coming across a pastoral scene, that strikes me, since it is mediated via a scene from Wordsworth, which has been a focus of your own reading. I'm wondering if there's any comment you'd like to make on this peculiar itinerary for you in your career and in your life. Have you reflected on it at all?

GH: You're right in crossing from that autobiographical sketch to my interest in the interrupted pastoral. I suppose it shows how drawn I am to resilience. Think of the children. And also to the resilience of the pastoral moment itself. And the idea, which is literal, or close to literal in Wordsworth, of rural nature as a shield, as giving some relief, a new chance or a renewed chance of recovery. But the

Holocaust was so traumatic, so interruptive an event, that, as you know well, because you've written about such experiences, it exists unintegrated alongside normal memories. So that not only is the pastoral interrupted, but you have a juxtaposition that probably can't be resolved. I'm reminded of Charlotte Delbo, who says (I paraphrase), "It's not right to ask how do I live *with* Auschwitz: I live *alongside* of Auschwitz." There it is still, a complete memory. It's not that I have a problem, because I want to integrate that memory. There is no chance of that: my Auschwitz place is here and my ordinary place, or post-Auschwitz self is here. And the survivor has to live on like that.

CC: Do you think that "alongside," or a reading of that alongside, could have been found already in Wordsworth, or is it precisely something alongside the Wordsworth for you? In other words, do you think your Wordsworth reading has prepared you for thinking about that, or is it rather that now you have to put something alongside your other reading?

GH: That would return us to a discussion of how trauma shows itself in Wordsworth or literature generally—and whether trauma can ever be "integrated." As to my personal case, please remember that since I did not myself pass through the full extent of collective trauma (I was not deported and in a camp), the sense, or recovery of the sense of trauma comes late. I suspect that my English countryside experience and Wordsworth's poetry converged, or helped me to think about, to articulate, whatever personal trauma there was, and that the much more severe issue of collective trauma, which after all was not my case, did not become an issue till much later still.

CC: When you were commenting on Wordsworth, and specifically on the pause, you said that there could have been something traumatic earlier, and in your pastoral, there was something earlier (your leaving Germany alone without your parents), and maybe partly that is what is emerging now. The pastoral scene wasn't your first experience, it came later.

GH: It is hard to say what came first, what came later. And knowledge always seems to be acquired knowledge. But to whatever my consciousness of the Holocaust speaks, its shock has grown on me. Yes, that happens too. It's not just that you start with shock and then try to move away from the shock, or to absorb or integrate it. There are times when the shock grows on you and becomes more severe.

Notes

Introduction

1. "Fifteen Who Fled Holocaust in 1939 Are Reunited," *New York Times*, July 28, 1983.

2. Geoffrey H. Hartman, "A Life of Learning," Charles Homer Haskins Lecture for 2000, ACLS Occasional Paper, no. 26.

3. Friedrich Nietzsche, *The Gay Science*, trans. Walter Kaufman (New York: Random House, 1974), par. 168.

4. Maurice Blanchot, *The Infinite Conversation*, trans. Susan Hanson (Minneapolis: U of Minnesota P, 1993), 232.

5. Ned Lukacher, "The Ring of Being: Nietzsche, Freud, and the History of Conscience," in *Intersections: Nineteenth-Century Philosophy and Contemporary Theory*, ed. Tilottama Rajan and David L. Clark (Albany: State U of New York P, 1995), 209–10.

6. Harold Bloom, *The Western Canon* (New York: Riverhead Books, 1994), 429–30.

7. Jacques Derrida, *The Gift of Death*, trans. David Wills (Chicago: U of Chicago P, 1995), 51.

8. Shoshana Felman, *Writing and Madness (Literature/Philosophy/Psychoanalysis)* (Ithaca, NY: Cornell UP, 1985), 17.

9. Alan Liu, *Wordsworth: The Sense of History* (Stanford: Stanford UP, 1989), 38; Emily Dickinson, "The Birds begun at Four o'clock—."

10. Andrzej Warminski, *Readings in Interpretation: Hölderlin, Hegel, Heidegger* (Minneapolis: U of Minnesota P, 1987), 189.

11. Franz Kafka, *Letters to Friends, Family, and Editors*, trans. Richard and Clara Winston (London: John Calder, 1978), 16.

12. Ian Balfour and Rebecca Comay, "The Ethics of Witness: An Interview with Geoffrey Hartman," *Lost in the Archives*, *Alphabet City* 8 (2002): 491–510.

13. Cathy Caruth, ed., *Trauma: Explorations in Memory* (Baltimore: Johns Hopkins UP, 1995), 8.

14. Paul de Man, "Time and History in Wordsworth," in *Romanticism and Contemporary Criticism: The Gauss Seminars and Other Papers*, ed. E. S. Burt, Kevin Newmark, and Andrzej Warminski (Baltimore: Johns Hopkins UP, 1993), 81.

15. Rudolf Eckstein and Elaine Caruth, "Keeping Secrets," in *Tactics and Techniques in Psychoanalytic Therapy*, ed. Peter Giovacchini (Northvale, NJ: Jason Aronson, 1993), 204n.

16. Jacques Derrida, *The Ear of the Other: Otobiography, Transference, Translation*, ed. Christie McDonald, trans. Peggy Kamuf (Lincoln: U of Nebraska P, 1985), and Derrida, "How to Avoid Speaking: Denials," in *Languages of the Unsayable: The Play of Negativity in*

Literature and Literary Theory, ed. Sanford Budick and Wolfgang Iser (New York: Columbia UP, 1989).

17. Claire Nouvet, "An Impossible Response: The Disaster of Narcissus," *Yale French Studies* 79 (1991): 121.

ONE: Reading: The Wordsworthian Enlightenment

1. M. H. Abrams singled out "The Aeolian Harp," also written in 1795 and first published (expanded) in 1796, as having established a new form, "the greater Romantic lyric." Its main feature is "the dramatic mode of intimate talk to an unanswering auditor in easy blank-verse paragraphs." Abrams, "Structure and Style in the Greater Romantic Lyric," in *From Sensibility to Romanticism: Essays Presented to F. A. Pottle*, ed. F. W. Hillis and H. Bloom (New York: Oxford UP, 1965). In Coleridge's *Poems* of 1797, "Reflections" follows "The Aeolian Harp." On the link between the two lyrics, see also Paul Magnuson, *Coleridge and Wordsworth: A Lyrical Dialogue* (Princeton, NJ: Princeton UP, 1988), 150–52.

2. Humphry House's *Coleridge* (London: Rupert Hart-Davis, 1962), chap. 3, rightly emphasizes the influence of what Coleridge named Cowper's "divine chit-chat" on a poet en route to "his own kinds of achieved simplicity" via a modification of Miltonic diction.

3. By far the most interesting description of the relation between Coleridge and Wordsworth is that of Jerome Christensen in a series of recent articles, especially the subtly Lacanian "Ecce Homo, Biographical Acknowledgment, the End of the French Revolution, and the Romantic Reinvention of English Verse," in *Contesting the Subject: Essays in the Postmodern Theory and Practice of Biography and Biographical Criticism*, ed. W. H. Epstein (West Lafayette, IN: Purdue UP, 1991). Christensen suggests that Coleridge creates, against the overly theatrical model by which revolutionaries portray the efficacy of persons, including the mob-as-person (crude representations of personified power, a sort of ecce-ism), a new possibility of biography and thence of autobiography, one that he then yields to Wordsworth by "biographical acknowledgment." Christensen's restitutive bias—correcting scholarship's failure to adequately recognize Coleridge's role in this transaction—does not lessen the heuristic daring of his genetic model of criticism, which is more focused on the reinvention of verse and less reductive of mediations than other contemporary attempts to specify historical factors. For a direct Bakhtinian reading of Wordsworth, see Don H. Bialistosky, *Wordsworth, Dialogics, and the Practice of Criticism* (Cambridge, MA: Cambridge UP, 1992).

4. "Affects," if synonymous with "pretends," could be a charged word pointing to social artifice, also perhaps to an anxiety about losing or lacking affection and so not realizing oneself as a complete human being. Coleridge's early and deep sense of being *spiritually* infantile (a condition of faith?) may be related to this problem of affect or social maturity. It is raised by J. Douglas Kneale in an essay that also clarifies the rhetorical relation of the poet's early "Effusions" in *Poems on Various Subjects* (1796) to the *genus sermoni*; see his "Between Poetry and Oratory: Coleridge's Romantic Effusions," *Romantic Aversions: Aftermaths of Classicism in Wordsworth and Coleridge* (Montreal: McGill-Queen's UP, 1999).

5. Yet when "Reflections" was published in October 1796, exactly a year after his marriage and pastoral honeymoon at Clevedon, Coleridge was already thinking of a new retirement. He was "determined to retire once for all and utterly from cities and towns," called politicians and politics "a set of men and a kind of study which I deem highly unfavorable to all Christian graces," and claimed to have "snapped my squeaking baby

trumpet of sedition" (*Letters of Samuel Taylor Coleridge*, ed. E. L. Griggs [Oxford: Clarendon P, 1956], 1:240). This does not mean, of course, that he gave up his essays on politics; as he wrote to Thelwall in December 1796: "I am not *fit* for *public* life; yet the light shall stream to a far distance from my cottage window" (Griggs, 1:277). In January 1797 he removed to Nether Stowey, not far from Wordsworth's Racedown, and in July 1797, at Alfoxden, their greatest year of poetic collaboration would begin. For the political history, including antiliberal agitation in the wake of the French Revolution, especially after the king's execution and the declaration of war between England and France—an agitation that forced Joseph Priestly into premature retirement and exile ("calm, pitying he retir'd, / And mus'd expectant on these promised years," Coleridge, "Religious Musings," 393–94)—see Nicholas Roe, *Wordsworth and Coleridge: The Radical Years* (Oxford: Clarendon P, 1988). Wordsworth's own bout with political journalism during this time probably lasted only a few months, from approximately February to the end of 1795. See Kenneth R. Johnston, "Philanthropy or Treason? Wordsworth as 'Active Partisan,'" *Studies in Romanticism* 25 (1986): 372–409, and Johnston, *The Hidden Wordsworth* (New York: Norton, 1998), chap. 18. Johnston argues that Wordsworth's "direct, personal involvement in some kind of *philanthropic* activity" in London during 1795 preceded the poet's retreat to Nature, from which he then "moved out again toward a revisionist love of mankind." "Philanthropy," it should be remembered, became in certain circles a politically charged word: its basic meaning of "love for mankind" was often associated with universalist or cosmopolitan tendencies that were held to undermine patriotism or to further the French rather than British cause. (The *Anti-Jacobin*'s "Friend of Man and the Knife Grinder," satirizing Southey's check, indicates the connotation of a phrase that may be linked to "*l'ami de l'humanité*" in honorary citizenship certificates voted by the French Assembly to foreign partisans.) For an overview of the career of "philanthropy" from Godwin through Coleridge to Shelley, see Frederick L. Beaty's "Philanthropy: Hopes and Limitations," in his *Light from Heaven: Love in British Romantic Literature* (De Kalb: Northern Illinois UP, 1971), 214–42.

6. For the full text, see the Appendix. The earliest, unpublished version dates from 1798 and is found in what has become known as the Two-Book *Prelude*.

7. All book and line references are to the 1850 *Prelude* except when otherwise noted.

8. The early phase of the French Revolution ("Bliss was it in that dawn to be alive, / But to be young was very heaven") could only have reinforced this pattern; but the link between joy and terror, as well as between joy, terror, and discontinuity, are too complex to be more than evoked here.

9. One labor of John Barrell in England and the New Historicists in the United States has been to demystify—in Wordsworth, too—this evasive and often religious rhetoric.

10. Cited by Willard L. Sperry, *Wordsworth's Anti-Climax* (Cambridge, MA: Harvard UP, 1935), 19.

11. Even when he resumes the classification game in his preface to the *Poems of William Wordsworth* (1815), "There was a Boy" heads "Poems of the Imagination," an unconventional rubric that could have embraced the Poem on his Life, which is at once of and about the imagination—indeed, as Stevens might have said, the "cry of its occasion." The problem of the relation of egotism to (ambitious) poetry, of allowing in the substance as well as in the rhetorical form of first-person experience—indeed, of seeing the latter as essential to imaginative poetry—also led to experiments with the ballad and the change from first-person reference in the earliest versions (MS JJ) of the Boy of Winander.

12. In Wordsworth accidents can impress "forms / That yet exist with independent life / And, like their archetypes know no decay." *The Prelude, 1798–1799, by William Wordsworth*, ed. Stephen Parrish (Ithaca, NY: Cornell UP, 1977), 259. The most striking of these accidents are the famous "spots of time." The imaginative feelings associated with those accidents always point to mortality as well as immortality. While the "accident" central to the Boy of Winander episode is fortunate (promoting development), the death of the Boy (aborting development) so laconically presented seems equally an accident. In *Prelude* 5, in which the episode follows a protest against Rousseauistic educational principles that would "control / All accidents" (5.357), Wordsworth's introduction of the accident of death may have a quiet—deathly quiet—irony.

13. I refer to intensely ambivalent experiences in which fear and beauty mingle. Wordsworth grew up "Fostered alike by beauty and by fear" (*Prelude*, 1.306ff.); this may suggest two different ministries, yet he also tells us that scenes were almost physically "fastened to the affections" and became habitually dear "By the impressive discipline of fear, / By pleasure and repeated happiness" (1.632–33). There does seem to have been a convergence; it is, in any case, such moments that may be called "traumatic." Though retrospectively the foundation of growth and strength "if but once we have been strong" (9.328), they can embosom—swallow up, capsize—human emergence.

14. Or preconversation, since it is the boy's mimicry that falters, and what it eventually calls forth is not "echoing song" but a "blast of harmony."

15. See Francis Jeffrey's notorious comments on *Lyrical Ballads* in the *Edinburgh Review* (1807).

16. My emphasis. For Wordsworth's full comment on "There was a Boy," see the "Preface" to *Poems in Two Volumes and Other Poems*, ed. Jared Curtis. The Cornell Wordsworth (1815; Ithaca, NY: Cornell UP, 1983).

17. See 1850 *Prelude*, 1.340ff. His thoughts about the dying hart in "Hart-Leap Well," that it was mourned by "sympathy divine," or the Doe's relation to Emily in *The White Doe of Rylstone*, are expressive of this deepest strain. Cf. the remarks on "passion" in my "Poetics of Prophecy," *The Unremarkable Wordsworth*, foreword by Donald G. Marshall (Minneapolis: U of Minnesota P, 1987), 178.

18. For this last and ultimate sense of ghostliness, see Susan Eilenberg, *Strange Power of Speech: Wordsworth, Coleridge, and Literary Possession* (New York: Oxford UP, 1992). She writes suggestively about the Lucy poems: "What we are asked to interpret in these texts is itself an act of interpretation in which the poet reads his own words as if they had been spoken by another. . . . He calls upon the reader to aid him against, or perhaps merely to witness, the stranger he discovers in himself, his own internal poetic rival" (110). Who that "internal poetic rival" may be is not clear, though in Eilenberg's triangular drama it must be Coleridge, unless it is a still more dispossessing "radical anonymity." Eilenberg also invents the extraordinary notion of "autoventriloquism" to describe how Wordsworth exorcizes by appropriation a voice or voices not his own.

19. For "epiphanic structure," see my *Fate of Reading and Other Essays* (Chicago: U of Chicago P, 1975), 126–37.

20. The issue of linguistic temporality is central to Paul de Man's shift from a phenomenological to a deconstructionist orientation. My own brief contribution to this matter must be limited to the following. Everything in the Boy of Winander portrait heightens our sense of the discontinuity and precariousness of human time compared to nature's more permanent presences. Man is the measure, but how does that affect a life that is

foreclosed? And is not every individual fate subject to foreclosure? "When he was ten years old" and that "long half-hour" look, are pseudo-specific measurements. A transitory life of fertile and fatal accidents is placed against Nature's deceiving backdrop, presences that suddenly come forward and overwhelm the individual consciousness they foster. Yet the episode, indeed Book 5 as a whole, recenters this pathos: it is not natural, external time, but the readerly consciousness with its more internal search for "timely utterance" that emerges.

21. The effect is a *nonsupernatural* ghostliness, often conveyed through a refinement of Gothic ballad or tale, its *quasi-supernatural* effects. In the Gothic genres it is the strange incidents, as it were, that surprise and do the exclaiming; but in the post-Gothic mode, with Wordsworth or James or Antonioni, the clues are subtler and less resolved. A semaphoric surplus hovers over them. There is a displacement from narrative speech to ghostly interstices that rarely interrupts formally yet points to an introspective and burdened imagination. Though incidents remain a plot necessity, they are subordinated to the search for sources of imaginative sympathy, for a "sacred fount" to replenish what is feared to be drying up.

22. "Essay, Supplementary to the Preface" of Wordsworth's 1815 *Poems in Two Volumes*, in *The Prose Works of William Wordsworth*, ed. W. J. B. Owen and J. W. Smyser (Oxford: Clarendon P, 1974), 3:81.

23. See Don H. Bialostosky, summarizing Michael Cooke, in *Wordsworth, Dialogics, and the Practice of Criticism* (Cambridge: Cambridge UP, 1992), 137.

24. Cf. my remarks in *The Fate of Reading*, 289–91. For another view of how this future reader is constructed (or the possibility of the act of reading itself), see Frances Ferguson, *Wordsworth: Language as Counter-Spirit* (New Haven, CT: Yale UP, 1977), 242–50. In Ferguson's subtle understanding, "The Boy of Winander" shows an affectional positing of the auditor-reader figure as a supplement to the self with the quality of a loved person. See also Paul de Man's more macabre twist, in "The Rhetoric of Temporality," *Blindness and Insight*, and "Time and History in Wordsworth," *Romanticism and Contemporary Criticism* (Baltimore: Johns Hopkins UP, 1993), 80–81. It is here too that the meta-rhetorical topic enters of the change from first person to second person (by the kind of formal apostrophe Douglas Kneale has clarified as "aversion"; see below, n. 25) or to third-person self-representation, as in Coleridge's epitaph on himself "Stop, Christian passer-by!" or tacitly in most narrative fiction. The tacit transformation especially haunts the act of reading.

25. The topos of the echoing landscape, of a sympathetic and responsive nature. Susan Eilenberg, thinking of the other as (mainly) Coleridge, writes of the conversational poems: "Even in [their] affectionate context, conversation meant something other than address and full response; one voice, one consciousness, seemed always to have to empty itself out for the sake of another," *Strange Power of Speech*, 25. On Wordsworth's apostrophe here, see Kneale, *Romantic Aversions*, on how the poet converts the conventional *exclamatio* into an *aversio*. He uses a "turn-tale" (in Puttenham's English) to invoke a preternatural though mute witness (the exemplary, classical case being the noble dead, fallen for their country, whom Demosthenes turned to in a famous speech). The transfusion of schoolboy learning into such a context is so incongruous that it disqualifies itself, yet an aura of "heroic argument" remains; even school rhetoric may have its true source in natural—untutored—experience. The most moving, and most literal, example of such a turn (which makes an absence present) is the opening of Wordsworth's sonnet calling to his dead child

Catherine: "Surprised by Joy, impatient as the Wind, / I turned to share the transport—O with whom / But thee, long buried in the silent tomb."

26. The full extent of Wordsworthian irony is disclosed when we take this phrase to be the obverse of "And few could know / When Lucy ceased to be." One of the lyrics now printed as a Lucy poem, "Three years she grew in sun and shower," gives us an explicit prosopopoeia in which Nature recounts the development of the girl whom she alone (or better than anyone else) "knew."

27. At the beginning of *The Prelude*'s book on "Books," which incorporates "There was a Boy," Wordsworth had evoked "The knowledge that endures" of poetry and geometry, "And their high privilege of lasting life / From all internal injury exempt"(1805, 5.65–67). This perspective compares the absence of internal contradiction, characterizing mathematic discipline, with the sublimation of psychic wounds that poetry ideally envisages. The fact that trauma also takes a political form in Wordsworth, that his description of betrayal by English politics (even more than by the French Revolution) uses an imagery of sudden inner "revolution," division, and discontinuity, does not have to be stressed here. Cf. *Wordsworth's Poetry, 1787–1814* (1964; repr., Cambridge, MA: Harvard UP, 1987), 116–18.

28. That Wordsworth does not always succeed in creating this integrated philosophical poetry is already suggested by Keats's objection to its "palpable design," John Hamilton Reynolds' preface to his ante-natal *Peter Bell*, and Charles Lamb's letter to Wordsworth (Jan. 30, 1801) objecting to the lecturing style of "The Cumberland Beggar."

29. While the question of poetry's relation to knowledge—of poetry's seriousness or mode of truth-telling—is raised by philosophy from its very start in Plato and Aristotle, it is not until after Kant that the task of philosophy comes to include a critical phenomenology sporadically open to the "presentations" of art. Philosophy now recognizes a reason burdened by reasoning and turns to *Anschauung*, or a similar faculty, as the province of a prereflective truth that cannot be presented because it is the source of representability. Yet philosophy does not give up its own rational method, its rigorous "transcendental deduction" (Kant) or "phenomenological reduction" (Husserl). The theme of a reduction of or resistance to meaning in poetry (i.e., to "a remoter charm / By thought supplied," "Tintern Abbey") has been an issue for, among others, me, when I emphasize the "modern" poet's emphasis on pure perception and nonrelational knowledge in *The Unmediated Vision: An Interpretation of Wordsworth, Hopkins, Rilke, and Valéry* (New Haven, CT: Yale UP, 1954); cf. "Was it for this? . . . Wordsworth and the Birth of the Gods," in *Romantic Revolutions: Criticism and Theory*, ed. K. R. Johnston et al. (Bloomington: Indiana UP, 1990); Thomas Weiskel, *The Romantic Sublime* (Baltimore: Johns Hopkins UP, 1976), chap. 7; Paul de Man, *The Rhetoric of Romanticism* (New York: Columbia UP, 1984), passim; and the recent work of Paul Fry and Cynthia Chase.

30. I allude to a dense Hegelian concept elaborated by Alexandre Kojève. See Denis Hollier, ed. *The College of Sociology 1937–39* (Minnesota: U of Minnesota P, 1988), 91.

31. Donald Davie says finely in his analysis of the first stanza of the Dejection Ode in *Purity of Diction in English Verse* (New York: Schocken Books, 1967), 129–30, that its "diction . . . mediates between conversation and rhetoric" and "the poem slides eloquently between [these poles] into the key which is to govern the whole."

TWO: Encrypted Sympathy: Wordsworth's Infant Ideology

1. Steven Connor, "Honour Bound," *Times Literary Supplement* 5 (Jan. 1996): 24; 24; see also "Introduction: Literature and the Return to Ethics," in *The Ethics in Litera-*

ture, ed. Andrew Hadfield, Dominic Rainsfird, and Tim Woods (London: Macmillan, 1999), 1.

2. Lawrence Buell, "Introduction: In Pursuit of Ethics," *PMLA* 114.1 (1999): 7.

3. Flyer for the International Seminar *"European Literature(s)," "World Literature(s)," and "Globalization,"* June 19–23, 2000, Leiden, organized by the Netherlands Graduate School for Literary Studies in cooperation with University College London and Aarhus University.

4. Martha Nussbaum, *Poetic Justice: The Literary Imagination and Public Life* (Boston: Beacon P, 1995), xvi; Nussbaum, "Exactly and Responsibly: A Defense of Ethical Criticism," *Philosophy and Literature* 22.2 (1998): 362.

5. The present essay is part of a more extended study of the ideology of sympathy which proposes to trace this faculty from its influential codification in Adam Smith's *Theory of Moral Sentiments* to contemporary revisions in largely "liberal" or "liberal-humanist" public discourse and practice, with specific emphasis on the deployment of literature as an ideological apparatus (though not, typically, a *state* apparatus). The centrality of the notion of sympathy to Wordsworth's thought, my principal concern in what follows, is well established, though I hope to further demonstrate the precarious nature of what David Simpson called Wordsworth's "politics of sympathy" (*Wordsworth's Historical Imagination: The Poetry of Displacement* [London: Methuen, 1987], 160) in specific textual detail in order to contribute to a reconsideration of its recovery today.

6. Geoffrey Galt Harpham, *Shadows of Ethics: Criticism and the Just Society* (Durham, NC: Duke UP, 1999), 37; see also Harpham, *Getting It Right: Language, Literature, and Ethics* (Chicago: U of Chicago P, 1992), 17.

7. Geoffrey H. Hartman, *The Fateful Question of Culture* (New York: Columbia UP, 1997), 7, 16 n.13.

8. Alfred Tennyson, *Tennyson: A Selected Edition*, ed. Christopher Ricks (Harlow: Longman, 1989).

9. On Wordsworth's posthumous role in the founding of *The National Trust for Places of Historic Interest or Natural Beauty in England, Wales and Northern Ireland*, see Stephen Gill, *Wordsworth and the Victorians* (Oxford: Clarendon P, 1988), 235–60.

10. See Geoffrey H. Hartman, *A Critic's Journey: Literary Reflections, 1958–1998* (New Haven, CT: Yale UP, 1999), xii, and Cathy Caruth, "An Interview with Geoffrey Hartman," chapter 16 in this volume; see also Harpham, *Shadows of Ethics*, 215–16.

11. *SSP*, xv. All quotations are taken from William Wordsworth, *The Salisbury Plain Poems of William Wordsworth*, ed. Stephen Gill. The Cornell Wordsworth (Ithaca, NY: Cornell UP, 1975). For convenience' sake, references will be given as follows: *SP* for *Salisbury Plain*, *ASP* for *Adventures on Salisbury Plain*, *GS* for *Guilt and Sorrow*, each time followed by the line number(s). References to the editorial matter and to manuscript transcriptions will be given as *SPP* followed by the page number.

12. Such, at least, was Wordsworth's evident intention ("The woman thus began her story to relate" [*ASP*, 261]), though the manuscript does not contain the story itself. The Cornell Wordsworth edition convincingly inserts the text that later appeared in *Lyrical Ballads* as "The Female Vagrant" instead.

13. For a richly detailed account of the shift from "the radical idiom of *The Rights of Man*" to "the insight of the imaginative poet" in the universe of discourse in which Wordsworth's Salisbury Plain poems were produced, see Nicholas Roe, *Wordsworth and Coleridge: The Radical Years* (Oxford: Clarendon P, 1988), 124–35. Alan Liu's advanced

mapping of this process as a "domesticat[ion of] political agon" (*Wordsworth: The Sense of History* [Stanford: Stanford UP, 1989], 222) remains exemplary.

14. John Rieder, *Wordsworth's Counterrevolutionary Turn: Community, Virtue, and Vision in the 1790s* (Newark: U of Delaware P, 1997), 97.

15. Toby R. Benis, *Romanticism on the Road: The Marginal Gains of Wordsworth's Homeless* (London: Macmillan, 2000).

16. Liu qualifies Wordsworth's comparison between savage and modern pain in these opening stanzas as "wholly insensitive to historical difference" (*Sense of History*, 183). Tracing the short-circuit between this comparison and the narrator's crisis in the face of "Unhappy man" in stanza 25 of *Salisbury Plain* (curiously glossed over in Liu's comments on the tropology of pain generated by the female vagrant's breasts [87–88]) may help to furnish a further history for this indifference.

17. This resistance, I would argue, must qualify Hartman's quiet integration of the child-beating in the narrative of Wordsworth's recovery of poetic faith through "the survival of his childhood strength of imagination" (Geoffrey H. Hartman, *Wordsworth's Poetry, 1787–1814* [1964; repr., Cambridge, MA: Harvard UP, 1987], 253).

18. All quotations from the Ode are from the reading text of the 1807 version in William Wordsworth, *Poems in Two Volumes and Other Poems, 1800–1807*, ed. Jared Curtis. The Cornell Wordsworth (Ithaca, NY: Cornell UP, 1983).

19. As Jared Curtis notes in the Cornell edition of the poem, "Probably some or all of stanzas 1–4 composed March 27, 1802. Further composition—possibly including some or, less probably, all of stanzas 5–8—on June 17, 1802. Most of the last seven stanzas probably composed, and the poem completed, early 1804, by March 6" (271).

20. Stanley Cavell, *In Quest of the Ordinary: Lines of Skepticism and Romanticism* (Chicago: U of Chicago P, 1988), 50.

21. Even the Intimation Ode's opening formula may be more precisely determined than as a mere marker of the retrospective reflex constituting literary composition; apart from echoing Coleridge's 1800 poem "The Mad Monk" (9–10), "Wordsworth's "There was a time when meadow, grove, and stream" also just about recalls the female wanderer's recollection of her young lover in *Salisbury Plain:* "There was a youth whose tender voice and eye / Might add fresh happiness to happiest days, / [. . .]: his voice of love / Charmed the rude winds to sleep by river, field, or grove" (*SP*, 271–72; 278–79).

22. Paul de Man, *The Rhetoric of Romanticism* (New York: Columbia UP, 1984), 81.

23. The revisions just quoted are transcribed in *SPP*, 111. For an alternative account, see Rieder, *Wordsworth's Counterrevolutionary Turn*, 98–101.

24. Another, more famous performance of the proverbial in times of crisis, including the natural trope of the "second birth," that would be well worth rereading here occurs in Book 10 of the 1805 *Prelude* (67–74). All references to *The Prelude* are to William Wordsworth, *The Prelude: 1799, 1805, 1850*, ed. Jonathan Wordsworth, M. H. Abrams, and Stephen Gill (New York: Norton, 1979).

25. For a further reflection on the "delusion bold" (1805 *Prelude*, 7, 308) central to the ideology of sympathy, see my "Suffering, Sympathy, Circulation: Smith, Wordsworth, Coetzee (But there's a dog)," *European Journal of English Studies* 7.2 (2003), 311–31.

26. Lisabeth During, "The Concept of Dread: Sympathy and Ethics in *Daniel Deronda*," in *Renegotiating Ethics in Literature, Philosophy, and Theory*, ed. Jane Adamson, Richard Freadman, and David Parker (Cambridge: Cambridge UP, 1998), 81.

27. Statement by William Hague in an address broadcast by the BBC on April 13,

2000. The gist of it was repeated in a preelection speech delivered in December 2000: "Conservatives believe high taxes damage prosperity, drive away tomorrow's entrepreneurs, undermine a good conscience, generosity, and a sense of personal responsibility and lead to a deep cynicism about the institutions that give our lives moral shape. Low taxes are not just the basis of a dynamic economy, but also the foundation of a compassionate, responsible and free society." Quoted from http://news.bbc.co.uk/2/hi/uk_news/politics/1055499.stm. That the underlying conception of the state in this compassionate conservatism barely differs from the conception of the state in Britain's New Labour may offer further evidence for Hartman's claim.

THREE: Romantic Memory

1. The importance of Locke's attachment to a versatile form of memory is, perhaps, most conspicuous in his *Some Thoughts concerning Education* in *The Educational Writings of John Locke*, ed. James L. Axtell (Cambridge: Cambridge UP, 1968), 285–88.

2. It would obviously be possible to describe the Lockean approach without adding in the question of whether the changes must inevitably be described in terms of progress. Yet that apparent addition is already implicit in this presentation of memory itself, because it is clear that rational choice frequently involves formulating an action less because of its necessity than because of a comparison between it and a past action. Whereas the notion of progress may not make sense on a societal level, it is clear that at least the Lockean account always suggests progress on an individual level.

3. Here I am obviously endorsing Ian Watt's extremely important identification of the novel as centrally concerned with psychology—if we understand psychology less as individual psychology than as generally committed to the importance of faculties such as memory and anticipation. Although Michael McKeon is accurate in pointing to the fact that Watt's book produces a tendentious account of what the novel is (in minimizing the role of Fielding by contrast with that of Richardson), Watt's approach stresses what is, I would argue, the most important aspect of the novel, its concern for depicting individuals coming to connect themselves with their experience. Ian Watt, *The Rise of the Novel* (Berkeley: U of California P, 1967). See Michael McKeon's *The Origins of the English Novel, 1600–1740* (Baltimore: Johns Hopkins UP, 1987) for a genetic account that takes issue with Watt's emphasis on formal organization.

4. See Steven Knapp's account of the difficulties that attach to many of the more familiar ways of moving between the individual and the collective in "Collective Memory and the Actual Past," chapter 5 of *Literary Interest: The Limits of Anti-Formalism* (Cambridge: Harvard UP, 1993), 106–36.

5. Rousseau provides a particularly important account of this issue in his discussion in Book 4 of *Emile* of the difficulties of teaching history. See Allan Bloom's translation (New York: Basic Books, 1979), esp. 237–43.

6. Discussions of evidence in the early modern period frequently cite the Old Testament to this effect. Patrick Mahony in *Cries of the Wolf Man* (New York: International UP, 1984), calls attention to Freud's awareness of the interest of doubled testimony by citing his remark in the Rat Man case (1909): "A witness who testifies to something before a court of law is still called 'Zeuge' [literally, 'begetter'] in German, after the part played by the male in the act of procreation; so that in hieroglyphics the word for a 'witness' is written with a representation of the male organ" (111). Mahony also cites the note that Freud

added in 1910: "The word 'witness' is expressed by the picture of the male genital. It may well be that the reason why two men have to testify is that a man with one testicle is not capable of begetting" (111–12).

7. I in no way mean to claim that things like death counts in war always involve actual agreement among witnesses. As Elaine Scarry pointed out in a discussion of this paper, there may be—and frequently are—significant differences between observers of even such dramatically accessible observations. What seems crucial to emphasize is the relative lack of specialization involved in the ability to produce a factual account and its contrast with what Freud describes as objects "not easily accessible to observation (such as a horse or a dog)." Freud's examples of such "not easily accessible objects" are those that are known, in the case of the Wolf-Man "only from stories and picture-books." See *Three Case Histories: The "Wolf Man," The "Rat Man," and The Psychotic Doctor Schreber*, ed. Philip Rieff (New York: Macmillan, 1963), 189.

8. See *Three Case Histories*, especially on the "sense of conviction that results from the analysis itself" (169); on seeing an event under conflicting rubrics, 202 ff.; and on the importance of "scenes from early infancy" as truthful if erroneous recollections, 206 ff. Freud's account is especially important for its claims that fantasies can only be derived from perceived material and that dreaming is a form of remembering, because it puts psychoanalysis in the position of producing neither a generally observable account nor a purely formal one that needs no correspondent in the world of actuality.

9. When Freud speaks of his patients and of himself as producing various editions of the same basic text, or when he employs the language of mathematics, he is obviously speaking of an analysis that needs to find no reference aside from the notion of a basic text. When he speaks of the urgency of the recollections of his patients, he links the formal claim with an empirical one.

10. Note Freud's exact distinction between the appropriateness of the patient's recounting received information—"the many stories about his childhood" that the patient was told "in his later years" (170)—and the inappropriateness of the analyst's receiving information from those other sources.

11. Freud's notion of *Nachträglichkeit*, the deferred recognition of something one has already experienced, is obviously pertinent to my concerns with memory here, but I would also want to include an expansive account of recognition that will extend past the range of experiences one has already registered (so that one could speak of accepting a connection with the consequences of one's actions, even if they weren't tied to an already complete experience).

12. In the area of Holocaust studies, such an anxiety about memories that are too good—in the sense of being too well-made or too aesthetically satisfying—to be true has been of particular concern to Aharon Appelfeld.

13. While it is certainly true that childhood memories come to us largely by report, one of the things that is especially important about the way memory comes to function is as an evaluation of the standard story (so that no one produces an account of how they remember the story of George Washington refusing to lie about having chopped down a cherry tree to show that they are confirming the story, but only to evoke, for example, where one was when one heard such a story). The aim of memory in these cases is not to produce a correct iteration of the traditional account or even to rehearse the truth as one sees it; it is, instead, to develop lines of connection between an individual and a particular action or account. Moreover, the importance of such psychological faculties is attested to

by the way in which modern law continually lays out its injunctions in combination with categories of exemption—specifications of the kinds of diminished capacity that would render one incapable of using the law as an extension of one's moral agency.

14. See Shoshana Felman, "Education and Crisis, or the Vicissitudes of Teaching," in *Testimony: Crises of Witnessing in Literature, Psychoanalysis, and History*, ed. Shoshana Felman and Dori Laub (New York: Routledge, 1992), 1–56; and Cathy Caruth, *Unclaimed Experience: Trauma, Narrative, and History* (Baltimore: Johns Hopkins UP, 1996).

15. See Geoffrey H. Hartman, "Preserving the Personal Story: The Role of Video Documentation," in *The Holocaust Forty Years After*, ed. M. Littell, R. Libowitz, and E. B. Rosen (Lewiston, NY: Edwin Mellen P, 1989), 53–60; "Introduction: Darkness Visible," in *Holocaust Remembrance: The Shapes of Memory*, ed. Geoffrey H. Hartman (Cambridge, MA: Blackwell, 1994), 1–22; "Learning from Survivors: The Yale Testimony Project," *Holocaust and Genocide Studies* 9.2 (Fall 1995): 192–207; and "The Cinema Animal," *Salmagundi* 106–7 (Spring-Summer 1995): 127–45.

16. Laura Mulvey, "Visual Pleasure and Narrative Cinema," *Screen* 16.3 (1975): 6–18; Mary Ann Doane, "Film and the Masquerade: Theorising the Female Spectator," *Screen* 23.3–4 (1982): 74–87.

17. See Bernard Williams, *Shame and Necessity* (Berkeley: U of California P, 1993) and Martha C. Nussbaum, *Poetic Justice: The Literary Imagination and Public Life* (Boston: Beacon P, 1995).

18. See particularly Geoffrey H. Hartman, "Learning from Survivors," in *The Longest Shadow: In the Aftermath of the Holocaust* (Bloomington: Indiana UP, 1996), 133, which opens on this theme.

19. I wish to distinguish between the woman's uncertainty and the suggestion that she might be disavowing her past and trying to distance herself from it here. The claim that I would make about the episode that Hartman recounts is analogous to Freud's claim in his discussion of the "Wolf Man" case, in that it does not concern itself with the exact provenance of the individual elements of the account but rather with the importance of a unique ability to make a particular connection among those materials. I would like to thank Zephira Porot of Tel Aviv University for having pointed out to me the importance of clarifying this point.

20. Matthew Arnold, "The Function of Criticism at the Present Time," in *Poetry and Criticism of Matthew Arnold*, ed. A. Dwight Culler (Boston: Houghton-Mifflin, 1961), 237–58, esp. 249.

21. Walter Benjamin, "Theses on the Philosophy of History" in *Illuminations*, ed. Hannah Arendt (New York: Schocken Books, 1969), 253–64.

22. Edmund Burke, *A Philosophical Enquiry into the Origin of Our Ideas of the Sublime and Beautiful*, ed. J. T. Boulton (Notre Dame, IN: Notre Dame UP, 1968), 34.

23. Geoffrey H. Hartman, "The Poetics of Prophecy," in *The Unremarkable Wordsworth*, foreword by Donald G. Marshall (Minneapolis: U of Minnesota P, 1987), 163–81.

24. Max Weber, *The Protestant Ethic and the Spirit of Capitalism* (New York: Macmillan, 1958). Weber's classic work is particularly useful for its account of how conscious beliefs enable practices with a range of consequences well past their initial entailments.

25. See Alexander Welsh, *Strong Representations: Narrative and Circumstantial Evidence in England* (Baltimore: Johns Hopkins UP, 1992). Welsh provides an important historical overview of the treatment of legal evidence that indicates how dramatically the notion of legal proof has shifted from the testimony of eyewitnesses to the testimony of circumstance.

26. See D. A. Miller, *The Novel and the Police* (Berkeley: U of California P, 1988), for a particularly compelling version of this view.

27. James Hogg, *The Private Memoirs and Confessions of a Justified Sinner* (1824; London: Oxford UP, 1969).

28. D. A. Miller's reading of *The Woman in White* is a particularly good example of the extensiveness of this process of seeing individual identity as continually open to redefinition. See his *The Novel and the Police.*

FOUR: Green to the Very Door? The Natural Wordsworth

1. See, e.g., Geoffrey Hartman, who cites the Isabella Fenwick "Intimations Ode" note to this end in his 1977 essay "A Touching Compulsion," in *The Unremarkable Wordsworth* (Minneapolis: U of Minnesota P, 1987), 20; hereafter cited as *UnRW.*

2. Paul de Man, "Intentional Structure of the Romantic Image" (1960); reprinted in *The Rhetoric of Romanticism* (New York: Columbia UP, 1984), 16. This is one of de Man's earliest formulations of the issue using the linguistic terms of his later work.

3. Alan Liu, *Wordsworth: The Sense of History* (Stanford: Stanford UP, 1989), 104. Liu's position gains its subtlety from the consciousness of reformulating without restructuring the purportedly hegemonic forms of antinaturalism in Wordsworth studies in order to redirect the course of interpretation. Marjorie Levinson somewhat comparably speaks of her political demystifications as "deconstruction" (*Wordsworth's Great Period Poems: Four Essays* [Cambridge: Cambridge UP, 1986]), while Tilottama Rajan elaborates a more complex compromise formation in arguing that deconstruction would have taken a different turn had it attended to narrative rather than lyric elements in Wordsworth (see her "The Erasure of Narrative in Post-Structuralist Representations of Wordsworth," in *Romantic Revolutions: Criticism and Theory*, ed. Kenneth R. Johnston, Gilbert Chaitin, Karen Hanson, and Herbert Marks [Bloomington: Indiana UP, 1990], 350–70).

4. See Jonathan Bate, *Romantic Ecology: Wordsworth and the Environmental Tradition* (London: Routledge, 1991), 9.

5. See my "Wordsworth's Severe Intimations," in *The Poet's Calling in the English Ode* (New Haven, CT: Yale UP, 1980), 133–61. Closer to the thematics, if not the techniques, of deconstruction, but already harboring, like the *Poet's Calling* essay, my present view of "nature," is "The Absent Dead: Wordsworth, Byron, and the Epitaph," *Studies in Romanticism* 17 (1978) ; 413–33. A position, finally, that most overtly resembles the one I work toward here is taken up in "Clearings in the Way: Non-Epiphany in Wordsworth," *Studies in Romanticism* 31 (1992); 3–19. Both the latter essays appear revised in my book *A Defense of Poetry: Reflections on the Occasion of Writing* (Stanford: Stanford UP, 1995), which provides them a fully developed context. See also my "The Diligence of Desire: Critics on and around Westminster Bridge, *Wordsworth Circle* 23 (1992): 162–64.

6. See Arthur Beatty (who cites Tinker's 1992 *Nature's Simple Plan*), *Wordsworth: His Doctrine and Art in Their Historical Relations* (Madison: U of Wisconsin P, 1922), 122.

7. See Joseph Warren Beach, *The Concept of Nature in Nineteenth-Century Poetry* (New York: Macmillan, 1936), 118.

8. Basil Willey, *The Seventeenth-Century Background: Studies in the Thought of the Age in Relation to Poetry and Religion* (London: Chatto & Windus, 1949), 304.

9. H. W. Piper, *The Active Universe: Pantheism and the Concept of Imagination in the English Romantic Poets* (London: Athlone P, 1962), 115.

10. William Wordsworth, *Home at Grasmere*, ed. Beth Darlington (Ithaca, NY: Cornell UP, 1977), MS. D., 816–81, 810 (p. 105).

11. Walter Pater, "Wordsworth," in *Selected Writings of Walter Pater*, ed. Harold Bloom (New York: Signet, 1974), 128, 130, 131. Pater almost certainly has in mind the passage in "Resolution and Independence" making the leech-gatherer a mediatory figure between a stone, a sea beast and a cloud—the passage Wordsworth cites in the 1815 Preface to illustrate the workings of the imagination.

12. William Hazlitt, *Lectures on the English Poets*, in *Lectures on the English Poets and The Spirit of the Age* (New York: Everyman, 1960), 163.

13. See Matthew Arnold, "Wordsworth," in *Poetry and Criticism of Matthew Arnold*, ed. A. Dwight Culler (Boston: Riverside, 1961), 343.

14. F. R. Leavis, "Revaluations (VI): Wordsworth." *Scrutiny* 3 (1934): 235.

15. See William Empson, *Seven Types of Ambiguity* (1930; rev. ed London: Chatto & Windus, 1949), 153–54, and Empson, *The Structure of Complex Words* (Ann Arbor: U of Michigan P, 1967), 304. That there appears to have been a "Cambridge School" of Wordsworth criticism, with Empson, Leavis, and Willey its chief exponents, has not to my knowledge been remarked. For de Man's opinion, see *The Rhetoric of Romanticism*, 88.

16. Basil Willey, *The Eighteenth-Century Background* (London: Chatto & Windus, 1940), 253.

17. Irving Babbitt, "The Primitivism of Wordsworth," *Bookman* (U.S.A.) 74(1931), 3, 10.

18. Geoffrey H. Hartman, *Beyond Formalism: Literary Essays, 1958–1970* (New Haven, CT: Yale UP, 1971), 311.

19. A. C. Bradley, "Wordsworth and the Sublime," in *Discussions of Wordsworth*, ed. Jack Davis (Boston: D. C. Heath, 1964), 47–62; G. Wilson Knight, *The Starlit Dome* (1943; repr. New York: Barnes & Noble, 1960), 16; D. G. James, *Skepticism and Poetry* (1937; repr. New York: Barnes & Noble, 1960), 141–69.

20. John Jones, *The Egotistical Sublime* (London: Chatto & Windus, 1954), 48. See Geoffrey H. Hartman, *Wordsworth's Poetry, 1787–1814* (1965; repr., Cambridge, MA: Harvard UP, 1987), 349.

21. See Geoffrey H. Hartman, *The Fate of Reading and Other Essays* (Chicago: U of Chicago P, 1975), 277.

22. Lionel Trilling, *The Liberal Imagination* (New York: Anchor, 1953), 140.

23. For the obvious truth of this fact, with its non-Marxist implications, one need look no father than the *National Geographic* for August 1994, with its gruesome article on pollution in the former U.S.S.R., "Lethal Legacy" (70–115). Interestingly, the lead article in this same issue, "England's Lake District," reflects Bate's Ruskinian view of that region: "Wordsworth called it 'a blended holiness of earth and sky'. Today this poetic rolling landscape receives 12 million visitors each year—and feels the strain" (1).

24. Anna Bramwell, *Ecology in the Twentieth Century: A History* (New Haven, CT; Yale UP, 1989). In support of Bate's (and Bramwell's) celebration of a specifically British grasp of the politics of nature, elaborated in Bramwell's chapter called "Back to the Northland," one might add that during the vogue among intellectuals for mountain climbing in the early twentieth century, the typifying charismatic figure in England was the leftist journalist Michael Roberts, friend of Richards, Empson, and others, whereas in Germany the comparable figure was Leni Riefenstahl.

25. P. D. James, *Devices and Desires* (New York: Knopf, 1990), 61–62.

26. I ought to say that in Bate's best chapter, "The Naming of Places," there are touches of an ontological perspective. See, e.g., the fine description of "Michael" on 105.

27. Alfred North Whitehead, *Science and the Modern World* (New York: Mentor, 1948), 80.

28. High praise, on this criterion, to Marshall Brown, "Wordsworth's Old Gray Stone," in *Preromanticism* (Stanford: Stanford UP, 1991).

29. See John Stilgoe, "The Kayak Elite, the String Bikini, and the Indoor Child," *Harvard Alumni Magazine*, Special Supplement, Summer 1994, 3–12.

30. See Alan Bewell, *Wordsworth and the Enlightenment* (New Haven, CT: Yale UP, 1989), 202.

FIVE: Poetic Knowledge: Geoffry Hartman's Romantic Poetics

1. Geoffrey H. Hartman, *The Unmediated Vision: An Interpretation of Wordsworth, Hopkins, Rilke, and Valéry* (New Haven, CT: Yale UP, 1954), hereafter cited as *UV*.

2. I. A. Richards, *Principles of Literary Criticism* (New York: Harcourt, Brace, [1925]), 273.

3. See Murray Krieger, *The New Apologists for Poetry* (Minneapolis: U of Minnesota P, 1956), esp. 123–55.

4. Susanne Langer, *Philosophy in a New Key: A Study in the Symbolism of Reason, Rite, and Art* (Cambridge, MA: Harvard UP, 1951), 79–102; René Wellek and Austin Warren, *Theory of Literature* (New York: Harcourt, Brace, 1948), 175–201; W. K. Wimsatt Jr., *The Verbal Icon* (Lexington: U of Kentucky P, 1954). See Eliseo Vivas's critique of Charles Morris's argument that poetry is made of "iconic signs," "Aesthetics and Theory of Signs," in *Creation and Discovery: Essays in Criticism and Aesthetics* (New York: Noonday, 1955), 249–65; Morris's essay, "Esthetics and the Theory of Signs," appeared in the *Journal of Unified Science* 8.1–3 (1939): 131–50. Cf. Allen Tate, "Literature as Knowledge," *The Man of Letters in the Modern World: Selected Essays, 1928–1955* (New York: Meridian Books, 1955), 34–63.

5. Northrop Frye, *Anatomy of Criticism* (Princeton, NJ: Princeton UP, 1957), 244: "Considered as a verbal structure, literature presents a *lexis* which combines two other elements: *melos*, an element analogous to or otherwise connected to music, and *opsis*, which has a similar connection to the plastic arts. The word *lexis* may be translated 'diction' when we are thinking of it as a narrative sequence of sounds, and as 'imagery' when we are thinking of it as forming a simultaneous pattern of meaning apprehended in an act of mental 'vision'."

6. Walter Ong, "Metaphor as Twinned Vision: The Phoenix and the Turtle," *Sewanee Review* 63 (1955): 193–201. Cf. Ong, "A Dialectic of Aural and Objective Correlatives," *The Barbarian Within* (New York: Macmillan, 1962), 26–40.

7. Elder Olson, "William Empson, Contemporary Criticism, and Poetic Diction," *Critics and Criticism, Ancient and Modern*, ed. R. S. Crane (Chicago: U of Chicago P, 1952), 55.

8. See Martin Jay, "Scopic Regimes of Modernity," *Vision and Visuality: Discussions of Contemporary Culture* 2, ed. Hal Foster (Seattle: Bay Press, 1988), 1–26.

9. This is the basic thesis of Harold Bloom's *The Visionary Company: A Reading of English Romantic Poetry* (Ithaca, NY: Cornell UP, 1961). Cf. Charles Taylor, *Sources of the Self: The Making of Modern Identity* (Cambridge, MA: Harvard UP, 1989).

10. Robert Langbaum, *The Poetry of Experience: The Dramatic Monologue in Modern Literary Tradition* (New York: Norton, 1957), 79. Compare Jacques Maritain, *Creative Intuition in Art and Poetry* (New York: Pantheon, 1953), 75–108, where poetry is understood as "connatural knowledge": "The content of poetic intuition is both the reality of the things of the world and the subjectivity of the poet, both obscurely conveyed through an intentional or spiritualized emotion. The soul is known in the experience of the world and the world is known in the experience of the soul, through a knowledge which does not know itself. For such knowledge knows, not in order to know, but in order to produce. It is toward creation that it tends" (90). Poetic knowledge is thus not anything mental; it is a species of practical knowledge that takes the form of poem. This is also close to Eliseo Vivas's view in "Literature and Knowledge," *Creation and Discovery*, 101–27.

11. Heidegger's thesis in "Der Ursprung des Kunstwerkes" is that poetry is an event in which things appear as things and not as objects of consciousness. Accordingly, "it becomes questionable whether the nature of poetry [*Dichtung*] . . . can be adequately thought of in terms of the power of imagination and image-making [*Imagination und Einbildungskraft*]" (*Gesammtausgabe* [Frankfurt: Vittorio Klostermann], 5:60); "The Origin of the Work of Art," *Poetry, Language, Thought*, trans. Albert Hofstadter (New York: Harper & Row, 1971), 72–73.

12. To avoid misunderstanding: the conception of subjectivity on the model of objective consciousness entails the concept of the unconscious, which is one of the basic inventions of Kant's *Critique of Pure Reason*, which describes the (inexperienced) workings of reason that make the experience of objects possible. The unconscious is not opposed to consciousness but is categorically continuous with it.

13. Emmanuel Levinas, "Éthique comme philosophie première," *Justifications de l'éthique* (Brussels: Editions de l'Université de Bruxelles, 1984), 42; "Ethics as First Philosophy," trans. Séan Hand and Michael Temple, *The Levinas Reader*, ed. Séan Hand (Oxford: Basil Blackwell, 1989), 76.

14. Emmanuel Levinas, "Langage et proximité," *En découvrant l'existence avec Husserl et Heidegger* (Paris: Librairie Philosophique J. Vrin, 1967), 227–28; Levinas, "Language and Proximity," *Collected Philosophical Papers*, trans. Alphonso Lingis (Dordrecht: Martinus Nijhoff, 1987), 118.

15. *The Journals and Papers of Gerard Manley Hopkins*, ed. Humphrey House and Graham Storey (London: Oxford UP, 1967), 269.

16. See Charles Bernstein's *ars poetica*, "The Artifice of Absorption," *Poetics* (Cambridge, MA: Harvard UP, 1992), esp. 86–87.

17. W. V. O. Quine, "Two Dogmas of Empiricism" (1951), *From a Logical Point of View: Nine Logico-Philosophical Essays* (Cambridge, MA: Harvard UP, 1961), 42.

18. See W. V. O. Quine, *Word and Object* (Cambridge, MA: MIT P, 1960), 238–43.

19. Paul Valéry, "The Poet's Rights over Language," *The Art of Poetry*, trans. Denise Folliot (Princeton, NJ: Princeton UP, 1958), 170–71.

20. Francis Ponge, *Le parti pris des choses* (Paris: Gallimard, 1948); hereafter cited as *PP*.

21. It should be added, with Kant in mind, that this preference for the near and the small is a tacit refusal of the beautiful. Kant at any rate thought that neither small things nor large could be beautiful: the one is trivial, the other is sublime. It is probably for this same reason that Ponge is one of the great comic poets.

22. *Francis Ponge: Selected Poems*, trans. C. K. Williams, John Montague, and Margaret Guiton (Winston-Salem, NC: Wake Forest UP, 1994), 29; hereafter cited as *SP*.

23. In *Signéponge*, for example, Derrida maps Levinasian ethics onto Pongean poetics in a single stroke: "Thus the thing would be the other, the other-thing which gives me an order or addresses an impossible, intransigent, insatiable demand to me, without an exchange and without a transaction, without a possible contract. Without a word, without speaking to me, it addresses itself to me, to me alone in my irreplaceable singularity, in my solitude as well. I owe to the thing an absolute respect which no general law would mediate: the law of the thing is singularity and difference as well. An infinite debt ties me to it, a duty without funds or foundation. I shall never acquit myself of it. Thus the thing is not an object; it cannot become one." See *Signéponge/Signsponge*, trans. Richard Rand (New York: Columbia UP, 1984), 14.

24. See Emmanuel Levinas, "La réalité et son ombre," *Les imprévus de l'histoire* (Montpellier: Fata Morgana, 1994), 135.

25. *Poems and Texts: An Anthology of French Poems, Translations, and Interviews with Ponge, Follain, Guillevic, Frénaud, Bonnefoy, Du Bouchet, Roche, and Pleynet*, trans. Serge Gavronsky (New York: October House, 1969), 41. Cf. Hartman, "The Voice of the Shuttle: Language from the Point of View of Literature," *Beyond Formalism: Literary Essays, 1958–1970* (New Haven, CT: Yale UP, 1970), esp. 342–43.

26. "Taking the side of things equals taking the side of words" (Francis Ponge, *Méthodes* [Paris: Gallimard, 1961], 20).

27. Francis Ponge, "The Pebble," *The Voice of Things*, trans. Beth Archer (New York: McGraw-Hill, 1972), 76.

28. Maurice Blanchot, *La part du feu* (Paris: Gallimard, 1949), 312–13; *The Work of Fire*, trans. Charlotte Mandell (Stanford: Stanford UP, 1995), 322–23. Hereafter cited as *PF* and *WF*. In a note Blanchot refers to Alexandre Kojève's lectures on Hegel's *Phenomenology of Spirit* delivered in Paris during the 1930s: "A. Kojève, in his *Introduction to the Reading of Hegel*, interpreting a passage from Hegel's *Phenomenology*, demonstrates in a remarkable way how for Hegel comprehension was equivalent to murder" (*PF*, 312; *WF*, 323).

29. Here it would be useful to consult Hartman's first essay on Blanchot, which he has never reprinted, "The Fulness and Nothingness of Literature," *Yale French Studies*, no. 16 (1955–56), where immediacy is said to be an "illusion" that literature at once produces by the power of its language and exposes by calling itself into question as, among other things, a discourse of signs and images (68–69).

30. Maurice Blanchot, "Le grand refus" (1959), *L'entretien infini* (Paris: Gallimard, 1969), 46–50; "The Great Refusal," *The Infinite Conversation*, trans. Susan Hanson (Minneapolis: U of Minnesota P, 1993), 33–36. Hereafter cited as *EI* and *IC*.

31. See esp. "Nietzsche et l'écriture fragmentaire" (*EI*, 227–34; *IC*, 151–60).

SIX: Wordsworth's Horse

1. All citations of Wordsworth are drawn from the excellent Norton Critical Edition, *The Prelude: 1799, 1805, 1850*, ed. Jonathan Wordsworth, M. H. Abrams, and Stephen Gill (New York: Norton, 1979); hereafter cited as Norton *Prelude*. The Horse passage, part of draft material from MS. W, appears on 498.

2. "It is a very characteristic piece of work. No one else could have written it—perhaps no one else would have wished to write it"; *William Wordsworth: The Borders of Vision* (Oxford: Clarendon P, 1982), 1–2. Jonathan Wordsworth opens his book with the Horse

passage, seeing it as emblematic of recurring concerns in the poetry: "Wordsworth's borderers, border conditions, states of mind, implications, words, are so numerous and ramified that they amount to a way of looking at his poetry as a whole. Or not quite the whole: the poetry of suffering stands a little to one side" (7).

3. Coleridge to Wordsworth, Dec. 10, 1798, *Collected Letters of Samuel Taylor Coleridge*, ed. Earl Griggs, 6 vols. (Oxford: Clarendon P, 1956–71), 1:452–53.

4. Paul de Man, "Time and History in Wordsworth," in *Romanticism and Contemporary Criticism: The Gauss Seminars and Other Papers*, ed. E. S. Burt, Kevin Newmark, and Andrzej Warminski (Baltimore: Johns Hopkins UP, 1993), 75.

5. I should mention here that Howard Erskine-Hill's reading of *The Prelude* analyzes, among other things, the shifting political valence of the figure of the horse and the equestrian not only in that poem, but in earlier works as well. For instance, the "Letter to the Bishop of Llandaff" excuses the excesses of the Jacobins by observing that "the animal just released from its stall will exhaust the overflow of its spirits in a round of wanton vagaries." In other manifestations, the instinctual energies of the horse are controlled and subordinated. See *Poetry of Opposition and Revolution: Dryden to Wordsworth* (Oxford: Clarendon P, 1996), chaps. 6 and 7.

6. What follows is a synoptic view of *Wordsworth's Poetry, 1787–1814* (1965; repr., Cambridge, MA: Harvard UP, 1987). The discussion of "boundary image" can be found on 198ff. Hartman also uses the term "border" interchangeably with "boundary" and cites the MS. W horse on 389 n.104.

7. In "The Ruined Cottage," for instance, both the narrator and the pedlar distance us from Margaret, who is a victim and a cautionary tale. Her imagination of hope, "which is radically in excess of the natural fact," becomes fixated on her specific place until a paralysis is produced: "Imagination cannot blend its power with nature's, because the concept of Nature has not emerged from the fixation on specific place, nor has that of the Imagination emerged from the blindness of fixed hope." Yet the role of the narrator is paramount, for by providing distance it "allows us to think about how passion—or vision—is to be faced." See Hartman, *Wordsworth's Poetry*, 138–39.

8. For a full exposition see ibid., 50ff.

9. Note that Nature in this sense as a divine continuum also becomes a standard for Art; cf. Pope, "An Essay on Criticism" (70–73):

> Unerring Nature, still divinely bright,
> One clear, unchanged, and universal light,
> Life, force, and beauty, must to all impart,
> At once the source, and end, and test of art.

10. Hartman, *Wordsworth's Poetry*, 198: "Man on Snowdon is not, however, a microcosm redeeming his alienated (macrocosmic) part. He is a mesocosm: at the boundary of all realms, and himself their boundary."

11. Christopher Norris, *What's Wrong with Postmodernism: Critical Theory and the Ends of Philosophy* (New York: Harvester Wheatsheaf, 1990), 18.

12. The phrase "critique of idealism" is Derrida's in a moment when he tries to explain what deconstruction and marxism have in common. See his *Positions*, trans. Alan Bass (Chicago: U of Chicago P, 1981), 62.

13. Wordsworth's opposition to the 1832 Reform Bill and Catholic Emancipation are surveyed in Stephen Gill, *William Wordsworth: A Life* (Oxford: Clarendon P, 1989), 362–63.

14. Mary Jacobus, "Afterword: Romantic Analogy; or, What the Moon Saw," in *Romanticism, Writing, and Sexual Difference: Essays on "The Prelude"* (Oxford: Oxford UP, 1989), 267–98.

15. This is the argument against metaphysical and religious claims. Cases in which mind and body are indeed reciprocal, without implying transcendence, would include psychosomatic symptoms.

16. See Ferdinand de Saussure, *Course in General Linguistics*, ed. Charles Bally and Albert Sechehaye, trans. Wade Baskin (New York: McGraw-Hill, 1966); and Jacques Derrida's lucid exposition of the structure of the sign in "Signature Event Context," in *Margins of Philosophy*, trans. Alan Bass (Chicago: U of Chicago P, 1982), 309–30.

17. In this connection it is worth noting that Jonathan Wordsworth, in his discussion of the sleeping horse in the opening of *Borders of Vision*, recalls how in "Tintern Abbey" the speaker has a vision while "laid asleep in body."

18. More precisely, as Frederick Pottle remarks, "the subject is a mental image [of an object] and the eye is that inward eye which is the bliss of solitude." See "The Eye and the Object in the Poetry of Wordsworth," *Yale Review* 40 (Autumn 1950), reprinted in *Romanticism and Consciousness*, ed. Harold Bloom (New York: Norton, 1970), 280.

19. The "Hartman" I am referring to here, and throughout, is the author of *Wordsworth's Poetry* (1964), not the later Hartman who absorbs and responds in complicated ways to poststructuralist theory. Hartman's "Words, Wish, Worth" (1979) takes up the issue of "the conflict between two kinds of reading: the direct or 'inner light' approach . . . and the learned, scientific, or philosophical approach, which sees all works, secular or sacred, as deeply mediated constructs, not available to understanding except through a study of history or of the intertextual character of all writing" (*Deconstruction and Criticism*, ed. Harold Bloom [New York: Seabury P, 1979], 187). This essay is a patient and subtle attempt both to admit and to blunt the force of intertextuality.

20. The question arises as to which was composed first. Two authorities on the composition history of *The Prelude* disagree on the precise dates of the lines in question in Book 1, part of what is called the post-Preamble. The Norton Critical edition states that Book 1 is "the creation of January 1804, more than half the material being new since 1799" (516). Mark Reed, editor of the Cornell edition of *The Thirteen-Book Prelude*, offers a different opinion: "The evidence is not decisive but appears to imply that most of I, 1–269, and thus most of the post-Preamble, had been composed before 1804" (17). Nonetheless, there is agreement that Snowdon and MS. W were written in February and March of 1804. Thus, although both Jonathan Wordsworth and Mark Reed would agree that the post-Preamble was composed before the Horse passage, a difficulty still exists. For while arguing for an earlier date, Mark Reed also tells us that the dating of the post-Preamble remains obscure because the earliest manuscript of the post-Preamble is the fair-copy MS. M sent to Coleridge in Malta (5), which included a version of the Snowdon episode with the MS. W Horse passage already revised out. Therefore, at least in terms of the extant manuscripts, the Horse passage would seem to be prior to the lines in Book 1. Nonetheless, I acquiesce in the opinion of the experts. See Mark Reed's introduction to *The Thirteen-Book Prelude*, 2 vols. (Ithaca, NY: Cornell UP, 1991).

21. The echo is noted by J. C. Maxwell in *The Prelude: A Parallel Text* (Harmondsworth, UK: Penguin, 1971), 540, as well as by W. J. B. Owen in *The Fourteen-Book Prelude* (Ithaca, NY: Cornell UP, 1985), 34.

22. The highly sophisticated critical literature on Wordsworth's intermittent revisions

of *The Prelude* over forty-five years concentrates almost exclusively on intratextual relations between manuscript versions. Thus, while Susan Wolfson, for instance, shrewdly observes that "manuscripts as well as memories" constitutes Wordsworth's past, I am attempting here to expand the notion of "revision" to include the ways a poet positions himself, not only in relation to his own past, but also in relation to the entire poetic tradition. For Wolfson, see *Formal Charges: The Shaping of Poetry in British Romanticism* (Stanford: Stanford UP, 1997), 104. For a compelling challenge to the idea that Wordsworth's revisionary activity implies an open-ended text (and self), see Zachary Leader's argument in *Revision and Romantic Authorship* (Oxford: Clarendon P, 1996).

23. See *Wordsworth's Pope: A Study in Literary Historiography* (Cambridge, MA: Cambridge UP,1995).

24. Hartman, *Wordsworth's Poetry*, 269; see also 399 n. 10, where the possibility of after-images acting like spots of time is raised.

25. Jonathan Arac, *Critical Genealogies* (New York: Columbia UP, 1987), 26. Hartman's phrase "suspensive discourse" is quoted from *Criticism in the Wilderness: The Study of Literature Today* (New Haven, CT: Yale UP, 1980), 274.

SEVEN: The New Historicism and the Work of Mourning

1. *The Letters of William and Dorothy Wordsworth*, vol. I, *The Early Years, 1787–1805*, ed. Ernest de Selincourt, 2nd ed. rev. Chester L. Shaver (Oxford: Oxford UP, 1967), 544–45, 546, 548.

2. Thomas Weiskel, *The Romantic Sublime: Studies in the Structure and Psychology of Transcendence* (Baltimore: Johns Hopkins UP, 1976), 6. Kevis Goodman brought this passage to my attention in a private communication.

3. Jean-François Lyotard, "A Postmodern Fable," talk presented on Nov. 11, 1992, at the University of California, Santa Barbara.

4. Jean-Luc Nancy, "Finite History," in *The Birth to Presence*, trans. Brian Holmes et al. (Stanford: Stanford UP, 1993), 155–56.

5. An allusion to the Borg society in the *Star Trek: The Next Generation* television series.

6. I am taking liberties here, of course, with Wordsworth's "Elegiac Stanzas Suggested by a Picture of Peele Castle."

7. This essay was originally a response to a session at the MLA convention in Toronto, Dec. 29, 1993. The session, which was organized by Kevis Goodman, included the following papers: Kevis Goodman, "Making Time for History: Wordsworth, the New Historicism, and the Apocalyptic Fallacy"; R. Clifton Spargo, "Facing the Other: Wordsworth's Critique of Subjectivity in 'Elegiac Stanzas' "; Leon Waldoff, "The Wordsworthian 'I' and the Work of Self-Representation in 'Elegiac Stanzas.' "

8. See chaps. 7 and 1 in Alan Liu, *Wordsworth: The Sense of History* (Stanford: Stanford UP, 1989).

9. I have taken all these terms of negativity from the pages of the New Historicism itself. Most of the words listed here, for example, can be found in the chapter on "Tintern Abbey" in Marjorie Levinson's *Wordsworth's Great Period Poems: Four Essays* (London: Cambridge UP, 1986). My own work often uses such vocabulary, especially "denial." For a discussion of the relation—and differences—between some of these terms, see 173 of my review article on David Simpson's *Wordsworth's Historical Imagination: The Poetry of Displacement* (*Wordsworth Circle* 19 [1988]: 172–81).

10. The very notion that "Elegiac Stanzas" "turns around and registers" loss, we recognize, mediates between the poet's and the critic's theaters of action. "Registration" is an eminently academic act.

11. And by contrast with more activist styles of cultural materialism, of course, even the subversion topos in Renaissance New Historicism is exorbitantly elegiac—as in the tone of the More chapter or the epilogue of Stephen Greenblatt's *Renaissance Self-Fashioning: From More to Shakespeare* (Chicago: U of Chicago P, 1980).

12. Freud, "Mourning and Melancholia," in *Standard Edition of the Complete Psychological Works of Sigmund Freud*, trans. James Strachey (London: Hogarth P, 1957), 14: 244.

13. Jean-François Lyotard, *The Postmodern Condition: A Report on Knowledge*, trans. Geoff Bennington and Brian Massumi (Minneapolis: U of Minnesota P, 1984), 80.

14. Lyotard, "What Is Postmodernism?" 80. I am indebted to Julie Ellison's talk titled "Someday Bridges Will Have Feelings, Too" (originally called "Between Regret and Assay") at MLA, New York, Dec. 28, 1992, for bringing to my attention the importance of this passage in Lyotard.

EIGHT: Making Time for History: Wordsworth, the New Historicism, and the Apocalyptic Fallacy

1. Virgil, *Eclogues, Georgics, Aeneid 1–6*, trans. H. Rushton Fairclough (Cambridge, MA: Harvard UP, 1986), *Georgics*, 4.564.

2. Wordsworth, *The Prelude, 1799, 1805, 1850*, ed. Jonathan Wordsworth, M. H. Abrams, and Stephen Gill (New York: Norton, 1979). Further references will be included, with the relevant *Prelude* text indicated by date. Recent studies of Wordsworth's ties to the georgic, including his apprenticeship as a translator of Virgil's poem, include Bruce Graver, "Wordsworth's Georgic Beginnings," *Texas Studies in Language and Literature* 33 (1991): 137–59; Graver, "Wordsworth's Georgic Pastoral: Otium and Labor in 'Michael,'" *ERR* 1 (1991): 119–34; and Kurt Heinzelman, "Roman Georgic in the Georgian Age: A Theory of Romantic Genre," *Texas Studies in Language and Literature* 33 (1991): 182–214.

It is worth noting that the inverted Virgilian phrase acts as a marker for the uneasy artistic conscience elsewhere in late-eighteenth-century poetry. William Cowper, for example, lashes out (with telling acrimony from the vantage of his cottage repose) at gypsies who "prefer / Such squalid sloth to honourable toil" (*Task*, 1.578–79), and Coleridge, in the 1795 "Reflections Upon Leaving a Place of Retirement," anticipates relinquishing the blissful existence of cottage life for more "honourable toil."

3. I am thinking primarily of Barrell's *The Dark Side of the Landscape: The Rural Poor in English Painting, 1730–1840* (Cambridge: Cambridge UP, 1980), but see also his earlier work, *The Idea of the Landscape and the Sense of Place, 1730–1740: An Approach to the Poetry of John Clare* (Cambridge: Cambridge UP, 1972), as well as more recent contributions: *English Literature in History: An Equal, Wide Survey* (London: Hutchinson, 1983) and the essays collected in *The Birth of Pandora and the Division of Knowledge* (London: Macmillan, 1992). Marjorie Levinson cites Barrell as exemplary in her introduction to *Wordsworth's Great Period Poems* (Cambridge: Cambridge UP, 1986), 3–4.

4. David Simpson, *Wordsworth's Historical Imagination: The Poetry of Displacement* (New York: Methuen, 1987); Alan Liu, *Wordsworth: The Sense of History* (Stanford: Stanford UP, 1989); Kurt Heinzelman, *The Economics of the Imagination* (Amherst: U of Massachusetts P,

1980); and Mark Shell, *The Economy of Literature* (Baltimore: Johns Hopkins UP, 1978). The "New Historicism" is at present an expansive category, including (in addition to Jerome McGann [note 6], Levinson, Simpson, and Liu) critics as diverse in their methodology as James Chandler (note 13), Marilyn Butler, Paul Hamilton, Clifford Siskin, Jerome Christensen, and Heinzelman. In what follows the emphasis falls on the work of Liu and Levinson.

5. See Liu's comments on the "embarrassment" of the postmodern intellect in "The Power of Formalism: The New Historicism," *ELH* 56 (1989): 721–71, esp. 740–47.

6. Jerome McGann, *The Romantic Ideology: A Critical Investigation* (Chicago: U of Chicago P, 1983), 91.

7. All quotations from *The Excursion* are taken from Wordsworth, *The Poetical Works of William Wordsworth*, ed. Ernest de Selincourt and Helen Darbishire, 5 vols. (Oxford: Clarendon P, 1940–49), vol. 5.

8. Geoffrey H. Hartman, *Wordsworth's Poetry, 1787–1814* (1964; repr., Cambridge, MA: Harvard UP, 1987). "Akedah" is Hartman's borrowing from Hebrew, but "Apocalypse" is a term with a long history in different schools of criticism, with different political valences and period interests. For a discussion of the pervasive rhetoric and politics of apocalypse in Romanticism in particular, see Steven Goldsmith, *Unbuilding Jerusalem: Apocalypse and Romantic Representation* (Ithaca, NY: Cornell UP, 1993).

9. See Levinson, *Wordsworth's Great Period Poems*, 68–79. Levinson's overt concern, although she is of course aware of Hartman's employment of the term, is with the presence of the biblical *Akedah* in "Michael"; she argues that the story provides a lever that shifts our attention away from material to spiritual history, from social critique to a wise passiveness.

10. The numerous discussions of the method include: Stephen Cole, "Evading Politics: The Poverty of Historicizing Romanticism," *Studies in Romanticism* 34 (1995): 29–49; Frances Ferguson, "Historicism, Deconstruction, and Wordsworth," *Diacritics* 17 (1987): 32–45 (reprinted in Ferguson, *Solitude and the Sublime: Romanticism and the Aesthetics of Individuation* [New York: Routledge, 1992], 146–71); Claudia Brodsky Lacour, "Contextual Criticism, or 'History' v. 'Literature,'" *Narrative* 1 (1993): 93–104; Marjorie Levinson, "Back to the Future," in *Rethinking Historicism: Critical Readings in Romantic History*, ed. Marjorie Levinson, Marilyn Butler, Jerome McGann, and Paul Hamilton (Oxford: Basil Blackwell, 1989), 18–63; Peter J. Manning, "Placing Poor Susan: Wordsworth and the New Historicism," in *Reading Romantics: Texts and Contexts* (New York: Oxford, 1990), 300–320 (an earlier version appeared in *Studies in Romanticism* 25 [1986]: 351–69); and David Simpson, "Literary Criticism and the Return to 'History,'" *Critical Inquiry* 14 (1988): 721–47. See also the articles by Liu cited in note 5 above and note 27. More vigorous and polemical dismissals of the method include Thomas McFarland's *William Wordsworth: Intensity and Achievement* (New York: Oxford, 1992), 1–33, and M. H. Abrams, "On Political Readings of *The Lyrical Ballads*," in *Romantic Revolutions: Criticism and Theory*, ed. Kenneth R. Johnston, Gilbert Chaitin, Karen Hanson, and Herbert Mark (Bloomington: Indiana UP, 1990), 320–49.

11. For a reading of the "passages of life" (1805, 11.269) as passages of text, see Thomas Weiskel, *The Romantic Sublime: Studies in the Structure and Psychology of Transcendence* (Baltimore: Johns Hopkins UP, 1986), 169.

12. Liu's comment (*Sense of History*, 456–57) can be compared with the following statement by McGann: "We may take it as a rule, then, that any criticism which abolishes the distance between its own (present) setting and its (removed) subject matter—any

criticism which argues an unhistorical symmetry between the practicing critic and the descending work—will be, to that extent, undermined as criticism" (*Romantic Ideology*, 30). For a fuller consideration of the problem of criticism's identification with its subject, see Liu, "The Power of Formalism," 730–40, and Levinson on "historicism's Hobson's choice of contemplation or empathy," in "Back to the Future."

13. For an argument that points to the ideological resonances, specifically the "implicit traditionalism," of a similar temporal structure, see James Chandler's discussion of *The Prelude*'s "spots of time" in *Wordsworth's Second Nature: A Study of the Poetry and Politics* (Chicago: U of Chicago P, 1984), chap. 8, esp. 206–15.

14. Important treatments of Wordsworth's use of *Othello* in this episode include Peter J. Manning, "Reading Wordsworth's Revisions," *Studies in Romanticism* 22 (1983): 3–28 (reprinted in Manning, *Reading Romantics*, 87–114), and Susan J. Wolfson, "The Illusion of Mastery: Wordsworth's Revisions of 'The Drowned Man of Esthwaite,' 1799, 1805, 1850," *PMLA* 99 (1984): 917–35. Wolfson is more suspicious than I am about the possibility of any mastery of traumatic experience by the power of books or by revisionary after-meditation.

15. Geoffrey H. Hartman, *Easy Pieces* (New York: Columbia UP, 1985), 148. Cf. Hartman's comments in "Words and Wounds," *Saving the Text* (Baltimore: Johns Hopkins UP, 1981), 145–48.

16. Kenneth Burke, *The Philosophy of Literary Form: Studies in Symbolic Action*, 3rd ed., rev. (Berkeley: U of California P, 1973), 61.

17. Cathy Caruth, ed., *Trauma: Explorations in Memory* (Baltimore: Johns Hopkins UP, 1995), 6, 8. For a fuller explication of the latter statement, see Caruth's "Unclaimed Experience: Trauma and the Possibility of History," *Yale French Studies* 79 (1991).

18. On the temporal dimension of the traumatic experience, see *Beyond the Pleasure Principle*, in *The Standard Edition of the Complete Psychological Works of Sigmund Freud*, trans. James Strachey, 24 vols. (London: Hogarth, 1953–74), 12:28, 31–32; hereafter cited as *SE*.

19. See Dominick LaCapra, *Representing the Holocaust: History, Theory, Trauma* (Ithaca, NY: Cornell UP, 1994), 14 n. 10.

20. It is not surprising that the issues I engage here concerning the paradox of historical representation—that is, our simultaneous need to establish an irreducible "reality" and our acknowledgment of the limits of realism (and presence of an aesthetic dimension) in historical narrative—have been most carefully considered by scholars of Holocaust. The most recent round of the debate may be said to begin with Hayden White's assertion that eighteenth-century theorists of a sublime history "had correctly divined that whatever dignity and freedom human beings could lay claim to could come only by way of what Freud called a reaction-formation to an apperception of history's meaninglessness" (*The Content of the Form: Narrative Discourse and Historical Representation* [Baltimore: Johns Hopkins UP, 1987], 72). The corollaries of White's emphasis on sublime narrative and historical emplotment have been addressed by LaCapra in *Representing the Holocaust* and at greater length by Saul Friedlander in a series of thoughtful essays: see esp. the introduction to *Probing the Limits of Representation: Nazism and the Final Solution*, ed. Saul Friedlander [Cambridge, MA: Harvard UP, 1992), 1–21] and Friedlander, "Trauma, Transference and Working-through in Writing the History of the *Shoah*," *History and Memory: Studies in Representation of the Past* 4 (1992): 39–59. Particularly relevant to my own discussion of Wordsworth is Friedlander's tentative solution to the particular difficulties of representing the Holocaust to present-day viewers or readers. He advocates a "distanced or allusive

realism": "Reality is there, in its starkness, but perceived through a filter: that of memory (distance in time), that of spatial displacement, that of some sort of narrative margin which leaves the unsayable unsaid" (*Probing the Limits*, 17).

21. Wordsworth, *The Prose Works of William Wordsworth*, ed. W. J. B. Owen and Jane Worthington Smyser, 3 vols. (Oxford: Clarendon P, 1974), 1:128–130.

22. "Mourning and Melancholia," *SE*, 14:244–45; "Remembering, Repeating, and Working-through," *SE*, 12:155 (Freud's emphases).

23. Benjamin, "The Storyteller," in *Illuminations: Essays and Reflections*, ed. Hannah Arendt, trans. Harry Zohn (New York: Schoken Books, 1968), 91. *The Excursion*'s relationship to the georgic genre has long been recognized. See, e.g., Annabel Patterson, "Wordsworth's Georgic: Genre and Structure in *The Excursion*," *Wordsworth Circle* 9 (1978): 145–54, and Hartman, *Wordsworth's Poetry*, 296–98.

24. For Empson on Gray's elegy, see *Some Version of Pastoral* (New York: New Directions, 1974), 5.

25. Orwell, "Politics and the English Language," in *A Collection of Essays* (New York: Harcourt, Brace, Jovanovich, 1946), 167.

26. Burke, *Philosophy of Literary Form*, 61 (Burke's emphasis); cf. 293–304.

27. Wolfson, " 'Romantic Ideology' and the Values of Aesthetic Form," *Aesthetics and Ideology*, ed. George Levine (New Brunswick, NJ: Rutgers UP, 1994), 190. Alan Liu includes an extensive list of intellectual historians, anthropologists, and literary critics who participate in what he calls "a *new rhetorical historicism*—that is, a method that views cultural discourse less as symbolic representation or figure than as performative act" ("Wordsworth and Subversion, 1793–1804: Trying Cultural Criticism," *Yale Journal of Criticism* 2 [1989]: 66). In this connection, I would also mention Michel de Certeau's emphasis on style and the literariness of historiography: *The Writing of History*, trans. Tom Conley (New York: Columbia UP, 1988).

28. James Chandler, *England in 1819: The Politics of Literary Culture and the Case of Romantic New Historicism* (Chicago: U of Chicago P, 1998), 5.

29. On "using," see Jerome Christensen, *Romanticism at the End of History* (Baltimore: Johns Hopkins UP, 2000), esp. chap. 7.

30. Chandler, *England in 1819*; Susan Wolfson, *Formal Charges: The Shaping of Poetry in British Romanticism* (Stanford: Stanford UP, 1997); Thomas Pfau, *Wordsworth's Profession: Form, Class, and the Logic of Early Romantic Cultural Production* (Stanford: Stanford UP, 1997); and Marc Redfield, *The Politics of Aesthetics: Nationalism, Gender, Romanticism* (Stanford: Stanford UP, 2003).

31. See, e.g., Alan Richardson, *British Romanticism and the Science of the Mind* (Cambridge: Cambridge UP, 2001), and Maureen N. McLane, *Romanticism and the Human Sciences* (Cambridge: Cambridge UP, 2000).

32. Both aspects of this argument are worked out in my *Georgic Modernity and British Romanticism: Poetry and the Mediation of History* (Cambridge: Cambridge UP, 2004), which begins with the late seventeenth century and concludes with Wordsworth. *Georgic Modernity*, however, is considerably more skeptical of "working through," or the therapeutic aspect of mediation. When, in the final chapter, it treats *The Excursion*, it insists on the dialectic between euphemism's "closing words" (*Exc.*, 7. 292) and its less pleasing "acoustical unconscious." More emphatically than this essay, it attends throughout to what George Eliot called "the roar that lies on the other side of silence" (*Middlemarch*, chap. 20).

NINE: Sound Government, Polymorphic Bears: *The Winter's Tale* and Other Metamorphoses of Eye and Ear

1. See Margreta de Grazia, "Homonyms before and after Lexical Standardization," *Jahrbuch der Deutschen Shakespeare-Gesellschaft West* (1990): 143–56, including 149–53 on Johnson and the term "pun." Unless otherwise noted, all quotations from *The Winter's Tale* and other plays of Shakespeare are cited from *The Riverside Shakespeare*, ed. G. Blakemore Evans (Boston: Houghton Mifflin, 1974).

2. See de Grazia, "Homonyms," 142–46, with Stephen Booth, "Exit, Pursued by a Gentleman Born," in *Shakespeare's Art From a Comparative Perspective*, ed. Wendell M. Aycock (Lubbock: Texas Tech UP,1981), 51–60.

3. For the above, see de Grazia, "Homonyms," passim and esp. 144–45 (on Antigonus); and, among others, Carol Thomas Neely, *Broken Nuptials in Shakespeare's Plays* (New Haven, CT: Yale UP, 1985), 191–209; Janet Adelman, *Suffocating Mothers* (New York: Routledge, 1992), 219–36; and Gail Kern Paster, *The Body Embarrassed* (Ithaca, NY: Cornell UP, 1993), 260–80.

4. See Stanley Cavell, "Recounting Gains, Showing Losses: Reading *The Winter's Tale*," in *Disowning Knowledge in Six Plays of Shakespeare* (Cambridge: Cambridge UP, 1987), 193–221; Michael Bristol, "In Search of the Bear: Spatiotemporal Form and the Heterogeneity of Economies in *The Winter's Tale*," *Shakespeare Quarterly* 42.2 (1991):145–67; and my "Temporal Gestation, Legal Contracts, and the Promissory Economies of *The Winter's Tale*," in *Women, Property, and the Letters of the Law*, ed. Margaret W. Ferguson and Nancy Wright (Toronto: U of Toronto P, 2004).

5. See Orgel, ed., *The Winter's Tale* (Oxford: Clarendon P, 1996), 155–56, which also cites several key discussions. For the Candlemas Bear, together with other responses to this notorious stage direction, see Bristol, "Bear," 158–62.

6. See Booth, "Exit," 51–60, with de Grazia, "Homonyms," esp. 152.

7. For the importance of this network of conveyance in the histories, *Merry Wives*, and other plays, see my *Shakespeare from the Margins* (Chicago: U of Chicago P, 1996), chaps. 4 and 5.

8. See Booth, "Exit"; and Kenneth Muir, "The Uncomic Pun," *Cambridge Journal* 3 (1950): 472–85.

9. Richard Halpern, *The Poetics of Primitive Accumulation: English Renaissance Culture and the Genealogy of Capital* (Ithaca, NY: Cornell UP, 1991), 243–45.

10. Tom Conley, *The Self-Made Map: Cartographic Writing in Early Modern France* (Minneapolis: U of Minnesota P, 1996), 32–34.

11. See Maureen Quilligan, *The Language of Allegory* (Ithaca, NY: Cornell UP, 1979), 48–51, who also cites the polyglot play here on *pésant* and "peasant," with de Grazia, "Homonyms," 148.

12. See Arvin H. Jupin, ed., *A Contextual Study and Modern-Spelling Edition of Mucedorus* (New York: Garland, 1987), esp. 86.

13. Quotations are from Henry Watson's early sixteenth-century English translation of *Valentine and Orson*, ed. Arthur Dickson (London: Oxford UP, 1937).

14. Stephen Dickey, "Shakespeare's Mastiff Comedy," *Shakespeare Quarterly* 42.3 (1991): 255–75, discusses the importance of bears and bear-baiting in *Twelfth Night*, including the connection between bear-baiting and theater important to the play.

15. Jonathan Bate, *Shakespeare and Ovid* (Oxford: Clarendon P, 1993), 224–27. For the

links between Ursa Major and Ursula—a name that was particularly resonant because of its counter-association with one of the most famous virgin saints—see, e.g., the choice of that name for a sexually rapacious female figure in Jonson's *Bartholomew Fair* and the Ursula called "Ursely" in *Much Ado about Nothing* (3.1.4), a Shakespearean plot of an innocent but sexually tainted woman.

16. For *Fasti*, 2.153–92, see the Loeb six-volume edition of Ovid, vol. 5: *Fasti*, trans. Sir James George Frazer, 2nd ed. rev. G. P. Goold (London: Heinemann, 1989), 68–71. For the "bearard that protects the bear," see *2 Henry VI* (5.1.210).

17. See Bristol, "Bear," 156.

18. Cited from 45–47 of *Ovid's Metamorphoses: the Arthur Golding Translation* (1567), ed. John Frederick Nims (Philadelphia: Paul Dry Books, 2000).

19. See Geoffrey Hartman, "Shakespeare's Poetical Character in *Twelfth Night*," in *Shakespeare and the Question of Theory*, ed. Patricia Parker and Geoffrey Hartman (New York: Methuen, 1985), 37–53, esp. 50, 45–46, 42, 41, and 49.

TEN: The Other Scene of Travel: Wordsworth's "Musings Near Aquapendente"

1. William Wordsworth, *The Thirteen-Book Prelude*, ed. Mark L. Reed (Ithaca, NY: Cornell UP, 1991).

2. T. S. Eliot, "Tradition and the Individual Talent," in *The Sacred Wood* (1920; repr., London: Methuen, 1960), 49.

3. Christopher Wordsworth, *Memoirs of William Wordsworth*, 2 vols. (London: Moxon, 1851), 2:329; hereafter cited as *Memoirs*.

4. Samuel Taylor Coleridge, *Biographia Literaria*, ed. James Engell and W. Jackson Bate, Bollingen Series 75, *The Collected Works of Samuel Taylor Coleridge*, vol. 7 (Princeton, NJ: Princeton UP, 1983), 75.

5. *The Letters of John Keats*, ed. Hyder Edward Rollins, 2 vols. (Cambridge, MA: Harvard UP), 1:394.

6. All quotations from "Musings Near Aquapendente" are taken from *Poems, Chiefly of Early and Late Years* (London: Moxon, 1842), where the poem lacks line numbers. The numbers in brackets are those from *The Poetical Works of William Wordsworth*, ed. E. de Selincourt and Helen Darbishire, 2nd ed., 5 vols. (Oxford: Clarendon P, 1952–63), 3:202–12; hereafter cited as *PW*.

7. Geoffrey H. Hartman, *Wordsworth's Poetry, 1787–1814* (1964; repr., Cambridge, MA: Harvard UP, 1987), 242. In subsequent essays Hartman explored Wordsworth's late, classicizing style; in particular, see "Blessing the Torrent," first published in 1978 and reprinted as chapter 6 of his *The Unremarkable Wordsworth*, foreword by Donald G. Marshall (Minneapolis: U of Minnesota P, 1987), 75–89.

8. William Wordsworth, *The Poetical Works*, ed. Thomas Hutchinson, rev. Ernest de Selincourt (London: Oxford UP, 1950), 753–54. Geoffrey H. Hartman, *Wordsworth's Poetry, 1787–1814* (1964; repr., Cambridge, MA: Harvard UP, 1987), 242.

9. A check of the Chadwyck-Healey database reveals enough instances in the Wordsworth circle and thereafter across the nineteenth century to establish the title "Musings" as a formal signal. Examples include Coleridge's "Religious Musings, A Desultory Poem, Written on the Christmas Eve of 1794," George Dyer's "Perambulatory Musings," Bernard Barton's "Summer Musings" and "Sea-Side Musings," Robert Southey's "Musings

on the Wig of a Scare-Crow," Wordsworth's own "Elegiac Musings: In the Grounds of Coleorton Hall," Winthrop Mackworth Praed's "A Member's Musings," and Aubrey De Vere's "A Wanderer's Musings at Rome."

10. The late composition may partly explain why the poem lacks the reflections on Italian nationalism which mark the succeeding poems in the sequence. On this aspect of the "Memorials," see John Wyatt, *Wordsworth's Poems of Travel, 1819–42* (Basingstoke, UK: Macmillan, 1999), 131–35.

11. Stephen Gill, "Wordsworth, Scott, and 'Musings Near Aquapendente'," *Centennial Review* 36 (1992): 222.

12. Michael Millgate, *Testamentary Acts: Browning, Tennyson, James, Hardy* (Oxford: Clarendon P, 1992).

13. This review of the relationship of Scott and Wordsworth is compiled chiefly from Edgar Johnson, *Sir Walter Scott: The Great Unknown*, 2 vols. (New York: Macmillan, 1970) and Stephen Gill, *William Wordsworth: A Life* (Oxford: Clarendon P, 1989).

14. *The Letters of William and Dorothy Wordsworth*, vol. 1, *The Early Years, 1787–1805*, ed. Ernest de Selincourt, 2nd ed. rev. Chester L. Shaver (Oxford: Clarendon P, 1967), 413–14; hereafter cited as *Early Years.*

15. *The Letters of William and Dorothy Wordsworth*, vol. 2, *The Middle Years, 1806–1811, Part 1*, ed. Ernest de Selincourt, 2nd. ed. rev. Mary Moorman (Oxford: Clarendon P, 1969), 264; hereafter cited as *Middle Years.* More than twenty years later Wordsworth was still irked by the misquotation: "W. Scott quoted, as from me, 'The swan on *Sweet* St. Mary's Lake Floats double, swan and shadow,' instead of *still*; thus obscuring my idea, and betraying his own uncritical principles of composition." Christopher Wordsworth Jr., from the summer of 1827, as quoted in Markham L. Peacock Jr., *The Critical Opinions of William Wordsworth* (1950; repr., New York: Octagon, 1969), 339.

16. John Lockhart, *Memoirs of the Life of Sir Walter Scott, Bart.*, 7 vols. (Edinburgh: Cadell, 1837), 1:405.

17. Quoted in Alice Pattee Comparetti, *The White Doe of Rylstone, by William Wordsworth: A Critical Edition*, Cornell Studies in English 19 (Ithaca, NY: Cornell UP, 1940), 44. Though quoting liberally from Whitaker, and even alluding to Scott's *Minstrelsy of the Scottish Border* (162), Wordsworth does not cite this compliment, or prompt. In its quarto format of narrative poem followed by notes, *The White Doe*, when published at last in 1815, looks a great deal like *The Lay of the Last Minstrel* and *Marmion*, a connection Wordsworth was still at pains to deny decades later in the notes dictated to Isabella Fenwick: "The subject being taken from feudal times has led to its being compared to some of Walter Scott's poems that belong to the same age and state of society. The comparison is inconsiderate. Sir Walter pursued the customary and very natural course of conducting an action, presenting various turns of fortune, to some outstanding point on which the mind might rest as a termination or catastrophe. The course I attempted to pursue is entirely different" (*PW*, 3:543). On this strand see "*The White Doe of Rylstone*, *The Convention of Cintra*, and the History of a Career," reprinted as chapter 8 of my *Reading Romantics* (New York: Oxford UP, 1990).

18. H. J. C. Grierson, ed., *The Letters of Sir Walter Scott*, 12 vols. (London: Constable, 1932), 1:390.

19. Quoted in Robert Woof, ed. *William Wordsworth: The Critical Heritage* (London: Routledge, 2001), 1:297–98.

20. All quotations from *Edinburgh Review* 24 (Nov. 1814): 1–30, as reprinted in Woof, 381–404.

21. All quotations from *Edinburgh Review* 24 (Nov. 1814): 208–43, as reprinted in *Scott: The Critical Heritage*, ed. John O. Hayden (New York: Barnes & Noble, 1970), 79–84.

22. On the contrast between the "basically sane and healthy Scott" and the weakness and subjectivity of the other Romantics, see J. H. Alexander, "The Treatment of Scott in Reviews of the English Romantics," *Yearbook of English Studies* 11 (1981), 67–86.

23. All quotations from the *Examiner*, Aug. 21, 28 and Oct. 2, 1814, 541–42, 555–58, 636–38, as reprinted in *The Selected Writings of William Hazlitt*, ed. Duncan Wu, 9 vols. (London: Pickering & Chatto, 1998), 2:321–40.

24. William Hazlitt, *Lectures on the English Poets* and *The Spirit of the Age*, ed. Catherine Macdonald Maclean (London: Dent, n.d.), 143–68.

25. I pass over their convergence in London in 1828. Haydon's comparison of the two men works a penetrating variation on the stock opposition: "Scott enters a room and sits at table with the coolness and self-possession of conscious fame: Wordsworth with a mortified elevation of head, as if fearful he was not estimated as he desired. Scott is always cool and very amusing; Wordsworth often egotistical and overwhelming. Scott seems to appear less than he really is, while Wordsworth struggles to be thought at the moment greater than he is suspected to be. I think that Scott's success would have made Wordsworth insufferable, while Wordsworth's failure would not have rendered Scott a whit less delightful" (*Autobiography*, quoted in Johnson, 1052).

26. *The Letters of William and Dorothy Wordsworth*, vol. 5, *The Later Years, Part 2, 1829–1834*, ed. Ernest De Selincourt, 2nd ed. rev. Alan G. Hill (Oxford: Clarendon P, 1979), 328; hereafter cited as *Later Years.*

27. I have written on this volume in *Reading Romantics*, in "Cleansing the Images: Wordsworth, Rome, and the Rise of Historicism," *Texas Studies in Literature and Language* 33 (1991): 271–326, and in "William Wordsworth and William Cobbett: Scotch Travel and British Reform," *Scotland and the Borders of Romanticism*, ed. Leith Davis, Ian Duncan, and Janet Sorensen (Cambridge: Cambridge UP, 2004), 153–69.

28. Text from *Yarrow Revisited* (London: Longman & Moxon, 1835), 9.

29. On this feature, see Jill Rubinstein, "Wordsworth and 'Localised Romance': The Scottish Poems of 1831," *Studies in English Literature* 16 (1976): 579–90.

30. On the envy see, e.g., the letter to Samuel Rogers announcing *The Excursion:* "I shall be content if the publication pays its expenses, for Mr. Scott and your friend Lord B. flourishing at they rate they do, how can an honest *Poet* [Wordsworth's differentiating italics] hope to thrive?" (*The Letters of William and Dorothy Wordsworth*, vol. 3, *The Middle Years, Part 2, 1812–1820*, ed. Ernest De Selincourt, 2nd ed. rev. Mary Moorman and Alan G. Hill [Oxford: Clarendon P, 1970], 148).

31. Wordsworth, "Essay on Epitaphs," *The Excursion* (London: Longman, 1814), 440–41.

32. See my "Wordsworth in the *Keepsake*, 1829," in *Literature in the Marketplace*, ed. John O. Jordan and Robert L. Patten (Cambridge: Cambridge UP, 1995), 44–73.

33. Text from William Wordsworth, *Last Poems, 1821–1850*, ed. Jared Curtis (Ithaca, NY: Cornell UP, 1999), 305; hereafter cited as *Last Poems.*

34. The representative utterance is from a letter of February 4, 1841, to Moxon (*The Letters of William and Dorothy Wordsworth*, vol. 7, *The Later Years, Part 4, 1840–1853*, ed. Ernest de Selincourt, 2nd ed. rev. Alan G. Hill [Oxford: Clarendon P, 1988], 176). The poem was then published in the *Athenaeum*, guaranteeing still wider diffusion.

35. The effect of the forty-eight-volume "Magnum Opus" edition of Scott (1829–33),

drawing into one uniform set the novels, poems, and assorted prose, together with fresh and appealing notes by the author, should also not be underestimated. See Jane Millgate, *Scott's Last Edition* (Edinburgh: Edinburgh UP, 1987).

36. See *Henry Crabb Robinson on Books and Their Writers*, ed. Edith J. Morley, 3 vols. (London: Dent, 1938) 2:524; hereafter cited as *HCR*.

37. *London and Westminster Review* 28 (Jan. 1838): 293–345, quoted in Thomas Carlyle, *Critical and Miscellaneous Essays*, 5 vols. (New York: Scribner's, 1904), 4:22–87.

38. *Letters and Journals of Lord Byron*, ed. Thomas Moore, 2 vols. (London: John Murray, 1830), 2:31–32.

39. Quoted in *The Fenwick Notes of William Wordsworth*, ed. Jared Curtis (London: Bristol Classical, 1993), 69–70.

40. Stephen Gill, "Copyright and the Publishing of Wordsworth, 1850–1900," in *Literature in the Marketplace*, ed. John O. Jordan and Robert Patten (Cambridge: Cambridge UP, 1995), 74–92.

41. Wordsworth's success in establishing the perception of the friendship between himself and Scott can be gauged by George Cattermole's painting of Scott and Wordsworth at Newark Castle. The source of this imaginative recreation must be Wordsworth's poems in *Yarrow Revisited* and the account of the final visit to Abbotsford that Wordsworth communicated to Lockhart for inclusion in his biography of Scott. I am still trying to track down the history of this image, which became widely known through the lithograph by James Duffield Harding. It is featured in the biographies of Wordsworth by Mary Moorman (1965) and Juliet Barker (2000).

42. "At last he rose, and twitch't his Mantle blue: / Tomorrow to fresh Woods, and Pastures new." Wordsworth immodestly claimed that of the finest elegiac compositions in English "Milton's *Lycidas* and my *Laodamia* are twin Immortals" (Alaric Watts, quoted in Peacock, 313).

43. I owe this parallel to Alan Richardson.

44. I am happy to call attention to the as-yet-unpublished dissertation of Peter Simonsen, "Word-Preserving Arts," defended at the University of Copenhagen in February 2003, for which I was honored to serve as a reader.

45. "A copy of the book presented, with autograph, by Rogers was in the Rydal Mount Library" (*PW*, 3:502). The chain of mediating print includes Samuel Rogers's poem, *Italy*, of which Wordsworth had read the anonymous first part in 1822 "with much pleasure" (*The Letters of William and Dorothy Wordsworth*, 2nd ed. rev. Alan G. Hill, vol. 4, *The Later Years, Part 1* [Oxford: Clarendon P, 1978], 153), and Rogers sent him the sheets of the sumptuous reissue and revision of the poem (1830), with illustrations by J. M. W. Turner and Thomas Stothard, "as the proofs came in" (P. W. Clayden, *Rogers and His Contemporaries*, 2 vols. [London: Smith, Elder, 1889], 2:9). Forsyth, whose book recounts his travels in Italy in 1802 and 1803, remarks of the scene of Wordsworth's poem: "On crossing the volcanic mountain of RADICOFANI, I remarked on its cone the ruins of a fort which was often conspicuous in the history of Italy. . . . On entering the Papal State, we were long fatigued with the same sad colour of dry clay. At length AQUAPENDENTE broke fresh upon us, surrounded with ancient oaks, and terraces clad in the greens of a second spring, with hanging vineyards, and cascades, and cliffs, and grottos screened with pensile foliage" (*Remarks on Antiquities, Arts, and Letters during an Excursion in Italy*, ed. Keith Crook [Newark: U of Delaware P, 2001], 70). The first edition of Forsyth appeared in 1813; the second, corrected and enlarged (the basis of Crook's text), in 1816, from John Murray,

Byron's publisher. Forsyth's work underlies both Canto 4 of *Childe Harold's Pilgrimage* and the "Memorials": Byron wrote Murray in 1820 that it and two other books "are all we have of truth or sense upon Italy," and he seems to have used it as a guidebook on his visit to Rome in 1817 (*Byron's Letters and Journals*, ed. Leslie A. Marchand, 12 vols. [Cambridge, MA: Harvard UP, 1973–82], 7:182, 5:221, 224, 227, 233). On "The Pillar of Trajan," see "Cleansing the Images," n. 26 above.

ELEVEN: Writing Criticism: Art, Transcendence, and History

1. I modernize the text of Philip Sidney, "An Apology for Poetry," *Elizabethan Critical Essays*, ed. G. Gregory Smith, 2 vols. (Oxford: Clarendon P, 1904), 1:156.

2. Neoplatonic allegorical interpretation gave poetry a role in the quest for transcendence but only as a propaedeutic. Recent critical theory does not reject the Platonic charge but glories in it: "(following Heidegger's analysis) poetry discloses or, more accurately, summons things, not as beings, but precisely as things — earthly, singular or nonidentical, opaque, refractory to the light, impenetrable to analysis, always withdrawing from view. Likewise, . . . poetry itself is thinglike discourse: material, dense (*dicht*), the dark saying where nothing is ever itself or capturable but is always interpretable otherwise, forever running loose, anarchic and dangerous" (Gerald Bruns, "Against Poetry: Heidegger, Ricoeur, and the Originary Scene of Hermeneutics," *Meanings in Texts and Actions: Questioning Paul Ricoeur*, ed. David E. Klemm and William Schweiker [Charlottesville: UP of Virginia, 1993], 42, and see 39–40). At full length, see Bruns, *Heidegger's Estrangements: Language, Truth, and Poetry in the Later Writings* (New Haven, CT: Yale UP, 1989).

3. Wesley Trimpi, *Muses of One Mind: The Literary Analysis of Experience and Its Continuity* (Princeton, NJ: Princeton UP, 1983); and Kathy Eden, *Poetic and Legal Fiction in the Aristotelian Tradition* (Princeton, NJ: Princeton UP, 1986).

4. *Kant's Life and Thought*, trans. James Haden (New Haven, CT: Yale UP, 1981), chap. 6, esp. 285–86.

5. Hans-Georg Gadamer, "Are the Poets Falling Silent?" in *On Education, Poetry, and History: Applied Hermeneutics*, ed. Dieter Misgeld and Graeme Nicholson, trans. Lawrence Schmidt and Monica Reuss (Albany: State U of New York P, 1992), 73; hereafter cited as "Silent."

6. Annabel Patterson, "Historical Scholarship," *Introduction to Scholarship in Modern Languages and Literatures*, ed. Joseph Gibaldi, 2nd ed. (New York: MLA, 1992), 185. I quote this phrase not to single out Patterson's intelligent essay but to document an idea whose wide distribution is demonstrated by the representative function this volume plausibly claims to play.

7. Jerome J. McGann's *The Romantic Ideology: A Critical Investigation* (Chicago: U of Chicago P, 1983) is the most widely influential and frankest statement of this position.

8. This measure was articulated most lucidly by Georg Lukács and enabled him to condemn Kafka while praising Thomas Mann, even though Mann failed to adopt a consciously socialist view. See "Franz Kafka or Thomas Mann?" *Realism in Our Time: Literature and the Class Struggle* (New York: Harper Torchbooks, 1971), 70: "Our apparently rather negative conclusion — that non-rejection of socialism is a sufficient basis for realism."

9. John Keats, *Complete Poems and Selected Letters*, ed. Clarence DeWitt Thorpe (New York: Odyssey, 1935).

10. In *Human Nature and History: A Study of the Development of Liberal Political Thought*, 2 vols. (Chicago: U of Chicago P, 1969), esp. chaps. 4 and 6, Robert Denoon Cumming underscores the modern historicist assumption that a text or event is only intelligible in relation to its immediate circumstances in contrast to ancient ways of conceiving history. While this contrast has the force of a penetrating critique, Cumming acknowledges very clearly how nearly impossible it is for us to extricate ourselves from historicism.

11. Obviously, I am following a Platonic procedure in pushing a contradiction to its extremes on both sides in the conviction that as a result of doing so something true will come into view. That artworks are things but not products and hence do not enter into the world of exchange and use, see Hannah Arendt, *The Human Condition* (Chicago: U of Chicago P, 1958), 167–74. Mikhail Bakhtin repeatedly protests against the reduction of works of literature or of human beings to their circumstances. As Gary Saul Morson and Caryl Emerson state his view, "individuals are in no sense wholly reducible to 'products of their era' " (*Mikhail Bakhtin: Creation of a Prosaics* [Stanford: Stanford UP, 1990], 405). It is instructive to notice that even in expounding his thought, Morson and Emerson fall back into the very historicist formulas that Bakhtin criticized, as, for example, when they assert that "each language reflects . . . the contingent historical and social forces that have made it," 141.

12. Vico, *The New Science*, trans. Thomas Goddard Bergin and Max Harold Fisch (Ithaca, NY: Cornell UP, 1968), 96 (par. 331); further quotations cite page and paragraph numbers of this translation.

13. Hans-Georg Gadamer, *Truth and Method*, trans. rev. Joel Weinsheimer and Donald G. Marshall, 2nd rev. ed. (New York: Crossroad, 1989), 231.

14. "What Is Enlightenment?" *Critique of Practical Reason and Other Writings in Moral Philosophy*, ed. and trans. Lewis White Beck (Chicago: U of Chicago P, 1949), 286–92.

15. *The Poverty of Historicism* (New York: Harper Torchbooks, 1964). Hannah Arendt remarks that "although history owes its existence to men, it is still obviously not 'made' by them" (Arendt, 185). Henry Kissinger writes, "When all is said and done, what Margaret Thatcher stood for was that man is not the product of circumstance but of choice, and that politics is not about expediency but about purpose" ("The Right to Be Right," review of *The Downing Street Years*, by Margaret Thatcher, *New York Times Book Review*, Nov. 14, 1993, 63). It would not be inconsistent to object to virtually everything Thatcher's government did in practice and yet to agree that the principle Kissinger states articulates the political reality that emerges after the collapse of political systems sponsored by historicist principles.

16. I take the liberty of paraphrasing what I wrote, following Cassirer closely, in "Kant and English Nature Poetry," *Iowa Review* 21 (1991): 83.

17. Hans-Georg Gadamer, "The Relevance of the Beautiful," in *Relevance of the Beautiful and Other Essays*, ed. Robert Bernasconi, trans. Nicholas Walker (Cambridge: Cambridge UP, 1986), 26; hereafter cited as "Relevance."

18. Derek Walcott, *Omeros* (New York: Farrar, 1990); hereafter cited as *Omeros*, book, chapter, section, and page number.

19. Gadamer, "On the Contribution of Poetry to the Search for Truth," in *Relevance*, 112; hereafter cited as "Truth."

20. Geoffrey H. Hartman, *Beyond Formalism: Literary Essays, 1958–1970* (New Haven, CT: Yale UP, 1970), 356–86.

21. *Aristotle's Poetics: A Translation and Commentary for Students of Literature*, trans.

Leon Golden (Englewood Cliffs, NJ: Prentice-Hall, 1968), 17, 1451b6–8; further quotations cite *Poetics* and Bekker numbers.

22. Geoffrey H. Hartman, *Minor Prophecies: The Literary Essay in the Culture Wars* (Cambridge, MA: Harvard UP, 1991), 202; hereafter cited as *Prophecies*.

23. My distinctions and remarks here are in part drawn from and are in part a response to Hartman's *Criticism in the Wilderness: The Study of Literature Today* (New Haven, CT: Yale UP, 1980) and, more recently, *Minor Prophecies*.

24. Alvin Kernan, *Printing Technology, Letters, and Samuel Johnson* (Princeton, NJ: Princeton UP, 1987), argues that Johnson was the first critic to accept his situation in the midst of mass communication and on this basis asserts Johnson's contemporary relevance.

25. That was already Plato's point in the opening book of the *Republic* against those who thought their superior skill gave them a right to dominate those subject to their expertise. See also Gadamer, "The Limitations of the Expert," in *On Education, Poetry, and History*, (see note 5 above) 181–92; hereafter cited as "Expert."

26. For a powerful attack on the liquidation of critical reading in the raging flood of "information," see Ben Agger, *Fast Capitalism: A Critical Theory of Significance* (Urbana: U of Illinois P, 1989).

27. Geoffrey H. Hartman, "History Writing as Answerable Style," in *The Fate of Reading and Other Essays* (Chicago: U of Chicago P, 1975), 101–13; hereafter cited as "History."

TWELVE: Gentle Hearts and Hands: Reading Wordsworth after Geoffrey Hartman

1. For the figure of prolepsis, see Quintilian, *Institutio Oratoria*, trans. H. E. Butler (London: William Heinemann, 1921), 9.2.16–17. Quintilian prefers the Latin term *praesumptio*, or "anticipation," to describe a rhetorical "genus" containing "several different species" of figures, including prediction, but also *occupatio*, or forestalling of objections, confession, self-correction, preparation, and qualification (9.2.17–18).

2. William Wordsworth, *The Poetical Works of William Wordsworth*, ed. Ernest de Selincourt, rev. Helen Darbishire, 5 vols. (Oxford: Clarendon P, 1952–1963), 3:77; hereafter cited as *PW*.

3. See, e.g., Hartman's discussion of the "westering" impulse of eighteenth-century English literature in "Blake and the Progress of Poesy," in *Beyond Formalism: Literary Essays, 1958–1970* (New Haven, CT: Yale UP, 1970), 196–205.

4. *Hamlet*, 2.2.516–18, in William Shakespeare, *The Complete Works*, ed. Alfred Harbage (Baltimore: Penguin, 1969); all subsequent references to works by Shakespeare are to this edition.

5. Strictly speaking, Hartman is referring to "psychoanalytically oriented criticism," but his point holds for criticism generally. See Geoffrey H. Hartman, "A Touching Compulsion," in *The Unremarkable Wordsworth*, foreword by Donald G. Marshall (Minneapolis: U of Minnesota P, 1987), 18; hereafter cited as *UnRW*.

6. Geoffrey H. Hartman, *Criticism in the Wilderness: The Study of Literature Today* (New Haven, CT: Yale UP, 1980), 1.

7. Paul de Man, *Blindness and Insight: Essays in the Rhetoric of Contemporary Criticism*, 2nd ed., intro. Wlad Godzich (Minneapolis: U of Minnesota P, 1983), 8.

8. The phrase "mournful iteration" is from Wordsworth's poem "A little onward lend

thy guiding hand" (*PW,* 4:92–94); see Hartman's essay "Words, Wish, Worth," in *UnRW,* 90–119, for a commentary. Yet is it not paradoxical that literary criticism is not to be repeated? One difference between so-called creative and critical acts is that creative acts are, in one sense, iterable performances. To take an example from popular culture: a singer-songwriter creates a Top Ten hit, and when you attend the concert, often named after the song, you expect to hear the performer sing it. Why is it, then, that critics never repeat their work? Alas, we do, all the time; critics get as much mileage as possible from a paper, often giving it several times to (hopefully) different audiences. But the situation changes once the paper has appeared in print. Why do we not read our essays that are already available to the public, in the way that a favorite author would repeat her most popular works or a singer his greatest hits? It makes one wonder who is closer, the poet or the critic, to Keats's figure "forever piping songs forever new." Does the noniterability of the critical act depend on more than style, perhaps on an isolatable gist of argument or "heresy of paraphrase" in a way that literature does not? Why might we have a reading of Hartman's *Akiba's Children* (Emory, VA: Iron Mountain P, 1978), but not of *Easy Pieces* (New York: Columbia U P, 1985)? While I cannot pursue these questions here, I would like—just in case my suggestion about critics repeating their published work is ever taken literally—to put my vote in for Hartman to perform his 1979 essay "Words, Wish, Worth: Wordsworth" (in *Deconstruction and Criticism,* ed. Harold Bloom [New York: Seabury P, 1979], 177–216).

9. "Wordsworth before Heidegger," in *UnRW,* 194. Hartman has written that "one of the highest aims of commentary" is "local illumination of the words of a text together with the foregrounding of a structure that provides a skeleton key for other poems and situates the object of analysis in generic terms" ("The Use and Abuse of Structural Analysis," in *UnRW,* 131).

10. This quotation, attributed to Hartman, is used by Michael Sprinker as the epigraph to his essay "Aesthetic Criticism: Geoffrey Hartman," in *The Yale Critics: Deconstruction in America,* ed. Jonathan Arac, Wlad Godzich, Wallace Martin (Minneapolis: U of Minnesota P, 1983), 43.

11. " 'Timely Utterance' Once More," in *UnRW,* 162.

12. Geoffrey H. Hartman, *Saving the Text: Literature/Derrida/Philosophy* (Baltimore: Johns Hopkins UP, 1981), 121.

13. I adapt three sentences here from my article on Geoffrey H. Hartman in *Encyclopedia of Contemporary Literary Theory: Approaches, Scholars, Terms,* ed. Irena R. Makaryk (Toronto: U of Toronto P, 1993), 354.

14. Geoffrey H. Hartman, *The Unmediated Vision: An Interpretation of Wordsworth, Hopkins, Rilke, and Valéry* (New Haven, CT: Yale UP, 1954), ix; hereafter cited as *UV.*

15. Geoffrey H. Hartman, "The Interpreter: A Self-Analysis," in *The Fate of Reading and Other Essays* (Chicago: U of Chicago P, 1975), 3.

16. Geoffrey H. Hartman, *Minor Prophecies: The Literary Essay in the Culture Wars* (Cambridge, MA: Harvard UP, 1991), 60.

17. This phrasing echoes Hartman in the title essay of *Beyond Formalism:* "Perhaps Wordsworth comes to reveal rather than teach" (49). Hartman has extended his interest in the phenomenon of "culture," in its various social, literary, and academic modes, in *The Fateful Question of Culture* (New York: Columbia UP, 1997).

18. William Wordsworth, *The Prelude: 1799, 1805, 1850,* ed. Jonathan Wordsworth, M. H. Abrams, and Stephen Gill (New York: Norton, 1979), 1.623; hereafter cited as

Prelude, with references to book and line number in the 1850 edition unless otherwise noted. Editorial and manuscript material will be cited as Norton *Prelude*, with page references.

19. William Wordsworth, *The Prose Works of William Wordsworth*, ed. W. J. B. Owen and Jane Worthington Smyser, 3 vols. (Oxford: Clarendon P, 1974), 1:138; hereafter cited as *Prose*.

20. A. Alvarez, ed., *The New Poetry* (Harmondsworth, UK: Penguin, 1962).

21. A. Alvarez, "English Poetry Today," *Commentary* 32.3 (Sept. 1961): 217–23. Alvarez altered the title to "The New Poetry or Beyond the Gentility Principle" for the introduction to his Penguin edition in 1962.

22. I quote from a sentence in the earlier version of Alvarez's essay published in *Commentary* (222). The sentence does not appear in the introduction to the Penguin edition.

23. See lines 65–68 of "Simon Lee" (*PW*, 4:63):

O reader! had you in your mind
Such stores as silent thought can bring,
O gentle reader! you would find
A tale in every thing.

24. *PW*, 2:504. For dating, see Mark L. Reed, *Wordsworth: The Chronology of the Early Years, 1770–1799* (Cambridge, MA: Harvard UP, 1967), 332, and Reed, *Wordsworth: The Chronology of the Middle Years, 1800–1815* (Cambridge, MA: Harvard UP, 1975), 166 n. 36. Hartman's reading of "Nutting" in *Wordsworth's Poetry, 1787–1814* (1964; repr., Cambridge, MA: Harvard UP, 1987), 73–75, while brief, implicitly contains the substance of many later discussions of the poem, a number of which I cite below.

25. E.g., David Perkins, in *Wordsworth and the Poetry of Sincerity* (Cambridge, MA: Harvard UP, 1964), says that "the general themes [of 'Nutting'] are the large concerns of the first two books of *The Prelude*" (184). For a discussion of the *ekphrasis* of the horse in MS. W (Norton *Prelude*, 498), see chap. 7 ("Symptom and Scene in Freud and Wordsworth") in my book *Romantic Aversions: Aftermaths of Classicism in Wordsworth and Coleridge* (Montreal: McGill-Queen's UP, 1999), 115–34.

26. See, e.g., Hartman, *Wordsworth's Poetry*, 73–75, and Frances Ferguson, *Wordsworth: Language as Counter-Spirit* (New Haven, CT: Yale UP, 1977), 70–76.

27. William Wordsworth, *Home at Grasmere*, ed. Beth Darlington (Ithaca, NY: Cornell UP, 1977), 97.

28. Harold Bloom, *The Anxiety of Influence: A Theory of Poetry* (New York: Oxford UP, 1973), 139–55.

29. Roland Barthes, *Empire of Signs*, trans. Richard Howard (New York: Hill & Wang, 1982), 83; italics in original. I am indebted to Tracy Ware of Queen's University, Kingston, for drawing my attention to this remarkable passage in private correspondence and subsequently in his essay "A Note on Roland Barthes and Wordsworth," *Wordsworth Circle* 19 (1988): 108.

30. "Diction and Defense," in *UnRW*, 127.

31. I would add that for Wordsworth the strength of Shakespeare is associated with the genre of the epitaph; his underpresence is a question of linkage between "the power of the man and the power of the monument" (see my *Monumental Writing: Aspects of Rhetoric in Wordsworth's Poetry* [Lincoln: U of Nebraska P, 1988], 144). The epitaphic element in

Wordsworth, so pervasive and so fundamental, is, I think, ultimately derived from Shakespeare. Milton, in other ways a far more obvious influence on Wordsworth, is secondary here. Shakespeare is the monumental poet, literally and figurally, and Wordsworth's epitaphic style, his composition of sonnet sequences, his recurrent tropes of voice and performance, and even his egotistical sublime have their origin in his response to the sweet swan of Avon, not to the lady of Christ's.

32. John Milton, *Complete Poems and Major Prose*, ed. Merritt Y. Hughes (New York: Odyssey, 1957), 728; hereafter cited as Milton.

33. See, e.g., Jonathan Wordsworth, *William Wordsworth: The Borders of Vision* (Oxford: Clarendon P, 1982), 49–50; and Roberts W. French, "Wordsworth's *Paradise Lost:* A Note on 'Nutting,'" *Studies in the Humanities* 5 (1976): 42.

34. A former student of mine, Frances Lister, has also noted an echo of Shakespeare's *Troilus and Cressida:* the boy has "a huge wallet o'er [his] shoulders slung"; Ulysses says, "Time hath, my lord, a wallet at his back, / Wherein he puts alms for oblivion" (3.3.145–46). Lister further observes that these occurrences of the word "wallet" are the only ones in Shakespeare and Wordsworth. In his analysis of Wordsworth's style and prosody, Bruce Bigley, while noting the metaphorical continuity between the stones being "fleeced with moss" and "scattered like a flock of sheep," is reminded of a classical image—"the mad Ajax surrounded by slaughtered sheep" in Sophocles' *Ajax* ("Multiple Voices in 'Nutting': The Urbane Wordsworth," *Philological Quarterly* 70 (1991): 443.

35. Wordsworth, writing to Sara Hutchinson in late February or early March 1801, records some responses to certain poems in the second edition of *Lyrical Ballads*—"For Coleridges [sic] entertainment I send the following harmonies of criticism"—and then goes on to cite reactions to "Nutting" by "Mr C. Wordsworth," who thought it "worth its weight in gold," and by "Mr Stoddart," who "can make neither head nor tail of it" (*The Letters of William and Dorothy Wordsworth*, vol. 1, *The Early Years, 1787–1805*, ed. Ernest de Selincourt, 2nd ed. rev. Chester L. Shaver [Oxford: Clarendon P, 1967], 1:319); hereafter cited as *Early Years.*

36. The motif of rising up in Wordsworth usually indicates a sublime or imaginative moment. First "the hazels rose / Tall and erect"; then the speaker says, "up I rose." In the note to Isabella Fenwick, Wordsworth says that "these verses arose out of the remembrance of feelings I had often had when a boy" (*PW,* 2:504).

37. It will be apparent to any reader of Hartman that by using "apocalypse" and "akedah" I am invoking terms that Hartman uses in *Wordsworth's Poetry,* passim.

38. Most critics have had something to say about the sexual imagery and rhetoric in "Nutting": see, e.g., David Ferry, who calls Wordsworth a "libertine" and "a sort of rapist and voluptuary in nature" in *The Limits of Mortality: An Essay on Wordsworth's Major Poems* (Middletown, CT: Wesleyan UP, 1959), 23, 25; Heather Glen likewise calls the boy a "voluptuary" and describes his excitement as "tumescent" in *Vision and Disenchantment: Blake's* Songs *and Wordsworth's* Lyrical Ballads (Cambridge: Cambridge UP, 1983), 272, 275, while Jonathan Wordsworth explicitly describes the boy's actions as "rape" (*Borders of Vision,* 48). Compare Frederick Garber in *Wordsworth and the Poetry of Encounter* (Urbana: U of Illinois P, 1971), 19; M. W. Rowe in "The Underthought in Wordsworth's 'Nutting,'" *English* 44 (1995): 20–21; and G. Kim Blank in *Wordsworth's Influence on Shelley: A Study of Poetic Authority* (New York: St. Martin's, 1988), 164, and Blank, *Wordsworth and Feeling: The Poetry of an Adult Child* (Madison, NJ: Fairleigh Dickinson UP, 1995), 163–66. In *Acts of Inclusion: Studies Bearing on an Elementary Theory of Romanticism* (New Haven,

CT: Yale UP, 1979), Michael G. Cooke speaks of "the idiom of a rape" (139), while Leslie Brisman, reading the poem as a scene of "oedipal fantasy" (cf. Wallace W. Douglas, *Wordsworth: The Construction of a Personality* [Kent, Ohio: Kent State UP, 1968], 76–84), terms the episode a "little rape" (*Romantic Origins* [Ithaca, NY: Cornell UP, 1978], 300, 298).

Other critics have explored the related issue of gender (through the Lucy figure) in the poem: see Marlon B. Ross, "Naturalizing Gender: Woman's Place in Wordsworth's Ideological Landscape," *ELH* 53 (1986): 391–410; Jonathan Arac, *Critical Genealogies: Historical Situations for Postmodern Literary Studies* (New York: Columbia UP, 1987), 34–49; Mary Jacobus, *Romanticism, Writing, and Sexual Difference* (Oxford: Clarendon P, 1989), 254–57; Margaret Homans, *Women Writers and Poetic Identity: Dorothy Wordsworth, Emily Brontë, and Emily Dickinson* (Princeton, NJ: Princeton UP, 1980), 50–54, and "Eliot, Wordsworth, and the Scenes of the Sisters' Instruction," *Critical Inquiry* 8 (1981): 223–24; Rachel Crawford, "The Structure of the Sororal in Wordsworth's 'Nutting,'" *Studies in Romanticism* 31 (1992): 197–211; Cooke, *Acts of Inclusion*, 138; Richard Bourke, *Romantic Discourse and Political Modernity: Wordsworth, the Intellectual and Cultural Critique* (New York: Harvester Wheatsheaf, 1993), 173–97; Gregory Jones, "'Rude Intercourse': Uncensoring Wordsworth's 'Nutting,'" *Studies in Romanticism* 35 (1996): 219–22; Susan J. Wolfson, "The Gatherings of 'Nutting': Reading the Cornell *Lyrical Ballads*," *Review* 17 (1995): 19–30; and Douglass H. Thomson, "Wordsworth's Lucy of 'Nutting,'" *Studies in Romanticism* 18 (1979): 287–98, which I also cite below.

39. Sigmund Freud, *The Standard Edition of the Complete Psychological Works of Sigmund Freud*, trans. and ed. James Strachey, 24 vols. (London: Hogarth, 1953–76), 7:150; hereafter cited as *SE*.

40. The term *Nachträglichkeit* occurs throughout Freud's writings. See, e.g., *SE*, 1:233, 356–59. See also the discussion of "deferred action" in J. LaPlanche and J.-B. Pontalis, *The Language of Psychoanalysis*, intro. Daniel LaGache, trans. Donald Nicholson-Smith (London: Hogarth, 1973), 111–14.

41. I take this version, found in Dove Cottage MS. 15, from Stephen Maxfield Parrish, *The Art of the Lyrical Ballads* (Cambridge, MA: Harvard UP, 1973), 30. For a detailed history of "Nutting" manuscripts, with photographs and transcriptions, see *Lyrical Ballads and Other Poems, 1797–1800*, ed. James Butler and Karen Green (Ithaca, NY: Cornell UP, 1992), esp. 554–55. A possibly related fragment is found in MS JJ:

> Then dearest maiden on whose lap I rest
> My head do not deem that these
> Are idle sympathies—

See William Wordsworth, *The Prelude, 1798–1799*, ed. Stephen Parrish (Ithaca, NY: Cornell UP, 1977), 78–79, for photographic copy and transcription. Even in this brief fragment, one hears a Shakespearean overtone of Hamlet's "country matters" dialogue with Ophelia—"I mean, my head upon your lap" (3.2.109). Interestingly, Cooke hears a similar echo in the published poem: "But if the 'cheek on . . . green stones . . . fleeced with moss' suggests Hamlet's 'head in the lap' and the *mons veneris*, the fleece also anticipates a scene of pastoral innocence" (*Acts of Inclusion*, 268 n. 31).

42. See, in particular, Hartman's two essays "Wordsworth, Inscriptions, and Romantic Nature Poetry" (*Beyond Formalism*, 206–30) and "Romantic Poetry and the Genius Loci" (311–36). Perkins says that "the last three lines [of 'Nutting'] are a mistake" because of

Wordsworth's "imperious temptation to find a moral in his experience and to state it" (*Poetry of Sincerity*, 185, 186). Marjorie Levinson echoes Perkins in her contention that "as the culmination of a syllogistic structure . . . the lines *are* a mistake" (*The Romantic Fragment Poem: A Critique of a Form* [Chapel Hill: U of North Carolina P, 1986], 64). But on the figure of "genius," as both poetic quality and nature-spirit, it is worth recalling John Wordsworth's letter of February 25–26, 1801, to Mary Hutchinson: "Wm says that the nutting and Joanna shew the greatest genious of any poems in the 2d Vol" of the 1800 *Lyrical Ballads* (*The Letters of John Wordsworth*, ed. Carl H. Ketcham [Ithaca, NY: Cornell UP, 1969], 96).

43. In the fragmentary version of "Nutting" found in Wordsworth's letter to Coleridge on December 14 or 21, 1798, the text is more explicit in referring to the "spirits." This version reads: "They led me, and I followed in their steps. . . . They led me far, / Those guardian spirits, into some dear nook" (*Early Years*, 241). In this context, Alan Grob has a strong reading, contra Perkins and Ferry, arguing that nature, "far from being a passive victim in this tale of mutilation, knowingly and lovingly leads the child to her quiet bower to receive his merciless ravage"—with a determination "to make a moral agent of this passionate child" ("Wordsworth's *Nutting*," *Journal of English and Germanic Philology* 61 [1962]: 827).

44. *Paradise Lost*, 9.663. As an aside, it should be noted that the prohibition against touching the tree of the knowledge of good and evil, as opposed to eating of it, is not mentioned by God in either Genesis or *Paradise Lost;* it comes from Eve, Adam, and the narrator (see Gen. 3.3, and *PL*, 7.46, 9.651, 663, 925).

45. For the sense of touch in Wordsworth and its relation to "psychoesthetic" or psychoanalytic criticism, see Hartman's essay "A Touching Compulsion," in *UnRW*, 18–30.

46. See Geoffrey H. Hartman, "The Use and Abuse of Structural Analysis," in *UnRW*, 129–51. On the tradition of poetic trees, see Albert Russell Ascoli, *Ariosto's Bitter Harmony: Crisis and Evasion in the Italian Renaissance* (Princeton, NJ: Princeton UP, 1987), 157–61. For other talking trees in Wordsworth, see, e.g., "The Oak and the Broom," in which the oracular tradition of a prophetic, talking oak is ironically undercut by a smaller, weaker bush (*PW*, 2:130–34). Arac mounts a challenging reading, opposed to Hartman's, which attempts to define Wordsworth's "modernity"—that is, the way that Wordsworth "rejected both poetic tradition and the social status with which it had come to be associated" (*Critical Genealogies*, 48). As I hear it, however, "Nutting" seems to invoke mutely these very things: the topos of gentleness looks before and after, toward both poetic tradition and social status. Cf. Charles Altieri, on the interpretive aspects of the unconscious as well as social modes of "spirit" in the poem: "There is a spirit in these woods, but its meaning and force are reserved for those who can learn to read it as the poem does" ("Wordsworth and the Options for Contemporary American Poetry," *The Romantics and Us*, ed. Gene W. Ruoff [New Brunswick, NJ: Rutgers UP, 1990], 190).

47. See *Vergil's* Aeneid, *Books I–VI*, ed. Clyde Pharr (1930; rev. ed., Boston: Heath, 1964), 6.441; and *As You Like It*, 3.2; see also my *Monumental Writing*, 72–99, on the topos of the *liber naturae* in Wordsworth. The intersection of poetry and trees also suggests, distantly, the topos of the suspended musical instrument, as in Wordsworth's "Vernal Ode" of 1817: "While thy tired lute hangs on the hawthorn-tree" (*PW*, 2:311).

48. For Hartman's comments on the presence of classical literature in Wordsworth's poetry, see "'Timely Utterance' Once More," which argues that "the theme of lost Hellenic grace or harmony [in Wordsworth] is not relevant except as it is also more than

Hellenic and recalls the 'echo' formula of a poetry at once pastoral and elegiac" (*UnRW*, 155); "Blessing the Torrent," which states that "in Wordsworth's style, early or late, the fallen sublimity of classicizing or poetic diction blends with the naturalism of elemental speech-acts" (*UnRW*, 87); and "Words, Wish, Worth," in which Hartman comments at length on Wordsworth's "regression, after 1801, to the Classics" (*UnRW*, 93)—a movement largely ignored by critics. As the present essay demonstrates, I am inclined to suggest an earlier date for Wordsworth's turn or return to classicism—indeed, back to the very beginning of his "Romantic" emergence in *Lyrical Ballads*. For an older view of classical influences in Wordsworth's poetry, see Douglas Bush, "Wordsworth and the Classics," *University of Toronto Quarterly* 2 (1933): 359–79. For Ariel in the "cloven pine," see Shakespeare's *Tempest* (1.2.250–99). As a relevant gloss on my reading of the spirit in the wood, I note Dorothy Wordsworth's reaction in 1805 to Sir Michael Fleming's proposal to cut down the trees on his property: "One who could do this wants a sense which others have. To him there is no 'Spirit in the Wood' " (*Early Years*, 638).

49. R. D. Havens's study *The Mind of a Poet: A Study of Wordsworth's Thought*, 2 vols. (Baltimore: Johns Hopkins P, 1941), while outdated in some aspects, is useful for the way it raises certain issues now obscured or forgotten, yet still haunting Wordsworth's poetry, even from the far side of theory today. In discussing "Nutting," for example, Havens sees Wordsworth's MS. reference to "those guardian spirits" who led him to the hazel bower as having "but one explanation: animism, the belief in spiritual beings who, like the dryads and nymphs of classical mythology, are associated with certain places, together with the belief in the possession of individual consciousness by each animate and perhaps each inanimate object. Such beliefs are universal and potent among primitive peoples. . . . Wordsworth is unusual in avowing them" (1:76). While I believe that Havens is on the right track here, I feel that he calls off the investigation a bit early, as we see a couple of pages later: "But any attempt to seek a literary source for Wordsworth's animism or to trace it to influences exerted on him after his return from France involves a fundamental misconception. It is as if one should attribute his mystic experiences to the reading of Plotinus or his love of nature to the reading of Thomson. Such things he did not learn from books" (1:78–79). Havens is right, in one sense: Wordsworth did not "learn" these feelings from books (though another "text," the *liber naturae*, was certainly instructive); rather, once the feelings sought to express themselves in answerable poetic forms and genres, there was available to him an entire literary tradition, as I shall demonstrate. Precisely how Wordsworth taps into and yet distances himself from that tradition is part of the question at hand.

50. James George Frazer, *The Golden Bough: A Study in Magic and Religion* (1913), 13 vols. (London: Macmillan, 1990). Turner's painting *The Golden Bough* was exhibited in 1834, although Turner had completed paintings on the subject as early as 1798 in his *Aeneas and the Sibyl, Lake Avernus*; his painting *Lake Nemi* dates from ca. 1828. See Martin Butlin and Evelyn Joll, *The Paintings of J. M. W. Turner*, 2 vols. (texts and plates) (New Haven, CT: Yale UP, 1977), plates: 214, 300, 334 (text: 121–22, 161, 186–87). Wordsworth compares Loughrigg Tarn to Lake Nemi in a couple of places; see the 1811 "Epistle to Sir George Howland Beaumont" (164–70; *PW*, 4:147) and the note to "Upon Perusing the Foregoing Epistle Thirty Years after Its Composition" (*PW*, 4:151). Compare Frazer's chapters on "The King of the Wood," "The Worship of Trees," "Relics of Tree-Worship in Modern Europe," and "The Worship of the Oak" in volumes 1 and 2. Of particular interest are Frazer's comments on trees "that bleed and utter cries of pain or indignation

when they are hacked or burned" (2:18). For Maybush and Maypole references in Wordsworth, see *The Prelude*, 8.128–63. While reading Wordsworth with Frazer turns up certain similarities—e.g., it offers to make the boy in "Nutting" into the ancient figure who sallies out to break off a branch from the sacred tree at Nemi, slay the rival priest, and become King of the Wood or *Rex Nemorensis* (Frazer, 1:11)—my own path takes a more specifically literary turn. Still, see James W. Pipkin, "Wordsworth's 'Nutting' and Rites of Initiation," *Interpretations: Studies in Language and Literature* 10 (1978) for the view that " 'Nutting' resembles the rite of initiation in picturing an encounter with the sacred that changes the young Wordsworth's fundamental mode of being" (11). Also see the sensitive "chthonic" reading by Anthony John Harding in *The Reception of Myth in English Romanticism* (Columbia: U of Missouri P, 1995), 108, especially the way that he relates metaphor and disguise in Wordsworth's boy to "the shaman who wears a caribou hide to attract, befriend, and control the spirits of the forest" (104).

51. Evelyn, *Sylva*, 5th ed. (London: J. Walthol et al., 1729), 280–318, 300, 301. Robert Woof, in editing T. W. Thompson, *Wordsworth's Hawkshead* (London: Oxford UP, 1970), adds in Appendix 4 the text of a reminiscence in which the son of Thomas Bowman, one of Wordsworth's headmasters, recounts his father's description of the young Wordsworth's reading habits, which included texts by Evelyn and Ovid: "He was one of the very few boys, who used to read the old books in the School Library, George Sandys' 'Travels in the East' and his Ovid's 'Metamorphoses', Fox's [sic] 'Book of Martyrs' & Evelyn's 'Forest Trees'. There were others, but these I remember" (344 and 344 n. 1). See also Duncan Wu, *Wordsworth's Reading, 1770–1799* (Cambridge: Cambridge UP, 1993), 56, 163, for agreement. In a letter to the *Morning Post* in 1844 on the Kendal and Windermere Railway, Wordsworth again speaks of Evelyn: "The accomplished Evelyn, giving an account of his journey from Italy through the Alps, dilates upon the terrible, the melancholy, and the uncomfortable; but, till he comes to the fruitful country in the neighbourhood of Geneva, not a syllable of delight or praise" (3:341–42). Wordsworth's point in referring to Evelyn's *Diary* of his travels is to show how "the relish for choice and picturesque natural scenery . . . is quite of recent origin" (*Prose*, 3:341). William Gilpin, in his 1791 *Remarks on Forest Scenery*, frequently cites Evelyn's *Sylva*, and also discusses the sacredness of groves, quoting a passage from Virgil's *Aeneid*, book 8, as an example of the *templum nemorale*, or "haunt of Gods" (*Remarks on Forest Scenery and Other Woodland Views (Relative Chiefly to Picturesque Beauty)* [1791], intro. Sutherland Lyall [Richmond, UK: Richmond Publishing, 1973], 1:205–7). Compare Susan Eilenberg's application of the ancient belief that "the ground was haunted and property was sacred" to a reading of Wordsworth's "place-naming poems" as "modern equivalents of these classical constructions" (*Strange Power of Speech: Wordsworth, Coleridge, and Literary Possession* [New York: Oxford UP, 1992], 69). For the role of prosopopoeia in allegories of writing and reading the book of nature, see Gilpin, 1:44, 103–5. For Tasso's account of Rinaldo in the enchanted forest and how he cut down the walnut/myrtle tree to break the spell, see *Godfrey of Bulloigne. A Critical Edition of Edward Fairfax's Translation of Tasso's* Gerusalemme Liberata, ed. Kathleen M. Lea and T. M. Gang (Oxford: Clarendon P, 1981), Canto 18.34–38.

52. Robert Frost, *Complete Poems of Robert Frost* (London: Jonathan Cape, 1951), 361.

53. See "Ode to Psyche" in John Keats, *Complete Poems*, ed. Jack Stillinger (Cambridge, MA: Harvard UP, 1982), 276, and Milton's "On the Morning of Christ's Nativity": "The Oracles are dumb" (Milton 48). In "Use and Abuse" Hartman comments on the "poetic tradition in which a tree or long-lived though mute object is made to speak:

perhaps an oracular oak, perhaps a ruined castle, perhaps a genius loci" (*UnRW*, 132). For Hartman's reference to Cowper's "Yardley Oak," which he calls "the nearest analogue" to Wordsworth's "Yew-Trees," see "Use and Abuse" (*UnRW*, 150).

54. William Cowper, "Yardley Oak," *The New Oxford Book of Eighteenth Century Verse*, ed. Roger Lonsdale (Oxford: Oxford UP, 1984), 608–12, lines 40–43. For another of these "kindred trees / Oracular," compare Wordsworth's address to "The Oak of Guernica" (*PW*, 3:136): "Oak of Guernica! Tree of holier power / Than that which in Dodona did enshrine / (So faith too fondly deemed) a voice divine / Heard from the depths of its aërial bower— / How canst thou flourish at this blighting hour?" (*PW*, 3:136). Wordsworth's demythologizing of the oldest oracle in Greece and his subtle reanimating of nature through the prosopopoeia implicit in an address to a tree clearly speak to the issue of imaginative metamorphosis in "Nutting."

55. De Selincourt thinks that Wordsworth's translation of Virgil's *Aeneid* belongs to 1823–24, though he also suggests that parts of the translation may have been undertaken as early as 1819 (*PW*, 4:469–71). Bruce E. Graver, in his edition *Translations of Chaucer and Virgil* (Ithaca, NY: Cornell UP, 1998), corrects earlier misdatings of the text, and convincingly demonstrates that Wordsworth's translation belongs to 1823–24.

56. Apropos of my claim for a "source" in *The Aeneid*, R. D. Williams states that "the grim and weird story of Polydorus and the drops of blood trickling from the myrtle shoots is not found in Classical literature before Virgil" (Virgil, *Aeneidos: Liber Tertius*, ed. R. D. Williams [Oxford: Clarendon P, 1962], 57). The relevant lines from Virgil read: "*Quid miserum, Aenea, laceras? iam parce sepulto, / parce pias scelerare manus*" (26). "*Pius*" is, of course, the epithet repeatedly applied to Aeneas. In the context of the Wordsworthian revisions, compare also Shakespeare's *Richard III*, in which Anne claims that "dead Henry's wounds / Open their congealed mouths and bleed afresh" in the presence of the murderer Richard (1.2.55–56). A wound becomes a mouth; voice, blood; and expression, effusion.

57. Edmund Spenser, *The Faerie Queene*, ed. Thomas P. Roche Jr., with the assistance of C. Patrick O'Donnell Jr. (New Haven, CT: Yale UP, 1981), 1.2.28–45. Spenser is also evoked in Wordsworth's phrase "milk-white cluster," which Wordsworth retained in "Nutting" from 1800–1836 (see *PW*, 2:211) but later changed to "tempting clusters," echoing Milton. He uses the phrase "milk-white" again in "Personal Talk" in a specifically Spenserian context: "heavenly Una with her milk-white Lamb" (*PW*, 4:74). In *The Prelude*, Spenser is called "gentle": "And that gentle Bard, / Chosen by the Muses for their Page of State— / Sweet Spenser" (3.281–83). Theresa M. Kelley sees similarities between the boy of "Nutting" and the allegorical figure of Proteus in Spenser's *Faerie Queene*, book 3 ("Proteus and Romantic Allegory," *ELH* 49 [1982]: 623–52).

58. Compare Wordsworth's "The Tuft of Primroses": " 'Stay your impious hand' " (*PW*, 5:361).

59. Dante Alighieri, *The Divine Comedy*, trans. Charles S. Singleton (Princeton, NJ: Princeton UP, 1970).

60. Leo Spitzer, "Speech and Language in *Inferno* 13," *Italica* 19 (1942): 88 n. 7.

61. E.g., "Wordsworth and Goethe in Literary History," in *UnRW*, 61.

62. Ovid has several references to the transformation of individuals into trees, including Daphne (1.518–57); Phaethon's sisters (2.330–66); the nymph in the oak tree sacred to Ceres (8.739–78); Dryope (9.357–97); and also Polydorus, mentioned in passing (13.618–58). See *The Metamorphoses of Ovid*, trans. Mary M. Innes (Harmondsworth, UK: Penguin, 1955). In other analogues, Tennyson curiously reworks the Arthurian legend of Merlin's

imprisonment by Vivien under a stone, causing Merlin to be confined in an oak tree (*The Works of Alfred, Lord Tennyson* [London: Macmillan, 1894], 395). In one modern retelling of the Orfeo story, Orfeo's breaking of a branch causes his wife pain and results in her being taken to the underworld (see *The Minstrel Knight,* retold by Constance Hieatt, illus. James Barkley [New York: Crowell, 1974]). Even Dorothy, in *The Wizard of Oz,* gets into trouble when she plucks an apple from the animated trees on the yellow brick road! For the relevant passages in Tasso's *Gerusalemme Liberata,* I turn, curiously, to Freud, who thought enough of the episode of Tancred's double slaughter of Clorinda in Cantos 12.64–67 and 13.38–45 to refer to it at some length in *Beyond the Pleasure Principle* in the context of the "compulsion to repeat." Freud's summary is worth quoting in full:

> The most moving poetic picture of a fate such as this [i.e., of the "perpetual recurrence of the same thing"] is given by Tasso in his romantic epic *Gerusalemme Liberata.* Its hero, Tancred, unwittingly kills his beloved Clorinda in a duel while she is disguised in the armour of an enemy knight. After her burial he makes his way into a strange magic forest which strikes the Crusaders' army with terror. He slashes with his sword at a tall tree; but blood streams from the cut and the voice of Clorinda, whose soul is imprisoned in the tree, is heard complaining that he has wounded his beloved once again.
>
> If we take into account observations such as these, based upon behaviour in the transference and upon the life-histories of men and women, we shall find courage to assume that there really does exist in the mind a compulsion to repeat which overrides the pleasure principle. (*SE,* 18:22)

See the translation of Tasso in *Godfrey of Bulloigne,* 378–79 and 398–400. Wordsworth knew his Tasso, as we can see from his reference to Erminia in *The Prelude,* where she is mentioned in the same breath as Ariosto's Angelica (9.451–3). I return to Wordsworth's Italian influences later.

63. Harold Bloom, *A Map of Misreading* (New York: Oxford UP, 1975), 17.

64. Ludovico Ariosto, *Orlando Furioso,* trans. William Stewart Rose, ed. Stewart A. Baker and A. Bartlett Giamatti (Indianapolis, IN: Bobbs-Merrill, 1968).

65. See Ben Ross Schneider Jr., *Wordsworth's Cambridge Education* (Cambridge: Cambridge UP, 1957), 103, for the claim that a pocket copy of *Orlando Furioso* was Wordsworth's "companion" in the summer of 1790; and Wordsworth's letter of October 17 and 24, 1805, to Sir George Beaumont (*Early Years,* 628). With the exception of a verse translation of the *Orlando Furioso,* Canto 1.5–14, dating from November 1802 (see *PW,* 4:473, and William Wordsworth, *Poems in Two Volumes and Other Poems, 1800–1807,* ed. Jared Curtis [Ithaca, NY: Cornell UP, 1983], 594–97), Wordsworth's later translations of Ariosto "have not survived" (*Early Years,* 628 n. 2). For further information about Wordsworth's reading and translation of Ariosto, see Reed, *Chronology of the Early Years,* 23, 77, 155, 303–4, 325, and 346; and Reed, *Chronology of the Middle Years,* 33, 201, 376. Some of these instances are summarized in Wu, *Wordsworth's Reading,* (7). Wordsworth's brother Richard writes May 23, 1794: "I have forwarded the Italian Gram., Tasso and Ariosto for you at Keswick" (*Early Years,* 120 n. 4). Wordsworth writes to William Mathews on March 21, 1796: "My Sister would be very glad of your assistance in her Italian studies. She has already gone through half of Davila, and yesterday we began Ariosto" (170). Recall also that at the time of the composition of "Nutting" in late 1798 Wordsworth was beginning *The Prelude,* which in its earliest drafts in MS. JJ opens with the famous question "Was it for this?"—a question that,

as correspondence in the *Times Literary Supplement* in 1975 showed, has a precedent in Virgil, *Aeneid*, 2.664–65 ("*Hoc erat . . . quod me . . . / eripis*": "Was it for this that you save(d) me. . . ?" [Pharr, *Vergil's* Aeneid, 131–32]); and Ariosto's *Orlando Furioso*, Canto 7.56–59. See Jonathan Wordsworth, " 'The Prelude' and Its Echoes," *Times Literary Supplement* 6 (June 1975): 627; Howard Erskine-Hill, " 'The Prelude' and Its Echoes," *Times Literary Supplement* 26 (Sept. 1975): 1094; and esp. John A. Hodgson, " 'Was It for This. . . ?': Wordsworth's Virgilian Questionings," *Texas Studies in Literature and Language* 33 (1991): 125–36, who thoroughly explicates the passage and its Wordsworthian adaptation. The connection between "Nutting" and *The Prelude* was made by Wordsworth himself in the Fenwick note, though the Ariosto link naturally remains unstated.

66. One critic who does refer to an Ariosto connection in a footnote is Douglass H. Thomson (see n. 38), though he does not mention Astolpho's metamorphosis. Thomson, however, comments at greater length on the presence of Shakespeare: the character of Orlando in *As You Like It* "furnishes a crucial analogue to the Lucy" of the manuscript fragment (291). Jean H. Hagstrum, discussing the ravaged grove of "Nutting" in *The Romantic Body: Love and Sexuality in Keats, Wordsworth, and Blake* (Knoxville: U of Tennessee P, 1985), writes that "literary context of sorts is provided by the attack on the trees of the forest by the loved-crazed Orlando of Ariosto's epic, but the differences outweigh the similarities" (95). I would argue that Shakespeare overlaps here with Ariosto not only in the connection with the name Orlando and the convention of reading and writing love poetry in trees, as in *As You Like It*, 3.2, but also in the Shakespeare-Ariosto connection of *The Taming of the Shrew* and *I Suppositi.* Thomson acutely notes that Wordsworth's consciously allusive epithets describing Lucy as " 'inland bred' " and having " 'some nurture' " are direct quotations from *As You Like It* (2.7.96–97). He also marks (290–91) the Shakespearean play on "gentleness" in *As You Like It:* "Your gentleness shall force / More than your force move us to gentleness" (2.7.101–2), which I take to be an example of antimetabole. More recently, Susan J. Wolfson has briefly noted the reference to Astolpho in "Gatherings of 'Nutting'," 27; Gregory Jones has followed suit in developing the Ariosto and Shakespeare links, though he does not refer to Thomson's and Hagstrum's earlier work or the Astolpho allusion. On the Ariosto-Virgil connection, see A. Bartlett Giamatti, *The Earthly Paradise and the Renaissance Epic* (Princeton, NJ: Princeton UP, 1966), who notes the allusion to Aeneas in Ariosto's use of the word "*pio*" in Astolpho's words to Rogero: "*Se tu sei cortese e pio*" (142–43).

67. My argument, which I can only sketch out here, is based on an observation in Reed's *Chronology of the Early Years:* in the Christabel Notebook, Reed writes, "A small amount of messy draft possibly based on Ariosto and a few lines of draft toward *The Danish Boy* (before 15 Oct. 1800; see Hale White 25–26; *STCL*, 1:637) conclude the book" (325). Reed states that this manuscript material must date from between October 6, 1798, and October 1800 (325). In his "Addenda and Corrigenda" in *Chronology of the Middle Years*, Reed writes that this draft " 'possibly from Ariosto' was probably toward W's 'ballad poem never written' for which *The Danish Boy* was to have served as a prelude (see *Danish Boy* IF note). (Information from Professor Paul Betz.)" (715). The Isabella Fenwick note to "The Danish Boy" reads: "Written in Germany 1799. It was entirely a fancy, but intended as a prelude to a ballad poem never written" (*PW*, 2:493). I am prepared to speculate that around the time that Wordsworth was composing "Nutting," he was rereading Ariosto's *Orlando Furioso* and specifically the Astolpho episode. The Virgilian, Dantean, and other contexts are, I believe, filtered through Ariosto.

68. This Ariosto reference in the preface to *The Borderers* is particularly interesting because it dates from around the year or so before the composition of "Nutting" in 1798. Wordsworth certainly seems to have had Ariosto on his mind during this period. I draw attention to a minor variant in Wordsworth's text, though one with implications for my reading: the Owen and Smyser *Prose* edition reads "the groves that *should* shelter him" (1:77), not "that *would* shelter him," as in Hartman's version (my emphasis in both cases). Robert Osborn, in his edition of *The Borderers* (Ithaca, NY: Cornell UP, 1982), also has "should" (63). Wordsworth is referring to Cantos 23.134–36 and 24.4 of *Orlando Furioso.*

69. Douglass H. Thomson has a fine reading of the early manuscript versions of "Nutting" in relation to the career of the figure "Lucy" in Wordsworth's poetry. He also notes that "the issue of whether or not the 'conclusion' [of "Nutting"] really did predate the 'beginning' of the poem (as Dorothy's letter suggests) involves a complicated bibliographical argument" (292).

THIRTEEN: "Reading After": The Anxiety of the Writing Subject

1. Roland Barthes, "The Death of the Author," in *Modern Criticism and Theory: A Reader*, ed. David Lodge (London: Longman, 1988), 172.

2. See Shelley, "Mont Blanc," 6. References are to the Norton Critical Edition, *Shelley's Poetry and Prose*, ed. Donald H. Reiman and Sharon B. Powers (New York: Norton, 1977).

3. See John Hollander, *The Figure of Echo: A Mode of Allusion in Milton and After* (Berkeley: U of California P, 1981).

4. Jacques Derrida, "Signature Event Context," *Margins of Philosophy*, trans. Alan Bass (Brighton, UK: Harvester, 1986), 313.

5. See the conclusion to "The Interpreter: A Self-Analysis," in Geoffrey H. Hartman, *The Fate of Reading and Other Essays* (Chicago: U of Chicago P, 1975), 19; hereafter cited as *FR.*

6. Geoffrey H. Hartman, *Criticism in the Wilderness: The Study of Literature Today* (New Haven, CT: Yale UP, 1980), 223; hereafter cited as *CW.*

7. See Wordsworth, "Lines written a few miles above Tintern Abbey," 107. References are to the Oxford Authors edition, *William Wordsworth*, ed. Stephen Gill (Oxford: Oxford UP, 1984).

8. See Coleridge, "Frost at Midnight," 64. References are to *The Complete Poetical Works of Samuel Taylor Coleridge*, ed. Ernest Hartley Coleridge, 2 vols. (Oxford: Clarendon P, 1912).

9. Jerome McGann, *The Romantic Ideology: A Critical Investigation* (Chicago: U of Chicago P, 1983).

10. See esp. *FR*, 289–92, and n. 6 above.

11. G. Douglas Atkins, *Geoffrey Hartman: Criticism as Answerable Style* (London: Routledge, 1990); Donald G. Marshall, "Secondary Literature: Geoffrey Hartman, Wordsworth, and the Interpretation of Modernity," in *Romantic Revolutions: Criticism and Theory*, ed. Kenneth R. Johnston, Gilbert Caihtin, Karen Hanson, and Herbert Marks (Bloomington: Indiana UP, 1990), 78–97.

12. The two words are etymologically connected, both deriving from Hermes, the Greek name for the messenger of the Gods. For the rise of hermeneutics, see Hans-Georg Gadamer, *Truth and Method*, 2nd rev. ed., ed. Joel Weinsheimer and Donald G. Marshall (London: Sheed & Ward, 1975). For the hermetic aspects of hermeneutics, see Umberto

Eco's discussion of medieval allegory in *The Role of the Reader: Explorations in the Semiotics of Texts* (London: Hutchinson, 1979), 51–52.

13. C. Falconer, *An Essay upon Milton's Imitations of the Ancients in his Paradise Lost. With some observations on Paradise Regain'd* (London, 1741), 61.

14. Edward Young, *Conjectures on Original Composition. In a Letter to the Author of Sir Charles Grandison* (London, 1759), 23.

15. "Annotations to *The Work of Sir Joshua Reynolds*," in *The Complete Writings of William Blake*, ed. Geoffrey Keynes (London: Oxford UP, 1966), 469.

16. Edmund Burke, *Reflections on the Revolution in France*, ed. Conor Cruise O'Brien (Harmondsworth, UK: Penguin, 1968), 119–20.

17. Thomas Paine, *The Rights of Man*, pt. 1, in *The Thomas Paine Reader*, ed. Michael Foot and Isaac Kramnick (Harmondsworth, UK: Penguin, 1987), 215.

18. See Harold Bloom, *The Anxiety of Influence: A Theory of Poetry* (London: Oxford UP, 1973).

19. "Bloom's is a dissident tradition, which he traces back largely to the radical Protestant stirrings of the English Civil War, and which then reaches forward to the young romantics and their thwarted hopes for the French Revolution" (Christopher Norris, *Deconstruction: Theory and Practice* [London: Methuen, 1982], 117).

20. "A Defense of Poetry" (Reiman and Powers, *Shelley's Poetry and Prose*), 493. For a parallel in Hartman's own writing, consider the following sentence: "The presence of greatness is what matters, a beforeness which makes readers, like poets, see for a moment nothing but one master-spirit" ("War in Heaven: A Review of Harold Bloom's *The Anxiety of Influence: A Theory of Poetry*"), in *FR*, 51.

21. Michel Foucault, "What Is an Author?" in Lodge, *Modern Criticism and Theory*, 196–210.

22. For the concept of the divided subject, see R. D. Laing, *The Divided Self: An Existential Study in Sanity and Madness* (Harmondsworth, UK: Penguin, 1959).

23. "Poetic anxiety implores the Muse for aid in divination, which means to foretell and put off as long as possible the poet's own death. . . . The poet of any guilt culture whatsoever cannot initiate himself into a fresh chaos; he is compelled to accept a lack of priority in creation, which means he must accept also a failure in divination, as the first of many little deaths that prophesy a final and total extinction" (Bloom, *Anxiety*, 61).

24. I use "antithetical" in the Bloomian sense, to refer to the active misreading by one poet of a precursor's work.

25. Kant's account of the sublime is bipartite: there is an initial stage of bewilderment or perplexity, as the mind is overcome by the grandeur of what it contemplates, and this is followed by a stage of recovery, as the mind realizes its own potential for grasping supersensible ideas. See *The Critique of Judgment*, trans. J. C. Meredith (1952; repr., Oxford: Oxford UP, 1978), 100.

26. "Battle between strong equals, father and son as mighty opposites, Laius and Oedipus at the crossroads; only this is my subject here" (Bloom, *Anxiety*, 11).

27. "Rather than submit to . . . 'openness' as an inescapable element of artistic interpretation, [the modern artist] subsumes it into a positive aspect of his production, recasting it so as to expose it to the maximum possible 'opening' " (Eco, *Role of the Reader*, 50).

28. See Tillotama Rajan, *The Supplement of Reading: Figures of Understanding in Romantic Theory and Practice* (Ithaca, NY: Cornell UP, 1990).

29. Jonathan Bate, *Romantic Ecology: Wordsworth and the Environmental Tradition* (London: Routledge, 1991), 107.

30. See Paul de Man, "Shelley Disfigured," in *The Rhetoric of Romanticism* (New York: Columbia UP, 1984), 93–123.

31. As on a number of occasions in *The Prelude*, Wordsworth draws attention to the division between past and present selves, while at the same time acknowledging the extent to which the past is readjusted by the present; see esp. 46–47: "unless I now / Confound my present feelings with the past."

32. Douglas Kneale comes close to suggesting something similar, though in his argument the stress falls on Wordsworth's own "gentleness" as a reader of precursor texts. (See his essay, "Gentle Hearts and Hands: Reading Wordsworth after Geoffrey Hartman," chap. 12 in this volume.)

33. Any allegorization of the poem, including the one I have offered, runs the danger of reductiveness. I am suggesting that Wordsworth's plea for "gentleness" on the reader's part is a warning against excessive closure, and that it exemplifies Eco's claim, cited in note 27, above.

34. A preoccupation with the *genius loci* (and other pre-Enlightenment phenomena) runs through Hartman's work, especially his writing on romanticism.

35. "Introduction," in *The Unremarkable Wordsworth*, foreword by Donald G. Marshall (Minneapolis: U of Minnesota P, 1987), xxvii; hereafter cited as *UnRW*.

36. Wordsworth's attempts to control the reception of his poems were many and various: they range from the careful categorization of texts within volumes (as in the divisions and subdivisions of *Poems, 1815*) to the instruction of individual readers. See, e.g., his response to criticism from Sara Hutchinson of his poem *The Leech-gatherer*: "I will explain to you in prose my feeling in writing that Poem, and you will be better able to judge whether the fault be mine or yours or partly both. . . . A person reading this Poem with feelings like mine will have been awed and controuled. . . . Everything is tedious when one does not read with the feelings of the Author" (*The Letters of William and Dorothy Wordsworth*, ed. Ernest de Selincourt, 2nd ed., rev. Chester L. Shaver, 2 vols. [Oxford: Clarendon P, 1967], 1:366). But Wordsworth depends on his readers honoring their side of a contract with him.

37. "Negative hermeneutics . . . reflects a supersensitiveness or hesitancy akin to thoughtfulness itself. . . . [It] doubts all final solutions, perhaps even any solution at all" (131).

38. Wolfgang Iser, "The Reading Process: A Phenomenological Approach," in Lodge, *Modern Criticism and Theory*, 212.

39. "Part of real understanding . . . is that we regain the concepts of a historical past in such a way that they also include our own comprehension of them. Above I called this 'the fusion of horizons' " (Gadamer, *Truth and Method*, 374).

40. Hans-Georg Gadamer, "On the Problem of Self-Understanding" (1962), *Philosophical Hermeneutics*, trans. and ed. David E. Linge (Berkeley: U of California P, 1976), 54, 55.

41. Wordsworth is by no means consistent on the question of the human mind's relation to nature; contrast, for instance, the implications of "Nutting" with the closing lines of the 1805 *Prelude*. Note also that in *The Prelude*'s "spots of time," Wordsworth presents a sequence of incidents in which a crime of some kind is committed against nature and that these incidents are seen as the source of imaginative nourishment. For further evidence of the poet's ambivalence toward the creative imagination, see Lucy Newlyn, *Paradise Lost and the Romantic Reader* (Oxford: Clarendon P, 1993), 209–13.

42. "Most of my readers will have observed a small water-insect on the surface of rivulets, which throws a cinque-spotted shadow fringed with prismatic colours on the sunny bottom of the brook; and will have noticed how the little animal *wins* its way up against the stream, by alternate pulses of active and passive motion, now resisting the

current, and now yielding to it in order to gather strength and a momentary *fulcrum* for a further propulsion. This is no unapt emblem of the mind's self-experience in the act of thinking" (*Biographia Literaria*, in *The Collected Works of Samuel Taylor Coleridge*, ed. James Engell and W. Jackson Bate [Princeton, NJ: Princeton UP, 1983]), 124.

43. See Wordsworth's discussion of *Resolution and Independence* in the "Preface" to *Poems, 1815:* "The stone is endowed with something of the power of life to approximate it to the sea-beast; and the sea-beast stripped of some of its vital qualities to assimilate it to the stone; which intermediate image is thus treated for the purpose of bringing the original image, that of the stone, to a nearer resemblance to the figure and condition of the aged Man; who is divested of so much of the indications of life and motion as to bring him to the point where the two objects unite and coalesce in just comparison" (*The Prose Works of William Wordsworth*, ed. W. J. B. Owen and Jane Worthington Smyser, 3 vols. [Oxford: Clarendon P, 1974], 3:33).

44. For Hartman's preoccupation with Satan's self-authoring, see, e.g., *FR*, 54, 123.

45. Hartman offers a much darker reading of "The Boy of Winander" in "Wordsworth and Goethe in Literary History," where he writes that "despite nature's generous, wild, even frighteningly deep response to the Boy's call, everything returns to silence. . . . His brief moment of vocal challenge — it cannot even be termed song — proves to be a deceptive mimicry, ending in muteness (*UnRW*, 61).

46. "The Boy of Winander" was originally composed in the first person, probably as an episode in the Two-Part *Prelude* of 1799, but was excluded by Wordsworth for reasons that are not entirely obvious. It was published as a discrete poem in *Lyrical Ballads* (1800), where the third person is introduced; and it appears in Book 5 of *The Prelude* (1805), where it is used to point up the contrast between a rural childhood and an urban one.

47. This, the sixth of Bloom's revisionary ratios, is defined by him as follows: "The later poet . . . holds his own poem so open again to the precursor's work that at first we might believe the wheel has come full circle, and that we are back in the later poet's flooded apprenticeship. . . . But the poem is now *held open* to the precursor, where once it *was* open, and the uncanny effect is that the new poem's achievement makes it seem to us, not as though the precursor were writing it, but as though the later poet himself had written the precursor's characteristic work" (*Anxiety*, 15–16).

48. Geoffrey H. Hartman, *Akiba's Children* (Emory, VA: Iron Mountain P, 1978), unpaginated.

49. Georges Poulet, "Phenomenology of Reading," *New Literary History* 1 (1969): 54.

50. Some of these similarities have been pointed out; see Marshall, foreword to *The Unremarkable Wordsworth*, ix, and Marshall, "Secondary Literature," 87–93.

51. Gadamer's description of the act of understanding corresponds closely to the interaction of boy and owls in "The Boy of Winander": "The understanding of a text has not begun at all as long as the text remains mute. But a text can begin to speak. . . . When it does begin to speak, however, it does not simply speak its word, always the same, in lifeless rigidity, but gives ever new answers to the person who questions it and poses ever new questions to him who answers it. To understand a text is to come to understand oneself in a kind of dialogue" (*Philosophical Hermeneutics*, 57).

FOURTEEN: Daring to Go Wrong

1. Geoffrey H. Hartman, "The Struggle for the Text," in *Midrash and Literature*, ed. Geoffrey H. Hartman and Sanford Budick (New Haven, CT: Yale UP, 1986), 8–9; hereaf-

ter cited as "Struggle." For the idea of criticism "as an extended conversation," see esp. "Tea and Totality," in Hartman, *Minor Prophecies: The Literary Essay in the Culture Wars* (Cambridge, MA: Harvard UP, 1991), 57–73.

2. Geoffrey H. Hartman, "The Voice of the Shuttle: Language from the Point of View of Literature," first published in the *Review of Metaphysics* (1969), reprinted in Hartman, *Beyond Formalism: Literary Essays, 1958–1970* (New Haven, CT: Yale UP, 1970), 351.

3. The King James Bible is cited except as otherwise noted.

4. *The Auroras of Autumn*, sec. 10, in Wallace Stevens, *The Palm at the End of the Mind*, ed. Holly Stevens (New York: Knopf, 1971).

5. Geoffrey H. Hartman, "Jeremiah 20:7–12: A Literary Response," in *The Biblical Mosaic: Changing Perspectives*, ed. Robert Polzin and Eugene Rothman (Philadelphia: Fortress P, 1982), 185.

6. Fragment I QS I.9, cited by O. J. F. Seitz, "Love Your Enemies," *New Testament Studies* 16 (1969): 50. See also W. D. Davies, *The Setting of the Sermon on the Mount* (Atlanta: Scholars P, 1989), 246.

7. The translation is discussed by Davies, *Sermon on the Mount*, 248–49.

8. *Paradise Lost*, 5:855.

9. H. W. Basser, "Midrashic Form in the New Testament: A Study in Jewish Rhetoric of Likes and Opposites," in *Approaches to Ancient Judaism: New Series 3: Historical and Literary Studies*, ed. Jacob Neusner (Atlanta: Scholars P, 1993), 147. Basser cites three previous publications of his as making the same argument: *Interpretation of the Song of Moses* (New York, 1984), 292; "Approaching the Text: The Study of Midrash" in *Methodology in the Academic Teaching of Judaism*, ed. Z. Garber (New York, 1986), 117; and *In the Margins of the Midrash* (Atlanta: Scholars P, 1990), 19.

10. Matthew Black discusses the word-play on *shalom* and *shalem* in *An Aramaic Approach to the Gospels and Acts*, 2nd ed. (Oxford: Clarendon P, 1954), 181.

11. Meir Sternberg, *The Poetics of Biblical Narrative: Ideological Literature and the Drama of Reading* (Bloomington: Indiana UP, 1985), 50. For a model of intolerance, see Sternberg's response to Fewell and Gunn in "Biblical Poetics and Sexual Politics: From Reading to Counterreading," *Journal of Biblical Literature* 111 (1992): 463–88.

12. David Rhoads, "Jesus and the Syrophoenician Woman in Mark: A Narrative-Critical Study," *Journal of the American Academy of Religion* 62 (1994): 360.

13. This is the formulation (but not the opinion) of P. Pokorn'y, "From a Puppy to the Child: Some Problems of Contemporary Biblical Exegesis Demonstrated from Mark 7.24–30/Matt 15.21–8," *New Testament Studies* 41 (1995): 324.

14. *The Gospels in Context: Social and Political History in the Synoptic Tradition*, trans. Linda M. Maloney. (Minneapolis: Fortress P, 1991), 75. Thiessen does not himself wish to claim that Jesus's words actually had this denotation, only that "surrounding this denotative kernel is an associative field conditioned by the historical situation." Like those cited by Pokorn'y, Thiessen can imagine a *logon* that comes not from the mouth of a literary artist but, as it were, out of the historical ground: "Perhaps Jesus . . . was able to make connections with a well-known saying shaped by this situation."

15. "The Realism of Numbers; The Magic of Numbers," in *Congregation: Contemporary Writers Read the Jewish Bible*, ed. David Rosenberg (San Diego: Harcourt Brace Jovanovich, 1987), 42.

16. *The Boyhood of Algernon Charles Swinburne: Personal Recollections by His Cousin Mrs. Disney Leith, with Extracts from Some of His Private Letters* (London: Chatto & Windus, 1917), 123.

17. *The Yale Edition of the Swinburne Letters*, ed. Cecil Y. Lang, vol. 4, *1877–1882* (New Haven, CT: Yale UP, 1960), 214.

18. This, and section 12 below, are cited from *The Poems of Algernon Charles Swinburne*, vol. 5 (London: Chatto & Windus, 1904).

19. *Swinburne: A Biography* (New York: Schocken, 1971), 248.

FIFTEEN: Rachel When from the Lord

1. Mark Calkins, *A la recherche de l'unité perdue: Genre and Narrative in Proust* (Ann Arbor, MI: University Microfilms, 1998).

2. Marcel Proust, A *la recherche du temps perdu*, ed. Jean-Yves Tadié, éd. de la Pléiade (Paris: Gallimard, 1989), 2:453–70; *Remembrance of Things Past*, trans. C. K. Scott Moncrieff (New York: Vintage, 1982), 2:157–75; hereafter cited as F and E, respectively.

3. Somewhat later in the chapter Marcel does not, apparently, understand the advances the Baron de Charlus makes to him when they leave Mme. de Villeparisis's reception together, or rather Charlus hurries to catch up with him (F, 2:581ff.; E, 2:294ff.).

4. See Margaret Morganroth Gullette, "The Puzzling Case of the Deceased Wife's Sister: Nineteenth-Century England Deals with a Second-Chance Plot," *Representations* 31 (summer 1990): 142–66.

5. As a matter of fact, when Rachel is first introduced, in the much earlier episode in the *Recherche* in which Marcel meets her in a brothel, the reader is told that the procuress "called her Rachel," "doubtless" to indicate that she is Jewish "(C'est sans doute à cause de cela qu'elle l'appelait Rachel)" (F, 1:567; E, 1:620). This suggests that her name is not really Rachel, that the procuress just calls her that. Later Marcel seems to take for granted that her name is really Rachel.

6. Ernest Newman, *More Stories of Famous Operas* (New York: Knopf, 1943), 320–40.

7. And so on for many more lines. Here is a literal translation: "Rachel! When from the Lord the tutelary grace confided your cradle into my trembling hands, I devoted my entire life to your happiness. Oh Rachel! . . . and it is I who delivers you to the executioner!" (Eugène Scribe, *Oeuvres Complètes* [Paris: Furne; Aimé André, 1841], 2:69).

8. See J. L. Austin, *How to Do Things with Words*, 2nd ed. (Cambridge, MA: Harvard UP, 1975), 17: "We may reasonably christen the second sort . . . *Misapplications.*"

9. See J. Hillis Miller, *Black Holes* (with Manuel Asensi's *J. Hillis Miller; or, Boustrophedonic Reading)* (Stanford: Stanford UP, 1999), 407–39, odd pages only. An extraordinary passage in Proust's *Recherche*, discussed in *Black Holes*, asserts that "the lie, the perfect lie [*le mensonge, le mensonge parfait*]," "is one of the few things in the world that can open windows for us on to what is new and unknown, that can awaken in us sleeping senses [*des sens endormis*] for the contemplation of universes that otherwise we should never have known" (F, 3:721; E, 3:213).

10. See Jacobus de Voragine, "Saint Mary Magdalene," *The Golden Legend: Readings on the Saints*, trans. William Granger Ryan (Princeton, NJ: Princeton UP, 1993), 1:374–83.

11. For accounts of some of these less orthodox (to say the least) versions, see chap. 15, "The Penitent Whore," in Marina Warner, *Alone of All Her Sex: The Myth and the Cult of the Virgin Mary* (New York: Vintage, 1983), 224–35; Michael Baigent, Richard Leigh, and Henry Lincoln, *Holy Blood, Holy Grail* (New York: Dell, 1983), 330–47; Margaret Starbird, *The Woman with the Alabaster Jar: Mary Magdalen and the Holy Grail* (Santa Fe, NM: Bear & Co., 1993), esp. 26, 49–52; 60–62; Ean Begg, *The Cult of the Black Virgin* (London: Penguin, 1996), 93–99; and Laurence Gardner, *Bloodline of the Holy Grail: The Hidden*

Lineage of Jesus Revealed (New York: Barnes & Noble, 1997), esp. 66–73, 100–142. I owe the first of these references to Linda Georgiana, the rest to Matthew H. Miller.

12. See G. W. F. Hegel, "The Spirit of Christianity and Its Fate," *Early Theological Writings*, trans. T. M. Knox (Philadelphia: U of Pennsylvania P, 1971), 242–44.

13. This essay is drawn from the draft of a book that will have this title.

SIXTEEN: An Interview with Geoffrey Hartman

1. See Geoffrey H. Hartman, "Literary Studies and Traumatic Knowledge," *New Literary History* (Summer 1995).

2. Geoffrey H. Hartman, "Reading and Representation: Wordsworth's 'Boy of Winander,'" *European Romantic Review* 5.1 (1994).

3. Ibid.

4. Ibid.

5. Geoffrey H. Hartman, "Christopher Smart's Magnificat: Toward a Theory of Representation," in *The Fate of Reading and Other Essays* (Chicago: U of Chicago P, 1975).

6. See also Geoffrey H. Hartman, "The Interpreter's Freud," in *Easy Pieces* (New York: Columbia UP, 1985). For an excellent elaboration of the idea of euphemism in another Wordsworthian context, see Kevis Goodman's essay, "Making Time for History: Wordsworth, The New Historicism, and the Apocalyptic Fallacy," chap. 8 in this volume.

7. See Cathy Caruth, "Unclaimed Experience: Trauma and the Possibility of History," *Yale French Studies* 79 (1991), reprinted in *Unclaimed Experience: Trauma, Narrative, and History* (Baltimore: Johns Hopkins UP, 1996).

8. Hartman, "Literary Studies and Traumatic Knowledge."

9. Geoffrey H. Hartman, "The Voice of the Shuttle: Language from the Point of View of Literature," in *Beyond Formalism: Literary Essays, 1958–1970* (New Haven: Yale UP, 1970).

10. Hartman, "I. A. Richards and the Dream of Communication," in *The Fate of Reading.*

11. See Geoffrey H. Hartman, "Reading the Wound: Testimony, Art and Trauma," in *The Longest Shadow: In the Aftermath of the Holocaust* (Bloomington: Indiana UP, 1996).

12. See Hartman, "Public Memory and Its Discontents," in ibid.

13. Hartman, "Public Memory and Its Discontents."

14. See Anna Deavere Smith, *Twilight—Los Angeles, 1992: On the Road: A Search for American Character* (New York: Anchor Books, 1994).

15. See Geoffrey H. Hartman, "Learning from Survivors: The Yale Testimony Project," *Holocaust and Genocide Studies* 9.2 (Fall 1995) and Hartman, *The Longest Shadow.*

16. Hartman, "The Longest Shadow," in *Testimony: Contemporary Writers Make the Holocaust Personal*, ed. David Rosenberg (New York: Random House, 1989).

17. "Introduction: Darkness Visible," in *Holocaust Remembrance: The Shapes of Memory*, ed. Geoffrey H. Hartman (Cambridge, MA: Blackwell, 1994).

Contributors

Leslie Brisman is the Karl Young Professor of English at Yale University. He is the author of *Milton's Poetry of Choice*, *Romantic Origins*, and *The Voice of Jacob*. His recent work has been mostly in biblical studies.

Gerald L. Bruns is the William P. and Hazel B. White Professor at the University of Notre Dame. He is interested in the relations between American and European literary cultures since the late nineteenth century, particularly in poetry, drama, and theater. His books include *Inventions: Writing, Textuality, and Understanding in Literary History; Heidegger's Estrangements: Language, Truth, and Poetry in the Later Writings; Hermeneutics Ancient and Modern; Maurice Blanchot: The Refusal of Philosophy;* and *Tragic Thoughts at the End of Philosophy: Language, Literature, and Ethical Theory.*

Cathy Caruth is the Winship Distinguished Research Professor of Comparative Literature at Emory University. She is the author of *Empirical Truths and Critical Fictions: Locke, Wordsworth, Kant, Freud* and *Unclaimed Experience: Trauma, Narrative and History*. She has also edited and introduced *Trauma: Explorations in Memory* and *Critical Encounters: Reference and Responsibility in Deconstructive Writing* (with Deborah Esch).

Ortwin de Graef is an associate professor of English Literature at Katholieke Universiteit Leuven (Belgium), where he also runs the master's program in literary studies. He is the author of two books on Paul de Man (*Serenity in Crisis* and *Titanic Light*) and has published on Romantic and post-Romantic writing and literary theory. His current research focuses on aesthetic ideologies of sympathy and the State in the post-Romantic condition.

Helen Regueiro Elam is an associate professor of English at the University at Albany. She is the author of *The Limits of Imagination: Wordsworth, Yeats, and Stevens* and has published on nineteenth- and twentieth-century poetry. She has edited and introduced a special issue of *Studies in Romanticism* and is currently finishing a book (*Strange Spaces*) on Plato, Dickinson, and Hölderlin.

Frances Ferguson has taught at the University of California at Berkeley, Johns Hopkins University, and the University of Chicago, where she is currently the George M. Pullman Professor of English Language and Literature. She is the author of *Wordsworth: Language as Counter-Spirit*, *Solitude and the Sublime: Romanticism and the Aesthetics of Individuation*, and *Pornography, the Theory: What Utilitarianism Did to Action*, as well as articles on eighteenth- and nineteenth-century topics.

Paul H. Fry is the William Lampson Professor of English at Yale. He is the author of *The Poet's Calling in the English Ode*, *The Reach of Criticism*, *William Empson: Prophet Against Sacrifice*, *A Defense of Poetry*, an edition of "The Rime of the Ancient Mariner", and numerous articles on Romanticism, the history of criticism, literary theory and aesthetics, the visual arts, and the philosophy of education. His book nearing completion is *Wordsworth and the Anthropology of Lyric*.

Kevis Goodman is an associate professor at the University of California at Berkeley and the author of *Georgic Modernity and British Romanticism: Poetry and the Mediation of History*. She has also published articles and reviews on topics in Romanticism, eighteenth-century poetry, and Milton in *ELH*, *MLQ*, *South Atlantic Quarterly*, and the *European Romantic Review*.

Robert J. Griffin is an associate professor at Texas A&M University. He is the author of *Wordsworth's Pope: A Study in Literary Historiography* and the editor of *The Faces of Anonymity*. *Anonymity and Authorship, 1695–1830* is under contract to Columbia University Press.

Geoffrey H. Hartman has just published with Fordham University Press a reader that contains selections from his work of fifty years. He has also recently coedited with Kevin Hart *Maurice Blanchot: The Power of Contestation*, a collection of essays by various hands. He is the Sterling Professor Emeritus of English and Comparative Literature at Yale and continues as project director of the university's Fortunoff Archive for Holocaust Testimonies.

J. Douglas Kneale is Professor and Chair of English at the University of Western Ontario. He is the author of *Monumental Writing: Aspects of Rhetoric in Wordsworth's Poetry* and *Romantic Aversions: Aftermaths of Classicism in Wordsworth and Coleridge* and the editor of *The Mind in Creation: Essays on English Romantic*

Literature in Honour of Ross G. Woodman. His essays have appeared in *PMLA*, *ELH*, *Studies in Romanticism*, *Ariel*, and elsewhere.

Alan Liu is a professor in the English Department at the University of California, Santa Barbara, where he has taught since 1988. He received his PhD from Stanford University in 1980 and taught in the English Department and British Studies Program at Yale University from 1979–87. His central interests include literary theory, cultural studies, information culture and new media, and British Romantic literature. He is the author of *Wordsworth: The Sense of History* and *The Laws of Cool: Knowledge Work and the Culture of Information*. He is the weaver of Voice of the Shuttle and principal investigator of the National Endowment for the Humanities–funded Teaching with Technology project at UCSB titled, *Transcriptions: Literature and the Culture of Information.* He is also a member of the board of directors of the Electronic Literature Organization.

Peter J. Manning is professor and chair of the English Department at Stony Brook University. He received his AB from Harvard University and his MA and PhD degrees from Yale University. He is the author of *Byron and His Fictions*, of *Reading Romantics*, and of several essays on writings of the British Romantic period. He is also the coeditor (with Susan J. Wolfson) of *Selected Poems of Thomas Hood, Winthrop Mackworth Praed and Thomas Lovell Beddoes*, of the *Longman Anthology of British Literature*, vol. 2A, and of *Lord Byron: Selected Poems*.

Donald G. Marshall is the Fletcher Jones Chair of Great Books at Pepperdine University. With Joel Weinsheimer, he revised the translation of Hans-Georg Gadamer's *Truth and Method*. He compiled *Contemporary Critical Theory: A Selective Bibliography* and has published articles on the theory and history of criticism and rhetoric. He edited *The Force of Tradition: Response and Resistance* (forthcoming). He has taught at University of California at Los Angeles, the University of Iowa, and the University of Illinois at Chicago.

J. Hillis Miller taught for many years at Johns Hopkins University and then at Yale University before going to the University of California at Irvine in 1986, where is he now UCI Distinguished Research Professor. He is the author of many books and essays on nineteenth- and twentieth-century English, European, and American literature, and on literary theory. His most recent books are *Others*, *Speech Acts in Literature*, *On Literature*, and *Zero Plus One*. He is at work on a book on speech acts in the novels and stories of Henry James. A *J. Hillis Miller Reader* has appeared from Edinburgh University Press and Stanford University Press.

Lucy Newlyn is a professor of English language and literature at Oxford University and a fellow of St. Edmund Hall. She has published widely on English Romantic literature, including three books with Oxford University Press and *The Cambridge Companion to Coleridge*. Her book *Reading, Writing, and Romanticism: The Anxiety of Reception* won the British Academy's Rose Mary Crawshay Prize in 2001. Married with a daughter and two stepchildren, she lives in Oxford and is currently working on the writings of Edward Thomas. She has coedited two volumes on Creative Writing in Academic Practice, and some of her poems appeared with Carcanet in the *Oxford Poets Anthology*, 2001. Her first collection, *Ginnel*, will appear with Carcanet in 2005.

Patricia Parker is the Margery Bailey Professor of English and Dramatic Literature and professor of comparative literature at Stanford University. Coeditor with Geoffrey Hartman of *Shakespeare and the Question of Theory*, she has edited numerous critical anthologies, including *Women, "Race," and Writing in the Early Modern Period* with Margo Hendricks. Author of *Inescapable Romance*, *Literary Fat Ladies: Rhetoric, Language, Culture*, and *Shakespeare from the Margins*, she is currently completing two new books on racial and religious configurations in early modern writing and editing new Norton and Arden editions of *Twelfth Night*, *Much Ado about Nothing*, and *A Midsummer Night's Dream*.

Index